Books by Bil Gilbert

GOD GAVE US THIS COUNTRY: *Tekamthi and the First American Civil War* (1989)

OUR NATURE (1986)

IN GOD'S COUNTRIES (1984)

WESTERING MAN: *The Life of Joseph Walker* (1983)

THE TRAILBLAZERS (1973)

CHULO (1973)

THE WEASELS (1970)

HOW ANIMALS COMMUNICATE (1966)

BEARS IN THE LADIES ROOM (1966)

God Gave Us This Country

God Gave Us This Country

Tekamthi and the First American Civil War

Bil Gilbert

ANCHOR BOOKS
DOUBLEDAY
NEW YORK   LONDON   TORONTO   SYDNEY   AUCKLAND

An Anchor Book
PUBLISHED BY DOUBLEDAY
a division of Bantam Doubleday Dell Publishing Group, Inc.
666 Fifth Avenue, New York, New York 10103

ANCHOR BOOKS, DOUBLEDAY, and the portrayal of an anchor
are trademarks of Doubleday, a division of Bantam Doubleday
Dell Publishing Group, Inc.

God Gave Us This Country was originally published
in hardcover by Atheneum, a division of Macmillan Publishing Company,
in 1989. The Anchor Books edition is published
by arrangement with Atheneum.

MAPS BY CORINNE OVADIA ELWORTH

Library of Congress Cataloging-in-Publication Data

Gilbert, Bil.
    God gave us this country: Tekamthi
and the first American civil war / Bil Gilbert.
    —1st Anchor Books ed.
        p.   cm.
    Originally published: New York:
Atheneum, 1989.
    Includes bibliographical references (p.   ).
    1. Tecumseh, Shawnee Chief, 1768–1813.
2. Shawnee Indians—Biography.   3. Indians of
North America—Northwest, Old—Wars.
4. Indians of North America—Wars—1750–1815.
5. Shawnee Indians—Wars.   I. Title.
[E99.S35T147   1990]
977'.00497302—dc20   90–156
[B]   CIP

ISBN 0-385-41357-2

FOR AMANDA KAY GILBERT,
the girl on the Huffy, whose continuing curiosity about why and how books are written has been a delight and inspiration.

Acknowledgments

Staff persons at the Library of Congress and the Wisconsin State Historical Society were invariably efficient and helpful. Kate and Lee Gilbert and Suzanne and Frank Sieverts gave special research assistance. Deborah Shaffer of the Mount St. Mary's College library in Emmitsburg, Maryland, went far beyond the professional call of duty in locating books, periodicals, and documents to be used as references. Her competence is impressive and her friendship is valued. Dr. Frank Zarnowski, also of Mount St. Mary's College, was generous in sharing his knowledge of and speculations about what has come to be called "primitive economics." Ann Finlayson, Tom Stewart, and Margaret Talcott devoted much time and effort to identifying literary and logical weeds, which sprouted in various drafts of this manuscript. As has always been the case with my writing the person who gave the most assistance with this book was my wife, Ann.

Contents

Maps on pages 32–33, 92, and 244–245

Prologue. He Who Waits as a Celestial Panther and a Shooting Star

In the 1760s North Americans, red and white, commenced a struggle for the control of the Ohio Valley and Great Lakes country, a region which came to be known as the Old Northwest. The fighting continued for about fifty years broken by occasional truces, treaties, and periods of uneasy peace brought about by the temporary exhaustion of the combatants. The confrontation is now often thought of as involving a series of small, disconnected, relatively trivial happenings which were subsidiary and tangential to the American Revolution, the founding of the Republic, the westward pioneering movement, and the War of 1812. In fact it was—to the extent any complex of events is—a separate, cohesive phenomenon of pivotal importance in the history of North America. When hostilities ended, the red people had been virtually eliminated—killed or exiled—from the territories which they had originally occupied. The total victory of the whites substantially influenced when, where, and how the United States was subsequently enlarged and developed. It can be reasonably argued, if not documented, that these events also had a lasting effect on the national psyche, shaping certain beliefs, biases, and self-images which are still significant in this country. The long, bitter conflict in the continental heartland seldom is, but might well be, called the first American Civil War.

Occasionally, for imperial reasons, the British took a hand, but the principal opponents were a dozen Indian nations and the United States and its colonial predecessors. Seldom were grand armies or strategies involved. Rather there were innumerable, scattered, guerrilla actions between irregular partisans who had at each other in the junglelike forests. In recent world history this was a confrontation of unique ferocity between members of two very alien races and cultures. There were some reds and whites who hoped otherwise, but generally the antagonists believed that this was a winner-take-all competition, that compromise and accommodation were neither possible nor desirable. Therefore not only soldiers and warriors but civilian noncombatants were regularly engaged and suffered many casualties.

People then living east of the Appalachians had a very imperfect understanding of where and how the forest campaigns of the late eighteenth and early nineteenth centuries were conducted. The savages—red and white—did things to each other which sensitive outsiders found unbelievable. The participants themselves had little inclination to explain or justify themselves. (Also many of the whites on the frontier and all the reds were illiterate.) In consequence few of those who made the history of this region were well known outside it in their own time, and most of them are now forgotten.

Of the thousands of red men who were engaged, the name of only one of them is still regularly mentioned in general histories. His own people, the Shawnee, who seldom used sibilants, called him Tekamthi or something close to that. (There are a number of other orthographic versions, including Tikamthe, Tecuptha, and Tecumseth.) English speakers found lisping awkward and unmanly and when, early in the nineteenth century, it became necessary to deal with the man, they spoke and wrote of him as Tecumseh. Since they made the records of the time, that is how he is commonly remembered.

Tekamthi was probably born in 1768. That year, more logically than any other, can be designated as the one in which the first American Civil War began. He was killed in 1813, and his death ended that war. During childhood he lived in and fled with his family from three villages that were sacked and burned by Long Knives, as white frontiersmen were often called by reds. His father, two brothers, other relatives, and many friends were killed in battles with the Americans. As a young man he was almost continually in the field, first as a warrior in the ranks and then as a rising junior chief directing partisan bands on scouting and scalping raids against the Long Knives. In 1794 after Anthony Wayne and his men won, at Fallen Timbers in Ohio, the first major victory for the United States in the west, many whites and reds thought the racial conflict had ended. But it continued for nineteen more years, mainly because of Tekamthi.

Sometime during the last fifteen years of his life Tekamthi conceived a plan for uniting the red people living between the northern Great Lakes and Gulf coast into a single federation. In this domain old national rivalries would be extinguished. Thereafter, purified of corrupting white influences, red people would live as their ancestors had, in accordance with their own traditions and the designs of their gods.

Tekamthi traveled extensively, explaining his ideas and recruiting supporters among the Indian nations: what remained of his own Shawnee, the Delaware, Iroquois, Miami, and Wyandot in the Ohio Valley; the Fox, Ojibwa, Ottawa, Sauk, and Winnebago of the northern lake country; the southern Cherokee, Chickasaw, Choctaw, and Creek; the Osage, Iowa, Kickapoo, Potawatomi, and Sioux of the prairies. In a series of great orations he gave them warnings: If they did not join together they would be separately defeated and either killed or dispossessed of their ancient homelands. If they tried to share the country peaceably with Long Knives, they would be used and herded as the white man did his dogs and cattle. They would live miserably until they were murdered by white thugs or lawmen, died of starvation or of the diseases and whiskey of white men. Even if the red resistance movement he proposed failed, it would bring them to a less painful and more honorable end. The time had come to test their fate, for assuredly their gods would not help those who did not dare to help themselves.

In retrospect it appears that Tekamthi and his followers had virtually no chance of establishing and defending an independent Indian state. There were fewer than 100,000 red people in the territories where Tekamthi proposed to create the new union. By no means all of them agreed that doing so was possible or desirable. Tekamthi's argument that the existing nations must yield their sovereignty to a racial federation antagonized most of the older, established chiefs. They feared for what they would lose if he succeeded. Others thought that continuing to resist the whites was suicidal. They turned away from Tekamthi, fearing a quick, brutal end more than they did the long, lingering one which he prophesied.

At the same time the United States had a population of seven million, including one million settlers already located west of the Appalachians. With few exceptions they were reflexively and violently hostile to Indians. In wealth, technology, and social organization the whites were more superior to the reds than they were in numbers.

These realities were, of course, far less apparent to the people who lived with them than they are to historians. In 1810 most believed that the outcome of the racial conflict was still in doubt and that therefore it had to continue. During the first decade of the nineteenth century, a principal reason for this opinion was that Tekamthi was taken very seriously by substantial numbers of reds and whites who felt that it was unwise to ignore his ambitions. The possibility that he might be a rare, dangerous sport, capable of skewing all reasonable projections, was touched on by William Henry Harrison who, as the federal governor and military commander in the western territories of the United States, was the American official most responsible for coping directly with the Indians. Harrison warned, in a confidential report to the War Department, that Tekamthi struck him as being comparable to the great empire builders of the past, "one of those uncommon geniuses which spring up occasionally to produce revolutions and overturn the established order of things."

Lewis Cass was another politician/soldier who campaigned against Tekamthi and, like Harrison, benefited from the association. (Chiefly because of his service against the Indians, Cass became the territorial governor of Michigan, Secretary of War, and a presidential candidate.) In his line of work, Cass was exposed to much speechifying, and though this was the golden age of American oratory, he among others thought that Tekamthi was the equal of the Calhouns, Clays, and Websters. Of one of Tekamthi's declamations, Cass observed, "It was the utterance of a great mind, roused by the strongest motives of which human nature is susceptible, and developing a power and labour of reason which commanded the admiration of the civilized as justly as the confidence and pride of the savage."

Others made more extravagant and dramatic claims. For example, the Creek in the far south said that after having traveled to their nation, seeking support, Tekamthi became angered at the faint-hearted, wait-and-see counsels of some of their chiefs. He said he would leave them to return to the north, but in one month, he would stomp his foot. The Creek would know when he did, and the doubters among them would be confounded. A month later the earth trembled, heaved, and split. The Creek in Alabama knew that Tekamthi was somewhere north of the Ohio and had made his sign. When whites heard this explanation for the New Madrid earthquake, which devastated the central Mississippi valley in 1811, they found it a ludicrous example of savage ignorance. Yet most of them firmly believed that Tekamthi held a commission as a general of the British Army. Reputable historians repeated this as a fact until well into the twentieth century when it was proved to be a fiction.

The two stories, beyond demonstrating the disparate allegorical styles of red and white reporters, seem to have been told to make the same point—that Tekamthi was a man of extraordinary abilities and possibilities. This opinion became widespread and caused many reds to hope and whites to fear that his uncommon valor, sagacity, and charisma might be sufficient to overcome the military, political, and economic factors which, rationally, indicated he must fail. In natural consequence there came to be great curiosity about the personality and formative experiences of Tekamthi.

In the days of their independence the Shawnee like most other native inhabitants of the eastern woodlands supported themselves by hunting, fishing, gathering wild edibles, and light agriculture. This mixed economy depended on harvesting things where and when they were most abundant and promoted a seminomadic but rhythmic existence. During the farming months the Shawnee lived in villages of several hundred people, usually along rivers (in the central Ohio Valley during Tekamthi's childhood) where corn, beans, and squash grew well in the bottom lands. If the soil remained fertile and there were no major natural or political catastrophes, these settlements might be occupied for decades, but seldom by all of their residents at all times of the year. In the proper seasons parties left the villages and temporarily lived elsewhere to take game, forage, make salt or maple sugar, and—after whites established a fur market—to trade.

Men and women contributed to the Shawnee economy about equally but separately, for they held rigid views about what their respective occupations should be. Women were the principal farmers and domestic-craft persons while men were hunters and traders. In times of emergency vocational roles might be altered or reversed but ordinarily one sex did not expect or permit the other to do its traditional work. Many social activities, religious obser- vances, and sporting events were also sexually segregated. After puberty men and women customarily spent more time in the company of their own sex than they did with the opposite one. They regarded these arrangements as natural and decent. There were no studies or surveys made about such intimate matters but by white standards of that time and certainly by contemporary ones, sexual activity was seemingly not of the highest priority.

Midsummer was the most convivial time of the year in the Ohio Valley. By then the hard work of planting fields was finished. Early corn and vegetables were ready, berries were ripe, the fishing good, small game of the year—rabbits, raccoons, woodchucks, waterfowl—was abundant in the woods around the villages. During these rich months, there was the time and wherewithal for family, clan, and national gatherings, sacred and secular festivals, foot races and ball games. (The Shawnee like many red peoples were inveterate sports and gamblers.) It was also naturally the season for flirtations, courtship, marriages, and matings. No taboos restricted sex to July and August; this was simply a good season for it, better than others when there was less opportunity and more pressing things to do. All of which does not verify that Tekamthi was conceived in the Green Corn month of 1767 but lends weight to the tradition that this was the case.

By then his mother, Methoastaske, and his father, Puckeshinwa, were mature, prominent people. She was at least in her mid- or late twenties, an industrious farmer, and a leader in the women's councils of the community. Puckeshinwa was older, perhaps twice as old. Ordinarily the Shawnee distributed authority on the basis of seniority, and he had lived long enough to have become one of the most important military men in the nation, a diplomat who had negotiated with the whites, and the principal civil chief of a village—named for him—on Darby Creek just above its junction with the Scioto River near what is now Columbus, Ohio.

Families of three or four children were the rule among the Shawnee, but Methoastaske bore at least nine, eight of whom reached maturity. (A rough, very approximate translation of her name is Turtle Laying Eggs in the Sand.) Tekamthi was the fourth. The eldest, another son, was born in 1760 or before. The youngest, a set of triplets—which was extremely rare and therefore a portentous happening among these people—were born in the early 1770s.

According to sketchy records left by British traders and Indian agents, 1767 was a relatively peaceful year in the Ohio Valley. Even so it is likely that in the early fall Puckeshinwa gathered together his men and went off to fight and raid, perhaps against the Kickapoo or Chickasaw, who were favored opponents. This was the custom and pleasure of Shawnee men and those of many other woodland nations who found small wars to be the most stimulating of diversions. An eighteenth-century Cherokee chief, in attempting to explain to a British agent why the idea of making permanent peace with neighboring nations was repugnant, said: "We cannot live without war. Should we make peace with the Tuscaroras, we must immediately look out for some other Nation with whom we can be engaged in our beloved occupation."

After the white invasion was well advanced, war became a grim business for red men, but traditionally the campaigns among them had been conducted somewhat like grand, high-risk sporting events. As a rule they fought for reasons of honor, to display their manhood and take trophies—scalps, coup, and prisoners—rather than for territorial or other material gains. The warriors favored hit-and-run raids, ambushes, and hand-to-hand melees which were usually brief, low-casualty affairs but offered good opportunities for individuals to win glory. Women might share in the excitement, rewards, and losses, but this type of warfare was exclusively a masculine occupation. Fall, Indian summer, was the traditional time for it since the weather was good and temporary agricultural surpluses made war games affordable.

Wherever he spent the early part of it, Puckeshinwa was no doubt back at the village on Darby Creek by the late fall, preparing for the winter hunt, which was imperative. The Shawnee did not produce large agricultural surpluses and did not have efficient means of storing them for long periods of time. In consequence during the winter months they depended largely on game. To get it, many of them left the villages, the move being dictated by ecological realities. In the 1760s the Scioto Valley was the center of the Shawnee nation, occupied by 3,000 or so people during the summer months. Had they all attempted to stay the winter and hunt from the farming communities, the nearby wildlife resources would have been exhausted in a season or so. Some who were weak, infirm, or conducting trade with whites might remain behind, but by the end of November, most of the residents of the Scioto villages left them. They traveled in small groups, sometimes for several hundred miles, to find sheltered camps in narrow tributary valleys where game was more plentiful and there was less competition for it.

The reputation and status of a Shawnee man was to a large extent based on his ability as a hunter. Those who lacked it were generally mocked and might be divorced by their wives—with the approval of the community—on the grounds that they were not only impoverished but shamed by living with such trifling persons. (For the same reasons, men were justified in breaking off marriages with women who were bad farmers or mothers.) As a matter of logic if not record, Puckeshinwa was a skillful hunter since incompetent ones did not become military or civil leaders. This being the case, the party he took out in the fall of 1767 was probably a sizable one, including several other families in addition to his pregnant wife and small children.

They traveled fifty miles westward from the Scioto to a small tributary of the Little Miami River near what is now Xenia, Ohio. A base camp was established in a protected valley, well set with rock maples. From it the men and older boys fanned out, sometimes being gone for a week or more. For food, their principal quarry were elk and deer, whose movements were restricted by the snow, denned black bears, and raccoons. By the mideighteenth century considerable efforts were also being made to take beaver, otter, lynx, and other smaller furbearers whose pelts could be traded to the whites. The men ate what they needed, field-dressed the rest of the game, and packed it back to the main camp, where the meat and furs were further processed by the women. In February when thaws, slush, and mud began to interfere with hunting, and furs were past their prime, the parties gathered at their base camp and began setting taps of hollowed sumac sections in maple trees, boiling sap, making and storing sugar.

In early spring of 1768, Methoastaske felt her time approaching. As was customary, she left the community, attended by a female relative or friend, to wait for the birth in seclusion. According to tradition, Methoastaske retired to a small, bowl-shaped hollow around a big spring, a mile southeast of Puckeshinwa's camp. This spring hole is now choked with vines and brush, unused, according to trail signs, except occasionally as an irregular playground for children from the suburbs of Xenia. However, cleared, improved with a shelter, blanket, and fire ring it would still make a pleasant place for entering the world. Tekamthi did so between the time of The Mouse-Eared Oaks and The Singing Frogs, as the Shawnee spoke of this season.

After giving birth, mothers remained alone with their babies for several days to prepare them to enter society and to make certain that they were capable of doing so. (Occasionally a child with severe birth defects was abandoned but cases of this sort of infanticide were apparently rare.) When the woman felt they were both ready, she brought back the baby to be admired by the father, family, and friends. Thereafter deliberations about what to call the new person commenced. Since Methoastaske bore this son at about the time when winter camps were usually broken, the selection of a name was probably delayed until the party returned to Puckeshinwa's village on Darby Creek, a better place for taking up a matter which the Shawnee considered extremely important.

Wise and pious elders were asked by the parents to recommend a name suitable for use not only in the family and community but by interested supernatural beings. They did so after studying the infant itself and considering the circumstances of his or her birth and ancestry. As a first function, the name placed the child in one of twelve groups which others have called clans but the Shawnee themselves spoke of as an *umsoma*—literally but inadequately "a good genius society." Except for certain outcasts, all Shawnee belonged to an *umsoma*. Each was represented by a totem animal whose attributes, it was thought, were to some extent shared by all members of the group. In given names, the *umsoma* reference was often so allusive as to be almost a code. Thus a boy might be called Leaper from Limbs or a girl Smooth Handsome Skin. For Shawnee, at least, this identified them as being members of the panther society. Male names made reference to the bolder, more active traits of the totem animals while softer, gentler ones were used for females.

Generally offspring belonged to the *umsoma* of their father. But occasionally the elders in charge of names might observe that the child of, say, a panther father and turtle mother (respectively the *umsomas* of Puckeshinwa and Methoastaske) had raccoon traits. This would be noted in the name and for social and ceremonial purposes the person would be a raccoon.

Also names often described notable physical or psychic traits of an individual and/or gave enigmatic hints about what this person might be or do in the future. In this latter regard, Shawnee names seem to have functioned as self-fulfilling prophecies somewhat as horoscopic and psychiatric projections do in our contemporary society. Thus it was assumed that a raccoon or turtle child would enjoy the water, would be encouraged in this direction, and draw confidence from his or her *umsoma* connection. Agility, strength, and boldness were looked for and, therefore, often found in panther people.

The Shawnee recognized that in such a complicated matter as selecting the right name, errors could be made. If so, they must be corrected. A name given at birth was often changed several times by the family and community before the proper one was discovered. A sickly infant might be given a new name in the first months of his life on the grounds that the first one had been so unsuitable that the effort of bearing it had sapped the baby's vitality. Or if a child first called Swift Deer grew to be a chubby, heavy-footed little boy, this was recognized by changing his name to something on the order of Deer in the Snow.

Even adults might receive new names to commemorate deeds or late-developing personality traits. This was the case with one of

Tekamthi's younger brothers. Names in this family often alluded to the panther, totem of Puckeshinwa's *umsoma*. It was believed that panthers were especially suited for war and politics, but as in nature, there were good, strong, brave panthers and bad, weak, cowardly ones. The child in question was first thought to be of the latter sort and was called Lalawethika. This signified that he was a slinky, timid creature who dragged his tail on the ground, whined and squalled in an unseemly fashion. The name was sometimes translated as the Loud Mouth or Rattle. For some years this seemed suitable. He grew into a very un-Shawneelike youth—an incompetent hunter, no warrior at all, and, when and for as long as trader's whiskey was available, an unpleasant drunk.

Sometime in his early thirties or thereabouts, Lalawethika had a powerful, epiphanic experience. While in a deep trance, he was visited, so he said, by the greatest being of the spirit world. The Master of Life told Lalawethika that it was His desire that red people turn aside from the evil, impious practices they had learned from the whites. Lalawethika was to purify himself and carry this message to others as the Master's earthly agent. Thereafter, Lalawethika did mend his ways; he became a teetotaler, a feared shaman, and the principal religious leader of the red resistance movement. His former derogatory name being unsuitable for such a personage, he came to be known as Tenskwatawa, the Open Door, a medium through which the highest authorities had chosen to make their wishes known to mortals. Whites called him the Prophet.

As for Tekamthi, the right name apparently was found early in his life, for he was so called as a boy of ten or twelve, which is when he was first noticed by those who left written records. Later when whites became convinced that he was the most formidable of all red men, they, having heard of the importance of names to these people, wanted to know what his meant. None had the opportunity or perhaps the nerve to ask the man himself, but other Shawnee speakers were questioned. They gave various answers: that Tekamthi could be translated as Man Who Waits, as the Crouching Panther, or the Shooting Star. Those who were interested accepted whichever seemed the most convincing and dismissed the other names as being offered by ignorant informants. After Tekamthi was killed and his people dispersed, it became safe and fashionable for linguists and ethnologists to return to the question. They decided that all of the earlier folk translations were partially correct, but none completely so, since Tekamthi was not, as Europeans understood it, a name in itself. Rather it was a word used to call to mind a complicated, metaphorical statement about this person, one which might be phonetically rendered as *nila ni tekamthi, manetuwi msi-pessi.*

Rumaging around in the cultural shards left by the Shawnee and the memories of their elders who would talk about such things, nineteenth-century students offered an interpretation. The first phrase—*nila ni tekamthi*—describes "one who lies waiting to cross the path of living creatures." The remaining words specifically identified the crouched being as a panther but one of supernatural origins. The *manetuwi msi-pessi* had immense magical powers and, although they generally kept to themselves, did on occasion take an unpredictable interest in human affairs. Ordinarily they lived beneath waters of deep lakes and rivers. When they did come on land—for example to lurk along a trail waiting to aid virtuous mortals or punish evil ones—they were invisible. Now and then, at night, for need or pleasure, one of them would spring into the sky. There it could be seen by humans but, because of its swiftness, only briefly as a streak of light flashing across the heavens.

To say of a man that he was like a magical beast crouched along a trail was also to say—at least to those who understood the natural and metaphysical observations of the elders who had named him—that he was like a Celestial Panther or Shooting Star. Tekamthi made a convenient, everyday name which summarized the full nominative metaphor. For ignorant foreigners one translation would do as well as the other, since each had an impressive ring to it.

This seems to me to be the right place to make mention of something which I think must be emphasized. It is a matter of record that William Henry Harrison, who became the principal American antagonist of Tekamthi, was born on July 12, 1773, at Berkeley, a plantation in Virginia. His parents were Elizabeth Basset and Benjamin William Harrison. He was christened according to the rites of the Episcopalian church, attended Hampden-Sidney College in Prince Edward County, Virginia, and then enrolled at the medical school of the University of Pennsylvania in Philadelphia. He left that institution because of financial reverses experienced by his family. Through the good offices of friends of his late father, who had once been the governor of Virginia, Harrison received, on August 16, 1791, a commission as an ensign in the 1st Infantry Regiment of the United States Army. His subsequent opinions about slavery, the United States Bank, federal land policies, home furnishing, the goodness of his wife, the alcoholism of his son, Andrew Jackson, Tekamthi, and an infinity of other subjects are known because he gave them in letters, government reports, and interviews which have been preserved.

The same sort of documentable things were never publicly known about Tekamthi. The Shawnee could not record vital statistics. Though they were dedicated and able oral historians, their chronicles tended to be more allegorical than actuarial, and they were less concerned than whites with exact details having to do with time, place, and such. The description offered here about the birth and naming of Tekamthi is based on what seems to be the most veracious of second, third, and even more distant accounts, on what is remembered of Shawnee customs of those times, and the surmise that his family behaved in customary ways. The same holds true in regard to many periods and events of his life. He left no personal papers nor did those who knew him most intimately: relatives, friends, lovers, aides, and counselors. Tekamthi did not confide in whites who might have been able and willing to transcribe autobiographical statements.

Only in connection with the last decade of his life are there Tekamthi records of a conventional sort. Even these are distorted because they were largely made and preserved by his adversaries, men who negotiated with or fought against him. Often these people had strong reasons of self-interest for editing and altering their accounts. Furthermore they usually were dependent on interpreters and translators of various abilities and loyalties.

If Tekamthi is considered only in terms of what he did and said as a matter of record, he becomes a small, flat figure of little consequence. Yet to treat him as such is obviously contrary to historical fact. Unless thousands of his contemporaries suffered from some sort of mass delusion, he was an unusually complex man of substantial significance in his own times and therefore in our history. For these reasons—that he seems to have led an important but largely undocumented life—this book is not intended as a conventional biography. Rather it is about Tekamthi: the few records, the many anecdotes, legends, and fictions associated with him; the people who were—and events which happened—around him; how he may have affected them and vice versa. What follows is an attempt to describe a shadow, the one Tekamthi made and the conditions of environment that caused him to cast it as he did.

This book is equally about what is here called the first American Civil War. This war was all about him from his infancy to death, and must have been an overriding, formative fact of his life. Once there were people who knew him under other circumstances—what he was like when he was playing games, hunting, praying, singing, making love—who joked with him, talked about the weather, the habits of deer, and nature of the universe. But those who did, so far as is known, made no mention of such matters. All that is left of him is the man of war. Considering the events of the red-white conflict in which he spent all of his life, this is now the only way to consider Tekamthi, even in part. Furthermore, a description of what is known of his experiences describes much of that conflict.

There is a second qualification having to do with the intent of this book. Beyond the fact that they left abundant records, William Henry Harrison and other white contemporaries of Tekamthi remain fairly comprehensible because they were people of European backgrounds and sensibilities. They were citizens of a constitutional republic, members of a Christian, entrepreneurial, and hierarchal society. Reasonable generalizations can be made about eighteenth-century whites because many of their institutions, modes of thinking, and systems of values are still operable, and their effects can be observed. The same is not true of Tekamthi. His culture was shattered and for the most part disappeared 175 years ago at about the time of his death.

With few exceptions the only surviving, first-hand reports of what the Shawnee were like as an undefeated, independent people are those made by foreigners who were generally unsympathetic observers. Sketchy and often biased as these accounts are, they agree on one important point. The traditional Indian culture produced people with mind-sets and behaviors which seemed profoundly alien to their contemporaries who were of European origin. By extension, a Tekamthi would presumedly have even less in common with present-day Americans than he did with whites who lived in this country during his own time.

Perhaps it is possible to draw a crude, incomplete, flickering likeness of this man as he sometimes was in some places. If the figure which emerges is quite clear and comprehensible, then it probably does not represent even a shadow of the Tekamthi who lived, is only that of a painted George Washington or, even more likely, one of us in feathers. I have tried to imagine and remember that He Who Waits as a Celestial Panther and a Shooting Star cannot be imagined or remembered as a William Henry Harrison can be.

I. The Meeting of Aliens

When whites began to settle in eastern North America, it was inhabited by some sixty native tribes or nations. Their traditions and customs were at least as diverse as those of Europeans, and their languages more numerous. However, just as Swedes and Spaniards were connected by certain common material interests, attitudes, and modes of behavior, so were the Shawnee and Susquehannocks. Confrontations between representatives of the two cultures—eastern North American and western European— commenced in the early seventeenth century and continued for the next two hundred years. There is no recent record of two peoples so alien who had to contend with one another for so long and were so little inclined toward mutual accommodation.

By the time they met the natives of the North American woodlands, Europeans had already encountered a good many residents of Asia, Africa, and South America who struck them as being bizarre in matters of dress and diet, manners and morals. However, they invariably found they shared some basic notions about what constituted rational and imperative human behavior, about such things as the creation and distribution of wealth, law and order, the need for social and political hierarchies. Therefore it was at least possible to work out a modus vivendi.

Where Europeans mounted invasions of foreign lands, there were conflicts, but they were essentially struggles over who would control the resources and people of a territory. By reason of superior technology and organization, Europeans were often triumphant. But except for members of the former ruling classes, this did not bring about drastic changes for the native peoples. After power was transferred, they were generally able to go about their ordinary business much as they had before. As they did so, there tended to be a mixing of Europeans and native cultures and bloods, the creation of new ones. This process is best illustrated by what resulted from the meeting of white and red (later black) people in Central and South America.

In North America what might be called the mestizo solution did not occur. Shortly after they met, reds and whites concluded that their traditions and ideas about what humans should be were so opposite as to make them absolutely incompatible. In fact, there was a considerable body of opinion among both that their races were only superficially related, stood to each other as, say, foxes do to coyotes. Many whites saw reds as not simply primitive, but as creatures whose development had been so arrested (by their environment or God) that they constituted a neotenic species, transitional between the higher beasts and lower humans. Red thinkers had more dramatic and specific theories: that whites were creative errors who had somehow escaped the scrap heap of the Maker of Life, that they were hybrids, the result of unfortunate matings of evil spirits or men with wolves, bears, or serpents.

Modern opinion inclines toward the view that reds and whites were more than ordinarily repugnant and incomprehensible to each other for historical rather than genetic reasons, specifically because they had come to have such disparate ways of exploiting their environment.

The red economy was based largely on harvesting naturally created surpluses, animal, vegetable, and mineral. To survive in this way, an Indian family required the resources of approximately as many square miles as a white one did acres. All the eastern woodland nations did some farming, but in comparison with European agriculture, theirs required small investments of labor and capital. They did not keep domestic stock, did little to enhance or maintain the fertility of the land, and worked it lightly. When it played out, they moved on to other naturally fertile places of which there was a great abundance. The importance of agriculture varied from nation to nation—the more settled Iroquois, for example, doing more farming than the nomadic Shawnee—but generally it was a supplement to foraging and hunting rather than the principal community activity. Among the Shawnee and other notable hunting nations, the function of agriculture was as much social as economic, since it gave wandering bands the wherewithal and excuse to stay together for a few months during the summer growing season.

For a millennium the Europeans had not been able to, or had not wanted to, live mainly from the natural bounty. Therefore they developed techniques of husbandry, land improvement, manufacturing, commerce, and foreign conquest to create additional resources or get them from others who had. Doing so had come to be equated with being civilized. From this perspective, Europeans saw North America in the seventeenth century as a howling wilderness that needed to be quickly and drastically improved if its potential wealth was to be utilized. For Indians the wilderness was wealth in place, a marvelous, self-replenishing storehouse given to humans by Providence. It was not owned, did not need to be managed by any individual or nation. Attempts to improve or expand it were pointless and impious. Generally reds believed that the Maker of Life was generous but not foolishly indulgent. He did not simply drop the good things of life in the laps of humans; they were expected to bestir themselves, to rummage around in the storehouse to find what He had put there for them. At times—to instruct the ignorant or punish the wicked—the bounty was reduced or withdrawn. In these cases the respectful response was to endure His or Her displeasure and by doing so, perhaps regain favor. This metaphysical tactic was explained to at least one sympathetic white man.

In 1755 British colonial authorities were attempting to build a military road westward through the mountains of western Virginia and Maryland, so as to deal with the French at Fort Duquesne (now Pittsburgh). James Smith, an eighteen-year-old farm boy, hired out for this work, but a few weeks after he joined, the construction crew was surprised and captured by a war party of Delaware, allied with the French. The warriors took Smith to the Ohio country and turned him over to the Wyandot. He voluntarily stayed with these people for four years—according to a remarkable memoir he wrote after he had somewhat reluctantly returned to white society. Among the Wyandot, Smith's mentor and foster grandfather was Tecaughretanego, who had once been a renowned warrior but had grown old and now hobbled with rheumatism. Smith came to love this old man and thought him the wisest and kindest he had ever known.

The winter of 1757 was an extremely severe one in Ohio. Game was scarce and hard to hunt because of the blizzards and ice storms. By January it became apparent that Tecaughretanego could not keep up and that attempting to assist him was handicapping the more vigorous men. It was mutually agreed that he would be left at a rude camp with a ten-year-old boy who was also slowing the party. Smith, who was not yet skillful enough to be of much assistance to the others, was detailed to remain with and try to care for the old man and boy.

He did his best, hunting frantically but unsuccessfully day after terrible day, driven by the knowledge that Tecaughretanego and the boy were rapidly weakening. Finally one evening when Smith was so exhausted that he said he did not even feel hunger, the old man took him aside and whispered that the time had come "to communicate to you the thoughts of my heart, and those things I know to be true." Smith recalled, "I told him I was ready to hear him." Then Tecaughretanego spoke as follows:

> Brother,
> As you have lived with the white people, you have not had the same advantage of knowing that the great being above feeds his people, and gives them their meat in due season, as we Indians have, who are frequently out of provisions, and yet are wonderfully supplied, and that so frequently, that it is evidently the hand of the great Owaneeyo [Creator], that doth this: whereas the white people have commonly large stocks of tame cattle, that they can kill when they please, and also their barns and cribs filled with grain, and therefore have not the same opportunity of seeing and knowing that they are supported by the ruler of Heaven and Earth.
> Brother,
> I know that you are now afraid that we will all perish with hunger, but you have no just reason to fear this.
> Brother,
> I have been young, but am now old—I have been frequently under the like circumstances that we now are, and that some time or other in almost every year of my life; yet, I have hitherto been supported, and my wants supplied in time of need.
> Brother,
> Owaneeyo sometimes suffers us to be in want, in order to teach us our dependence upon him, and to let us know that we are to love and serve him: and likewise to know the worth of the favors that we receive, and to make us more thankful.
> Brother,
> Be assured that you will be supplied with food, and that just in the right time; but you must continue diligent in the use of means—go to sleep and rise early in the morning and go a hunting—be strong and exert yourself like a man, and the Great Spirit will direct your way.

The next morning, Smith came upon a buffalo cow grazing through the snow in a protected thicket. He killed the animal, immediately gorged himself, then cut off as much meat as he could carry and returned to the camp. After fasting for so long, Tecaughretanego wisely ate sparingly and bade the boy do the same. When they had finished their first snack, Tecaughretanego "delivered a speech upon the necessity and pleasure of receiving the necessary supports of life with thankfulness." Smith said that he himself considered at the time (and continued to do so often throughout his life) "how remarkably the old man's speech had been verified in our providentially obtaining a supply."

Accumulating property, a central preoccupation for Europeans, was a much lesser one for reds. They had relatively few personal possessions—weapons, tools, clothing, some small artistic or ceremonial objects—and owning more items was not a means for an individual to gain status or power. There is no reason to think that a peculiar racial asceticism was involved. Rather this was again a reflection of the manner in which they responded to their environment.

The natural bounty on which the reds depended was never so large as to encourage or enable them to convert much of it into nonconsumable goods, say, elaborate household furnishings. As they traveled about, they contrived what they needed in the way of shelter and utensils and abandoned them when they moved elsewhere. Even the farming villages which might be seasonally occupied for many years needed little guarding or maintenance. If a family returned in the spring and found their pole and bark cabin of the previous summer had been flattened by heavy snows, it was a matter of only a day or two of fairly light work to build another, equally serviceable one.

The natives did not as a rule accumulate more or bulkier possessions than they could conveniently carry on their backs or in canoes. Having, by the time Europeans met them, lived in this fashion for many generations, the reds were convinced that it was a good and true way of life, that people should make do with nature as they found it, not make more of it. As Tecaughretanego pointed out to James Smith, the white life-style—rushing about making and hoarding things, filling paddocks with tame cattle and cribs with grain—seemed to thoughtful reds to be exceedingly unpleasant and also irreverent, since it showed a profound lack of trust in the good nature of the Maker of Life. To progressive, entrepreneurial-minded Europeans, the economic fatalism of the reds demonstrated that they were mentally and spiritually retarded.

The stereotype of poor, starving, shivering Indians is largely drawn from the situation of these people in the nineteenth century after their traditional economies had been greatly disrupted. When the Europeans first met them (and presumably for centuries previously) they seem to have enjoyed a relatively high and secure standard of living. Available reports have suggested to modern students of what has come to be called primitive economics that in terms of basic physical welfare—calorie intakes, longevity, and general community health—nearly all of the red people lived about as well as the white middle classes, better than the white urban and rural poor of the time.

The income of native communities was very small by European standards, but so were their collective expenses. Since reds largely supported themselves by immediately consuming naturally created surpluses, they did not have to divert capital to collect, store, and distribute their wealth—or for the people to do this directly unproductive work. As a homely example: in colonial North America building fences was a continuing, fairly costly (in terms of labor) activity for whites but not for their red contemporaries.

Reds paid little or nothing for the upkeep of kings, presidents, ministers, parliamentarians, judges, lawyers, inspectors, assessors, police, or the facilities they require. They had small need for these functionaries, again because they had so little capital wealth, the management of which was an essential purpose of European-style governments. For the same reason, reds did not need to make elaborate and expensive arrangements to maintain and distribute political power, which was the other principal function of white governments.

In the European system, authority flowed from wealth. Those who controlled it could command others by giving or withholding property. In red societies wealth was found, not created, and was more or less equally available to all. Among them the critical element for power—the ability of some to require services and obedience from others—was missing. The lack of authority and hierarchical organizations based on it astonished and shocked most whites who had an opportunity to visit red communities while they were still operating in their traditional manner.

One of those who did was the Rev. David Jones, a Welsh Baptist from New Jersey. He was a vigorous divine of evangelical inclinations and certainly a bold man. During the Revolutionary War, to encourage a regiment of Washington's continental line under heavy British pressure, Jones, a fighting chaplain, was said to have bellowed out: "A shad would as soon be seen barking up a tree, as a Revolutionary soldier turning his back on the enemy or going to hell." The story may be apocryphal, since these sentiments seem too complicated to serve as a battle cry, but it perhaps illustrates the temper of the man.

In 1772, Jones was seized by the ambition to bring the word of the Lord to the western Indians, especially to the Shawnee, who had the reputation of being the most savage of the lot. In the late winter of 1773, after many delays and hardships he reached a village at the confluence of the Scioto River and Paint Creek, which Jones understood was called Chillicothe. (More accurately, it was a *chillicothe*, the Shawnee word for a considerable settlement.)

Jones arrived exhausted and famished from his hard trip. Though he was the first white man of God to visit these settlements, he was well received, being given food and shelter by various families. Jones remarked in his journal that they "may be said to possess some degree of hospitality." He noted that in many other respects these people were very uncivilized. They appeared to build their houses wherever it pleased them rather than on properly owned plots of ground. They did not exchange sacred vows when marrying, practiced no-fault divorce, and lacked jails.

After recovering his strength, Jones expressed his desire to go among the citizens of Chillicothe and preach. He was told that before doing so he should consult with a man named Yellow Hawk, who would soon return to the village from a hunt. After a few days he did and met with Jones who told him "that my chief business was to instruct them from GOD, for his mind was revealed to us [i.e., white Baptists], &c." Jones went on to outline the sermons he intended to offer. The gist of them was that he would tell the people how and why to mend their savage ways.

Yellow Hawk listened and then replied ("not with a very pleasant countenance, nor the most agreeable tone,") that the Maker of Life had long before explained to the Shawnee how He wanted them to live and that it would be blasphemous for a white man to speak contrary words in public. Yellow Hawk said Jones could stay for a time in the village but he was not to raise the "subject of religion." If he did, he would be immediately expelled or worse. Observing that the weather was bad, that he had no horse or food, and that the Shawnee seemed like "lions," Jones decided to be silent and live to evangelize another day. Fortunately he did. His account of the weeks he spent in Chillicothe is one of the best and earliest descriptions of the domestic life of the Shawnee.

Jones's first thought was that Yellow Hawk was a king or at least a high priest. Later he learned that he was simply a respected citizen who others thought would know how to deal with the white medicine man who had unexpectedly turned up in their midst. This discovery led Jones to some reflections about savage government, which were much more perceptive than those made by most white observers. He commented:

They are strangers to civil power and authority; they look on it that God made them free—that one man has no natural right to rule over another. . . . Every town has his head-men, some of which are called by us kings; but by what I can learn this appelation is by the Indians given to none, only as they learned it from us. The chief use of these head-men is to give counsel, especially in time of war; they are used also as most proper to speak with us on any occasion, especially if it be important.

This political philosophy prevailed among most of the natives of eastern North America. In each community and nation there were men and women whose opinions carried special weight, as Yellow Hawk's did, and who might command others when it came to settling domestic disputes, farming, hunting, fighting, or conducting foreign relations. However, they had no real coercive powers; they were followed and obeyed only to the extent that their directions seemed to make good sense to others. Certain perks and marks of respect might be extended to principal men and women, but they received no substantial material rewards for their public services. Even the greatest of them were obliged to support themselves and their families in the same way that less prominent citizens did.

The Rev. David Jones, despite finding many abominable customs in Chillicothe, was on the whole a sympathetic observer. He noted that while their style of government or nongovernment was practically ridiculous, it did seem in an odd way to agree with the ideals of "our greatest *politicians*, who affirm that a ruler's *authority extends* no further than the PLEASURE of the people."

For most other whites, the apparent willingness of these people to live in anarchy, without established rulers or hierarchies, was additional proof of how childish, irresponsible, and dangerous they were. Reds had a different but equally low opinion of white governments, which seemed to them to be autocratic arrangements which worked to make a few the masters of many.

Excepting for some Europeans of very strong puritanical convictions, both reds and whites valued leisure, and the former, because of their economic system, had much more of it than the latter. There is a sense in many of the early reports that nothing quite so annoyed whites as did the amount of free time the natives had on their hands. It appeared that very little of what the savages did amounted to real labor. They did not have bosses to get them up, set them to, and keep them working. They seemed to bestir themselves as it pleased them, did only enough to satisfy their immediate wants, and gave the impression of enjoying themselves in the process. For example their farming—with gossipy women in charge, their children playing in the fields, the men often doing nothing but lolling about laughing and cracking jokes—struck whites as being more like a community frolic than serious agriculture. Even hunting, an imperative and arduous work for nearly all red men, seemed fairly frivolous to Europeans, among whom, for some centuries, the pursuit of game had been a sport for the rich and powerful or a criminal activity of outlaws and poachers. William Byrd, of the great Virginia plantation family, remarked that red men "are quite idel, or at most emply'd only in the *Gentlemanly* Diversions of Hunting and Fishing."

To some like Byrd it was unseemly that half-naked savages should cavort about the woods acting as if they were gentry. Others had more serious moral and practical objections to the free and easy native life-style. Regularly, early white observers such as David Jones made the point that these people appeared to ignore or willfully flout the First Rule: that man must earn his daily bread by the sweat of his brow. Clearly they had to be taught or forced to labor as whites did before they could be Christianized, civilized, or turned into safe, useful neighbors. Reds came to analyze the situation in much the same way: that if they had to spend their days working at the dull, demeaning jobs of whites, they could no longer be what they had been and wanted to be; that the prospect of being civilized, as the whites defined it, was intolerable.

In their spare time reds enjoyed many pursuits that were very similar to white ones. At a sensual level, this made the abundant leisure of the former even more galling to the latter. David Jones noted that all day, "almost every night until near twelve o'clock," the Shawnee visited neighbors, took potluck, gossiped, sang, danced, played musical instruments and games, gambled at cards and dice, engaged in practical jokes and theatricals. (Jones was beset by a strolling band of mummers, dressed in outlandish animal costumes. At first he was badly frightened, mistaking the masqueraders for a troupe of devil worshippers.) "It appears," Jones observed reprovingly, "as if some kind of drollery was their chief study."

Jones visited Chillicothe in the late winter as its residents were reassembling after making their winter hunts. In consequence he made no mention of the warlike games and more or less sporting wars which in the summer and fall were a chief study of the Shawnee and other red peoples. These diversions were somewhat similar in purpose and even practice. For example, the Ball Game, the ancestor of modern lacrosse, was the most important sport in most of the woodland nations where it was sometimes called, with good reason, the Little Brother of War. Major contests between villages or clans might continue from dawn to dusk or for several days. In them, players were frequently crippled, and it was not uncommon for a few to be killed accidentally in the heat of competition. So far as warfare was concerned, reds among themselves sometimes fought for serious (from the European standpoint) reasons—to control hunting and foraging territories. More often these conflicts resembled international sporting events, organized and conducted to give men and communities an opportunity to gain glory and honor. Successful warriors often came home with transportable loot and prisoners, but the value of this booty was more symbolic than material, approximately equivalent to that of wreaths, palms, or trophies won by athletes.

At times certain classes (but seldom entire communities or nations) of Europeans had been similarly engrossed. However, the interest in affairs of honor had greatly declined by the time the invasion of North America commenced, particularly among the types who conducted it. Therefore how seriously the reds played games and how lightly they warred (somewhat in the fashion of medieval European jousters) was taken by white North Americans as another sign that the natives were congenitally backward. One historian was to claim that the time, energy, and resources they devoted to these useless activities constituted "economic insanity," and was an affliction which stifled their material progress. However, for Indians it was white economic concerns which were trivial as well as dismal. Reds were instructed from early childhood that the end-all and be-all for a man was to live heroically, and that of women to help men to do so. According to their traditions, heroes were made or recognized in big games and small wars.

Perhaps because they had more leisure, metaphysical and religious interests seem to have been more general and intense among reds than whites. The Indian approach to these matters was again essentially a heroic one. Theological beliefs varied between nations, but it seems that nearly all the reds were deists, acknowledging an omnipotent, first being who had created and ordered the world. As a practical matter, the Maker of Life was too high and mighty to take much interest in routine temporal happenings but He or She had created a sizable company of lesser noncorporeal beings whose job it was to do so. These spirits were more bizarre in form and behavior than Christian angels, devils, or saints, often appearing as animals, plants, geological or meteorological phenomena. Also they were apt to involve themselves with people in direct, physical, and emotional ways, becoming angered or amused by humans, dealing with them in loving, deceitful, or vengeful ways. Naturally, red men and women were much concerned with identifying these spirits, learning about their habits, how to win their good opinion, or if necessary contend against them.

All of which whites, in the main, initially dismissed as the fantasies of ignorant, superstitious savages. More recently, different opinions have been advanced. One of them is that the religious beliefs and practices, the heroic games, wars, and ideals, to some extent the political philosophies of the native North Americans rather closely resembled those of the early Greeks of whom Homer sang. Historians have suggested that a more sympathetic and attentive study of the red culture—while it was still intact—might have provided instructive insights into the origins and components of European civilizations. However, at the time, in the field so to speak, reds seemed so alien and dangerous that few whites had either the inclination or opportunity for such intellectual work. Commentaries on both sides were largely devoted to cataloging the bad manners, stupidities, and general wickedness of the other race.

Guesses—and nothing more has ever been possible—about the size of the native population of North America when Europeans arrived, range from less than one to more than ten million. Even if the highest estimates are accepted, the numbers are surprisingly low, given the size and resources of the country and the length of time it had been occupied (for at least 10,000 years in the eastern woodlands). There is no evidence that the North Americans were innately less fertile, long-lived, or vigorous than other peoples. As noted, they often were at war but compared to those of other places, theirs were brief, low-casualty affairs. Also there are no indications that they suffered more than Europeans from famines and epidemic diseases.

Ecology rather than sociology may provide the best explanation of why North America was so sparsely settled in the sixteenth and earlier centuries. For generations the natives had supported themselves in a satisfactory manner, basically by consuming naturally created surpluses. In consequence they were not greatly motivated to augment them by developing more exploitive habits which elsewhere—including South and Central America—had permitted and required people to become more numerous. In short, the North Americans had attitudes and appetites which allowed, or forced, them to live within the carrying capacity of their lands.

The traditional red system constituted a successful environmental adaptation, until it was exposed to the white one. Contrary to various genetic and moralistic claims, this did not occur because whites were naturally more intelligent, energetic, or pious than reds—or, as has been suggested in the last few decades, were inherently more cruel, greedy, and depraved. Rather, for historical reasons white culture had come to contain elements which proved to be absolutely incompatible with, and eventually fatal to, red culture as it had evolved.

A botanical happening serves as an analogy. The American chestnut was a splendid tree, so well suited to the local environment that it once made up some 40 percent of the forest cover east of the Mississippi. Early in the twentieth century a chestnut blight virus was accidentally brought to this country from abroad. It swept through the eastern forest like an enormous biological fire, killing millions of chestnuts, leaving only a few thousand scattered survivors. This happened not because one of the organisms was more or less vigorous or effective than the other, but rather because of the evolved properties each possessed. White and red cultures stood to one another somewhat as did the chestnut blight virus and the American chestnut tree. The consequences of their meeting were quite similar.

Most obviously, the whites brought with them a terrible collection of poxes and fluxes, flus and fevers for which the reds had little or no natural immunity. (The whites did because of long previous exposure.) Within a few years after the arrival of disease-bearing Europeans, native communities along the Atlantic coast were devastated and depopulated by these contagions. As the survivors fled, they took the seeds of the scourges with them. Epidemics raged among more westerly people even before they came in contact with whites. On the basis of anecdotal accounts and circumstantial evidence, it has been estimated that in the seventeenth century the native population of eastern North America was reduced 50 percent or more by diseases introduced by whites.

Where similar catastrophes had occurred, it could at least be claimed that certain material benefits resulted. Though it presumedly brought them little comfort, those who remained after the Black Death plagues swept over Europe were wealthier than they had been before, since there were so few left to use the available resources. This was not the case with the native North Americans. The whites brought other things, a great array of new material goods, which had the effect of increasing red appetites and their resource needs.

The utility of some of the white possessions—guns, horses, metal weapons, tools, and utensils—was immediately apparent to reds.

Many other items appealed to them for sensual reasons, because they were so novel, cunningly contrived, and beautiful.

Reds immediately coveted European goods but they did not have traditions or skills which inclined them to get them as whites did, by laborious manufacture. Their economy was based on finding and taking more or less ready-made things. This tactic naturally suggested itself in regard the whites, but they proved to be so well armed and (shortly) numerous that looting was dangerous and ineffective. The only other alternative was to barter, to which whites were very agreeable. The one thing the natives had in abundance and whites wanted was wild animals, that is, the furs of some of them. For the next 150 years the relationship between the two races largely revolved around the exchange of peltries for manufactured goods.

A popular stereotype pictures unscrupulous white traders seducing innocent reds into commercial transactions, cheating them, and then riding home chortling about how they had obtained a small fortune in furs for nothing more than a handful of cheap trinkets. Such things happened infrequently. Customarily a few white traders entered red communities and did their business, politely, while surrounded by armed, pugnacious hunter-warriors, who had little affection for them. If the reds on reflection did not like the bargains they first struck, they could intercept the white merchants before they had left their territories and make, by force, a new deal. More often it was reds who gloated about how they had horn-swoggled or intimidated stupid whites into giving them two marvelously sharp axes and a keg of rum that would provide hours of delight for a pack of common hides. The fur trade, like any other, continued because both buyers and sellers thought it profitable.

To trade with the whites, reds stepped up their harvest of naturally created surpluses and began converting them into foreign exchange. Though the luxurious furs of beaver, mink, otter, and other small animals were individually more valuable, the bulk item in this commerce was the hides of white-tailed deer, the animal most used in red communities for food and fabric. In 1770, the first year from which comprehensive records survive, about 800,000 pounds of deerskins were exported from the American colonies. At the same time, thousands of deer were being taken for domestic use by reds and whites.

The time sequence varied from place to place, but rather quickly the surpluses were exhausted, and red hunters began dipping into what might be called their natural capital—i.e., to harvest animals faster than they could renew their populations. This brought about immense changes in the woodlands, affecting not only furbearers but all animals, plants, and humans connected with them by intricate ecological webs. So far as the people were concerned, what was happening was masked for a time. In part because of greater need and also because they were equipped with white weapons and tools, red woodsmen ranged farther and hunted harder than had been their custom. Therefore harvests remained large, but the rate at which wildlife populations—and everything associated with them—were declining became more rapid.

By the latter part of the eighteenth century, game had become noticeably scarcer in many regions east of the Mississippi. Red residents were increasingly hard-pressed to get the wherewithal to trade for white goods, many of which had come to be regarded as necessities, and at the same time feed, clothe, and otherwise support themselves. Especially during the winters, famines began to occur, and generally reds came to be—and to recognize that they were—poorer than their ancestors had been. Having no expertise or desire to farm as whites did, they dug deeper into their natural capital, eating up, literally and figuratively, the resource base which for centuries had produced their wealth.

The long-range effect of the fur trade was to undercut the traditional red economy. The process was accelerated by white determination to own and develop lands controlled by reds. For the nations west of the Appalachians, this pressure commenced to be felt in the period just prior to the Revolutionary War and thereafter became steadily more intense.

During the seventeenth century, Europeans were largely occupied with settling and improving a narrow, 100-mile or so wide strip of flatland along the Atlantic coast. (Disease more than war or trade cleared this territory of its native inhabitants.) However, the white population in what is now the United States grew from about 250,000 in 1700 to more than 1.5 million in 1760. Immigrants—particularly Scotch-Irish and lowland Germans—accounted for much of this increase. These newcomers were desperate to obtain land of their own, but on arriving found that nearly all of the coastal properties were already owned by earlier, mostly English, emigrants. The migration of the Scotch-Irish and, to a lesser extent, Germans was directed toward the west where there was an abundance of land, vacant except for a few savages. British authorities concerned with maintaining the lucrative fur trade—and therefore the wilderness animals and peoples who supported it—did little to facilitate the westward movement of these white peasants. In fact they periodically tried to suppress it with edicts and proclamations, but were unable to do so. Land-hungry whites, like an irreversible tide, began to flow into and then across the mountains. After the

Revolution, encouraging this migrating, wresting the lands by purchase, negotiation, or force from the reds became the principal domestic concern of the government and people of the United States. Neither had much interest in the fur trade. Even before their independence, the trade had employed and profited only a few colonists, and after the Revolution it remained under the control of the British, based in Canada.

There were exceptions, red nations and communities who voluntarily gave up their territories and hoped for the best. But, generally the reds chose to resist, convinced that they could not share the land with the whites and continue to live as they wanted, or at all, for long thereafter. White feelings were substantially the same: that free Indians made dangerous and thoroughly undesirable neighbors. Therefore, in and to the west of the Appalachians, the forest wars between the two races began in the 1760s and continued intermittently for the next fifty years.

Though seldom noted in the histories of the time, it was the military prowess of red men which made the conflict such a long and bitter one. From early childhood onward they were inspired to become heroic warriors. They commenced taking part in minor actions while in their early teens. By the time they reached adulthood, they were superbly trained in both battle and woodcraft: to go to war carrying only a small pack of supplies and live off the land for weeks or months; to move rapidly and surreptitiously through the forests; to maintain their morale while enduring fatigue, hunger, and pain. For the most part these students and lovers of war were opposed by white farm boys, factory hands, and clerks who were paid or forced to fight. They had few heroic ambitions and, as a rule, little experience at fighting, living, or even traveling in forests. They were often led by civilians, distinguished from their troops only by the fact that they had become more prosperous and respected in peacetime pursuits. Professional military men among the whites usually were wedded to strategies devised for European campaigns of maneuver in open country. In time a few Scotch-Irish frontiersmen learned something of Indian tactics, but even the best of them, the Boones and Kentons, were no more able than ordinary warriors.

The results were not surprising. In hundreds of small skirmishes and occasionally a major battle, the more mobile and skillful warriors defeated larger companies of whites. Beyond immediate advantage, these successes created a balance of terror, which benefited the reds. Often the invasion was slowed, or sometimes halted for substantial periods, because whites so greatly feared the warriors that they imagined them to be more terrible and numerous than they were. Conversely their victories made the warriors excessively contemptuous about the courage and character of white men, overconfident about being able to go on indefinitely routing any number of them.

However, the mathematics of the situation greatly, inexorably favored the whites. Given the overall disparity in numbers and the fact that whites were constantly reinforced—as the reds were not—by new immigrants to the frontier war zones, the warriors were individually more valuable to their communities than white soldiers were to theirs. Therefore, though red casualties were consistently lighter than white ones, the consequences were heavier. Warren Moorehead, a local Ohio historian, spent the winter of 1893–94 working through old military records and journals trying to compile a body count for the forest wars in that state. He concluded that 12,002 whites and 7,837 reds were killed. Though it speaks well of their martial ability, even such a ratio was, in the long term, disastrous for the reds.

Economically, proportionate to the wealth they had, the forest wars were much more costly for the defenders than they were for the invaders. Red communities were obliged to allocate ever more substantial portions of their dwindling resources to keep warriors in the field during the long-drawn-out campaigns the whites were able to conduct. The warriors were also the hunters. During much of the year they were the principal food producers, and the loss of them or even their prolonged absence resulted in immediate and severe hardship for their dependents. Finally, though furbearers were much scarcer than they had been, the wars made it even more necessary for reds to trade with the whites. Most obviously, they had an imperative need for guns and ammunition, which they could not fight without but could not manufacture. They got them and other commodities by increasing the rate at which they exported their natural capital.

It has been argued with justification that had not fur traders, supported by British political and military agents, continued to arm and eventually feed the red resisters, the forest wars would have been less lengthy and bloody than they were. But again, it was not a matter of innocent primitives being seduced and corrupted. The parties to these transactions had similar self-interests in halting the westward advance of the white Americans.

As the two races struggled to control the land, they advanced, as is customary, explanations to justify what they were doing. Whites, who ordinarily paid little attention to it, used natural law as a basis for their case, asserting that it was wrong that a few savages should continue to enjoy exclusive possession of the continent's rich resources. In 1802 as the red resistance was weakening, the point was summarized, in a series of rhetorical questions, by John Quincy Adams: "What is the right of a huntsman to the forest of a thousand miles over which he has accidentally ranged in quest of prey? . . . Shall the fields and vallies, which a beneficent God has formed to teem with the life of innumerable multitudes, be condemned to everlasting barreness?"

Red counterclaims rested on a bedrock principle of human law. The land was theirs because they were there first.

Even now both cases seem unassailable. Contemporary environmental theory fully supports the proposition of Adams: that it is right, an evolutionary imperative, that creatures pioneer into new territories, adapt to them, compete with earlier occupants, diversify, and multiply. It is difficult to argue on ecological or moral grounds that, once having found North America, Europeans should have turned away or left it as it was. On the other hand, just as reds claimed, in virtually all human societies, there is a fundamental legal principle to the effect that it is unjust and immoral to force those who have first title to a property to give up their rights to use it as they see fit.

The paradox is interesting, but the confrontation beween reds and whites in the forests of North America was not settled in accordance with moral or social law. The bottom line, so to speak, was that having become what they were, the reds ultimately could not afford to be at peace with the whites—to share the land and trade with them—or to remain at war with them.

II. To Be Shawnee

Anthropologists with taxonomical interests divided the red nations of North America into "families," based on similarities in their languages. The Shawnee were placed among the Algonquians, whose thirty or so members included the Delaware, Penobscot, and Powhatan of the Atlantic seaboard, Miamis, Kickapoos, Illinois, and many others in the middle of the continent, the Arapaho, Blackfeet, and Cheyenne of the far west.

This classification was a matter of absolute indifference to the natives involved who did not know there was an Algonquian family or that they were of it. That their languages had common roots—often fewer and less obvious ones than those of the languages of Europe—did not allow them to converse easily and did not promote any special feelings of affection. Throughout their recorded history the Shawnee, for example, got along much better with the Creek and Wyandot (members respectively of the Muskogean and Iroquoian language families) than they did with the Kickapoo, Illinois, and other Algonquians.

According to archaeological evidence, red people commenced to move into eastern North America, from the south or west, 10,000 to 12,000 years ago. In the centuries immediately preceding the Christian era, some of them began building substantial earthen memorials and tombs. Enough of these works survived into modern times to give the name "Mound Builder" to an entire culture, which in fact had many different components. The consensus is that the most immediate, identifiable ancestors of the Shawnee were members of what is now called the Fort Ancient culture. These people were, commencing about 1000 A.D., mound builders

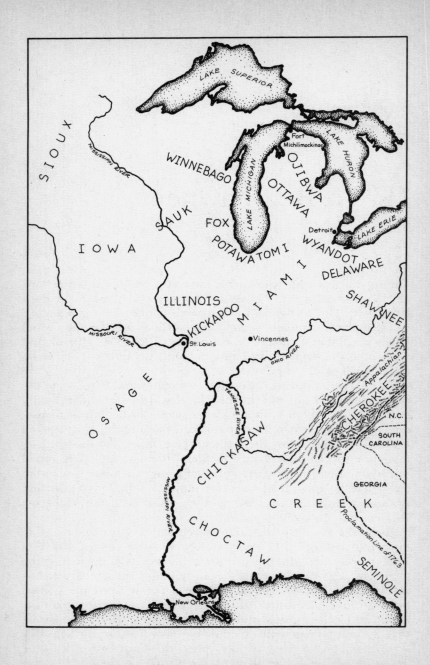

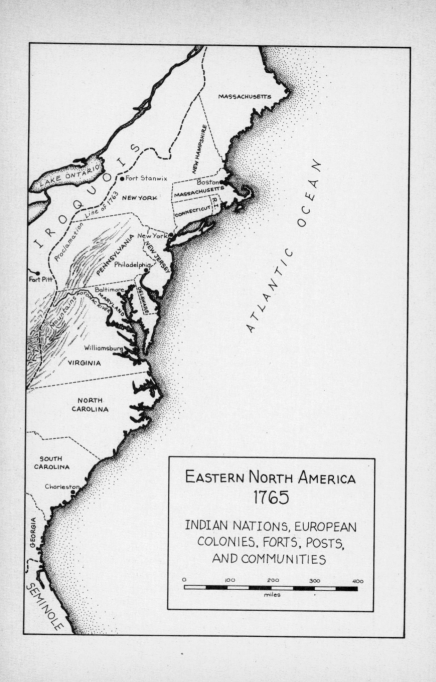

EASTERN NORTH AMERICA
1765

INDIAN NATIONS, EUROPEAN
COLONIES, FORTS, POSTS,
AND COMMUNITIES

0   100   200   300   400
miles

in the Ohio River drainage system. Shawnee of the historic period were aware of these prominent, antique earthworks and thought they had been built by their ancestors. They made no particular use of the structures and seem to have been less curious about them than were white archaeologists.

In other respects the Shawnee were extremely interested in who they were and from where they had come. The longest surviving account of their prehistory—by one who lived when the Shawnee were free and their youths were traditionally instructed in the subject—was made by Tenskwatawa, the Prophet and brother of Tekamthi. Tenskwatawa possessed a powerful and manipulative personality but not by Shawnee standards a heroic one. After the death of his brother and the ruination of the resistance movement they had led, he spent much of the rest of his life ingratiating himself with the victorious whites. To this end, in 1824, he agreed to talk to a Charles Trowbridge about the history of the Shawnee. Trowbridge was an energetic, ambitious young man who sometimes worked as an Indian agent for Lewis Cass, then the governor of Michigan. Cass had campaigned against Tekamthi but later had developed an avocational interest in ethnology. Therefore he had persuaded the federal war department to provide funds so that Trowbridge could interview, before they passed on, various Indian leaders who had been prominent while their people were still free.

Tenskwatawa commenced by speaking to Trowbridge of the creation of the Shawnee. He said:

> When the Great Spirit made this Island [the planet] he thought it necessary to make also human beings to inhabit it, and with this view he formed an Indian. After making him he caused him to stand erect, and having surveyed him from head to foot he pronounced the work defective, and made another, which he examined in the same manner with great care and particularity and at length pronounced him well made & perfect. But previous to making the second he discovered that one of the Principal defects in the other consisted in misplacing the privates to the forehead instead of the middle of the body, and seeing this he immediately took apart the limbs and reformed them. In this second formation he placed the privates under the arm of a man, and of a woman, whom he also made at the same time, and finding this would not do he became vexed and threw away the different members of the body. After some time employed in reflecting about the means necessary to accomplish the desired end, he set himself again at work to put them together, and at last made them as they now are, and was satisfied. Then his mind was a good deal troubled to know how this man & woman should commence to increase. He placed

them together side by side & retiring a few paces seated himself to survey them. He thus changed their position to each other frequently, at each change seating himself to examine the effect, until they faced each other and by dint of changing or moving became connected in the act of copulation. When he saw this he deemed it good, and having told them how to proceed left them to their will. After some time the woman was discovered to be pregnant & in about a year was delivered of a child. The Great Spirit then told the man & woman that they should live, increase & multiply in that manner, that he had made them & thereafter they must make themselves. He then opened the door of the skies & the Indians looking down saw this Island. By this time there were 12 Indians at the residence of the Great Spirit. They were all Shawanese, but the roots of 12 tribes. He told them they must come down to live upon this Island, that it would take them 12 days, which days were equal to years of the Indians, and that in the mean time he would finish every thing to be created upon the earth. That means must be provided for their subsistence on the earth where they were to live and that as he had taken his time to make *them*, he must also proceed gradually in forming all things below. That he would give them a piece of his heart, which was good, and would *mix it* with the hearts which they had, so that a part of their hearts at least should be good. "Now" said the Gt. spirit, "I can hear, and I will give you ears that you may distinguish the least noize. I can speak, & I will give you tongues that you may communicate with each other. I will also give you of my teeth to chew your food—which shall be corn, beans, cucumbers, squashes, melons—& Elk, Deer, Bear, Buffaloe, Turkey & Raccoon & small game. Of vegetables you shall have twelve kinds, and of meats twelve kinds. And now I have finished you and all things else. Remember who made you & these and do not at any time attribute the formation to any but me. Your age shall be 200 years, and then your head shall become white like mine, and you will drop down. When you become thus advanced you must tell your children all that I have told you that it may be transmitted to the latest posterity.

The Great Spirit again opened a door of heaven and allowed the first people to peer down at His works. They saw what he had described, but also a grotesque. It was a being somewhat in their own shape but of a bad, pallid color, hairless and circumcised. The Maker told them that the creature was not one of His, that it had been created by another sort of spirit. He therefore had no control over this white man or its descendants. Furthermore He predicted that eventually the white spirit, working through the mortals he had made, would attempt to do mischief to the reds and "would certainly exert himself to change the period of their existence from 200 years to a shorter time."

However, these difficulties lay in the future and the immediate purpose of the first twelve reds was to become "comfortably situated" on earth. To lead them on this great endeavor the Maker created two old men, Kweekoolaa, and his second in command, Maakweekeelau. Then He packed all fourteen humans into a large basket, carried them to and deposited them in the world. They wandered about for a time and came to the edge of a great ocean. There Kweekoolaa made prayers and was advised by the Great Spirit that it was His wish that they cross the sea and go to a northern land. To enable them to do so He temporarily parted the waters, making a smooth path of sand. However He also commanded that Kweekoolaa must remain behind. The First Twelve were then led by Maakweekeelau who, upon arriving on the far shore, counseled the people that they must move farther to the north, but he would stay behind "to look on his friend Kweekoolaa who remained on the opposite side of the sea." These two old men became, said Tenskwatawa, two rocks. They will stand, one at each end of the miraculous trail which the Shawnee used to reach North America, so long as the earth survives.

Left to their own devices, the People continued to march northward. As they did so, the women bore many children, and each of the men developed special skills and separate responsibilities for making travel arrangements, hunting, security, conducting religious services, etc. The descendants of one of the original six couples did not prosper and this line expired. However, the other First men became the founders—and their progeny members—of the five permanent divisions or tribes of the Shawnee nation. They were the Chalaakaatha, Mekoche, Thaawikila, Pekowi, and Kispoko. In historic times all Shawnee identified themselves as belonging to one of these divisions each of which, according to tradition, had different roles to play in both peace and war. However, villages, traveling bands, war parties, and marriage might be mixed in terms of these divisional affiliations. Puckeshinwa, the father of Tekamthi and the Prophet, was, for example, a Kispoko, while their mother, Methoastaske, was a Pekowi.

To return to Tenskwatawa's account. In due time the original group, much increased in numbers, came to a large river. While camped there, they were visited by the Great Spirit. He told them that they had reached the place he had intended for them and that the river was to be known as the Shauwonoa, as they themselves should be. He said that He would not return in person to them again, that they henceforth "must think for themselves." He advised them that to serve as their special protector he had created an old woman whom they should know as their Grandmother and who would receive their prayers.

Having settled in along the river, the Shawnee began to explore and found that for purposes of His Own, the Great Spirit, after having made them, had created inferior Indian nations and placed them in this country. They decided to visit some of these secondary people, but on approaching them were warned not to come farther.

> But the Shawenese fearlessly approached, disclosing to the Creeks (for such were the newcomers) their origins etc. When they came to the description of the medicine the Creeks pretended to doubt the truth of the story, whereupon, the Shawenese, vexed, destroyed all of the Creeks by virtue of the medicine. The next day however they brought some of them to life by the same means and compromised with them, calling them thereafter their brothers.

In subsequent travels the Shawnee met the Catawba, Chippewa, and other people, all of whom first vexed them and then were soundly beaten. In time, the Six Nations of the Iroquois sent 7,000 men against the Shawnee:

> They attacked the Shawanoa village at break of day, and had well nigh killed the whole of their warriors, when the remaining few took the weapons & habiliments of those killed and putting them upon the women, the latter joined the party and by their numbers and appearance so much deceived the 6 Nations that they supposed themselves attacked by a fresh force and fled.

Other secular and sacred historians of the Shawnee who spoke to white recorders added information, or did not mention some of the things which Tenskwatawa did. However, all confirmed the main points of his account, particularly that the Shawnee had been made before and better than any other people. Some argued that the Great Spirit had indeed manufactured the whites, but quickly and of very coarse materials. The Shawnee were molded from His heart (or brain, in other versions), but He used bits of His chest for the French and English, toes for the Dutch, hands for the Americans, etc. That they are specially and divinely endowed has occurred to many other people, but few have been so convinced about their superiority and arrogant about flouting it as were the Shawnee.

Also like Tenskwatawa, other oral historians insisted that the Shawnee had come to North America after making an immense journey, which required them to cross the sea. Apparently no other woodland natives had this belief. Perhaps in rather recent times the Shawnee had made such a unique migration—or, for inexplicable reasons, the passage of man from Asia to North America, which others had forgotten, remained fixed in their collective memory. It is also quite possible that the story was a fiction, flowing from their sense of being so special. Whatever the case, no artifacts have been found which support—or deny—their claims.

White records and Shawnee traditions differ greatly in specifics —names, dates, places, numbers, etc.—but are compatible so far as general themes are concerned. For example, just as Tenskwatawa observed, the Shawnee always seem to have been a singularly restless people. In the seventeenth century when Europeans first began to hear of them, they were irregularly scattered in small bands and villages through the eastern half of the continent. They might appear anyplace between Florida and the Great Lakes, the Atlantic Coast and the prairies, remain for a few years or generations, and then move on to another place often hundreds of miles distant. The anthropologist Charles Callender wrote:

> The Shawnee during their recorded history were never united into a single society. Their fragmentation, combined with the extent and frequency of their movements, make it difficult to assign them to a specific area . . . and it seems impossible to associate them with any one type of environment.

Another ancient trait of his people, their consistent belligerency, was mentioned by Tenskwatawa. Many others, both red and white, thought this was their most distinguishing characteristic. So far as their known history goes, there are few periods when the nomadic Shawnee—some of whom seemed to be always trying to establish themselves in the homelands of more settled people—were able or inclined to be truly at peace. Tenskwatawa told Charles Trowbridge that of all the nations they knew of, there were only three with whom the Shawnee had *not* fought. Even this stretched the truth a bit, for he included (along with the Delaware and Wyandot) the Creek on the grounds that, though the Shawnee had first annihilated them, they had reconstituted these people and ever after lived at peace with them.

As for whites, the Shawnee said they immediately mistrusted them, unlike other nations who on first meeting these strangers thought they might be benign or even semidivine. According to Shawnee oral historians, the first contact with Europeans had been made by a band of their people camped on an Atlantic beach. One day they sighted a huge misshapen canoe, driven by sails attached to the trunks of trees. From one of the trees flew a forked pennant which the Shawnee took to be the insignia of the Great Serpent, which they had long understood embodied evil. The craft landed and, as foretold, out of it came white men. The Shawnee advanced to meet these repugnant beings who, pacifically, opened a keg of strong drink and offered to share it. Fearing neither men nor devils, the Shawnee drank the liquor, which brought tears to their eyes. When they had recovered, an old man, acquainted with the ancient lore, concluded that the drink was a poison like the venom of the Serpent. He prophesied, "This is what is to destroy our young men."

It is possible that this was a stylized description of a real event. Interpretations of the reports made by the De Soto expedition to Georgia in 1540 and those of the Roanoke colonists in Virginia, forty-five years later, suggest that the Shawnee were among the first natives encountered along the beaches. Aside from these wispy stories of contacts in the south, the earliest European reports about the Shawnee were made by the French. As their explorers and traders traveled west, they were told by residents of a roving, troublesome people more to the interior. This nation was variously spoken of as the Sawana (by the Miamis), Osawanow (Menominee), Chaoanos (Illinois), and Shawunogi (Fox and Sauk). In all languages the name meant, approximately, "persons from the south." The French decided to call them Chaouanons. The English tried such forms as Savana and Satana before fixing on Shawano and then Shawnee.

The Shawnee entered the formal history of North America in the midseventeenth century as a result of their becoming embroiled in a series of wars with the Iroquois—i.e., the Mohawk, Oneida, Onondaga, Cayuga, and Seneca. (In 1722 the Tuscarora, who migrated to New York from North Carolina, were admitted as junior members of this confederation, which came to be called the League of Six Nations—but is more properly referred to as Five Nations prior to 1722.) All were members of the Iroquoian language group, which included among others the Cherokee. For three centuries the affairs of the Iroquois (hereafter used to designate only these Five or Six Nations) were to have a great influence not only on those of the Shawnee but all other people, red and white, in eastern North America.

When the French came to the St. Lawrence valley in the sixteenth century, the Iroquois inhabited central and western New York. The confederacy was formed to defend against larger, hostile nations—Huron, Erie, Mohican, Susquehannock, who ringed the Iroquois on all sides. The most powerful of these enemies were the Huron who, with more than 30,000 people, were at least twice as numerous as the Iroquois and well situated strategically at the head of the river. The French formed an alliance with these people and to show solidarity with them sent soldiers along with a Huron war party, which met and routed a company of Mohawk warriors.

Fortunately for the Iroquois, the Dutch and later British shortly turned up on their doorsteps in the Hudson valley. Both were eager to trade and to form anti-French alliances. By 1630 the Iroquois appetite for European goods and weapons had increased but furbearers in their limited territories had declined to the extent that they were having great difficulty raising foreign exchange. The obvious place to get more fur was in the Great Lakes region to the north and west of them, but these parts were occupied by nations who were already sending their pelts, through the Hurons, down the St. Lawrence to the French. The Iroquois became ambitious of filling the same profitable middleman role. Since neither the French nor the Hurons had any interest in sharing this lucrative commerce, the only option for the Iroquois was to enter the business by force. To do so, the Iroquois commenced what is remembered as the Beaver Wars. They were quite different from previous international conflicts between North American natives, being fought, at least by the Iroquois, for material and strategic gain. Once they understood the aims of the Five Nations, the Dutch and the British strongly approved, and supported them with arms and political and military advice.

Initially the Iroquois tried hijacking canoe flotillas which brought the furs to Montreal, but had indifferent success with these tactics. Therefore in 1649, breaking with red military tradition, the Five Nations launched, in midwinter, a blitzkrieg-like attack. It so punished and demoralized the Huron that this nation ceased to exist as an organized political community. (Huron refugees wandered for a time in the upper Great Lakes region. Eventually their descendants settled in southern Michigan and Ohio, where they became known as the Wyandot.) Subsequently the Iroquois dealt in similar fashion with the Erie and Neutrals—nations to the west of them in Ontario and Pennsylvania—and with the Susquehannocks who occupied territories to the south along the river which was named for them.

These preemptive strikes cleared away some of their neighbors but otherwise did not make the Iroquois more secure or prosperous than they had been.

To the north the French increased their military presence and reorganized the fur trade so that the Nipissing and Ottawa replaced the Huron as middlemen in the region east of Lake Superior. Once again the Iroquois were barred from the fur trade and found themselves on the defensive against the French and their red allies. The Five Nations responded, in the latter part of the seventeenth century, by striking off in a new direction—into the Ohio Valley country. They came too late with too little, finding that the French had already begun to build posts south of the Great Lakes and that the natives of the area were much more difficult to subdue than the Hurons had been.

In the 1680s Iroquois warriors, never more than 500 of them at one time, threatened and occasionally fought the Miami in Indiana, a confederation of Illinois nations, and, everywhere, the Shawnee. The Five Nations won some battles and seized some furs but were unable to conquer, overawe, or establish exclusive trade relations with any of the locals. In the 1690s they withdrew their war parties and, though their agents and diplomats continued to circulate, were not thereafter a military factor in the region.

Back in New York the Iroquois hit upon a brilliant idea. They declared that their western adventures had been so successful that the Ohio Valley nations were now their vassals. This claim was later expanded. A Mohawk chief announced: "We are the six confederate nations, as the Heads and Superiors of all Indian nations of the Continent of America."

Since none of the western people admitted to being or behaved as Iroquois subjects, the ploy would have amounted to no more than an interesting face-saving exercise except for the response of the British and their colonial representatives. These authorities not only accepted the Iroquois claims but helped to expand and enforce them. They did so not because they were excessively gullible but because they were philosophically comfortable with imperial concepts and found it convenient to have a red empire, even if it was mostly fictitious.

By treating with the Iroquois as if they were the "heads" of the rest, the English were able to ignore many of the other savages. If, for example, they signed a treaty with the League giving them trading or territorial rights in country traditionally occupied by the Delaware or Shawnee, the Iroquois—because they had been paid to—would help to enforce its provisions. The arrangement gave the English a satisfying sense of having done things in a legal, ethical way. Third parties who objected to whites occupying their lands could be told that it was done in accordance with a valid diplomatic contract made with their imperial masters, the Six Nations.

The Iroquois alliance was also valuable to the British as a

bargaining chip in games of power politics played with France, Spain, and later the United States. No mean illusionists themselves, the British after a time declared that the League of the Six Nations was their tributary, a client state. Therefore, according to European custom and law, they held de jure title to all the territories, at least up to the Mississippi, which the League said it owned by right of conquest. In this inexpensive, painless way, the British came to have claims in the Ohio Valley which other whites took seriously.

The Iroquois themselves did very well because of these arrangements. In return for giving title to things which they had never previously owned, they received lump-sum settlements, long-term subsidies, special trading privileges, and arms. Sometimes reality —other peoples refusing to go along with the imperial charade— intruded. However, the British already were, and the Iroquois became, adept at ignoring and explaining away awkward facts that contradicted useful fictions. A certain temperamental affinity seems to have contributed to the success of this odd partnership.

The Iroquois have been generally remembered as the most bloodthirsty and ferocious of the North American natives. They are indeed worth remembering but not for those reasons. After their initial victories in the Beaver Wars, they did not often fight. In fact, the cornerstone of their policy was to avoid war by negotiation and bluff. When they were forced into battle they were not particularly successful. Nevertheless, they remained a significant force for two centuries after the European invasion commenced. They did so essentially by using their wits and becoming the most geopolitically astute of all the red nations.

As for the Five Nations and the Shawnee, their relations seem to have been consistently bad. The more settled, sophisticated Iroquois clearly found the wandering bands of Shawnee uncouth and troublesome. They spoke of them as the Ontoagannha, "persons of unintelligible speech." League representatives told the British that when it came to land titles and trading privileges, the Ontoagannha should be ignored because they were barbarians, "mere hunters without communities or Chief men." There are no recorded statements directly explaining how the Shawnee felt, but their behavior indicated that they thought of the Iroquois as greedy, treacherous, and later as running dogs of the English.

If Tenskwatawa's statement is at all factual, Shawnee and Iroquois commenced fighting before whites arrived. If not, they were doing so shortly thereafter, for Capt. John Smith of Virginia reported in 1607 that the two nations were engaged in a fierce war along the Susquehanna River. Thereafter, the Shawnee fought occasionally with the Eries, Neutrals, and Susquehannocks against the Iroquois in the Beaver Wars and later in the Ohio Valley. Beyond being nomadic, the Shawnee were widely engaged because they came to be mercenaries of sorts. As a "restless people delighting in war" (so observed a Mohican chief), bands of Shawnee were sometimes asked to relocate within or near to the territories of other nations, with the hope that they would help against the enemies of their hosts.

Most of the information about Iroquois–Shawnee confrontations in the seventeenth century came from the former. In formal eastern councils, the League declared that they were so often victorious that the Shawnee had been added to their roll of subjects. This was propaganda concocted for whites. More objective communiqués indicate that after a century of fighting, the irregular Shawnee were if anything more troublesome than ever. In 1683, the Five Nations threatened to invade the Miami because they had sought assistance from the Shawnee. Later a white agent returning from a meeting with the Iroquois told colonial authorities in New York that the savage Shawnee, some of whom had moved east, were in a "public war with the Iroquois, who show great displeasure because the government makes peace with these Indians."

Because of the Iroquois wars, or perhaps to escape plagues, the Shawnee became especially migratory in the latter part of the seventeenth century, spreading out in all directions from the lower Ohio Valley, where many of them had congregated in the early 1600s. Some moved to Alabama where they established villages within and at the pleasure of the Creek nation. Others, at the request of the Cherokee, moved through the territories of that nation to settle in South Carolina. (This was by no means new country for the Shawnee. In times past they had occupied villages along the Carolina, Georgia, and Florida coasts and traded with the Spanish before they did with either the French or British.) After arriving, the Shawnee destroyed, more or less as commissioned, a local nation, the Westo. Then they entered into the business of capturing other reds and selling them to white slave dealers in South Carolina. Eventually the Cherokee, Catawba, Natchez, Chickasaw, and other nations of the midsouth formed an alliance and, in 1700 or thereabouts, drove the Shawnee from the region. The coalition was partly motivated by economic interest, since some of its members, particularly the Chickasaw, were themselves prominent slavers and did not want to share the market with such newcomers as the Shawnee. The southern trade in Indian slaves, most of whom were transported to the Caribbean, flourished at this time. The English buyers justified it, in part, on theological grounds. Catholic missionaries, working from French posts on the lower Mississippi, were then proselytizing among the Indians of this region. The English argued that if left in freedom and igno- rance, these people might well fall into the clutches of the papists, a fate, so far as their souls were concerned, much worse than being enslaved by protestants who would at least expose them to sound Christian doctrine.

Other Shawnee migrated northward. Some settled for a time in the vicinity of Fort St. Louis, then the westernmost French strong point on the Illinois River. They were encouraged to do so by Réné Robert Cavelier de La Salle, who built the post in 1682 to promote French trade and keep the Iroquois and British out of the region. La Salle formed a high opinion of the intelligence and character of the Shawnee, taking two warriors, as the best representatives of the red race, with him on a visit to France.

In 1685 there were nearly 1,000 Shawnee gathered on the upper Illinois, but shortly they became restless once again. Some re- turned south to join the enclave of their people among the Creek. Some relocated along Lake Erie, in areas which had been largely depopulated by the Beaver Wars. Another band of particular historic importance turned east.

In 1690 five Delaware showed up near Fort St. Louis with the design of drumming up business for themselves and English traders in Pennsylvania and New York. They approached a Shaw- nee chief, Opeththa, and urged that his group establish a village on the upper Delaware river. Opeththa made prudent inquiries about the nature of that countryside and especially about how the Iroquois might react if he and his people appeared. The Delaware assured him that it was a fine location and there was nothing the League could or would do to them. Opeththa then agreed to make the move, saying, "We have been everywhere and could find no good land."

These conversations were reported to Henri Tonty, one of La Salle's aides, then in charge at Fort St. Louis. Not wanting to lose the Shawnee, their warriors, and furs, Tonty came out to make medicine of his own. Among other things he directly warned the Delaware agents: "All the Indians that you take along will be killed and yourself also."

The Delaware leader was not intimidated, replying, "Come, tomorrow I will depart for New York. If you can, kill me. I fear you not."

Opeththa then settled the matter by saying to the Delaware, "If you go, I'll go along; and I shall stop Monsieur Tonty's ears. . . ."

(This, at least, is how the Delaware later reported the meeting to the English.)

Opeththa, seventy-two warriors, one hundred women and children packed up and left, taking along with them six Cherokee captives and a French outlaw, Martin Chartier, who had escaped imprisonment by joining the Shawnee and had married a woman of that nation. Chartier and later his son Peter remained with the Shawnee and became useful for dealing with whites.

Opeththa and his people made a leisurely trip east. They stopped to plant crops and hunt in Ohio, spent some time in Virginia, and did not arrive in Pennsylvania until 1692. As promised, they were hospitably received by the Delaware and Susquehannocks. Authorities of Penn's colony were at first alarmed by the appearance of this new lot, whom they spoke of simply as the Strange Indians, but after visiting with them decided they would be good for business. The Iroquois were less pleased. The League informed the Pennsylvania governing council that these newcomers were their enemies and that they might march south with the "design of carrying off the Shawanah Indians."

The Shawnee may never have heard of this threat. If they did, it did not seem to concern them much, for they went on living where they were and trading directly with the whites. However, the Pennsylvania administrators were stirred to send gifts to the League and messages, which explained that while they regarded the Strange Indians as "our friends and allies," they also recognized that they were titular subjects of the Five Nations. Thus the forms were respected, the Iroquois were mollified.

In the first decades of the eighteenth century, more Shawnee from Illinois, Ohio, and the Carolinas migrated to eastern Pennsylvania but the country did not prove as good as they had hoped. Increasing white settlement and sharp trading practices set them on the move again. Bands began to travel west, first into the mountains beyond the Susquehanna, then to the upper Ohio Valley. The loss of their trade to the French disturbed Pennsylvania's whites. They offered gifts and better treatment, but the Shawnee continued to leave. Then the Pennsylvanians went to the Iroquois, saying, in effect, that if indeed they had imperial authority they should exercise it by making the Strange Indians return. The League stalled and referred the matter to various councils, but eventually—in 1735, for a fee—sent a delegation of sachems to talk with a large band of Shawnee then settled on the Allegheny River. As the League was later forced to report to the Pennsylvania governing council, the mission was a disaster.

The Iroquois said they had been "very pressing" with the Shawnee "to return toward the Sasquehannah, assuring them that the Six Nations would take them under their Wings & protect them [but] the Shawnee had entirely refused to leave that place [the Allegheny] which they said was more commodius to them."

Worse was to follow. One of the leaders of the delegation, a Seneca chief, "pressed so closely that they [the Shawnee] took a great Dislike to him . . . and they seized on Him & murdered him cruelly."

The bloody conclusion of these negotiations dealt a blow to Iroquois prestige, which to a considerable degree was based on the assumption that lesser people who were impudent to the League would be swiftly punished by its ferocious warriors. In this case, the Iroquois were unable or unwilling to retaliate for the ultimate insult given their emissaries.

Commencing in the 1730s, Shawnee from all points of the compass began gathering in the territory north of the Ohio, between the Muskingum and Miami rivers. During the next forty years more of them came to live there than had ever before in their recorded history assembled in the same place at the same time. They found the land not only "commodious" but largely unoccupied as a consequence of the Beaver Wars. For the same reasons, the Miami from the west and the Wyandot from the north entered the region. Informally, and rather amicably, the three nations divided most of what is now Ohio and Indiana among them. The Shawnee sector was in the south, where they built villages along tributaries of the big river and hunted both to the west and south, in Kentucky and the Virginias.

Intermingled in Ohio with the three major nations were the Delaware—who like the Shawnee had left the east—and Mingo. (Mingo was a catchall term referring to mixed groups of Iroquois-speaking peoples. Some were remnants of the Eries and Neutrals, while others were originally Senecas, the most westerly of the Six Nations, who had become dissatisfied with the policies of the League and no longer accepted its authority.) Also, among the Shawnee there was at least one permanent village of Cherokee, the two nations having resolved most of their previous differences.

During the first half of the eighteenth century, these and all other nations east of the plains were drawn into the competition between France and England for the control of the fur trade. Though North America was a theater of operations in the global struggle taking place between the European powers, neither of them had any appreciable armed forces west of the Appalachians prior to the 1750s. Their interests were advanced by traders, intelligence agents, military advisers, and occasionally missionaries. The general objective of these Europeans was to monopolize trade with individual red nations and employ them to defend against or attack the allies of their opponents. Acts of commercial double dealing and diplomatic treachery were common. Fighting was sporadic, and most of it was done by the reds in their traditional raid-and-skirmish fashion.

Despite the conniving and violence, there were fairly stable alignments between some of the settled red nations with imperative territorial interests and one or the other of the European powers. For example, though they were quite willing to court and be courted by the French, the Iroquois were generally on the side of the British, as were the Cherokee and Chickasaw in the south. The Ottawa, Nipissing, and other western Great Lakes people, the Illinois and Choctaw along the Mississippi, were in the main pro-French.

The mobile Shawnee bound to no place or power were notable for their inconstancy. The Iroquois, who had a wealth of unpleasant experience with them, warned the English that these people "are remarked for their deceit and perfidy, paying little or no regard to their word and most solemn engagements." With justification, other reds and whites came to much the same conclusion. Who the Shawnee traded with and fought for or against was determined solely by their immediate self-interest. They quickly changed sides when the other made it worth their while. Also, at any given time separate bands of Shawnee might pursue quite different policies in different parts of the country. By way of illustrating the tactics and temper of some of them:

. . . In 1739, Shawnee mercenaries joined a French-led expedition, which went down the Mississippi to attack the pro-British Chickasaw. Then 500 Shawnee warriors raided the Catawba, trading partners of the English colonists in South Carolina. Beyond material rewards, these campaigns were satisfying for heroic reasons to the Shawnee, since there had long been bad blood between them, the Chickasaw, and the Catawba.

. . . In the 1740s the Shawnee attacked a French post on the Wabash. To the east they opened their villages to British and even Iroquois agents and with them attempted to detach the Miami from their long-standing alliance with the French. By the end of the decade Pierre de la Jonquière, governor of New France, was writing to Paris that it "would be in our interest to destroy these Chaouanons [Shawnee] . . . they are always trying to disturb the nations that are our allies."

. . . In the early 1750s the Shawnee sent diplomats to both the French and British, inquiring about what their friendship and services were worth. They received the best offer from the French and most of the Shawnee joined them at the outbreak of the French and Indian War, the American theater of the Seven Years War. In 1755 a contingent of Shawnee took part in the annihilation of the army led by Edward Braddock and George Washington. During the next three years, both British and Iroquois agents made numerous attempts to secure at least the neutrality of the Shawnee but were rejected. Repeatedly their warriors came out of the Ohio country to raid English-speaking settlements from Pennsylvania to the Carolinas. This marked their first important confrontation with the Long Knives—their generic term for white frontiersmen—and earned them the reputation which they kept for the next sixty years of being the most formidable of all the savages.

. . . In 1758, when the military balance between the Europeans had clearly shifted, the Shawnee, looking to their supply lines, made a truce with the British. However, in 1763 they enthusiastically joined what whites called the Conspiracy of Pontiac. (It was a violent reaction of the western nations, led by Pontiac, an Ottawa war chief, to what they considered a conspiracy against them: their abandonment by France and the mean trading practices the British instigated after they eliminated their European competitor.)

. . . Pontiac surrendered in 1765. The Shawnee branded the Ottawa a coward—and may have arranged his assassination—but again started doing business with the British. Along with furs they collected and sold prisoners, Frenchmen and their sympathizers who still remained in the western territories. Aside from some heroic-type skirmishing with the Chickasaw, Kickapoo, and the most exposed Long Knives, they were generally at unaccustomed peace for a decade. Then they commenced their longest and last war against the Americans—as the whites who would shortly organize the United States began calling themselves.

Prior to the mid-eighteenth century, when most of them congregated in southern Ohio, the Shawnee had been a guerrilla people, perhaps for many generations, as Tenskwatawa indicated. Often surrounded by hostile neighbors, they had not occupied fixed territories for long and customarily operated in small bands which could not easily be caught and cornered. This history marked their society in a variety of ways.

A Shawnee man took up arms as soon as he was strong enough to carry them and continued to bear them until his death. Kishkalwa, famous for both his valor and longevity, recalled that he had fought his first battle in about 1750 against a party of Chickasaw who were ambushed as they were preparing to attack a French post in Illinois. Though only seventeen, Kishkalwa seized the medicine bag of an enemy chief, a feat somewhat comparable to a European soldier capturing the regimental standard of an enemy.

At the head of a straggling refugee band which had been driven to a reservation in Kansas, Kishkalwa made and won his last fight in 1818 (when he was eighty-five), leading a war party against the Osage. Except for its length, Kishkalwa's career was not exceptional. There were no doubt others, but of all Shawnee men of whom biographical records survive, only one—Tenskwatawa, the prophet—was not a warrior.

The Iroquois, Huron, Cherokee, Creek, and other permanently located nations built open towns in places well situated for farming, hunting, or trade. Their interest was to protect these centers by fighting or negotiating on their frontiers, or better, in the lands of their neighbors. Since they generally lived in enclaves granted by or taken from foreigners, the Shawnee could not employ such defense-in-depth strategies. They placed their villages in natural strong points from which they would go out to farm, hunt, or raid and retreat to when under attack. Within Shawnee communities, family cabins were flimsy—pole frameworks roofed with bark— and could be abandoned without great loss. But, in the center of villages occupied for any length of time, there was a sizable log structure. It was used as a council and ceremonial hall but also as a fort and supply cache in which villagers could rally and defend themselves.

The Shawnee political system was generally simpler but more autocratic than that of more settled nations. In bands and villages, they coalesced around strong individuals of proved courage and wisdom. "To the decisions of the chief and principal men," said Tenskwatawa, "the nation at large cheerfully submit, and as the general interest & their own popularity are equally connected they seldom fail to choose aright."

War and peace chiefs, with ad hoc committees of councillors, were recognized by the Shawnee. However, unlike the Iroquois whose military men could not by tradition serve as civil sachems, the same man might fill both positions among the Shawnee, as was the case of Puckeshinwa, Tekamthi's father. When the offices were held separately, war chiefs were usually more influential. Being so often in a state of military alert, the Shawnee apparently became accustomed, even in brief periods of peace, to taking direction from their war masters.

Peace chiefs, responsible for domestic order, were sometimes hereditary but succession was by no means automatic. No man was thought fit for leadership until he was at least thirty years old, and thus there was ample time to determine, empirically, whether or not a son possessed the good qualities of a noted father.

War chief was an earned office. Before a man could be considered for the position, he was expected to organize and lead—by persuading other young warriors to follow him—at least four free-lance raids, bringing back from each of them one or more scalps and all of his men alive.

When separate bands and villages came together to conduct joint operations, their war chiefs selected overall leaders. If successful, these men might be recognized as national general officers and remain so throughout their lives, as did the remarkable Kishkalwa. While expeditions were being considered, individuals, even entire villages, were free to withdraw if they disagreed with the leadership or tactics. However, once in the field, the authority of Shawnee chiefs was greater than that of their counterparts in many of the other red nations. Europeans, as observers and combatants, were frequently impressed by the singular discipline of Shawnee war parties, the ability of their commanders to plan and the willingness of their warriors to execute concerted maneuvers.

Shawnee women were organized as were the men, having their chiefs and "principal matrons" who directed agricultural operations, certain ceremonies, and the affairs of their own sex. Though they did not go into battle with the warriors, women recognized as war chiefs helped with the logistics of expeditions. Female peace chiefs sometimes acted successfully, according to Tenskwatawa, to restrain hot-blooded, glory-hungry young warriors, "bent on some undertaking not countenanced by the nation." Though they did not take direct part in the deliberations of the men, women exercised a kind of veto power over them. Their contributions to the community were recognized as substantial, and Shawnee tradition held that no adult citizen, regardless of sex, could be forced to act unwillingly.

A distinctive and—given their Gypsy-like status—surprising collective characteristic of the Shawnee was their cultural conservatism. Wherever they lived, whomever they associated with, they resisted outside influences, changed their behavior and minds slowly and reluctantly. This became most apparent after Tekamthi fell and the beaten Shawnee were driven west of the Mississippi as dependents and quasi-prisoners of the United States. In similar circumstances, the remnants of other dispossessed red nations bowed to the inevitable and made attempts to learn and practice white ways. Generally the Shawnee did not. To the exasperation of white authorities responsible for them, they continued to roam, trying to hunt and practice subsistence farming even as the country grew more settled. Many of them refused to learn English, to send their children to white schools, or listen to Christian missionaries.

Joab Spencer, a white minister and amateur folklorist, who became acquainted with them in Kansas during the middle part of the nineteenth century, remarked with some resignation, "The Shawnees cling to their old customs, seemingly more reluctant to abandon their ancient rites than any other civilized tribe." At greater length other students were to say much the same thing, and this trait may be the key one for understanding, imaginatively, the complicated history of these people. Their wanderings and wars did not bring them much in the way of wealth or security. But in retrospect it seems that these were not the things they most coveted. The constant, crucial ambition of the Shawnee was to remain Shawnee, which they were unshakably convinced was much better than being anybody else. Considering how long they were able to do so under such adverse circumstances, they must be reckoned as impressively successful people.

Sometime in the mid-1820s Tenskwatawa spoke again to a white man about Shawnee history, on this occasion illustrating it with an account of the doings of his own immediate ancestors. It may be that this was a continuation of his conversations with Charles Trowbridge, but the white interviewer was never clearly identified. However, his notes eventually came into the hands of Thomas McKenney, a sympathetic Quaker, who had been appointed by President Monroe to the Bureau of Indian Affairs, then an agency of the War Department. Later McKenney published the "loose memoranda of the original transcriber" (whoever he was) as "the story of Tenskwatawa as related by himself."

The original transcriber had said that Tenskwatawa said that his paternal grandfather was a Creek, not a Shawnee. As a young warrior, the Grandfather (he was never given a name in the interview) was part of a Creek delegation which made a peaceful visit to the whites of Charleston, South Carolina, in about 1700. While they were conferring with the governor of the colony, his beautiful young daughter happened to come to the council grounds. Thereupon she "conceived a violent admiration for the Indian character; and . . . determined to bestow herself upon some 'warlike lord' of the forest." In privacy the young woman explained her passion to the governor. He was apparently both a doting father and an exceptionally broad-minded man. The next day "finding that she persisted in this singular predilection, he directed her attention to a young Creek warrior [the Grandfather], for whom, at first sight, she avowed a decided attachment."

The governor then told the assembled Creek of his daughter's desire and said he would give his consent to the match. The Grandfather "was not so ungallant as to refuse." Along with his bride, the Grandfather took up residence with the whites, becoming a slaveholder and a popular sporting man. The couple had two daughters and then a son, whose birth so pleased his grandfather, the governor, that "he called his friends together, and caused thirty guns to be fired."

In his early teens this son went wild, returning to live first with the Creeks and then with the Shawnee, whom he more admired. They gave him the name Puckeshinwa. He became so attached to the Indian mode of life that when the governor sent for him, he refused to return. Eventually Puckeshinwa (the father of Tenskwatawa and Tekamthi) married Methoastaske (their mother), a Shawnee living among the Creeks. When her people determined to migrate north to Ohio, Puckeshinwa agreed to go with them. Upon hearing of this plan, his adoring grandfather, still the governor of South Carolina, called Puckeshinwa to him and "gave him a written paper and told him that upon showing it at any time to the Americans, they would grant any request which he might make— but that he need not show it to French traders, as it would only vex them, and make them exclaim, Sacré dieu!"

Unfortunately for the annals of both American history and true romance, no one interested in this family tree has accepted Tenskwatawa's account as being true or even as a garbled version of the truth. Beyond the many and large intrinsic improbabilities, he was an oral historian. If he did not invent the story, he had to have heard it from somebody else. However, Tenskwatawa did not tell this story until after the rest of his immediate family was dead, and before him, nobody made mention of these happenings. Nor, even later, when there was great curiosity about Tekamthi, did anyone step forward and say that he or she had heard of these things. What with the handsome young red, the passionate white virgin, thirty-gun salutes, and the rest, this tale makes that of Capt. John Smith and Pocahontas seem like a tepid social note. Had anybody, in fact three generations of bodies, heard even rumors of such carryings on, then as certainly as gossip is juicy, more or less the whole world would have heard of them.

Perhaps it occurred to Tenskwatawa that establishing himself as a member of a family who had long had good relations with Americans, intimate ones with some of the greatest of them, might do him some good. There is another simpler explanation for this fine yarn. Tenskwatawa was always greatly skilled at playing with other men's minds, for serious purposes and entertainment. At the time, having been reduced to giving interviews to junior white ethnologists, his circumstances and prospects were poor. Inventing the story about the Grandfather, which jabbed at white pride in a vital area, no doubt brightened up one of his days.

Nearly a century later, Gaynwah (Thomas Wildcat Alford), a literate great-grandson of Tekamthi, attempted to write a history of the Shawnee and of his own family. He never completely finished it, saying to a white friend who published some of his notes, "I have great difficulty in getting at the truth; so many statements of your people are at variance with our tradition and vice versa, that at times I get almost discouraged."

Gaynwah had nothing to say about the Grandfather and the Daughter of the Governor but did think that Puckeshinwa, the known founder of his line, had been born somewhere in the south. As a youth he had moved to Pennsylvania, living at times along the Delaware River and then in a Shawnee community high up on the Susquehanna near the New York border. Puckeshinwa, apparently good at languages, served as an interpreter in councils among his own people, the Delaware, and whites. In 1749 he was one of the negotiators who arranged to transfer a parcel of land east of the Susquehanna to the Pennsylvania colonists. As the French and Indian War approached, Puckeshinwa told a Delaware chief that he was moving to Ohio because he feared the English had "very bad designs" against the Shawnee. However, according to Gaynwah, Puckeshinwa and his band remained neutral in the war. (If so, this is surprising since most Shawnee leaders who later became renowned, as Puckeshinwa did, fought at this time against the English.) In 1758, after Gen. John Forbes retook Fort Duquesne, Puckeshinwa was among those negotiating a truce with the British.

Puckeshinwa then made a trip to the Shawnee village which had long been established among the Creek in Alabama. There he met and married Methoastaske. Later there were stories that she was a Creek or even a Cherokee, but those who personally knew the family and left records of it thought she was pure Shawnee, a woman of the Turtle *umsoma* and Pekowi division of the nation. The couple's first son, Cheesekau, was born about 1760. He was followed by a girl, Tecumpease, and another boy, Sauwaseekau. Before 1768 the family must have migrated to Ohio, since, while they differ as to the exact place, the best red and white accounts agree that Tekamthi was born along the upper valley of the Little Miami River. Tekamthi himself confirmed this tradition in his only known autobiographical statement. In 1805, riding with some of his advisers and several white men to a council with the governor of Ohio, he said casually as they crossed the Little Miami that he had been born and spent much of his early boyhood along it. One of the whites, Duncan McArthur, seized on this tidbit of information and later recorded it.

III. 1768

When Tekamthi was born in 1768, his people were in the middle of something of a golden era. It lasted for only a decade but things had seldom gone so well for them—and never would again—as they did in those years.

During the French and Indian wars, most of the Shawnee had fought on the losing side but, as was their custom, independently. Their own campaigns against isolated white settlements in Pennsylvania and Virginia had been successful, and the warriors gained a formidable reputation, which intimidated others of both races as that of the Iroquois had in the previous century. Their casualties were moderate, and while many nations were losing people and land, the Shawnee were gaining both as their in-gathering toward southern Ohio continued. By 1765 at least 3,000 of them were living north of the Ohio between the Scioto and Miami rivers. They controlled hunting lands which extended to the south and west well into what is now West Virginia, Kentucky, and Indiana. For the first and only time in their recorded history the Shawnee were the most numerous and dominant people in a sizable territory. It was one which was then particularly rich in natural resources. Because of the political turmoil which had commenced with the Beaver Wars, the central Ohio Valley had been lightly settled and hunted during the previous century, and game remained relatively abundant. Also it was convenient to competing white traders from Ontario, New York, Pennsylvania, and Virginia, which gave the Shawnee special leverage for jacking up fur prices.

When David Jones visited Chillicothe in 1773, he found the residents had many guns, a fine herd of horses, plentiful iron tools and utensils, milled blankets, glass beads, and other fashionable ornaments of white manufacture, chocolate to drink, and pasteboard cards for gambling.

Secure and prosperous as life was then for the people in the Scioto villages, 1768, in retrospect, also marked the formal beginning of the end of their good times and nation. In that year at Fort Stanwix (near present-day Rome, New York) the British and Iroquois, playing at imperial games, reached an agreement which drastically altered the political map of North America and commenced the first American Civil War. The treaty of Fort Stanwix came about as follows:

After the defeat of the French, the British turned their attention to managing their greatly expanded North American possessions. Among other things, in 1763 a boundary was established by proclamation which extended from Iroquoia in New York southward along the crest of the Appalachians to Georgia. White colonists were to stay east of the Proclamation Line and devote themselves to developing the coastal and piedmont regions as a source of cheap agricultural commodities for the motherland. They were not encouraged or in many instances not permitted to create their own industries or trade with foreign nations. The policy was designed to give English entrepreneurs an exclusive North American market for their manufactured goods. It was also thought reasonable that the colonists pay certain taxes and fees so that the British government would not have to bear the expense of administrating this closed mercantile system. As to the wilderness west of the boundary line, this was envisioned as a vast, royal, Indian reservation. The reds would remain in it and continue to support the lucrative fur trade, selling the pelts they took only to agents of British firms.

All of which, as conceived and drawn on maps in London, was tidy and rational, but in terms of the realities of the North American frontier it was fantastic. Thousands of poor immigrants from Europe were arriving each year in the Atlantic port cities. Rather than docilely remain along the coast to provide cheap labor, the boldest of them—in the main Scotch-Irish—continued westward looking for land. When they found an attractive spot in the forest, they began to clear it, asking no one's permission, establishing their title by what came to be called Tomahawk Rights. Even those who had heard about it did not give a tinker's curse about the Proclamation Line of 1763.

One who had a number of unpleasant experiences with these unruly pioneers was John Murray, Earl of Dunmore and the last

British governor of Virginia. In a dispatch home, Dunmore complained:

> The Americans acquire no attachment to Place: but wandering about seems engrafted in their Nature. . . . In this colony Proclamations have been published from time to time to restrain them. But . . . they do not conceive that Government has any right to forbid their taking possessions of a Vast tract of Country, either uninhabited, or which serves only as a Shelter for a few scattered Tribes of Indians. Nor can they easily be brought to entertain any belief of the permanent obligation of Treaties made with those People, whom they consider but little removed from the brute Creation.

Few serious efforts were made to halt the westward movement of the squatter classes, since it was feared, justifiably, that doing so would lead to messy, costly insurrections all along the border. In consequence red nations of the Ohio Valley—who had at first thought the 1763 boundary line a very good thing—concluded that the British had lied about their intention to keep whites out of their lands or were too weak and timid to fulfill their promises. Therefore the reds began to defend the boundary themselves, sending out warriors to pick off the most exposed white families and communities.

The settlers made appeals for aid and punitive counterattacks, but colonial authorities felt under no obligation to protect people who, once they had crossed the Proclamation Line, were officially criminals. This neglect did not halt the migration of the frontier whites but did make them, in addition to Indian haters, rabidly anti-British. How strong and general these feelings were became apparent and of considerable importance a decade later during the Revolutionary War.

There was another group, a small but economically potent one, which was much opposed to British policies and had considerably more leverage than the frontier settlers for doing something about them. It was made up of land speculators. They had no inclination to blaze trails or fight Indians, but as a class these entrepreneurs were, for a century or more, to have an inordinate influence on the timing and direction of the westward movement of Americans.

Throughout the eighteenth century, Pennsylvania merchants, Virginia planters, and other prominent colonists accumulated titles to lands in and to the westward of the Appalachians. Some of the grants were purchased, from the crown, very cheaply. Others were gifts given to demonstrate royal favor or in return for political good works. The size of their holdings was often impressive but initially they were almost worthless. At the time there was plenty of good, secure land remaining in the coastal plain and little demand for unsurveyed tracts in the inaccessible, exceedingly dangerous western wilderness. The expulsion of the French and the arrival of thousands of land-hungry immigrants from Europe changed the North American real-estate market. It occurred simultaneously to many of these speculators that their western properties might be made valuable if the wilderness lands were legally opened to settlement and cleared of Indians. Among the land speculators were many well-educated, broad-minded humanists who had nothing personally against the savages and in fact often took a lively scientific and even affectionate interest in them. However, this did not alter the fact that it would be bad for business to allow many Indians to live on lands that could be sold and developed.

The 1763 boundary line was an anathema to these large land speculators. "I can never look upon that proclamation," Washington wrote to a business associate, "in any other light (but I say this between ourselves) than as a temporary expedient to quiet the minds of the Indians." (In 1760, Washington and some other of the Virginia gentry working through agents in London had received a royal grant for 2.5 million acres located in the Ohio valley. The 1763 proclamation had quashed these titles.)

Benjamin Franklin was less circumspect in his objections to the crest-of-the-Appalachians boundary. Speaking to the British House of Commons in 1766, he forthrightly explained that Americans wanted land, not furs or Indians.

> The trade with the Indians, though carried on in America, is not an American interest. The people of America are chiefly farmers and planters; scarce anything that they raise or produce is an article of commerce with the Indians. The Indian trade is a British interest: it is carried on with British manufactures, for the profit of British merchants and manufacturers. . . .

Many other men of property shared these opinions and began to agitate for a drastic revision of the 1763 proclamation. They made effective lobbyists. Most were members of the various colonial councils, and those who were not had kin or close friends who were.

By the mid-1760s it had become apparent to royal ministers that the Appalachian boundary was causing such unrest in North America that trying to hold to it, even on paper, was not worth the trouble. As a first step toward change, it was decided to do what had often been done previously—talk to the Iroquois. The League of the Six Nations was eager to do so, for its own problems had become more critical than those of the British.

Though they had often opposed them in the preceding 150 years, the French had been very useful in a strategic way to the Iroquois. By hinting that they were considering establishing closer, warmer ties with them, the League had often been able to pry subsidies and concessions from the British. This sort of leverage disappeared when the French did. Worse, the Iroquois immediately became an island in a sea of British territories. So weakened and surrounded, the Iroquois had a desperate need to find new means for maintaining their imperial status and keeping whites out of their homelands. When British agents mentioned the possibility of rearranging land titles and political boundaries in eastern North America, the Six Nations were very receptive.

After preliminary discussions, a great council was convened at Fort Stanwix in the fall of 1768. Representatives of some other red nations were invited to attend, but the main business was done in executive sessions between Iroquois sachems and commissioners from New York, New Jersey, Pennsylvania, and Virginia. The master of ceremonies was Sir William Johnson, commissioned by the Privy Council in London as the Crown's superintendent of Northern Indian Affairs. Having settled in the Hudson Valley about 1740, he had become, as a landowner and trader, one of the richest and most influential men in New York. Also Johnson had been adopted by the Mohawk, taken two wives from among these people, and come to be an informal ambassador and viceroy to the Six Nations.

After several weeks of negotiation, it was agreed that the Proclamation Line of 1763 would be abolished from Tennessee northward. Furthermore, as the imperial owners of the territories involved, the Six Nations would cede to the crown portions of western Pennsylvania and most of what is now West Virginia and Kentucky.

As a result the British were immediately spared having to listen to the continuing complaints of the colonists about the 1763 Proclamation. After Fort Stanwix, administrators could tell the restless frontiersmen that it was now legal for them to migrate through the mountains, as they had been doing illegally for the previous five years. Furthermore, the land speculators were unleashed, so to speak, to survey, advertise, and find buyers for their western holdings.

At least in the short term, the rewards for the Iroquois were greater and more material. First, £10,000 had been appropriated so that the British negotiators could buy trade goods which would be distributed proportionately among the various red nations who gave up their territorial claims. At the end of the negotiations the Iroquois demanded and were given the entire purchase price—by the standards of the time an enormous one. (They paid out a few hundred pounds' worth of goods as bribes and hush money to individual representatives of other nations.) More importantly, by ceding territories far to the south and west of them, the Iroquois were able to direct the course of white settlement away from Iroquoia. All of this was accomplished without cost to the Six Nations. They did not have and never had had any use for the lands they sold; nor had they been put to any expense to conquer or occupy them. Their title to the property was valid and valuable only because the British accepted it as such. Few negotiators ever, anywhere, made such a fine bargain for their nation as the Iroquois sachems did at Fort Stanwix.

Though not mentioned at the proceedings, it was understood by the parties involved that the real cost of the treaty would be borne by the Shawnee (and to a lesser extent by the Cherokee of northern Tennessee) whose hunting territories the Iroquois had sold. Though Sir William Johnson among others said that he saw no reason why they should attend, some Shawnee showed up at Fort Stanwix. They were not warmly received and had no formal role in the deliberations. At the end of them, in November, the Shawnee came before Johnson, who summarized the treaty. He told them that they should feel guilty about the way they had previously treated Englishmen and should go home and "pay due regard to the Boundary Line now made." To cheer them up they were given £27 but were advised to divide this tip with the Delaware.

When these observers returned to the Ohio country, the Shawnee found their report preposterous and at first thought they had misunderstood what had happened. Therefore other emissaries were sent to the Iroquois to ask for an explanation and to demand, if the incredible rumors proved correct, that the Six Nations disavow the Fort Stanwix treaty. They were coldly told that it was all true, that a bargain was a bargain, and that the Shawnee must accept it and should not take up their hatchets, "which you run about with doing Mischief." They were also told that, if they caused trouble, a great Iroquois army would march into Ohio and the "consequences would be fatal" for the Shawnee. Reporting to William Johnson, a Mohawk sachem, Abraham, assured him that all the treaty provisions would be respected. "As to the pretensions of any inconsiderable people, behind our backs, we shall soon silence them, and we desire that you may assure the King that it was our property we justly disposed of, that we had full authority to do so."

Past experiences had made the Shawnee contemptuous of the Iroquois ability to carry out such threats, and they ignored those made after Fort Stanwix. However, their reception by the Six Nations and Johnson convinced them that, no matter how just their cause, they would lose their hunting territories in the Virginias and Kentucky unless their warriors could defend them against invading whites.

The agreement at Fort Stanwix immediately set a few of the bolder frontiersmen (as well as astute land speculators to the east) to thinking about the western country. The first party, in 1769, to get well beyond the mountains was led by John Findley. He was a peddler and small fur buyer who during the previous twenty-five years had traded frequently and amicably with the Shawnee along both sides of the Ohio River. (During the 1750s Findley sometimes made use of a cabin near what is now Lexington, Kentucky. The trade goods he picked up in the east were wrapped in English hay. After packing them to his depot, he unwrapped them, throwing away the hay and the seeds it contained. Thus, at least in folk history, Findley is credited with bringing blue grass to Kentucky.)

Findley and the five others with him were Long Hunters, of a type which was later too much glorified as the intrepid explorers and trailblazers who first led the American people west. In truth they were little motivated by public service and were generally rather antisocial men. As a group their most notable characteristics were that they did not get along very well in the rude frontier settlements, could not abide hoeing corn, splitting rails, colicky babies, and such. They made their Long Hunts principally so they could support themselves for months, sometimes years, while wandering about the woods free of civic and family responsibilities. As they did so, they developed Indianish skills and attitudes.

One of the men in the Findley party, Daniel Boone, was a classic Long Hunter. He and Findley first met in 1755 when they were serving as teamsters in Braddock's ill-fated campaign against the French and Indians. Escaping this debacle, Boone drifted south, took up some land in the Yadkin valley of North Carolina, married and started a family but did not spend much time with it. Beyond roaming about in the Great Smoky Mountains region, he wandered into eastern Kentucky and at least twice to Florida. He was home early in 1769 when Findley, trading horses in a small way, stopped by his cabin and suggested that since it had been officially opened to whites, they should take a look at his old stomping grounds in central Kentucky. Boone was eager to go and had no difficulty finding four other men in the area of similar temperament. On the first of May the six of them started west. Finding a good route through the Cumberland Gap, they spent the summer in the rolling limestone country of north-central Kentucky. The beauty of this place and its bountiful game delighted them. Boone later reported that the "buffalo were more frequent than I have seen cattle in the settlements, browsing on the leaves of cane, or cropping the herbage on those extensive plains."

Late in the fall the six men were surprised by Shawnee warriors. One of them was killed, but the others were captured alive and treated rather gently, considering who and where they were. As a matter of course, the furs the whites had collected were taken from them as were most of their weapons and supplies. However, they were left with enough so that they could get back across the mountains to North Carolina and were told to do that immediately. Before they were released, the Shawnee leader, a man whites came to call Captain Will, gave Boone some advice: "Now Brothers, go home and stay there. Don't come here any more, for this is the Indians' hunting ground, and all the animals, skins and furs are ours; and if you are so foolish as to venture here again, you may be sure the wasps and yellow-jackets will sting you severely."

The Shawnee had no national councils or ministers to issue ultimatums or policy statements. In effect, Captain Will's warning to Boone and Findley was the de facto proclamation they made in response to the treaty of Fort Stanwix.

For ordinary reasons of honor and chauvinism, the warriors were outraged by the casual, arrogant trespasses of the whites. The crucial matter for them was defending the wilderness itself, and, as Captain Will pointed out, the quality of hunting within it. By then the Shawnee had learned that, when whites came into a territory, they first reduced the game by direct—and by red standards wasteful—consumption. Next, when they commenced to settle they greatly inconvenienced both the native wildlife and people by altering springs and water courses, felling and burning trees, fencing clearings for their stock and crops. Once they so developed a piece of land, they claimed exclusive use of it and became very belligerent about keeping other men and beasts off their property.

In 1773, a delegation of Shawnee visited Fort Pitt to report to Alexander McKee, the British superintendent of Indian affairs, about what was happening in the eastern part of their hunting territories. Fort Pitt was the hub of the western British fur trade, and McKee, a veteran fur buyer, was principally concerned with promoting this commerce. Therefore he was particularly sympathetic to the Shawnee. Also, as a Pennsylvanian he was not overly concerned about the fate of the would-be Kentucky pioneers, most of whom were from Virginia and North Carolina. McKee asked the chiefs why their young men were running around with their hatchets. A brief answer summed up the Shawnee case. Their warriors, said the spokesman, "are disappointed in their hunting and find the Woods covered with White People." McKee said that he understood their anger but could not personally give them any satisfaction. However, he agreed to pass their complaints along to higher authorities and advised that they be patient until a decision was made in their case.

In 1769 they had no choice but to get out of the country as fast as they could but neither Boone nor Findley later paid any attention to Captain Will's threat. Boone returned to Carolina in the winter. He remained there only long enough to find more supplies and tell his neighbors about the marvels of the Kentucky country. In the spring he headed back to take another look. He spent considerable time hiding in canebrakes and lost some caches but was not caught by the Shawnee on this trip.

In 1773 Boone was again in Carolina. There he sold his Yadkin Valley farm and, with the backing of cagey real-estate speculator, Richard Henderson, recruited five families to migrate with his own and forty single men to central Kentucky. While still in the mountains, this group was stung hard by the Shawnee. Six of the party, including Boone's eldest son, were killed and their stock rustled. The survivors retreated to the white settlements on the Clinch River (in present-day Tennessee). There they were to regroup and get ready to go west again two years later. As for John Findley, after the 1769 trip, he returned to his sometime home in western Pennsylvania, but also shortly went back on the trails again, heading when last seen for Kentucky. He was never heard of again.

The experiences of Findley and Boone stirred rather than quelled the migratory urges of similar people. In backwoods communities all along the border, Kentucky came to be imagined as an earthly paradise, and the most restless frontiersmen began organizing parties to enter it. Those from Maryland and central Virginia generally struck north toward Fort Pitt with the intention of going west down the Ohio River. More southerly mountaineers chose to follow the Findley-Boone wilderness trail through Cumberland Gap. Wherever they went, they were met by the Shawnee. Those caught on the move or in the open were mauled and turned back as Boone's first group was. However, the warriors had neither equipment nor experience for siegecraft. When the invaders could fortify a strong position and were willing to remain close to their palisades and blockhouses, they were able to survive. These private posts became staging areas for the next advance. Thus, erratically and slowly but irreversibly, the tide of whites flowed west.

During the early 1770s, what is now Wheeling, West Virginia, became the most westerly secured area on the Ohio. By the early spring of 1774 several hundred whites had assembled there in response to an announcement of Dunmore, the Virginia governor, that he would commence issuing patents for land on both sides of the river. (White Pennsylvanians in the Pittsburgh region to the north hotly disputed his authority to do so. In the jurisdictional quarrel that followed, officials of the two colonies slandered, harassed, and occasionally tried to arrest each other.)

Most of the Virginians who gathered at Wheeling that spring were not themselves prospective settlers but rather surveyors representing eastern speculators. Michael Cresap, a failed fur trader, was there, intent on claiming an area near the confluence of the Ohio and Kanawha rivers, 150 miles below Wheeling, where he hoped to develop a pioneer community. George Rogers Clark and William Crawford represented the Ohio Land Company, formed by prominent Virginians looking for at least 200,000 acres in the valley. George Washington was part of this combine but also engaged John Floyd to advance his individual interest. Washington's instructions were specific. He wanted, he wrote, to get about 10,000 acres, preferably along the Scioto River—in the heartland of the Shawnee nation. However, if there were difficulties there, "I would go quite down to the Falls [the present Louisville] or even below; meaning thereby to get richer and wider bottoms, as it is my desire to have my lands run out on the banks of the Ohio."

Cresap and Floyd set off from Wheeling as soon as the ice broke on the river. The members of their crews were more explorers and partisans than technicians—hard, heavily armed backwoodsmen prepared to fight off either Indians or rival land prospectors. By then the Shawnee had come to understand the nature of surveyors—Red Flag men they called them—and that once they appeared, settlers soon followed. (Another sign of the same thing were honeybees, who ranged in feral swarms about 100 miles ahead of the European settlement line. Reds spoke of them as the white man's fly.) Early in 1774, the Shawnee killed several of Floyd's men but sent another back to Wheeling with a provocative message. They told the man to tell his compatriots that George

Croghan, a trader and Alexander McKee's deputy at Fort Pitt, had told them to "kill all the Virginians they were to find on the River." Whether this was true or not, it confirmed the dark suspicions of the Virginians about the Shawnee, fur traders, and Pennsylvanians. A week or so later, Dr. John Connolly, whom Dunmore had appointed as Virginia's magistrate of western Pennsylvania, circulated a letter advising his supporters that it was their right and duty to take up their rifles and avenge the insults given them.

Michael Cresap was in the woods when he received Connolly's unofficial declaration of war. He said he was well pleased with it and "would put every Indian he met on the River to Death." As it happened, the next day Cresap and his men were able to bushwhack and scalp several Shawnee chiefs. They were members of a conciliatory minded group and were returning from Fort Pitt where they had asked Alexander McKee if by negotiation the surveyors and the bloodshed could be halted. The killing of these diplomats put an end to the peace movement. The Shawnee then commenced to send emissaries seeking military assistance from other red nations, arguing that if they did not help stop the whites on the Ohio, their own territories would soon be invaded. The Miami, Wyandot, and Ottawa listened respectfully, but answered, in effect, that Kentucky was a great distance from their own lands and defending it was a Shawnee problem.

The Delaware, the Shawnee's nearest neighbors and allies in the French and Indian wars, did not even offer moral support. Having been bribed and browbeaten by agents of Sir William Johnson and the Iroquois to obey the provisions of the Treaty of Fort Stanwix, Delaware sachems unctuously told the Shawnee that it would be better for all if they swallowed their pride and made peace with the Long Knives. The Shawnee representaves replied that once they had beaten back the Virginians, they "would then Blaze a Road to New Comer's Town [the principal Delaware community] to determine whether the Peace was so strong Between the White and the Delawares as they Pretended."

Initially the Mingo, the dissident Iroquois living in southern Ohio, were also inclined to neutrality, but were driven by bloody circumstances to aid the Shawnee. A principal man among the Mingo was called John Logan by whites and was regarded as an especially friendly and trustworthy Indian. The son of a prominent Cayuga chief, Logan, after settling in Ohio, had married a Shawnee woman. In the spring of 1774, with his family and a few others, he was camped along the Ohio where it was joined by Yellow Creek, near the present site of Steubenville.

On May 3, while Logan and the other warriors were absent, a

drunken party of Cresap's men came across the river from Virginia to this camp. (Whether or not Cresap was among them became a matter of controversy among frontiersmen and later historians. Logan thought he was. Cresap and others said he was not.) Led by one Daniel Greathouse, a particularly unsavory border thug, the whites killed thirteen red women and children, including all of Logan's immediate family. News of this happening quickly spread to the more settled regions of Virginia, where it shocked and revolted politer members of colonial society. Thomas Jefferson said it was "inhuman and indecent," Charles Lee that it was "a black, impious piece of work." Governor Dunmore admitted that the deed on Yellow Creek was "marked with an extraordinary degree of cruelty and inhumanity."

Despite these protestations, no official effort was made to catch and punish the killers or indemnify the surviving relatives of the victims. A few weeks later, Logan gathered together eight Mingo and Shawnee warriors and went across the river to obtain closely calculated justice. Ignoring Pennsylvania whites, he returned to Ohio bearing the scalps of thirteen Virginians.

Logan's raid so terrified settlers that some of them began to flee east, fearing a general Indian uprising was imminent. On June 10, under heavy pressure from real-estate men to pacify the upper Ohio so that they could get on with the business of selling it, Governor Dunmore formally declared that Virginia was at war with the Shawnee. During the summer he raised 3,000 militiamen to invade and destroy the Shawnee communities on the Scioto River in Ohio. The expedition left for the west on September 8. The original plan of campaign was that Dunmore, with 1,500 men from the tidewater and piedmont areas, would proceed to Fort Pitt. From that point, using traders' canoes and flatboats, they would descend the Ohio to its juncture with the Kanawha, a stream flowing north out of the mountains, near the present site of Gallipolis. There Dummore would rendezvous with Andrew Lewis, who was to recruit 1,500 more men from among the western Virginia settlers and bring them directly through the mountains to the Ohio. (Lewis had served as a major in the campaign of Braddock and thereafter became a prominent frontier politician and land holder.) The combined forces would then cross the Ohio on Dunmore's boats and march northwest to the Shawnee villages.

Shawnee scouts kept track of these maneuvers almost from the time they began. By stripping the Scioto villages of virtually all their men, including very old and young ones, the Shawnee were able to raise 400–500 warriors to oppose the invaders. They were joined by Logan and some of his Mingos, a few Wyandot and

Delaware who disagreed or were ashamed of the pacific policies of their chiefs. In all, the red force numbered no more than 700 men. The overall command was given to Cornstalk, a Shawnee war chief who had been fighting the British and Long Knives since the 1750s. His principal lieutenants were Black Hoof, Black Fish, Blue Jacket, and Puckeshinwa, the father of Tekamthi. Puckeshinwa brought with him his eldest son, the fourteen-year-old Cheesekau.

The Earl of Dunmore had much the easier route but proved to be an exceedingly deliberate campaigner. Despite having with him some of the better white woodsmen, George Rogers Clark, Cresap, Simon and James Girty (brothers who had gone Indianish as fur traders), Dunmore after leaving Fort Pitt became anxious about his flotilla being ambushed. Shortly, he abandoned the plan to meet Lewis at the Kanawha. At the mouth of the Hocking River he disembarked his army and started it marching cautiously—overland toward the Scioto.

Lewis was more energetic. He got his frontiersmen (about 1,000 of them) across the mountains and to the agreed-on meeting place by October 6. He camped and waited for Dunmore at Point Pleasant, a high, narrow neck of land surrounded on three sides by the Ohio, Kanawha, and a tributary of it, Crooked Creek. Apprised of these movements, Cornstalk and his councillors decided for the time being to ignore the slow moving, apparently timid Dunmore and send all the warriors against Lewis before he could cross the Ohio. They believed that if they could destroy or rout these Long Knives, the prospects were good that they could then turn on Dunmore, harass and cut up his command as it tried to move through the heavy forests.

On October 9, Simon Girty arrived at Point Pleasant with a message for Lewis from Dunmore. Explaining that he would not be coming downstream with his boats, the commander in chief ordered Lewis to cross the Ohio as best he could and hurry north to meet Dunmore somewhere in the vicinity of the Scioto. Though greatly exasperated, Lewis told his men to get a good night's sleep and in the morning they would ford the big river and commence marching north as the Earl had directed.

Later in the same day, Cornstalk and his men arrived on the north bank of the Ohio. During the night, a short distance above Point Pleasant, they swam and rafted across the river undetected. The war chiefs were informed by scouts that Lewis was on the very tip of Point Pleasant but appeared to be preparing to leave this natural cul-de-sac the next day. Cornstalk and the others decided to launch the warriors in the morning when this camp was being broken. The plan was to overwhelm Lewis' pickets and then deal with the milling whites like so many buffalo trapped in a dead-end ravine. Given the advantage of terrain, surprise, and the experience of their men, they might well have done what they hoped to, had they not been frustrated by some very bad luck.

George Washington, Anthony Wayne, Andrew Jackson, and other American military leaders were to note that while frontiersmen sometimes fought well enough, they usually made poor soldiers. Lewis' men were apparently no exception, but in this case an unsoldierly act saved the entire command. Lewis had ordered that at dawn the men should commence preparations to cross the Ohio. However, two of them, remembered only as Robertson and Hickman, decided to forgo this work and make a hunt to improve their breakfast mess. Looking for squirrels, coons, groundhogs, or whatever, they came over a rise and saw, on the flat below, Cornstalk's warriors gathering. A Shawnee sharpshooter immediately picked off Hickman, but Robertson escaped, sprinted back to his camp, and told Lewis he had seen "a body of the enemy covering four acres of ground as closely as they could stand by the side of each other."

Lewis had learned a lot about Indian fighting since his service with Braddock. He sent two companies, led by his brother Charles, up Crooked Creek with orders to hide in the brush along the stream. Col. William Flemming was directed to take two more companies and do the same along the Ohio. When the Indian army advanced, these two units were to attack its flanks, and perhaps encircle it. However, when the warriors came howling up the peninsula, they quickly discovered and overwhelmed these would-be ambushers, killing Charles Lewis and badly wounding Flemming.

Nevertheless, the resistance these companies made bought Lewis some time, which he used to set the rest of his men to work felling trees across the narrow neck of Point Pleasant, making a crude breastwork. Though such assaults were not their style, Cornstalk's men attacked this line in waves. A Capt. John Stuart who was there said the action was "extremely hot" all morning and that the defenders could hear Cornstalk (his voice identified by one of the whites who had been a Shawnee prisoner) shouting to his men, "Be strong. Be strong."

By noon the warriors had cut a small breach in the log wall, but they did not have enough men to expand it nor much inclination for such a foot-by-foot advance. Cornstalk then ordered a sudden retreat, attempting to lure the whites into an impetuous pursuit, which would leave them vulnerable to a counterattack once they were outside the breastworks. Lewis did not take this bait but held his men in good order. Then using their advantage in numbers the Long Knives began pushing the Shawnee slowly back down the peninsula. By late afternoon it was apparent to Cornstalk that neither further maneuvering nor bloodshed would serve to dislodge the whites. Under fire he and his men retreated north across the Ohio. Lewis was content to wait and regroup on the south shore.

Veterans of both sides who had fought at Point Pleasant had two general but vivid memories of the battle; that it had been a beautiful day, the fall foliage being scarlet; that by nightfall the ground beneath the trees was in many places red with their blood. The white body count was 222 men either killed or seriously wounded. As was their custom, the Shawnee carried off as many of their dead and wounded as they could, but it was generally estimated that their losses had been a half, or a bit more, of those suffered by Lewis' men. Among the warriors lost was Puckeshinwa. Later, whites heard that he had been terribly wounded as the Shawnee fought their way to the river in the afternoon. The fourteen-year-old Cheesekau carried him across the Ohio. On the north shore, Puckeshinwa died in his son's arms.

Cornstalk led his surviving men back to Chillicothe on the Scioto. While the wounded were nursed, the dead buried and mourned, he called the war and peace chiefs to council. According to summary reports of white traders living among the Shawnee, Cornstalk said, "The Long Knives are upon us by two routes. [Dunmore by then had advanced to the eastern edge of the Scioto plains and was waiting there in a fortified position, Camp Charlotte.] Shall we turn and fight them? Shall we kill our squaws and children and then fight until we are killed ourselves?" None, it was said, answered Cornstalk, who then sunk his hatchet in the war post in the middle of the council ground and said, "Since you are not inclined to fight, I will go and make peace."

Cornstalk with several aides then went to Camp Charlotte, believing that it would be easier to deal with the English governor than with Lewis and his Long Knives. Later a report circulated along the Virginia border that vengeful frontier troops arrived eager to storm Chillicothe and put a quick, final end to the Shawnee problem. Lewis was only stopped, at sword point, because of a direct confrontation with Dunmore. The story that Dunmore faced down Lewis with 800 or so partisans at his back seems unlikely. It is more plausible that Lewis and his men, sore and subdued after Point Pleasant, had no great enthusiasm for trying to force their way alone into Chillicothe, that any threats they made in this regard were exercises in half horse—half alligator backwoods brag.

No written records of the negotiations at Camp Charlotte were preserved, and the two sides had different versions of what was said. Dunmore and most whites claimed that Cornstalk accepted the Fort Stanwix boundary line and gave up Shawnee rights to their former hunting territories south of the Ohio. Also, the Shawnee pledged to trade thereafter with the whites in accordance with the "King's regulations." In return, Dunmore recognized that lands north and west of the Ohio, beyond Wheeling, belonged to the Shawnee and other Indians. Some whites and the Shawnee said that no mention of such territorial adjustments had been made, that a truce had been declared and there had been talk that white traders would be required to deal more fairly with Indians than they had in the past.

Whatever the oral agreements, after the Camp Charlotte council, Dunmore took his troops and Lewis' back to Virginia. Cornstalk and his warriors temporarily put down their hatchets. However, shortly all parties went back to doing what they had been doing—whites trying to press farther into the Ohio valley and reds trying to keep them out—paying very little attention to any settlements negotiated at Camp Charlotte.

Point Pleasant ended the opening phase of the first American Civil War. During it the Shawnee enjoyed great success in many small border raids. The battle against Lewis and his men at the mouth of the Kanawha was a military draw. Even so, the overall campaign had gone against the Shawnee. Their warriors had not been able to keep settlers out of Kentucky or to destroy the forces sent to aid them. By the mid-1770s there were nearly 10,000 whites in Kentucky. Most of them were in the eastern parts of the territory but appreciable numbers occupied fortified communities farther west. In consequence Kentucky was much less valuable to the Shawnee for hunting than it had been in 1768.

Though their forces were superior to his, Dunmore and Lewis had not been able to defeat Cornstalk, but they had inflicted losses which were more serious to the Shawnee than greater losses were to the whites. Simply by appearing, the Virginia expedition demonstrated to Cornstalk and others how numerous and rich the colonists were and that they were able to extend their power west of the mountains. The Dunmore-Lewis expedition increased the influence of Virginia along the Ohio and decreased that of the Pennsylvania traders at Fort Pitt, who were more conciliatory to the western Indians. Also, before returning to Virginia, Dunmore built and garrisoned a post, Fort Randolph, near Point Pleasant.

The Shawnee recognized these realities and, though not abandoning their claims to the territory, thought it prudent to put more distance between themselves, Kentucky, and the Long Knives in it. After the Camp Charlotte truce, they began migrating westward to the valleys of the two Miami rivers. By 1777 their principal community, another Chillicothe, was located on the Little Miami near Puckeshinwa's former hunting camp, the birthplace of Tekamthi.

Even on the Miamis it is doubtful that the Shawnee could have remained secure for long had the white invasion of the west continued as it had during the previous decade. However, it did not. Coincidentally, in the same week of September 1774 in which Dunmore had left with his expeditionary force for Ohio, the first Continental Congress of rebellious colonists was convened in Philadelphia. The battles of Concord and Lexington were fought seven months later in Massachusetts and the Revolutionary War followed. This conflict dramatically improved the situation of the Shawnee.

For most of the next seven years the Americans (as the former colonists will henceforth be called) were thoroughly occupied with the British along the coasts, drawing men and resources from the frontier districts for eastern campaigns. So far as there was a formal American Indian policy, it was to placate the reds in hopes that they would remain neutral. The British, on the other hand, immediately set about to create a second, western front, by raising the Indians to strike the Americans from New York to the Carolinas. The Shawnee in particular were courted and flattered, given special trading privileges, arms, ammunition, and, in time, British military advisers and sometimes artillery. So encouraged and supplied, their warriors eventually reentered Kentucky, wiped out or forced the abandonment of some of the American settlements, and commenced raiding as far to the east as the Shenandoah Valley. In this work they were fully supported by the Delaware, Miami, Wyandot, and other western nations who after the outbreak of the Revolution were no longer under pressure from the British or Iroquois to respect the Treaty of Stanwix.

Beyond the grief it caused, the death of Puckeshinwa did not greatly disrupt the lives of his widow, Methoastaske, or their children. Shawnee villages were, in effect, extended families in which caring for the kin of fallen warriors was a traditional community responsibility. So that they would have an adult patron of suitable stature to represent their interests, Tekamthi and Tenskwatawa were adopted by Black Fish, Puckeshinwa's longtime companion in arms and a prominent civil and military leader.

Methoastaske went on about her business as a leading farmer and matron among the women. Cheesekau, who had proved himself a warrior at Point Pleasant, became the role model and guide for his younger brothers—particularly Tekamthi, for whom he developed, according to later stories and happenings, a special fondness. Tecumpease, the eldest daughter, apparently had similar feelings. Though she took responsibility for all her younger brothers and sisters, Tekamthi, an appealing and promising child, was said to be her clear favorite.

IV. Red Boys

When David Jones visited Chillicothe in 1773, he reckoned that there were about twenty whites in the village. The same situation existed at the time throughout the Ohio Valley, where there were few communities which did not have some birthright whites living with and as reds—voluntarily and quite happily, according to many firsthand reports.

Some of these foreigners had come as traders or for other business reasons, as did Moses Henry, the resident gunsmith who with his Shawnee wife boarded Jones for a few days. But most whites in the villages first appeared as prisoners-of-war, who, after proving themselves congenial, educable people, had been adopted by red families. Often they replaced a relative who had been killed. After an initiatory period, these former prisoners enjoyed the same rights and privileges as the native-born residents. This custom—of maintaining their strength and compensating for wartime losses by recruiting and naturalizing captives—was common among most of the woodland nations long before the coming of whites. It became more prevalent during the white wars, which created more need for new, ready-made citizens and more prisoners.

There were fifty or sixty whites living with the Shawnee in Chillicothe-on-the-Little Miami. In addition to adopted captives, there were assorted British political agents, traders, and their families. In this white community were three preadolescent boys— Benjamin Kelly and a set of brothers, Abraham and Stephen Ruddell—who had been taken prisoner in Kentucky and adopted by red families. In Chillicothe at the same time was another boy, Anthony Shane, the son of a French-Canadian trader and a Shaw-

nee woman. The four of them are now remembered only because
they were acquainted with Tekamthi and because Stephen Ruddell
and Shane left accounts of this association.

Through his mother Shane was related to Tekamthi, but Stephen
Ruddell may have been closer to him. (As an adult Shane was not
fully accepted by either reds or whites, and there is a sense that this
also may have been the case in his youth.) Ruddell was a large,
active boy whom the Shawnee called Big Fish. He took to their
ways quickly and enthusiastically. Ruddell said that he first met
Tekamthi when they were both twelve years old and the two of
them became "inseparable" chums.

Shane and Ruddell wrote of their youth when they were men and
Tekamthi had become famous. Both showed an understandable
inclination to enhance their own importance by trading on their
connection with the celebrated Shawnee. Ruddell's account is
especially effusive, somewhat like those offered by early biogra-
phers of the young George Washington. Ruddell remembered
Tekamthi as always, in everything, the leader of the village boys—
the bravest, most honorable and considerate, the best athlete,
apprentice hunter, and warrior. Although somewhat more re-
strained, Shane said much the same—that Tekamthi was particularly adept with the bow and arrow and war club and "always had a
set of followers who were ready to stand or fall with him."

Beyond testifying that their friend was precocious and person-
able, neither Ruddell nor Shane gave much specific information
about him. However, though they were the only ones to leave any
record of his early years, it is not necessary to consider the boyhood
of Tekamthi as though it began when their accounts of it did. He
was a member of a prominent family in a very conservative society.
Both logic and the later events of his life make it clear that he was
reared—saw, heard, was taught, and did—approximately as children of this nation had been for many previous generations. Some
of the Shawnee traditions about the care and training of their youth
are still remembered and therefore some of his experiences can be
imagined.

Shawnee infants spent most of their first months strapped to a
cradleboard. This practice allowed mothers to go about their
regular business and was thought to promote straight backs and
patience. Crying or other outbursts were considered bad habits (a
loud baby could ruin a hunt or imperil a fleeing band), and bawling
children disgraced their parents. They were taught to hush by
being rocked, crooned to, or fed, before they became noisy. Young

Shawnee grew up little inclined to wail, whine, or throw tantrums, and as adults were contemptuous of people who so expressed themselves.

Throughout their lives, commencing as nursing infants, Shawnee ate as much and as often as they wanted when there was food. Settled in villages or camps, families took the morning meal together. During the rest of the day, women kept stews simmering over low fires. Not only their immediate kin but neighbors and casual visitors were welcome to dip into the pots, snack on fresh or preserved edibles. A successful couple such as Methoastaske and Puckeshinwa might set, so to speak, a better table than others. This would earn respect for their skill at farming or hunting but, because of the communal customs, it elevated the general standard of living, not just that of their own family.

Private hoarding was contrary to tradition. If anybody was poor, then everyone was, including the most prominent and industrious. Since even in the best of times the natural economy was chancy, most children by an early age had experienced hunger pangs and, again, were expected to bear them without self-pity or complaint. This control was probably easier for them to develop than it was for residents of European communities, in which it was possible and permissable for some to feast while others went without. So conditioned, Shawnee when necessary could travel, hunt, make war on very short rations for considerable periods of time. According to reports of foreigners, they seemed able to do so with much less physical and psychic discomfort than was experienced by those who fed—or thought they should—more regularly and rhythmically.

As toddlers, children were permitted to roam about villages and camps, doing and getting into more or less whatever they pleased. At an early age they learned to recognize their names as they were whistled, a distinctive note for each syllable, Te-kam-thi. This odd, pretty practice was also an instructive one. Hunters and warriors used the whistling code, expanded by bird and mammal sounds, which they were adept at mimicking, to keep in touch with each other while fooling their quarry or enemies. There are many accounts of white frontier people being terrified by whistling birds which they mistook for Shawnee warriors. There are other stories of parties being surprised because the birds were singing so sweetly that it seemed there could be no danger in the woods.

Parents and older brothers and sisters were directly responsible for the welfare of children, but all members of a community helped them learn skills and manners. Contrary to the white approach— where some children were taught more or less than others to

prepare them for different occupations and stations in life—
Shawnee education was universal in several senses. All children
were trained in the same way to be the same thing, a competent and
respectable Shawnee man or woman. Despite white opinion that
they were simple creatures of nature, this was a complicated
process. It is unlikely that a human could, or ever did, behave as a
true Shawnee without a great deal of guidance. The people themselves reckoned it required about twenty-five years to educate a
young person properly. Until that age—though they might already
be mothers, farmers, hunters, and warriors—youths were regarded
as apprentices who needed to be supervised by their elders.

Occasionally when they were intolerably rude or destructive,
Shawnee children were whipped or deprived of privileges, but the
common mode of instruction was permissive. This struck John
Heckewelder as a key element in the red culture. (Heckewelder, a
keen-eyed Moravian missionary, came to the Ohio Valley in the
1760s and for the next fifty years was a sympathetic student and
defender of the natives of that country.) Of the relationship between adults and children, he noted:

> No punishments, no threats are ever used to enforce commands
> or compel obedience. The child's *pride* is the feeling to which
> an appeal is made, which proves successful in almost every
> instance. A father needs only to say in the presence of his
> children: "I want such a thing done; I want one of my children
> to go upon such an errand; let me see who is the *good* child that
> will do it!" The word *good* operates as it were, by magic, and
> the children immediately vie with each other to comply with
> the wishes of their parent.
>
> In this manner of bringing up children, the parents are
> seconded by the whole community. If a child is sent from his
> father's dwelling to carry a dish of victuals to an aged person, all
> in the house will join in calling him a *good* child. They will ask
> whose child he is, and on being told, will exclaim: what! has
> the Tortoise, or the Little Bear (as the father's name may be) got
> such a good child? . . . On the other hand when the child has
> committed a bad act, the parent will say to him: "O! how
> grieved I am that my child has done this bad act. I hope he will
> never do it again."

Most other whites—few of whom had the opportunity or mind-
set to make the sort of observations the Reverend Mr. Heckewelder
did—thought the lack of discipline among red children was shocking if not sinful, that they would be greatly improved with hard,
regular beatings. However, considering the nature of the society
these children were expected to enter, the system described by
Heckewelder was a sensible one. Within Shawnee and other red

communities, there was no public apparatus for forcing individuals to behave contrary to their wishes. (As it did to David Jones, the lack of jails struck many whites as being very significant.) Therefore praising and rewarding children for good deeds was probably more effective than coercion as a means for producing adults who would voluntarily behave themselves. Heckewelder, commenting on this point, said, "The whole of the Indian plan of education tends to elevate rather than depress the mind, and by that means to make determined hunters and fearless warriors."

During their first years, children of both sexes were mainly in the company of and instructed by women as they farmed, foraged, built shelters, worked hides, cooked, collected, and prescribed medicines. (Among both whites and reds, Shawnee were renowned as physicians, there being among these contentious people perhaps more than ordinary need for and opportunity to practice healing skills.) Since when they were grown, they would often be without women, it was thought appropriate for boys to learn something about domestic crafts. When boys were five or six years old, their education became the responsibility of their fathers and brothers and other men of the community. The youngsters were given scaled-down but functional pieces of adult sporting equipment, tools, and weapons and turned loose to use them experimentally. They did so in enthusiastic imitation of great athletes, hunters, and warriors. Considerable property damage and not infrequently bodily injuries resulted. However, unless the mischief became absolutely intolerable, the boys went undisciplined, since aggressiveness was thought to be a promising trait of character which should be cultivated. In consequence, packs of small but formidable boys roamed every woodland village. One John M'Cullough spent eight years as a member of one of these youth gangs and later wrote a remarkable memoir, a true—so he said—Huck Finn kind of account of what it was like to be a red boy by adoption 230 years ago.

M'Cullough's family had moved from York, Pennsylvania, to the vicinity of what is now Chambersburg, then the most westerly region settled by whites. In the early summer of 1756, when he was eight years old, playing in the woods beyond the family cabin, he was kidnapped by a party of Shawnee and Delaware warriors passing through the area after having lifted white scalps in the country to the east. The warriors took M'Cullough to Fort Duquesne, the military stronghold of the French and their red allies. There his captors gave him as a gift to Ketoohalend, a warrior whose own younger brother had been killed and who was looking for a boy to take his place. Ketoohalend and two of his friends took

M'Cullough into the middle of the Allegheny River, pushed him into the water and held him underneath it "until I was almost smothered. This they repeated several times." The terrified child, certain that he was to be drowned like an unwanted puppy, began to squall and struggle. Ketoohalend signed for him to be quiet, that he was being washed, not killed.

Most captives being considered for adoption went through a similar ritual washing, the symbolic intent of which was to remove foreign taints. Other prisoners, generally grown men, were required to run between two lines of their captors, who whipped and reviled them. Occasionally these gauntlets were designed as a form of torture, and there were cases of men being broken and killed in them. More commonly this was a rough form of initiation in which the captors tried to determine what kind of person, brave or cowardly, they had. James Smith, who became the foster grandson of Tecaughretanego, endured a gauntlet and, when he finished it, asked a warrior why he had been so roughly treated. The man, amused, told him not to take it personally, it was a kind of red greeting, "like how do you do."

Ketoohalend and his friends scrubbed off as much of M'Cullough's whiteness as custom decreed, cut his hair, and dressed him Indian fashion. Then they took him to a large encampment on the Muskingum River, southwest of Fort Duquesne, which was being used by the Shawnee, Delaware, and Mingo as a staging area for military operations against the English. Ketoohalend introduced M'Cullough into his extended family and directed that he be treated the same as any other child of his age. This was done. M'Cullough makes no mention of his ever being discriminated against because of his race or former nationality. Chiefly his memoir is devoted to describing what a grand time he and the other boys had running free in the villages and camps.

Perhaps because Ketoohalend and the other men who would normally have supervised them were often absent fighting the English, the deportment of M'Cullough and his companions fell far short of that of the "good children" described by John Heckewelder. Also, with considerable provocation, the women and old men left in the village sometimes showed less than traditional patience in dealing with these little hellions. Even so, M'Cullough, though he got into at least as much trouble as the others, remembered being punished only twice.

In one instance his foster sister-in-law asked M'Cullough to baby-sit her two-year-old son while she was working in the corn. As soon as she left, M'Cullough sneaked away to play ball with his friends. Abandoned, the infant crawled off into the fields, became alarmed, and started to cry. His mother eventually found the child and, after comforting him, set off looking for M'Cullough. She yanked him out of the game and then felled him with one smart blow of a hoe handle. Several days later Ketoohalend returned. After hearing from both parties, he said that he was shocked that his wife should have forgotten how disgraceful it was for a woman to strike a boy of this age and perhaps inhibit his emerging manliness. Thereupon Ketoohalend cut a bundle of switches and whipped his wife, with the approval of all other relatives. Thus reminded of her manners, the woman, M'Cullough recalled with satisfaction, never laid a hand upon him again.

Later, on a summer day, the gang of boys was catching and killing turtles by a creek. In the course of things one of them grabbed a handful of rank turtle guts and threw it in M'Cullough's face. He responded by picking up a large rock and laying open the head of the prankster. Unfortunately, the victim had a bachelor uncle, Mussoohwhese, who was fishing nearby. Like communities everywhere, Indian villages had some bad, bent characters in them. Mussoohwhese was one. He was a known murderer (having treacherously stabbed a friendly trader to get his horse) and something of a sadist who made a habit of following the boys in M'Cullough's set and devising ways of tormenting them. Hearing the commotion, Mussoohwhese came up to investigate. By then, M'Cullough had prudently hidden himself in the reeds. Mussoohwhese called out that he would catch him if it took a year. The boy decided that he might as well come out and take his punishment. When he did, Mussoohwhese stripped him and stood him against a tree, then raked his back and legs until they bled, with the jawbone of a gar pike in which the sharp teeth of this fish were still set.

Ketoohalend was absent, but on his return, he again sided with M'Cullough. He said that retaliating for a faceful of turtle with a well-aimed stone was reasonable and showed spirit. It was certainly nothing that entitled someone outside the family to punish him as dishonorably as Mussoohwhese had. Ketoohalend announced publicly that had he been present he would have buried his war hatchet in Mussoohwhese's skull. Apparently the threat was taken seriously, for M'Cullough makes no further mention of himself or his mates being molested by this wicked uncle.

When he was ten, M'Cullough got into his most serious scrape. He, a boy, Watook, and his younger brother went into the cabin of a warrior who, feeling poorly, had gone to a village doctor to be treated in a sweat house. In the cabin the boys found a large horse pistol. Together they loaded the piece. Much excited, Watook began waving it about, threatening "for diversion" to shoot the other two. The younger brother ran off and hid but M'Cullough argued with Watook that things had gone too far. Finally Watook agreed and asked M'Cullough to help him lower the cock and unload the gun. While they were trying to do so, the pistol went off, instantly killing Watook.

M'Cullough thought that he would be executed and his body "thrown into the creek to be devoured by fish or left above ground to be devoured by vermin," as had happened to two other wanton murderers. Soon villagers gathered and rather calmly interrogated M'Cullough. He said, of course, that it was not his fault. A young woman, who unbeknownst to the boys had been nearby and witnessed part of the incident, testified in his behalf. The ad hoc jury decided that the death was accidental, the regrettable but more or less unavoidable consequence of boys being boys. This officially settled the matter, but M'Cullough said that afterward "the little fellows" with whom he ran would sometimes tease him as being a killer, but more, it seems, in admiration than horror.

In 1760, having learned from a trader that his son was still alive, M'Cullough's natural father visited the Indian camp during a lull in the hostilities. He found Ketoohalend, gave him gifts, and arranged for his son to return with him. When young M'Cullough found out about this, he threw a tantrum and physically resisted being taken back to the white settlements. Finally his father tied him to a horse and, as they traveled east, kept him in ropes when they stopped to camp. On the third night M'Cullough wriggled free and disappeared into the forest. Several days later he came home to Ketoohalend, who regarded the whole incident as a stroke of good fortune since it ended with him retaining his adopted brother as well as his ransom.

M'Cullough continued to live red, traveling and hunting between the Great Lakes and Ohio for the next three years. In 1763 Brig. Gen. Henry Bouquet's invasion of western Pennsylvania put an end to the uprising of Pontiac. The Shawnee and Delaware sought a truce. A non-negotiable demand was that they return all their white "captives," who Bouquet and the other officers assumed were being cruelly abused. Finally about two hundred men, women, and children (including M'Cullough) were brought to a depot on the Muskingum and turned over to the soldiers. Many of them "shed torrents of tears" as they begged to stay with their red husbands, wives, and friends. "Every captive," said a military observer, "left the Indians with regret."

Bouquet was unmoved. He ordered the captives to be put under guard and tied up if necessary, to ensure that all could be brought home and freed. Perhaps because Ketoohalend explained that this was a serious political matter and he would not be welcomed back if he tried any funny business a second time, M'Cullough went along docilely. (On the march at least two women, Rhoda Boyd and Elizabeth Studibaker, managed to escape and return permanently to their Indian families.) Thereafter M'Cullough remained with the whites, became a farmer and merchant. But throughout his life he looked back on the eight years he had spent as an Indian as the most interesting part of it.

M'Cullough's experiences and reactions were by no means unique. Among those who became interested in the phenomenon of white "captives" was Jean de Crèvecoeur, a gentleman farmer and essayist who is still regarded as one of the most astute commentators on American society in the latter half of the eighteenth century. Writing in 1782, he claimed there were thousands of whites living voluntarily as Indians, but on the other hand, "We have no examples of even one of these Aborigines having from choice become Europeans." Later historians have accepted de Crèvecoeur's impressions as being substantially correct.

All of which was shockingly contrary to many important European dogmas and policies which were based on the conviction that white civilization was patently superior. The conventional wisdom was expressed by a Philadelphia minister, William Smith, who remarked, "For easy and unconstrained as the savage life is, certainly it could never be put in competition with the blessings of improved life and the light of religion, by any persons who have had the happiness of enjoying and the capacity of discerning them."

The facts—that there was an ongoing informal referendum in which those who participated showed strong preference for the red life-style—were so unsettling that most white authorities ignored them, as did the Reverend Mr. Smith. Those who gingerly took up the question usually concluded that while it was clearly better, materially and spiritually, to be civilized, it was a difficult thing to manage, required more brains and gumption than all reds and a good many baser whites possessed. So thought Benjamin Franklin, who commented in 1753 that whites who got a taste of Indian living were very apt to "become disgusted with our [European] manner of life, and the care and pains that are necessary to support it and take the first good Opportunity of escaping again into the Woods, from whence there is no reclaiming them."

Some who became, as Franklin once put it, White Savages had more pragmatic reasons for their behavior. Mary Jemison, taken prisoner in Pennsylvania as a young girl, lived a happy life as a Seneca wife (married to the same warrior for fifty years) and mother. She said of her husband that "he uniformly treated me with tenderness and never offered an insult." Also she found that the "cares" of red matrons were not "half so numerous nor great" as those of their white counterparts.

The attraction of the red life for white men was more obvious. As a Shawnee, Delaware, or Wyandot, they could hunt, fish, ramble, play games, gamble, gossip, and fight in a fashion which only the richest and most powerful Europeans were permitted or could afford. De Crèvecoeur, who sometimes fantasized about going red (but was essentially too refined to do so) interviewed two long-time white savages, one originally an Englishman, the other a Swede. Though the essayist probably dressed up their language a bit, they explained their motives very clearly, telling him that they remained red because they enjoyed "the most perfect freedom, the ease of living, the absence of those cares and corroding solicitudes which so often prevail with us [whites]."

Ideally a hunter or warrior was expected to bear hardships so lightly that the fear of fatigue, pain, and even death did not deter him from acting heroically. Therefore very early, adult men began to condition boys to be hardy and self-controlled.

His adopted brother, Ketoohalend, being on the warpath, John M'Cullough's training during his first months as an Indian boy was supervised by an "uncle," a veteran warrior who

> was blind in one eye—a very good natured man. In the beginning of winter he used to raise me up by daylight every morning and make me sit down in the creek up to my chin in the cold water . . . [when] he thought I had been long enough in the water, he would bid me dive. After I came out he would order me not to go near the fire until I would be dry. I was kept at that until the water was frozen over, he would then break the ice for me and send me in as before.

Being so new to this educational system, M'Cullough first felt he was being punished and did not understand that the old man thought him so precocious that he deserved a chance, though only eight, to demonstrate his bravery. In contrast, Gaynwah (Thomas Wildcat Alford), a birthright Shawnee, recalled that on the first cold morning when his father took him to the creek and ordered him to plunge in, "I knew that my father had begun to train me to be a man, a brave, possibly a chief. Pride filled my heart! I did as my father told me, the other children looking on with admiration and respect. Every morning during that winter I repeated that performance, breaking the ice when it was necessary."

As soon as they could walk, Shawnee boys were encouraged to wander about in the woods beyond the village clearings. This was directly useful since they frightened off deer, coons, crows, and other thieving creatures from the women's fields. More importantly, as they roamed they commenced the study of natural history, which preoccupied Shawnee males throughout their lives. The basic skills—learning the habits of animals, reading signs, being patient—required to find a snapping turtle hiding under a creek bank were much the same as those necessary for getting a denned bear.

In time, these exercises for developing woodcraft and character were formalized. At ten or twelve, a boy was directed to go off alone and not return until he was able to bring back some sort of edible game. Before leaving, his face was smeared with charcoal to show anyone he met that he was on a quest and should not be given aid or advice. Gaynwah recalled that on the first day of his black-face test he did not find anything to shoot or eat. On the second day he was lucky—because his hands were unsteady from fatigue and hunger—to bring down a quail with an arrow. He ran home with the bird, bringing honor to himself and his father.

These tests were progressively lengthened and made more difficult. An unmanly response to them—giving up because of pain or exhaustion, showing fear, lying about or blaming others for failure—was one of the few offenses for which responsible men physically punished boys. The whippings, often severe and bloody, were administered to publicize the boy's disgraceful behavior and also to give him an opportunity to redeem himself by enduring the beating bravely.

Boys so conditioned became exceptionally impassive men, who in moments of crisis suppressed signs of their inner feelings so as not to alarm their companions or give satisfaction or encouragement to their enemies. Since whites mostly met them in adversarial situations, they understandably thought of red men as being almost pathological stoics. The grim, unfeeling brave, occasionally grunting a bestial "ugh," became a general stereotype. The few whites who came to know them in easier, relaxed circumstances were astonished at how overtly emotional red men and women were; by the abandoned way in which they danced, sang, played games, mourned, worshipped. Most particularly, they were forever giggling, hooting, and howling in fits of amusement. Of the Shawnee he met in 1773, the Rev. David Jones thought "both men and women in laughing exceed any nation that ever came under my notice."

The Shawnee had a special taste for parables and allegories in which animals acting like humans were the principal characters. This anthropomorphic style was natural for them since each person was thought to possess some of the characteristics of the totem animal of the *umsoma* to which he or she belonged. "The stories relative to one's Umsoma, or against the Umsomas of other parties was one phase of the story telling that gave vent to the wit and humor of the narrator," said Gaynwah. He added that while traveling or hunting, there was a lot of good-natured banter. Apparently it was somewhat similar to that of modern sports fans bragging about their teams and ridiculing others. For example, when crossing a river, turtle and raccoon people customarily went first and joked about why and how panther and rabbit people were lagging behind.

There was a mocking element in many Shawnee stories aimed at subtly commenting on the behavior of others. Since all Shawnee were theoretically free to do as they pleased, open criticism of an individual was impolite. However, telling a story about a clumsy, lazy, greedy, or rude animal to a person who seemed to have the same traits was thought to be a good way of correcting these failings.

Though they took an active, affectionate interest in training boys, hunters and warriors in their prime were often absent. Therefore, after they were of an age when it was thought unseemly for them to be supervised by women, the youths were thrown much into the company of old men. Tenskwatawa remembered that he and other boys were "taught when very young to carry little birds, squirrels, &c., which they kill to some of the aged people in the village . . . and few grew up without feeling the necessity of paying a good deal of attention to those whose advice and opinion may be of essential service to them."

Among the conservative Shawnee, the only important, permanent hierarchy was based on age, and not only children but adults regularly sought the "advice and opinion" of their seniors. This behavior was based on the conviction that Shawnee customs were more or less perfect and that longevity in itself demonstrated how well a person understood them.

John Heckewelder observed that when a boy did something commendable, say, killed his first deer, a proud father would not boast about his son's ingenuity or how well he himself had trained the youngster. Rather he would say that the boy "must have listened attentively to the aged hunters, for, though young he has already given proof that he will become a good hunter himself." If he failed, the boy might be reprovingly told that "he did not pay attention to the discourses of the aged."

The relationship between the young and old was a sensible, symbiotic one. As Tenskwatawa noted, boys physically assisted the old men. In return they were shown and told how to make and maintain tools and weapons, draw the pictographic script (with which hunters and warriors left substantial messages for each other in the field), dress and paint themselves fashionably, conduct themselves properly at religious and ceremonial functions, treat with women. Furthermore, though they might not still be able to practice the most manly arts, the veterans could talk inspiringly for hours about such things as stalking and dispatching a buffalo, a Chickasaw, or Long Knife. Tenskwatawa said that in his boyhood there were "particularly happy old men [who would] sit up a whole night or employ a whole day recalling the scenes of their youth, their warlike adventures, their courtships, hunting excursions . . . traditions or fabulous stories of the ancient days."

In these sessions Shawnee youths were given much practical how-to information while learning history and cosmology. Listening to the old men, they also began to appreciate the power of their language, which Joab Spencer, the Shawnee missionary, among others, thought was more "expressive, stately, eloquent and beautiful" than any other. Witty conversation was a chief entertainment of the Shawnee. Tekamthi's younger brother (one of the set of triplets which included Tenskwatawa) was called Kumskaukau, Star over the Great Water. Little is remembered of him other than that Anthony Shane recalled he was a "jolly" youth who "always had a party around him because of his good humor and stories."

Composing and delivering stirring orations was a major Shawnee art form. Those who could hold the rapt attention of a village or nation for hours as they spoke of serious matters were counted as great men. These oral performances earned somewhat the same sort of respect that outstanding feats of hunting or war did. Years later when Tekamthi began to speak publicly of his ambition to create an independent red nation, whites were astonished that an ignorant savage was so well informed about wars and treaties of the past, could marshal the facts in such an orderly fashion and state his case so powerfully. These listeners attributed the remarkable performance to his special genius. No doubt this was a factor, but also Tekamthi had benefited from a splendid, classical Shawnee education. As a boy, he had listened and learned from the greatest men of the nation—his own father, Cornstalk, Black Hoof, Black Fish, and Blue Jacket. In such subjects as natural and social history, military affairs, theology, and public speaking, Tekamthi's education had been longer, probably as good as, or better than, that received by Harrison, Cass, or any other of his white adversaries.

Whether they were intended to be instructive or entertaining, the stories the old men told boys invariably included moral lessons: passages that noted the rewards which came to those who were brave, loyal, and self-sacrificing, the punishments which befell those who were not. This emphasis was imperative, for the Shawnee depended on civil manners rather than civil law to maintain domestic order. Gaynwah said that even in his day there survived a short code of conduct which summarized the moral philosophy of his people. He translated it as: Do not kill or injure your neighbor, for it is not him that you injure, you injure yourself. But do good to him, therefore add to his days of happiness as you add to your own. Do not wrong or hate your neighbor, for it is not him you wrong, you wrong yourself. But love him, for Moneto [The Master of Life] loves him also as he loves you.

The Shawnee did not regard these precepts as applicable when dealing with foreigners. Gaynwah, apparently a gentle, broad-minded man, made this very clear, stating, "Our people believed that they were only responsible for their conduct toward their own race, especially their own tribe. . . . To the white man they owed nothing, except to return in kind the treatment they received."

As Christians sometimes have ignored their golden rules, the Shawnee were not always able or willing to live according to the fine principles described by Gaynwah. There are records of domestic disputes, malicious termagants, sadistic bullies, and occasional murderers—though no rapists or thieves—among them. As a rule difficulties were resolved privately, but juries of principal men and women were convened to consider the most serious cases. They might go so far as to sentence a killer to public execution, but once a decision was reached, all the involved parties were expected to forgive and forget. The Shawnee were too few and often in such precarious circumstances that they could not tolerate simmering, disruptive feuds.

According to those who lived in both, Shawnee villages ordered by traditional rules of etiquette and ethics were generally at least as peaceful and secure as white communities governed by formal laws and professional enforcers of them. However, there were two notable, if sporadic causes of exceptional violence—the abuse of alcohol and foreign prisoners. Whites, of course, had considerable experience with drunkenness and torture, but in these regards red behavior—and the consequences of it—was singular.

There were some Indian women and even children who became drunkards but from the beginning men had and caused the greatest problems. Alcohol easily meshed with the heroic codes of conduct. Warriors were trained to be impassive and self-disciplined in the face of danger, but it was also thought very manly for them to be wild and frenzied in their leisure pursuits. They soon discovered that the strong drink of whites could produce almost instant abandon, and this was the purpose for which they most often used it. They did not tipple to be convivial but to become roaring drunk as quickly as possible. There is no evidence that red men had naturally weaker heads than whites or that booze had a worse effect on their constitutions. Yet, as a generality, they were probably the more dangerous drunks. Most obviously there were no farm hands, lawyers, or ribbon clerks among them. Almost to the man they were warriors, conditioned to violence, contemptuous of pain and injury, exceptionally prickly about insults, real or imaginary. The consequences were frequently disastrous. James Smith, John M'Cullough, John Heckewelder, and many others who lived in Indian communities told stories of men who were wise and kindly when sober murdering and maiming each other when drunk, of terrified women and children hiding from besotted husbands, fathers, and friends.

Red communities had no drunk tanks or authorities to escort troublemakers to them. Furthermore, there were strong traditions which prohibited one person from restraining or correcting the behavior of another. For a man to clap a drinking companion on the back and advise him that he had had enough, should go home and sleep it off, would have been extremely rude, quite possibly suicidal. The opinion evolved in most red nations that inebriation was a form of temporary insanity and men could not be held responsible for their acts when so afflicted. However, as time passed, thoughtful chiefs and councillors became very aware of how serious this mental-health problem was.

The Shawnee claimed they were the first North American natives to drink—somewhere on an Atlantic beach—and to learn that white spirits were poisonous. If this was not the case, they were, as a matter of record, among the first to become formally interested in prohibition. As early as 1701, meeting with whites, Shawnee negotiators asked that the whiskey trade be suppressed. At other councils in 1734 and 1753, the request was repeated. Many white authorities (including Benjamin Franklin who represented Pennsylvania at the bargaining sessions in 1753) were sympathetic. So too, contrary to much folk history, were many fur traders whose concerns were commercial, not moralistic. Bartering with the western reds was always risky and dealing with drunken ones made it much more so. No effective embargo was ever established. The whiskey continued to flow, essentially because red men wanted it. If they could not get it from established traders, they turned to rash irregulars and renegades who took the risks so as to work their way into the profitable business. Not infrequently, when the whiskey kegs were opened, otherwise good men were at the head of the line, unable for manly reasons or weakness to practice what they preached about the evils of strong drink. The careful consideration of consequences before acting is not a prominent trait among heroes or would-be ones.

As noted, the great majority of prisoners of war met one of two reasonably benign fates. Either they were held for ransom (a business which picked up greatly during the white wars) or were naturalized and adopted by their captors. In both cases, as hundreds of accounts testify, they were treated as humanely and enjoyed more freedom than did prisoners held in white jails of the time. However, a few captives were now and then put to slow, horrible deaths, a practice which, like prisoner taking itself, had originated before the coming of Europeans. Traditionally the victims were enemy warriors executed in retaliation for acts they or their nation had committed against their captors. Sometimes this was done in anger by the war parties immediately after they took a prisoner. Others were brought back to the villages to be ceremonially tortured. When this occurred, women generally took the lead in these rites, which gave them an opportunity to vent their anger and grief for the losses of their own men by practicing cruelties on foreign ones.

Customs varied from nation to nation, but as a rule war criminals were ritually shaved and painted, then secured loosely, so as to allow some interesting freedom of movement, to a post around which slow-burning firewood had been piled. Before and after the flames were lighted, victims were stoned, slashed, and partially dismembered, care being taken so that these preliminary torments did not bring about their untimely end. Skillful torturers could keep a man, or at least the charred, mutilated hulk of one, alive for many hours. Somewhat like hangings and witch or heretic burnings among Europeans, these were great public occasions which engaged the entire community and were thought to be instructive particularly for youths. Prisoners who died badly, screaming and begging, served as a warning against cowardice. Those who remained self-controlled provided positive role models.

Men of all nations recognized that they might someday come to the stake and hoped to meet such an end honorably. It was accepted that by outwardly showing no fear or pain a warrior demonstrated contempt for his torturers and erased the dishonor of having been captured. Therefore he would live on in the memory of his own people as a hero and no doubt be accepted as such in the next world. Many were able to meet their end in this ideal fashion. An Iroquois veteran being torn apart by Hurons asked sarcastically, "Must I, who have made the whole earth tremble, now die by the hands of children?" The answer was yes, but his response became legendary. A Shawnee bound and driven through a Cherokee torture gauntlet was left bloody and broken at the end of it. He staggered to his feet and entered it once again, saying that, if this was not a nation of infants, he had been shamed by receiving such soft caresses. An impressed Cherokee warrior brained him with a war club on the grounds that a man of such valor and élan deserved to be treated with honor.

Gruesome as these ordeals were, they were founded on a kind of logic—that of revenge and the heroic codes. During the white wars, because of a new sort of racial animosity this was corrupted. In some communities innocent prisoners were terribly tortured, not to satisfy the national honor or the grief of survivors but simply to provide a few hours of frenzied public entertainment. There was, for example, the case of Martha Moore and her family. After their men were killed defending a farm in southwestern Virginia, they were captured by Shawnee raiders led by a minor chief, Black Wolf. Two of the children, a crying infant, Peggy, and a retarded son, John, were immediately killed. (The first hours after capture were very dangerous ones for prisoners. The adrenaline of the warriors was flowing, and they usually had need to get out of an area quickly. Captives who made difficulties or were feeble were often dispatched for the same reason a useless horse was.)

Returning to his village in Ohio, Black Wolf found a band of Cherokee visiting there. They had also been raiding but without success and were consequently sore and disgruntled. To cheer them up, Black Wolf made a present of Martha Moore and her daughter Jane. (Another daughter, Mary, and a servant girl, Martha Evans, were kept by the Shawnee and treated well until they were ransomed several years later.) The Cherokee tied the women to a stake and commenced to roast them very slowly. Martha Moore cried out and begged to be released quickly, but her pleas were directed toward her own God. They were heard by a Shawnee matron who, disgusted by the unheroic sport of the Cherokee, entered their fire ring and with two quick hatchet blows ended the ordeal of the Moore women.

Such horrible happenings became increasingly frequent and involved the Shawnee as well as Cherokee and other nations. Both Tenskwatawa and Black Hoof (who was also interviewed by Charles Trowbridge) said that there came to be a society of outcast witch women, who stole prisoners from their rightful captors to torment and even cannibalize them. The two men made it clear that they and other respectable people regarded these practices and people as despicable. There are other accounts in which grateful prisoners told of leading men or women stepping in to save them by outfacing bloodthirsty mobs. For decent-minded reds the occasional, slow, painful execution of an enemy warrior was one thing, an act of public policy, but burning women and children, torturing purely for pleasure, dishonored ancient traditions and was a sport for degenerates.

It was known that as a man Tekamthi personally loathed drunkenness and the senseless torture of prisoners. Furthermore, he preached to his followers that they must give up these practices, because they rotted character and made men less able to serve the red cause. There is no record of him reminiscing about particular early events which led to those opinions. Nevertheless, in these and many other matters the conduct of his life, particularly the public part of it, constituted a commentary on the general experiences of his boyhood and their powerful effect on him.

He was born toward the end of the last generation who knew Shawnee society when it was strong and operating essentially as it had for many years previous. As he attempted to rally his people and give them hope, the first premise of Tekamthi's case was that life in the forests, hunting camps, villages, and families of his youth had been so sweet and right that trying to preserve the conditions which supported it was worth every sacrifice. But he also grew up when the failure of some of the traditions was becoming apparent. The second premise of Tekamthi was that reds must strengthen and purify themselves to survive. To save the best and most important of the old ways, they must give up some of them which were the cause of their difficulties and corruption. Most particularly, Te-kamthi urged that reds must become unified, like a single family, to shield themselves against whites. This could only be done if individuals and nations sacrificed some of their ancient freedoms and heroic ideals, became more disciplined in acting collectively to advance their common, racial welfare.

There is no connection of record between the experience of the boy and the convictions of the man. However, for a few years around 1768, among the Shawnee there was a mixing of the sweet traditional life with portents of the bitter times which were shortly to come. This was the peculiar social environment of a bright, observant boy, one who displayed charismatic qualities at an early age and was educated to be a hero-leader. Other fates may have been possible for him, but it is difficult to imagine that the boy could have become something other than what Tekamthi, as a man, was—both a passionate reactionary and revolutionary.

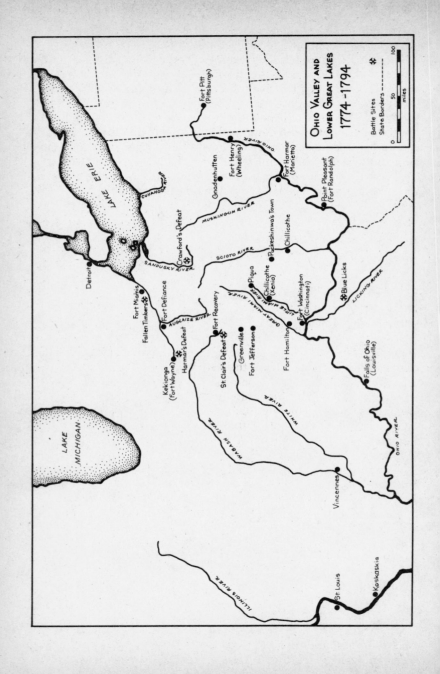

OHIO VALLEY AND
LOWER GREAT LAKES
1774-1794

Battle Sites ✤
State Borders -------

0   50   100
miles

LAKE ERIE

LAKE MICHIGAN

Detroit

Fort Miamis
Fallen Timbers ✤
Fort Defiance
Kekionga (Fort Wayne)
Harmar's Defeat
Fort Recovery
St. Clair's Defeat ✤
Greenville
Fort Jefferson

CUYAHOGA RIVER
Crawford's Defeat ✤
SANDUSKY RIVER
AUGLAIZE RIVER
GREAT MIAMI RIVER
LITTLE MIAMI RIVER

Gnadenhutten
Fort Henry (Wheeling)
MUSKINGUM RIVER
Fort Harmar (Marietta)

Fort Pitt (Pittsburgh)

OHIO RIVER

SCIOTO RIVER

Buckeshinwa's Town
Chillicothe
Piqua
Chillicothe (Xenia)
Fort Washington (Cincinnati)
Fort Hamilton

Point Pleasant (Fort Randolph)

✤ Blue Licks
LICKING RIVER

WABASH RIVER
WHITE RIVER

Falls of Ohio (Louisville)

OHIO RIVER

Vincennes

ILLINOIS RIVER

St. Louis
Kaskaskia

V. The Making of a Warrior

The natives of the Ohio Valley knew little about the economic and political issues which set the whites to fighting in the American Revolution. However, short- and long-term self-interest inclined the majority of them toward the British.

. . . Obtaining European goods had become vital for the reds. At the outbreak of the Revolution the established St. Lawrence trading routes and the important western posts—except Fort Pitt— were controlled by agents of the British who for the most part were veterans of the fur business. Alexander McKee, who came to head the British Indian service in the west, had a Shawnee wife as did his deputy, Matthew Elliott, another Tory trader. The Girty brothers were naturalized reds, and nearly all the men in this service had some native connections. In contrast, there were few Americans whom the reds had previously known and respected. Furthermore the new nation lacked access to world fur markets and had little capacity to manufacture goods, except whiskey, for the Indian trade.

. . . Maj. William Croghan, stationed at Fort Pitt in the early years of the war, observed that the great issues of the Revolution did not much engage the civilians in western Pennsylvania and Virginia. "The country talks," he noted, "of nothing but killing Indians and taking possession of their lands." By then many reds had concluded that such sentiments were universal among frontiersmen whom they knew as land-thieving surveyors, murderous thugs of the

Cresap-Greathouse stripe, or formidable Indian fighters like Andrew Lewis and his men. Between them and the Long Knives there was already much spilled and bad blood. Irrespective of British–American differences, westerners of both races were ready to have at each other in their own ways and wars.

. . . Croghan's remarks emphasized the absolutely irreconcilable matter. The British wanted furs and were willing to give something in exchange for them. The Long Knives wanted Indian lands and had demonstrated that they would take and occupy them by force. The Revolution did not change this or even immediately slow the white invasion of the Ohio valley. In fact, it was the opinion of Col. Daniel Brodhead, another American at Fort Pitt, that many whites migrated west to avoid militia duty and taxes in the east. Whatever their reasons, in 1775–76 several thousand new settlers spread out into what is now West Virginia and down the Ohio below Wheeling. Along with lesser stations, three major fortified communities were established in central Kentucky: Logan's Fort, Harrodsburg, and, by the persistent Daniel, Boonesboro.

In consequence at the beginning of the Revolution most of the Iroquois, Wyandot, and Mingo, along with factions within other nations, aligned themselves with the British. There was virtually no genuine pro-American sentiment, but some reds held that they should, at least temporarily, stay out of this strange war and let the whites maul each other. This was the first opinion of many of the Shawnee. They had taken the lead during the previous decade in resisting the Long Knives but had never formed, like the Iroquois, strong attachments to the British. Though bands of young, freelance warriors joined the Wyandot and Mingo in raiding white settlements, the nation as a whole remained neutral in 1775–76. The wait-and-see party was headed by Cornstalk who, because of the way he had fought at Point Pleasant and negotiated afterward, was the single most influential man among his people.

Cornstalk's policies were in keeping with the Shawnee tradition of never being completely on anyone's side but their own. With British agents, who spoke of the advantages and gratifications which would follow if the Shawnee took to the warpath against the Long Knives, Cornstalk was evasive, refusing to make firm commitments but hinting at enough to maintain trade relations. At the same time, he talked to Americans from Fort Pitt about his support for the truce arranged at Camp Charlotte. American authorities in the west were themselves very conciliatory. Daniel Brodhead went so far as to send troops to drive off a colony of whites—mostly Virginians for whom he had little regard—who had squatted north of the Ohio on Indian lands. It was a diplomatic gesture but had no real effect. As these whites were being removed, more were arriving.

This double game bought some time for the Shawnee, which they used to recover from Point Pleasant and relocate in more secure areas along the Miami rivers. Still it was clear to Cornstalk that neutrality could only be a diversionary tactic, that halting the invasion of their lands remained the life-and-death issue for his people. In preparation for the day when they would again have to confront the Long Knives, he began looking for allies. Early in the summer of 1776 he left the Ohio country, unbeknownst to the Americans who had begun to think that this great man had become their Indian. With emissaries representing the Iroquois, Delaware, and Ottawa, he traveled south to meet the Cherokee and persuade them to join an anti-America alliance. The council was held at Muscle Shoals on the Tennessee River and lasted for more than a week. The Iroquois, who had come the greatest distance, told of what they had seen between the St. Lawrence and the Tennessee. They said, according to John Stuart, a British agent present, that "where we could once see only deer and buffalo we found the country thickly inhabited . . . [with] large numbers of white men around salt springs and buffalo grounds."

On or about July 4—as the Americans were declaring their independence—Cornstalk delivered the crucial speech of the council. Behind him, aides extended a great, ceremonial belt of purple beadwork wampum, said to measure nine feet long. On it Cornstalk dashed a blood-red dye, to illustrate dramatically the substance of his message. Then he said that much of the land on which the Shawnee had formerly hunted was covered with forts, settlements, and armed white men whose clear intention it was to exterminate the Indians. He advised, as recorded by Stuart:

> It is better for the red men to die like warriors than to diminish
> away by inches. Now is the time to begin. If we fight like men,
> we may hope to enlarge our bounds. The Cherokees have a
> hatchet that was brought to you six years ago. Your brothers the
> Shawnese hope you will take it up and use it immediately.

Cornstalk ended his speech in a typically Shawnee way: "If any nation shall refuse us now, we shall hereafter consider them the common enemy of all red men. When affairs with the white people are settled, we shall fall upon such nations and destroy them."

Despite Cornstalk's eloquence and warning, the Cherokee were divided. Those living in the eastern part of the nation had been contending for some time and not very successfully against white settlers in the Carolinas and Tennessee. Recently they had ceded some of their former lands for a price and peace and were reluctant to break this truce. The unsubdued Cherokees, called the Chicka-mauga, were led by a war chief, Dragging Canoe. In due ceremo-nial time, Dragging Canoe rose at the council, accepted the great belt of wampum from Cornstalk, and promised to send his warriors into the field—which he shortly did.

Cornstalk with his entourage returned to Ohio, where later in the summer he met with Col. George Morgan, who had been appointed by the Continental Congress as its representative to the western Indians. Morgan, a Philadelphian with some experience as a trader, was a bold, forthright man but not, like many of the American agents, by red standards a diplomatic or well-mannered one. He came into the Ohio country demanding that the nations send delegations to Fort Pitt to sign peace treaties with the Americans. Cornstalk gave him no immediate satisfaction but did help him escape from the village where they met. The act probably saved Morgan's life since the area was crawling with warriors in a very anti-American mood.

For most of the next year, 1777, Cornstalk continued to talk neutrality to the Americans while presumably waiting for the right time to make war. However, it became increasingly difficult to restrain the young men, many of whom slipped away to run around with their hatchets in Kentucky with Wyandot, Mingo, and Cher-okee warriors. In midsummer these mixed raiding parties made a series of attacks in the Wheeling area. Less concerned with the plight of the settlers than by the prospect of British-Indian forces striking east out of the mountains, the American Congress detached Brig. Gen. Edward Hand to deal with the situation but was unable to send any additional troops with him. (At the time there were about 200 Continental soldiers stationed in the west at Fort Pitt and lesser posts. Among the white settlers in the western part of Pennsylvania, Virginia, and eastern Kentucky, there was a pool of 1,000–1,500 men able but by no means all willing to serve in the militia.) Hand was an energetic, conventional-minded soldier but poorly acquainted with the politics and geography of the west. After taking command he commenced to gather men with the intention of marching north to destroy a depot (on the Cuyahoga River, upstream from the present Cleveland) which the British were establishing to supply the Indians.

Upon hearing of this, Cornstalk, his son, and another man traveled to the nearest American post, Fort Randolph at Point Pleasant. His purpose was to tell the soldiers there—and through them Hand—that if the Cuyahoga expedition was carried out, it would bring the Shawnee and other western nations directly into the war on the side of the British. Capt. Matthew Arbuckle, the commander at Fort Randolph, paid no heed to the warning but, rather, imprisoned the Shawnee, holding them as hostages to guarantee the good conduct of their nation. On November 10, 1777, a party of white frontier hunters came down the Kanawha River. Hearing that the great Cornstalk was being held under light guard, they decided to take vengeance for past wrongs done to their people by his. As they approached the prison cabin, a friendly white woman ran to warn the prisoners.

The son, Elinipsico, "trembled with fear," witnesses said, but Cornstalk was calm, saying: "I am here among you, and you may kill me if you please. I can die but once, and it's all one to me now or at another time."

Arbuckle attempted to protect the hostages from the vigilantes, but only by persuasion. They brushed him aside. Breaking into the cabin, they shot and mutilated the unarmed Shawnee, putting seven or eight bullets, it was said, into the body of Cornstalk.

The killing of Cornstalk outraged eastern whites as had that of Logan's family, but more for tactical than humanitarian reasons. Patrick Henry, the governor of Virginia, wrote to his western militia commander, Col. William Flemming, that "The Murder of the Shawnanese Indians will no doubt bring on Hostilities with that People. In order to ward off the Stroke it is necessary to have every Gun in your County put into good order & got ready for Action." He went on to rail that the work of a handful of lawless frontier "assassins" had altered public policy and would "oblige our People to be hunting after Indians in the Woods instead of facing Gen. Howe in the field." Henry issued a formal apology to the Shawnee nation, but the delivery of it was impossible. A few months later he was able to bring Cornstalk's killers to trial in a Virginia court, but they were acquitted because no witnesses from Fort Randolph would testify against them.

At Fort Pitt General Hand assessed the situation much as did Henry. In his report to the Secretary of War about Cornstalk's murder, he predicted, "From this event we have little reason to expect a reconciliation with the Shawanese for if we had any friends among them, those unfortunate wretches were so."

Assuming that Cornstalk's murder was a de facto declaration of war, Hand went ahead with his plan to capture the British-Indian supply depot on the Cuyahoga River. In February of 1778 he gathered 500 men, mostly newly recruited militia, and started marching north. Hand was ignorant of the true nature of this country then, and it is difficult even to imagine it now, for this was a great temperate jungle of a sort which disappeared everywhere more than a century ago. What is now Ohio, Indiana, and Michigan was covered with hundreds of miles of virtually unbroken virgin forest. The standing and fallen trees were lashed together with ropes of vine and thickets of brush. Slow-moving, steep-banked rivers and streams meandered through the forests, draining millions of acres of bog and swampland. Native animals and people had laid trails through this jungle, but they made bad paths for white soldiers even when they could find them.

Without reaching the Cuyahoga or finding any warriors, Hand and his men thrashed through the Ohio wilderness for several weeks before turning back, famished and frozen. Less than fifty miles from Fort Pitt, they came upon a camp where the Delaware had left a few people too feeble to take part in the winter's hunt. There Hand's militiamen killed a small boy, two women, and one old man, who it turned out was the brother of a Delaware chief still neutral as between the British and Americans. They also captured two other women and took them back to Fort Pitt. Returning from this campaign, which along the frontier came to be known derisively as the Squaw War, Hand resigned as the western commander of American forces and returned to the fighting in the east for which he was better suited.

As Hand was struggling through the Ohio jungle, Shawnee chiefs formally joined the British, accepting a war belt of wampum from Henry Hamilton, the commandant at Detroit. A few weeks later, Black Fish and Black Hoof led out their warriors. Their first objective, for obvious reasons of revenge, was Fort Randolph at Point Pleasant. In May this post was surrounded by Black Fish and 400 of his men. After several weeks, unable to take the fort, they left behind a small detachment to keep the garrison pinned down inside the palisade. Breaking into smaller parties, they raided up the Kanawha River, east into Virginia as far as the Shenandoah Valley. By then the red rising was general in the west. Warriors of the Wyandot, Mingo, Delaware, and Miami and some Kickapoo and Ottawa from the Great Lakes were either raiding with the Shawnee or conducting similar, independent operations. George Morgan, the putative American Indian superintendent, thought that between them these nations could muster about 3,500 warriors, but he was lobbying for reinforcements, and his estimates were probably on the high side.

Among the prisoners taken by Black Fish during 1778 was Daniel Boone, caught early in the year along with twenty-five other settlers who were trying to mine salt at a lick. Because of similarities in skills and attitudes, there was often considerable mutual admiration between Long Hunters such as Boone and the Shawnee.

Black Fish evidently thought Boone was a good man and adopted him and some of the others in that batch of captives. Boone later recalled that he hunted and rambled with the Shawnee and "At Chelicothe, I spent my time as comfortably as I could expect . . . and had a great share in the affection of my new parents, brothers, sisters and friends. I was exceedingly familiar and friendly with them. . . ."

As another ward of Black Fish, one of Boone's new brothers was Tekamthi. The white man and red boy seemingly left no particular impression on each other or at least did not later remark on it. However, Black Fish extended his protection to another of these captives, the boy, Benjamin Kelly, who stayed four years in this extended family. After rejoining the whites, he left a very brief record of the experience, saying only that he had enjoyed it, had run with Tekamthi, and found him a fine companion.

Boone remained with the Shawnee for three months but then, according to his version, learned of a plan to make a surprise attack on Boonesboro. Thereupon, he "escaped," and hurried back to Kentucky to warn the settlers at the fort and help them defend it. They did so successfully, but questions were raised about what Boone had been doing all spring while his frontier companions had been fighting and dying.

As Patrick Henry had predicted, the murder of Cornstalk and the general Indian war that followed drew American forces away from the fighting against the British in the east. In the late spring, though he could ill spare them, Washington ordered two regiments of his Continental line to Fort Pitt. By July of 1778 the Americans had assembled 1,400 troops, about half of them Virginia militia, in the west, but they did not have much immediate impact. The dangers and difficulties of trying to find and fight the Indians in the open were such that the Continental commanders prudently restricted themselves to establishing several new forts and reinforcing those which they still held.

In the fall of the year, there was something of an American counterattack, though a very irregular one, the purposes of which were and have remained unclear. As an early surveyor and land speculator, George Rogers Clark had become a prominent western political figure but remained well connected with the Virginia gentry establishment, of which he was a birthright member. In the summer he traveled east to discuss the frontier situation with, among others, Thomas Jefferson and Patrick Henry. He came away from these meetings with two sets of orders. Those made public called for him to raise 500 militiamen to aid the settlements in Kentucky. Clark also carried secret instructions to invade the

Illinois country, an expedition which seemingly had little to do with protecting Kentucky from Indians or generally forwarding the American war effort. (There was and has remained a suspicion that Henry and Clark were chiefly interested in establishing, for future exploitation, Virginia's land claims in this distant region.)

Clark was a hard, aggressive man, much better acquainted with the western wilderness than the other commanders the Americans had sent into it. In the summer of 1778 with 180 recruits he started down the Ohio in boats, passing through the war zone on the upper river, heading west. Some of his men, finding that he did not intend to help in the defense of Kentucky, turned back but were replaced by backwoodsmen met along the river. In Illinois, Clark occupied Kaskaskia, a trading community established when the territory was still claimed by France and whose residents remained French-Canadians and anti-British.

Late in the fall Henry Hamilton, the British commander at Detroit, came south to Vincennes on the Wabash River, so as to be in position to deal with Clark the next spring. Hamilton (infamous among American frontiersmen as the Hair Buyer, who encouraged Indians to bring in white scalps) came with about 200 white troops, mostly Canadian militia and some 300 Indians of mixed nationalities. After settling in at Vincennes, he assumed there would be no more campaigning that winter and released many of his troops, including all of the warriors, to avoid having to supply them. Learning of this, Clark decided to strike overland against Vincennes, a march which Hamilton thought impossible. Setting out in early February of 1779, Clark and his badly equipped and clothed men struggled through 200 miles of half-frozen swamps. They arrived at Vincennes on February 23, having performed a feat which still stands as a major monument to human endurance. After some brief skirmishing, Hamilton, with fewer than 50 effective soldiers, surrendered Vincennes. Clark then sent messages back to Virginia asking that a new militia force be raised to join him in the spring for an attack on Detroit, the center from which the British were arming the Indians.

In military terms, the forces involved and the results achieved were insignificant. However, Clark's "conquest of the Northwest," as the campaign was publicized and thereafter remembered by Americans, had important psychological repercussions. Encouraged by his success and the increase of American troops along the upper Ohio, settlers became bolder about moving west. In the spring and summer of 1779, 300 flatboats of pioneers started down the river and other whites entered Kentucky through the southern mountains. In the first months of the migration season, they met with relatively little resistance, for the manner in which Clark had dealt with the British gave the Indians pause for thought. Arent De Peyster, who became the new commandant at Detroit, observed: "Mr. Hamilton's defeat has cooled the Indians in General."

In particular, the renewed American activity influenced a debate about national strategy which was going on among the Shawnee. By 1779 many residents of the villages along the Miami rivers thought the time had come to make a major migration to get away from the Long Knives. This was in keeping with tradition, for throughout their known history these nomadic, nonterritorial people had tended, when hard-pressed in one area, to relocate in another. Their stubborn defense of Kentucky in the 1760s and 70s was atypical behavior. In the spring a thousand or more Shawnee made this choice. Following Yellow Hawk, the chief who had prohibited David Jones from evangelizing along the Scioto, they moved to southern Missouri. It being the inalienable right of their citizens to go and do as they pleased, the parting was amicable.

Methoastaske went with Yellow Hawk to Missouri, taking along her youngest daughter. Tekamthi and the other children remained on the Little Miami with Black Fish and his people. Among the restless Shawnee, for whom communal ties were sometimes stronger than family ones, such separations were not uncommon or apparently traumatic. By then Cheesekau was a rising young brave and her other sons were of an age when men of the village, not Methoastaske, were primarily responsible for their upbringing. Her eldest daughter, Tecumapease, had married an established warrior, Wasegoboah, and the couple made room in their cabin for Tekamthi. (Though not specifically mentioned, the other children very likely also took meals and slept there.) As the Shawnee looked at things, if Methoastaske thought it wise to migrate west with members of her clan there was no practical reason for her to feel guilty about doing so or for her children to think that they had been cruelly abandoned and rejected.

In light of the events of the next few months, the Shawnee who moved to Missouri made a timely choice. As they were leaving, Virginia authorities approved George Rogers Clark's plan to advance on Detroit. A frontier militia commander, Col. John Bowman, was directed to recruit the men Clark needed. Bowman gathered about 300 militia but, instead of taking them to Clark, decided to attack the Shawnee along the Little Miami River. This plan struck his men, who were mostly Kentuckians, as being far safer and more sensible than making a long march to Detroit. Also it offered Bowman an opportunity to win glory as an independent partisan commander.

Early in the morning of May 28, Bowman crossed the Ohio, and two days later, under the cover of darkness, his 265 men worked their way, undetected, to within a mile of Chillicothe. The village was then occupied by about 200 people, living in cabins scattered over an open prairie between the Little Miami and the big spring where Tekamthi had been born. The recent departure of the Missouri-bound migrants had greatly reduced Shawnee strength, and, though they could still muster some 500 warriors in the Miami valleys, only about thirty of them were in Chillicothe that morning. This was the reckoning of Gaynwah, the Shawnee who later recorded oral histories of his people. Joe Jackson, a white captive in the village who watched the action from the Shawnee side, made much the same estimate. On the other hand, Bowman in his subsequent report said there were at least 100 warriors. Gaynwah suggested that these extra seventy-five men were the products of "the fear and imagination of Bowman's invaders."

Just before dawn on the thirtieth, a returning Shawnee hunter discovered the lurking Long Knives. Trying to break through their lines to warn the village, he was shot and then scalped. The commotion woke Black Fish. With several warriors who had been sleeping near his cabin, he ran toward the Americans and began firing at them, briefly halting their advance. During the exchange Black Fish received a terrible wound. He was carried back to the village, but ordered the warriors to stand and if necessary die together. Black Fish's sortie allowed some of the Shawnee noncombatants to escape into the woods, but others fell back to the council lodge, a sixty-foot-square building made of hickory logs. Within this strong point, the women and small children screamed and whooped defiantly. Assatakoma, a notable conjurer thought to be nearly 100 years old, chanted prayers to encourage the twenty-five warriors and "about fifteen boys who," according to Joe Jackson, "could shoot."

No direct mention was made of the eleven-year-old but Tekamthi, as a member of Black Fish's family, was almost certainly in the village that morning. Possibly he escaped with the others while Black Fish made his first stand but more likely, being a leading boy, he was with the fifteen who fought with the warriors at the council house.

Bowman's men made an effort to take this building but soon withdrew, later saying that only cannon could have reduced it. Then they spread out to loot cabins of clothing, tools, and silver ornaments or to round up Shawnee horses on the prairie. While so engaged, they came across a black woman, a former slave living with the Shawnee, who told them that Simon Girty was rapidly approaching with 100 warriors. This figure was increased to 500 by the time Bowman heard the story. Having already had nine men killed (the Shawnee lost three in the defense of Chillicothe) and wanting to keep their booty, the Long Knives began a hasty and somewhat panicky retreat. The men and boys who had defended the council house came out and took the offensive, harassing the invaders for twenty miles or so, picking off a few more of them. Two days later Bowman with his surviving men and a herd of 163 captured horses got back across the Ohio. In Kentucky the militiamen sold their loot at a public auction, which netted each survivor $500 in Continental currency. Then they went home, showing no further interest in marching on Detroit. Clark, for lack of men, was forced to give up this campaign.

On the Shawnee side, a week or so after the battle, Black Fish died of his wounds, but beyond that the raid did virtually nothing to impair their ability to continue the fight against the Long Knives. After Bowman's retreat the residents of Chillicothe rebuilt their cabins and were able, the season being early, to replant whatever crops had been trampled. They were soon able to replace the horses, for that summer Shawnee raiders—with Black Hoof and Blue Jacket emerging as the principal chiefs—struck at white settlements throughout the Ohio Valley. Americans were forced to abandon Fort Randolph, where Cornstalk had fought and died, as well as two other posts, Laurens and MacIntosh, closer to Fort Pitt. Later the warriors effectively closed the Ohio River to American traffic. In October, near the present Cincinnati, Matthew Elliott, the Girty brothers, some 130 Shawnee, Mingo, and Wyandot came across a flotilla of military flatboats. They were loaded with ammunition which had been purchased in New Orleans and was being shipped upstream for the hard-pressed troops around Fort Pitt. The raiders sent out several men in canoes as bait, and the American captain, David Rodgers, took it. Pursuing the canoes in hopes of picking up a few easy scalps, he brought his cumbersome barges close to the shore, where they were boarded by the warriors waiting in ambush. Of the sixty Americans, only fifteen escaped. Rodgers and forty others were killed, while five survivors were taken back to the Shawnee villages as prisoners.

After the ambush of Rodgers and his munitions boats, the American Congress, having barely enough resources to maintain armies in the east, in effect withdrew from the war in the west. In March of 1780, George Washington advised Daniel Brodhead, then the Continental commander in the Ohio country, that he was on his own and must find men and provisions from among the white settlers. Joseph Reed, the president of the Pennsylvania Council, lamented, "The Frontiers exclaim with Anguish, & we are now reduced to the painful Necessity of listening to Distress we cannot relieve & Claims we cannot satisfy."

For the remainder of the Revolution the American hope was that the frontiersmen, by their own devices, could hold back the Indians and British long enough for Washington and his Continentals to win a victory in the east. Eventually this strategy of necessity worked, but it turned out to be a very close thing. During the next three years the tide of the frontier war ran strongly against the Long Knives, who were reduced to defending isolated, armed camps. Within these enclaves, living conditions were terrible, and doubts grew about how long they could or should hang on—at least as Americans. Brodhead, at Fort Pitt, sent back a gloomy report: "I learn more and more about the disaffection of many of the inhabitants on this side of the mountain. The King of Britain's health is often drunk in companies; & I believe those wish to see the Regular Troops moved from this department, & a favorable opportunity to submit to the British government."

Like Brodhead, other American leaders railed about the lack of genuine patriotism or any but the most base material motives among the frontier people. However, in the end it was the land hunger of the backwoods settlers and their doubts about whether the British would respect their property claims that saved the west.

In the spring the British organized an ambitious western expedition. Under a veteran officer, Henry Bird (with McKee, Elliott, and the Girtys acting as liaisons to the Indians), about 200 men were sent south to the Shawnee villages along the Miami rivers. There they rendezvoused with 700 warriors from various nations of the west. April was no doubt an exciting time for the boys of Tekamthi's set, for, in addition to the gathering of foreign soldiers, the British brought with them six pieces of light artillery, the first such weapons deployed in the region.

In May, Bird loaded the guns on rafts, descended the Miami, crossed the Ohio at what is now Cincinnati, and started up the Licking River into Kentucky. During the first week of June, they invested two fortified white settlements, Ruddell's and Martin's. Both stations surrendered after only brief resistance. Except for about twenty who were killed, all of the 350 residents were taken prisoner. A few, including the two Ruddell boys, Stephen and Abraham (whose father, Issac, had developed the station), were taken home by the Shawnee. More were brought back to Detroit by Bird. Some were ransomed and repatriated but others took up land in Ontario and settled there voluntarily as British subjects. Issac Ruddell was a special case. In Kentucky he had the reputation of being a hard, grasping real-estate shark. At Detroit it was rumored he was an informer for the British and received 900 guineas for spying on his fellow captives. The pay seems high for such insignificant work, but the story was commonly believed in Kentucky. When Issac Ruddell returned there after the war, a man by the name of McCune, who had been a fellow prisoner, "went out and got a hoop-pole, of which he had a parcel, and wore it out on Riddle [Ruddell]," so said a contemporary. Ruddell survived both the beating and gossip that he was a traitor. He stayed in Kentucky and it was reported that he "got an island and 16 milk cows, . . . made a great deal of money there."

Originally the British and Indians intended to take their cannon through Kentucky, doing to other fortified stations what they had done to Ruddell's and Martin's. This plan was aborted because of the disparate military customs of the allies. After the first spectacular success, the warriors broke up into smaller parties and fanned out, looking for prisoners, horses, cattle, and other loot. Bird, as was often the case with both British and American officers in the west, became concerned about his supply line and started back toward Detroit.

The most combative and competent American leader in Kentucky was George Rogers Clark. As the British Indian force dispersed, he determined that at least a defiant gesture was in order, but found that other frontiersmen were much less belligerent. On his own authority, Clark put armed guards on the trails leading out of the region, to turn back settlers fleeing to the east. Also he closed the land offices, thus putting a temporary halt to real-estate dealing, which interested Kentuckians much more than chasing Indians. Then, essentially by force of character, Clark raised 1,000 militiamen. It being too late and risky to pursue the British-Indian raiders, Clark, in August, did what Bowman had done the summer before—attacked the Shawnee villages in the Miami Valley.

In this instance the Shawnee had plenty of warning, and before Clark reached Chillicothe, they evacuated and burned it, retreating to Piqua, another of their communities, ten miles to the north. Clark pressed ahead and began skirmishing in front of Piqua. Later it was accepted as fact along the border that Tekamthi was there when his home village, for the second time in a year, was stormed. Again there are understandably no eyewitness accounts of what the boy did. Probably it was very little, for the action was light. Having no interest in defending easily replaceable property, the villagers slipped away into the forest, with the warriors fighting a rear-guard action. Clark's men burned the cabins and took whatever loot they could find. One of the few casualties of this campaign was Clark's nephew, Joseph. The young man had been previously captured by the Shawnee and was living with them in Piqua when it was attacked by his uncle's troops. When the fighting started, Joseph Clark ran out of the village, but before he could identify himself, he was shot and killed by the Kentuckians.

Clark's raid, like Bowman's, had virtually no effect on Shawnee resistance. The warriors remained on the offensive and, the next spring, extended their raiding area. The principal difference between the campaign of 1781 and those of previous years was that the British did not contribute soldiers or cannon, things having turned bad for them in the east. In the fall, word began to trickle west that the great Red Coat war chief had been beaten by the Americans and the King's men turned on their backs like turtles. Matthew Elliott and other British agents told the Indians that stories about the defeat of Cornwallis by Washington were ridiculous fictions. Whether or not these denials were believed, the British surrender at Yorktown had no immediate consequences in the west. In fact, things got much worse for the Long Knives, who came to speak of 1782 as the Year of Blood. It began with a happening terribly in keeping with that name.

John Heckewelder and the other gentle Moravian missionaries had been evangelizing in Ohio for more than a decade. They had their greatest success with the Delaware, the most pacific of the western nations. At Gnadenhutten (on the Tuscarawas River, near the present-day New Philadelphia) the Moravians established a commune of some 200 Christianized Delaware, whom they taught to farm and raise cattle in white fashion. This peaceful, neutral community was treated atrociously by both warring sides. In 1781, the British decided that the missionaries and their Indians might be supplying food and information to the Americans. Therefore Matthew Elliott and a mixed Wyandot-Shawnee party was sent to Gnadenhutten. They stripped the communards of their possessions and herded them back to a grim concentration camp on the Sandusky River. The white missionaries were eventually taken to Detroit for interrogation, but in the winter of 1782 the Christian Delaware, very nearly starved, were allowed to go back to Gnadenhutten to try to plant a spring crop. To the south, Americans in the Wheeling area heard of their return and were angered by it on the grounds that these people had, during their captivity, probably been turned into hostiles. To do something about this threat, a frontier bravo, David Williamson, organized a company of militia which much more resembled a lynch mob than a military unit.

Arriving on March 8 at Gnadenhutten, Williamson's "rangers" drove the unarmed Delaware (twenty men and about seventy women and children) into their council house. There Williamson ordered their execution, explaining, "For when they were killed the country would belong to whites, and the sooner this was done the better." The Delaware congregation knelt down and began to sing psalms. In this position they were dispatched with hand weapons and tools. A principal butcher was Charles Builderback, said to be a very fat as well as black-hearted man. A barrel maker by trade, he had brought along a cooper's mallet on the expedition. With it he brained, literally, thirteen of the Delaware. Then he stopped and turned the hammer over to another of the militiamen, saying, "My arm fails me. Go on in the same way. I think I have done pretty well."

In terms of numbers, greater massacres were committed, by both sides, during the red-white wars: 360 white settlers were killed by the Iroquois on a single day in the Wyoming Valley of Pennsylvania; 500 more died when Fort Mims in Alabama was overrun by the Creek; 200 Cheyenne were slaughtered by white militia at Sand Creek, Colorado. In these and other instances many of the victims were unarmed noncombatants. There was nothing to choose between the behavior of their killers, whether red or white. However, as an exercise of unprovoked, cold-blooded sadism, Gnadenhutten was the worst of the atrocities. Years later, as he called for them to unite and defend themselves against the whites, Tekamthi told his people that the absolutely fundamental reason for doing so was that "They do not think the red man sufficiently good to live." After Gnadenhutten there were few reds who doubted that this was the stark truth. When word of this massacre spread, the western nations were united in their desire to take revenge. Very shortly opportunities to do so occurred.

In the spring, William Crawford, Washington's surveyor and real-estate associate, raised a ragtag militia force with which he hoped to make a preemptive strike against the Indians in central Ohio before they began their summer raids. His second in command was David Williamson, the Gnadenhutton butcher. Crawford left the Steubenville area in May with 500 men. They reached the Sandusky during the first week of June, and there they were surrounded by a large force of Delaware, Wyandot, and Shawnee. At this point, Williamson and his Wheeling thugs prudently turned tail and ran. Before they fled, they stripped the bark from a tree and on it scrawled a message: "No quarter to Indians, man, woman, or child."

The warriors struck on the fourth of June. Crawford and his

remaining men fought for a day, but then commenced a retreat which turned into an every-man-for-himself rout, during which more than a hundred men were killed or captured. (On the other side, the total casualties were four warriors and one British agent.) Among the prisoners was Crawford, who after being recognized as the white leader was turned over to the Delaware. They shaved him and blackened his face with charcoal. While this was being done, a Delaware chief, Wingemund, approached. Having been previously acquainted with him, Crawford asked if he remembered that they had been friends. Wingemund (who shortly afterwards spoke to John Heckewelder, giving his version of what happened) said he did remember, and they would still be friends if "you were in your proper place and not here."

Crawford asked for an explanation. Wingemund said that Crawford had got himself into a fix where no former friends could help him. Because of the "cruel murders of the Moravian Indians who would not fight and whose only business was praying," his own people, the Wyandot and Shawnee, were crying aloud, "Revenge, revenge."

Crawford said the anger was justified, that he himself thought the Gnadenhutten murders were despicable, but he had had no part in them. Wingemund agreed this was true and that he personally thought Crawford a good man. However, Crawford had made no effort to punish the "execrable man, Williamson," and in fact had gone to war with him against the Indians. Williamson was the man they wanted, said Wingemund, but unfortunately he and his fellow cowards "ran off in the night at the whistling of our warrior's balls, being satisfied that now he had no Moravians to deal with, but men who could fight and [with] such he did not want to have anything to do." Regretfully, concluded Wingemund, Crawford must now pay for Williamson's crime because he had not "attended to the Indian principle, that as good and evil cannot dwell together in the same heart, so a good man ought not to go into evil company."

Crawford was stripped and beaten with clubs. Then warriors, removing the lead from their charges, fired seventy rounds of black powder into his naked body. His ears were cut off and he was tethered in the fire ring which was lighted. Relatives of the Gnadenhutten dead prodded him with burning sticks, while others shoveled hot coals on his face and stomach. At first Crawford begged to be killed quickly but was answered derisively. Finally he sank into a coma and seemed to feel little pain during the last three hours of his life.

A Dr. Knight, the expedition's surgeon, was captured with Crawford and forced to watch his torture. When it was finished, he was slapped in the face with Crawford's scalp and told that much the same would be done to him, but he would be sent south to the Shawnee villages so that the nation could revenge Gnadenhutten according to its own customs. While he was being taken to the Miami, Knight escaped his guards and eventually reached Fort Pitt alive. There he told of Crawford's awful end, and his story was soon generally known to Americans. Though the two cruelties were quite different, quantitatively and qualitatively, the ordeal of Crawford affected whites somewhat as the Gnadenhutten killings had the reds. Crawford had not been some border thug like Williamson, but rather a cultured Virginia gentleman, a member of the American establishment and friend of George Washington. There was a subliminal sense that his status and character should have made some difference to his captors. Because it had not, the opinion held by frontier Long Knives—that the only good Indian was a dead Indian—became common among Americans of all classes.

Williamson escaped, and Crawford died for his sins, but later there was a serendipitous happening, which suggested that there were inhuman forces of justice and retribution. By 1789, Charles Builderback, who had stood literally in Delaware blood and brains while bashing in the heads of the praying Indians at Gnadenhutten, had become a well-to-do settler and militia captain. One day he was rounding up cattle along the Ohio. There he and his wife were captured by a party of Shawnee, who recognized him as the fat murderer of the Delaware. Putting aside his wife—who was not physically injured—they very slowly emasculated and otherwise dismembered the "big Captain." They kept him alive for a long time and then, taking turns, smashed his skull with hatchets. During the Indian wars few men of either race died more horribly than Builderback. At least from the red standpoint, no man more deserved such an end.

The Year of Blood, 1782, continued as it had commenced. After disposing of Crawford's force, the warriors fanned out, overrunning small forts and farms, taking scalps and prisoners from western Pennsylvania to southern Virginia. Along the frontier during the summer, it was common to hear bellowing cows who had either been abandoned or whose owners did not dare come outside the stockades to milk them. In August, Black Hoof, Blue Jacket, Simon Girty, and a British captain named Caldwell along with several hundred Shawnee, Potawatomi, and Wyandot struck at Bryan's Fort (Lexington) in Kentucky. The siege was brief and unsuccessful but served as something of a feint. The attackers lurked nearby until the whites gathered 180 men from other stations in the region; the warriors then began a leisurely retreat, drawing the Long Knives after them like a fox playing with hounds. At Blue Licks on the far side of the Licking River, the raiders found a suitably narrow and heavily wooded ravine. Leaving a good trail into it, they took positions on the slopes above and waited. When the whites came up, they halted on the stream to study the terrain. Daniel Boone was among them. He said the place smelled like a trap and advised that they scout ahead very carefully.

Boone's opinion was disputed by Hugh McGary, thought to be an exceedingly "rash and Insubordinate" man driven by "an unreasoning hatred of the Indians." Even by border standards, McGary was a rough piece of work. A neighbor said of him:

> McGary was a creature without consideration. Was by nature a savage. He married a Yocum. She had a bastard child as well as he. He went to drive her bastard off; she said drive off both; and they did.

McGary stood up and said that Boone was growing old and had always been soft on Indians, that the red devils were clearly on the run, that any white man who failed to follow him in pursuit was a coward. McGary then spurred his horse into the Licking River, and the rest of the company, fearing to turn down his dare, followed him. During the next few hours seventy of them were killed and a few more taken prisoner in the bloody ravine. Isaac Boone died there, but Daniel, his father, and Hugh McGary were among those who escaped the ambush. (On the other side, ten warriors and one member of the British Indian service were killed.)

After he became celebrated, the story surfaced that Tekamthi saw his first offensive action at Blue Licks. By then he was fourteen, the same age that his brother Cheesekau had been when he fought with their father at Point Pleasant. Sometimes there was an addendum to this report: that Tekamthi fled, terrified, from his first battle. If he ran, the failure of nerve was obviously thought to be excusable, since no Shawnee who was regarded as a coward was followed and respected as Tekamthi later was. In fact the point of this story was laudatory not derogatory—that Tekamthi had normal human weaknesses but because of his strength of character overcame them to become the bravest of the brave.

If Tekamthi did not first go to war against the Long Knives in the ravine at Blue Licks, then he probably did so in a smaller engagement which occurred the next year. In the 1780s, capturing flatboats of the white pioneers was a regular military chore and substantial source of income for the Shawnee. According to

Stephen Ruddell, Tekamthi, when he was fifteen, took part in one of these ambushes on the Ohio River. It was successful, and several prisoners were taken. One of them was singled out to be tortured and killed on the spot by the war party. After this was done, Tekamthi stepped forward, said Ruddell, "and expressed in strong terms his abhorrence of this act and it was finally concluded by the party that they would never burn any more prisoners."

It is difficult to imagine a fifteen-year-old berating warriors about their behavior and persuading them to make a no-torture pledge. What seems more plausible is that Tekamthi privately told Ruddell how he felt later—or perhaps did so at the torture camp, since there is an interesting question about where the Big Fish (as Ruddell was known among the Indians) was while this was happening.

In telling the story, Ruddell was not at all specific about times and places, which is understandable, since Big Fish lived with the Shawnee for nearly fifteen years, until they were beaten and dispersed following the battle of Fallen Timbers. Then, with a Shawnee wife, he rejoined white society, became a farmer and ordained Baptist missionary. Thereafter he talked freely about his experiences as a naturalized Shawnee, in fact became locally famous because of them. But, with one exception—to be taken up in due course—Ruddell was vague about what he was doing while his "inseparable" companion Tekamthi and other red friends were fighting Long Knives. Most whites who came back to the settlements after having lived red were similarly reticent, with good reason. Being held "captive" was common and more or less acceptable, but turning into a renegade warrior was not. Those who did and were later found out often were punished vigilante fashion, roughly and sometimes terminally.

In regard to Ruddell and the flatboat, there was a particularly delicate matter. In these operations the Shawnee frequently put an adopted white on an open river bank or sand bar. He or she would hail a passing boat party, shouting that they were escaped prisoners, fleeing the savages. If a decoy lured a boat into shore, the hidden warriors pounced on it. Women and boys worked especially well for this purpose. Ruddell would have presumably been very leery about admitting that he had been present at one of these ambushes.

Ruddell's story was retold by whites as the years passed and cited as evidence that Tekamthi was a uniquely compassionate and humane savage. In fact his objection to orgiastic torture was by no means singular. Tekamthi's adopted father, Black Fish, saved Boone, among others, from the ordeal. Logan, the Mingo, did the same for Simon Kenton, another notable Long Hunter who came as a captive to Chillicothe. Black Hoof, toward the end of his long life, said that only twice had prisoners been tortured in his presence— the implication being that he did not tolerate such behavior. Another Shawnee war chief, Biaseka (the Wolf) had the same principles. Returning after several months' absence, he found a rabble of villagers burning a captive for sport. Biaseka "passed through the crowd without speaking to anyone, and approaching the prisoner, placed the pistol to his head, and blew out his brains—coolly remarking, that he disapproved of the torture of a defenceless person."

There were many similar cases. Tortures such as those inflicted on Crawford and Builderback were sometimes judged to serve a serious public purpose. But for an honorable man the casual tormenting of a prisoner was despicable entertainment. Tekamthi was from one of the great warrior families, steeped in stories about Shawnee champions, somewhat as upper-class English boys were in tales about King Arthur, Richard the Lionhearted, and Robin Hood. On that day along the Ohio (if Ruddell's account was indeed based on an actual happening) such a fifteen-year-old may have found the base conduct of the torturers more abhorrent than the agonies of their prisoner. This at least was his attitude when he was older.

Toward the end of the Year of Blood, the doughty George Rogers Clark organized another token offensive. In November, gathering together some militia, he invaded the Shawnee villages along the Miami rivers—with the usual, inconsequential results. After Clark retired, the Shawnee again reoccupied their communities and began making plans to retaliate. However, when they approached the British to get munitions and supplies for the next campaigning seasons, they met with a shocking response. After much ceremonial palaver, Arent De Peyster, the Detroit commandant, told them that regrettably he could not aid them as he had in the past. Furthermore, he said that he had been asked by his own chief (the ranking British military commander, Gen. Frederick Haldimand) to tell them that at least temporarily they should not "push the War into the Enemies Country." Haldimand had received his own instructions from London and passed them along to De Peyster, saying, "Nothing is more natural than this desire [of the Shawnee to continue on the offensive]. Yet under the express orders I have received it is impossible I can comply with their Request."

The Shawnee left empty-handed and baffled. Neither De Peyster nor Haldimand thought it politic to explain that British, American, and French diplomats were then negotiating a peace treaty in Paris. For reasons of general global policy, the British did not want these talks disrupted by a pack of savages running about with their hatchets in the Ohio Valley.

VI. A Fair Land but Dark and Bloody

The Treaty of Paris, signed in September 1783, formally ended the American Revolution for the white belligerents. As part of the settlement, the British transferred their claims in the Ohio Valley and lower Great Lakes to the United States. They did so with their fingers crossed. Recognizing that the Americans were too exhausted and impoverished by the Revolution to do anything about it, British garrisons and administrators, contrary to the treaty, did not leave Detroit and other lesser forts west of the mountains. From these posts they continued to monopolize the fur trade and to treat independently with the Indians.

Though they were not specifically mentioned in the peace negotiations, how to handle the natives of the region was a major post-Revolutionary concern for both Britain and the United States. The American position was straightforward: having defeated the British, they had also—in principle if not in the field—defeated their red allies. Henceforth, the Indians south of Canada and east of the Mississippi were conquered subjects of the United States, who no longer rightfully owned the lands they occupied.

The British interest in the Indians was more complex. Immediately, they needed them for the fur trade. Also they envisioned that in the future the reds would make political and military instruments for overturning the Treaty of Paris as it applied to the west. This was a project which British strategists began to consider even while the peace negotiations were underway and continued to entertain for the next thirty years. The short-term imperial policy during the 1780s was to keep the Indians generally hostile to the Americans and maintain them as fur gatherers and partisans-in-waiting. The Indian service was willing to give warriors sufficient supplies that they could continue to harass frontier settlers with small raids, but they did not want a major confrontation, which would be injurious to larger British policy interests and bad for the fur business.

After the Revolution British agents circulated among the western nations, explaining the new situation to them somewhat as follows: The English had of course not given away the lands of their red friends to the Americans; they had only withdrawn—perhaps very temporarily—their own claims in the area. During the next few years it might be necessary to make some concessions to the Americans, but if these greedy, treacherous people became too aggressive, English soldiers would come to help the reds defend their lands, or at least some of them. For the moment the natives should be patient, put their trust in the goodness of the English King, and continue to bring their pelts to the fur posts. Such experienced operatives as McKee, Elliott, and De Peyster naturally put it less plainly, but their underlying ambition was to control the western Indians like a pack of formidable dogs, keeping them reasonably fit and mean. Perhaps these savage creatures would never be unleashed, but the threat that they might would have a good, intimidating effect on the Americans. For some years it did.

When they began to hear of it, bit by bit, the western natives formed a very different opinion from that of either the British or Americans about the Treaty of Paris. The general feeling was that, like the war the whites had fought in the east, the peace agreement should and did not have much to do with reds. The soldiers of the English King may have been defeated on distant battlefields, but the warriors in the west had not been. To the contrary, they had generally been victorious against the Long Knives and remained free and sovereign people. As to questions about territorial sovereignty, a Shawnee chief, Kekewepellethe, answered, "God gave us this Country. We do not understand measuring out the land. It is all ours."

Virtually all the Indian leaders believed as Kekewepellethe did, but there was also a growing awareness that their power to defend themselves independently against the Americans had been reduced by events of the previous two decades. Prior to 1768, the Ohio Valley nations made war regularly but on a part-time basis. Their traditional campaigns were brief and seasonal, allowing the men to spend most of their time hunting, trapping, educating their sons, supporting and protecting the women farmers. After the white invasions commenced, the warriors were in the main successful because individually they were much more adept at forest warfare than their white opponents. However, to cope with the persistent, ever more numerous Long Knives, they became full-time soldiers. They were able to do so because their communities altered their traditional way of life and endured considerable hardships to keep them in the field. Also, the British government had subsidized their war effort; as Arent De Peyster had observed, "They cannot hunt to furnish themselves while they take part in the war."

The British employed entire nations in the Ohio Valley somewhat as they did Hessian soldiers in the east. They were given arms and munitions and, as the fighting grew heavier, grain, cattle, clothing, tools, and utensils. Because of their heroic traditions and loathing of the Long Knives, the warriors made willing, effective, and cheap mercenaries. In consequence a generation of natives became significantly dependent on white goods and accustomed to getting them as compensation for fighting Americans. (Looting grew to be another fairly important source of income and military supplies.)

At the end of the Revolution, when for a few years it served British interests to curtail their aid, the dilemma of the western reds became obvious and grim. If they returned to their traditional employments, hunting, subsistence agriculture, and trading furs for British goods and weapons, they could not go on fighting Americans as they had. But if they did not continue—in fact increase—this resistance effort, the Americans would soon overrun their lands.

By 1785 there were 45,000 settlers in Kentucky and several thousand more located north of the Ohio. As the number of whites had increased the population and wealth of the Indians had declined because of epidemic diseases, warfare, and the ruination of their hunting territories. Nevertheless, the Ohio Valley natives were by no means helpless or subdued at the end of the Revolution. Their great assets were the military prowess of the warriors and the fear they inspired. Furthermore they still had considerable leverage for obtaining aid from the British, who could not entirely abandon them without abandoning their fur trade and hopes for using Indians to frustrate the western ambitions of the United States.

In the summer of 1783, as peace negotiations proceeded in Paris, American authorities were also working on a national Indian policy. No debate was necessary about the final objective, which was to clear the red people from lands which the United States wanted. There were, however, differences of opinion about means—how to, as George Washington wrote the Congress, "induce them [the savages] to relinquish *our* territories and remove to the illimitable regions of the West."

The frontier whites, hungry for both land and racial revenge, generally favored a simple, direct solution to the problem. No longer occupied by the British, the United States should turn on the western Indians and exterminate them, making further discussions about land titles unnecessary. As did many other eastern officials, Washington had a low regard for rabid, Indian-hating backwoodsmen like Williamson, Builderback, and McGary. "Banditti," he sometimes called them and warned that their rash, violent inclinations might draw the new nation into dangerous and undesirable adventures. Beyond the loss of life which it would involve, Washington noted that the United States could not then afford a full-scale Indian war. He proposed a much safer and inexpensive plan to the Congress. Efforts should be made to establish many new settlers along the frontier. Revolutionary war veterans should be especially encouraged, with grants of free or very cheap land. The presence of these ex-soldiers might overawe the savages, and if worse came to worse, they would make superior militia. The pioneers would clear the wilderness and reduce game, making the country less useful and attractive for the Indians who, Washington reasoned, would then become "as eager to sell [their lands] as we are to buy."

The role of the United States government was to be that of a broker; that is, its agents would initially negotiate with various Indian nations to purchase, "for trifling amounts," their lands which would then be sold or given to private citizens for development. Washington had some specific tactical suggestions about how to bargain with the savages. The government agents should first point out that as former allies of the British (nothing was said about those who had not been) they were a conquered people without civil rights. However, the United States was prepared to be generous. If Indians did so obligingly, they would be paid something to leave the lands they presently occupied and would be given new ones farther to the west. Furthermore, Washington advised, the government commissioners might pledge that the United States "will endeavor to restrain our People from Hunting or Settling" in the new territories allotted to the Indians. Washington made it clear that whatever the reds might think, these guarantees would be only temporary. As sections of the country filled up, the bolder settlers would naturally want to pioneer into new territories. To accommodate them, negotiations would be reopened with the natives and, the boundaries between white and red lands pushed farther west.

Washington cautioned that, in dealing with the Indians, American representatives, while obviously paying no more than was absolutely necessary, should behave politely, be patient, and not try, too quickly, to "grasp at too much. . . . That," Washington summarized, "is the cheapest as well as the least distressing way of dealing with them."

Washington's plan was accepted by the Congress as proposed and immediately put into operation. The first natives to be dealt with, in 1784, were Iroquois, whose circumstances made their case a simple one to settle. Toward the end of the Revolution, in the only truly successful Indian campaign conducted by the Americans, the Six Nations were defeated, their homelands invaded and occupied. Some of the Iroquois retreated across the St. Lawrence and were given sanctuary by the British, but those left within the United States were surrounded by white settlements, and without political or military power. Therefore the American commissioners had no need to be patient or generous. The remaining Iroquois were allotted some small, scattered parcels of land in central New York and northern Pennsylvania but surrendered their territorial claims elsewhere. Individually, as free-lance warriors and politicians, some Iroquois continued to play a role in red-white affairs, but collectively, as a nation and pseudoempire, they were thus eliminated.

In the following year American negotiators turned their attention toward the Wyandot and Delaware, who were also vulnerable because their homelands were directly adjacent to large white settlements in Pennsylvania and New York. At Fort McIntosh, near Pittsburgh, some of the chiefs of these two nations, having received certain threats and compensation, agreed to give up their claims to eastern and southern Ohio and remove with their people west of the Cuyahoga River to land which they were assured would be exclusively theirs.

The Shawnee, regarded as the most hostile of the western Indians, did not, as requested, appear at Fort McIntosh. Therefore Richard Butler, the principal American commissioner, along with George Rogers Clark and others proceeded to Fort Finney, a post newly built at the confluence of the Ohio and Greater Miami rivers. From there, word was sent to the Shawnee asking them to come in and negotiate. (The messenger was Wingemund, the Delaware chief to whom William Crawford had spoken just before he was tortured and executed.) For several months there was no response from the Shawnee, but in January of 1786, 300 of them appeared at Fort Finney. The band was led by Kekewepellethe, who proclaimed, "All the land is ours." He had few warriors with him, but many women and children who were cold and hungry because the corn harvest and hunting had been very bad that year.

To "honor" these bedraggled people, Butler ordered the garrison to fire a military salute over and around them as they entered Fort Finney. Then he began the talks with Kekewepellethe and his counselors, saying, "We plainly tell you that this country belongs to the United States—their blood hath defended it, and will forever protect it. Their proposals are liberal and just . . . and you should be thankful for the forgiveness and offers of kindness of the United States."

What Butler proposed was that Kekewepellethe, on behalf of his entire nation, agree to give up all territorial claims in the Miami Valley. The Shawnee would then move to northwestern Ohio and take up lands near the reservations which had been set aside for the Delaware and Wyandot. In return, there would be peace, and as immediate compensation, the Americans would give Kekewepellethe and his people some corn, blankets, and miscellaneous presents. At first Kekewepellethe resisted, responding, "You say you have goods for our women and children; you may keep your goods, and give them to the other nations, we will have none of them." Then he laid a black wampum belt, signifying hostility, on the conference table. Immediately the American commissioners rose in anger and left the room. Before he did, George Rogers Clark, using his cane, knocked the wampum belt on the floor and ground it to bits under his boot.

Kekewepellethe and his people were left alone for a few hours to consider their circumstances. When the bargaining resumed, Butler said that his first offer still stood, that Kekewepellethe could either take it or leave it. Rejecting the terms would mean war, which Butler hinted broadly might begin almost immediately, saying, "The destruction of your women and children or their future happiness, depends on your present choice." So intimidated, Kekewepellethe surrendered, agreeing to all of Butler's demands. Thereupon the atmosphere improved. Food and other gifts were distributed and, according to Butler's report, "liquor was given to the Indians and they got drunk. The business was conducted with great care and gave the Indians perfect satisfaction."

When other Shawnee heard of the business done at Fort Finney, they were contemptuous and enraged. They made it clear to the Americans that Kekewepellethe (called Tame Hawk by English speakers) was a weak man who spoke only for himself, that they, the free, unsubdued Shawnee would pay no attention to the so-called Treaty of Fort Finney. They did not, and in fact took up their hatchets and once again began attacking Long Knives along the Ohio and far to the south of it. Mary Moore, so cruelly tortured in the Shawnee villages, was taken prisoner in July of 1786 by Black Wolf and a party of warriors raiding in southwestern Virginia, less than 200 miles from Richmond.

As Washington had pointed out, the United States was ill prepared to fight a general Indian war and did not then have the manpower or resources to back up the bluffs made by Richard Butler at Fort Finney. After the interlude in 1784–86, when all parties pondered the significance of the Treaty of Paris, this inability of the United States government to act forcefully in the Ohio Valley became obvious to all the other parties. Encouraged by the weakness of the Americans, the red nations grew increasingly belligerent. The British began to aid them once again, though not quite so openly as they had during the Revolution. The land-hungry Scotch-Irish continued to pioneer across the Appalachians, to take up land without reference to national policies and hold it by tomahawk rights. This migration, much more than specific military actions, was the crucial frontier happening during the post-Revolutionary period.

Little by little, without formal agreement, even the Shawnee, the most intransigent of the western nations, came to recognize that they had lost their former hunting grounds south of the Ohio. They continued to fight in Kentucky as a means of bringing the war home to the Long Knives, but no longer had any real hope of regaining the territory. With this strategic difference, the civil war in the west continued much as it had during the previous two decades.

In the fall of 1786, George Rogers Clark raised the largest militia army, 2,000 men, ever assembled in Kentucky. With more than half this force, Clark headed toward the Wabash Valley, having heard that large numbers of Shawnee, Miami, Ottawa, and other warriors were gathering there with British agents to form a great anti-American alliance. Within a few days 300 of the volunteers deserted. The remainder continued on, growing hungrier and more nervous about Indians as they marched north. After about three weeks, during which they saw no action, they also turned homeward, arriving back in Kentucky it was said "in vile disorder." (His troops laid most of the blame for this botched campaign directly on Clark, who they claimed was often drunk and confused.)

While Clark was thrashing about in Illinois, Col. Benjamin Logan led the remainder of the militia army, 800 men, up the Miami River to do what had been done three times before—attack the Shawnee villages. Again these communities were largely undefended since Black Hoof, Blue Jacket, and most of the warriors were elsewhere raiding or hunting. The first village Logan and his men came to was Mackachack, whose residents were of the band who had turned themselves in to the Americans at Fort Finney earlier in the year. One of them, an aged man, Moluntha, had served as a counselor to Kekewepellethe and left his mark on the treaty made there. A few weeks earlier, an American agent had reported to Richard Butler, the peace commissioner, that the people of Mackachack "had done all in their power to keep the Shawnee from going to war."

On the October morning when Logan's raiders stormed into the hamlet, Moluntha, though old and feeble, stepped out confidently to welcome them. He carried a peace pipe, wore a cocked hat, and stood under an American flag which flew from the ridgepole of his cabin. The latter two items had been given to him at Fort Finney, where he had been assured that ever afterward he and his people would be "included among the friends of the United States."

Unfortunately Hugh McGary, the frontier bully who had led the militia into the bloody ambush at Blue Licks four years before, was with Logan's advance party, which surrounded Moluntha. As Moluntha was making peace signs, McGary pushed forward and asked if he had been at Blue Licks. Moluntha had little English and was confused by age and the circumstances. He understood only that the American was asking a question. Wanting to be obliging he nodded his head vigorously saying, "Yes, yes." McGary bellowed, "Godamn you, I'll give you Blue Lick play." Then he grabbed the hatchet from his belt, brained Moluntha, and lifted the old man's scalp. A Col. James Trotter tried to stop him in this bloody work, but McGary outfaced this officer saying, reported witnesses, "By God, he would chop him down or any other man who should attempt to hinder him from killing Indians at any time." (Several months later McGary was brought to trial in a Kentucky court. He was found guilty of murdering Moluntha and of behaving in a "disorderly manner." He was sentenced to being suspended from his rank of militia captain for a period of one year. Thereafter he was promoted to major.)

After Moluntha was killed, Mackachack and several other Shawnee villages located nearby were sacked and burned. The only significant resistance was put up by a single warrior. He had been making a night hunt and was unaware of what was happening until, carrying a deer across his shoulders, he came to the outskirts of his village. There he was spotted by half a dozen mounted Kentuckians, who started to pursue him. The warrior dropped down in

the tall prairie grass and from this cover, shot and killed first a Capt.
William Irvine and then another of the Long Knives. While he was
reloading his musket, the remaining troopers rode him down and
took his scalp. Later another American died, and three more were
wounded while twenty-five Indians were being killed. In addition
to those who were scalped, the militiamen took twenty-six women
and two children as prisoners. Also they captured two warriors. The
first was stripped, smeared with gunpowder, and burned. The
second, a young Delaware who had come to the village to marry a
Shawnee girl, was slowly strangled before being scalped. After two
days, growing increasingly concerned about the whereabouts of the
Shawnee warriors, the Long Knives retired to Kentucky, bringing
back considerable negotiable loot.

Though not much of a military engagement or triumph, Logan's
raid had more than ordinarily significant consequences. Most
importantly it served to destroy the small Shawnee peace party.
Those members of it who were not killed, as Moluntha was, were
convinced that further attempts at negotiation were insane, that the
only good Americans were dead ones.

The great pan-Indian council of which Clark had heard rumors
was held shortly after the sack of the Miami villages—but near
Detroit rather than in Illinois. At it the Shawnee along with the
Miami were the hard-liners, urging the other nations to join them in
the defense of the Ohio River line and "to exterminate all the
Americans who might be in those lands." Immediately the Shawnee began acting on this policy. Two months after Logan's raid, a
frontier militia officer reported that "There are now more Shawnee
on the south side of the Ohio River than have been discovered at
one time for two years past."

Logan's raid unified the Shawnee but also created hardships for
them. Coming just at harvest time, Logan's troopers destroyed
15,000 bushels of corn, leaving the residents on short rations that
winter. The Shawnee reoccupied the villages, but in the spring,
after the maple-syrup season, decided that because of its proximity
to the Kentuckians, the Miami area was no longer a good military
base or a secure place for the women to farm and raise children.
Most of them (1,000 to 1,500 people) left this region and migrated to
the upper Maumee River valley—in the vicinity of what is now
Fort Wayne, Indiana. There at the invitation of their hosts, they
settled adjacent to Kekionga, a sizable cluster of Miami villages.

The Miami—a confederation of Algonquin people closely associated by tradition, blood, and language—had moved into the area

during the preceding century from the western Great Lakes. During the Revolution they fought against the Long Knives but played a secondary role in the Ohio River campaigns. Only after the collapse of the Wyandot and Delaware brought the enemy uncomfortably close to their homelands, did the Miami assume a leading role in forming the anti-American coalition. With a population of 2,500 to 3,000, they were the most numerous of the remaining front-line nations. Also, they were well connected with peoples to the north and west of them, the Ottawa, Chippewa, Kickapoo, and Potawatomi, and used their influence to draw them into the alliance.

Kekionga, the principal Miami settlement, was strategically located at the point where the St. Joseph's and St. Mary's rivers joined to form the Maumee, which gave easy access to Lake Erie and Lake Huron. A network of other streams within short portage distance provided water routes to the Wabash, Miami, and Ohio rivers, to Lake Michigan, the Illinois and Wisconsin country. In consequence this junction had long been an important trading center, the French establishing the first European posts there early in the eighteenth century. By the 1780s Kekionga, called by the Miami "the glorious gate," was the most cosmopolitan community in the region. In addition to the Miami and Shawnee, there were permanent enclaves of unsubdued Delaware and Wyandot, a few Ottawa and Cherokee, a steady flow of visitors from nations to the west and north. The villages, interspersed with large—200-to-300-acre—cornfields, gardens, and orchards, extended for nearly twenty miles.

Along with some white Americans living as naturalized reds in Kekionga, there were 150 or so Canadians, both French and English speaking, who had come as traders or artisans and settled with their racially mixed families. Members of this British, more or less, colony led comfortable and socially active lives, according to Henry Hay, a young commercial traveler who visited there in the winter season of 1789. In his journal Hay mentions attending skating parties, a wedding reception, dances ("with the Gentlemen and Ladies all dressed in their best bibs & Tuckers"), serenading and then kissing "young ladies and women of the village." ("Miss Rivarr is a very pretty girl, but rather awkward.") He thought the food was excellent and varied. Game—bear, deer, raccoon, porcupine, and turkey—could be purchased daily from Indian hunters and wild salad greens from the women. Cheese, pickles, tender veal, and Madeira wines were brought up the Maumee from Detroit and Canadian farms in Ontario. A Mrs. Adamhers, who shared Hay's interest in flute playing, served him excellent and therapeutic coffee one day when he was suffering from a terrible hangover, contracted while sitting up all night playing cards and getting "infernally drunk." The same lady told Hay that since it was difficult for a young traveling man to get his laundry done in Kekionga, she would have her Negro maid wash his linens. (At the time, blacks, taken as prisoners from their owners in Kentucky, were not uncommon in the region. Those kept by the Indians were ordinarily naturalized as whites were. However, the British often continued to use them as slaves. While campaigning with the warriors in the south, Matthew Elliott collected fifty or more blacks with whom he worked his large farm in southern Ontario.)

George Ironside was an enigmatic, erudite man who had been educated at Kings College in Aberdeen, Scotland, and then drifted to Kekionga. He prospered there as an intelligence agent, trader, and apparently as an informal banker, for Hay was able to cash a check with him. Hay also met Blue Jacket and Little Turtle, respectively the leading war chiefs of the Shawnee and Miami. He thought them both impressive and congenial men. Some of their warriors showed him an interesting curio, "the Heart of a white prisoner—it was quite dry, like a piece of dried venison, with a small stick run from one end of it to the other and fastened behind the fellow's bundle that killed him, with also his scalp."

During the spring and summer of 1787 the Shawnee moved into the upper Maumee Valley and began building cabins, clearing fields, and putting in crops. (They settled on the north side of the river in bottomlands downstream from Kekionga proper.) Cheesekau and Tekamthi traveled with their family and neighbors and helped with this work but did not stay long after the new villages were established. Later in the year the two brothers, with four companions, left on a long wandering trip. Tekamthi was to be gone from the Ohio country for more than three years. Cheesekau never returned to it.

Such extensive travels, grander versions of the long hunts of white frontiersmen, were traditional for young Shawnee, the final rites of passage into and proofs of manhood. Cutting themselves loose from family and community ties, they roamed, seeking exciting places, people, and experiences. Often they met with hardship and danger, but these things were intrinsic to questing and reasons for it. Now it is difficult to imagine how free six young Shawnee such as these were and probably felt. More than half a continent was open to them. They were a school of human fish, able to live and cavort however they fancied in the great forest seas.

The condition of their people, the lands and forests were shortly to change so drastically that these Shawnee braves were among the last to adventure in this way of their fathers and grandfathers. For Tekamthi, the three-year ramble was the only period of his adult life which he devoted largely to pursuing the pure joys of existence. After it was over and he returned to Ohio, his freedom of action was increasingly restricted by obligations to his followers and by the maneuvers of his opponents.

When the party left, Tekamthi was about twenty years old, at least in physique a man such as was subsequently described by literate whites. There were wild claims that he was a giant in stature, but men who stood next to him and had no interest in myth-making said he was about 5 feet 10 inches, rather tall for a Shawnee, who tended to be slight people. Ruddell, Shane, and other acquaintances agreed that he was of greater than ordinary strength and endurance, very quick and well coordinated in his movements. Shane said that, among all the frontier reds and whites he knew, Tekamthi was the best bird shot both with a gun and bow. He also could wield a war club skillfully and told Shane that because this had been the favorite weapon of ancient Shawnee heroes, it was his.

Tekamthi was light-complexioned, more of an olive-tan than red shade, whites thought. The face was roundish and symmetrical. The nose and mouth were both straight and prominent. Several mentioned that he had an exceptionally fine set of large, white, regular teeth. In easy circumstances, he had a pleasant, warm smile. Some thought the eyes were the most striking facial feature. They were hazel in color, deep-set, and a bit hooded by his brows, giving him a habitual—from what whites saw—intense, brooding expression.

Cheesekau, Tekamthi, and their four mates left the Maumee in the fall on horseback. Members of such parties customarily traveled light, taking only the clothes they wore—long, belted hunting shirts, breech clouts, leggings and moccasins—a bundle of worked leather for repairs and an all-purpose blanket-poncho. They carried a small bag of parched corn and jerked meat for emergency rations. Each man had his own medicine pouch containing both remedies and magical talismans. Several hatchets and knives were tucked under belts. On long expeditions, bows and bolas (with which Shawnee hunters were adept) were still favored over guns, which were heavier, not so easy to maintain in the field, and in many circumstances less effective. Firearms could be traded for or stolen all along the frontier when they were needed for serious work.

The group headed first toward the prairies of western Illinois to take buffaloes, which at that time of year were making their fall migration to the south. The Shawnee hunted and gorged for several weeks, and then Tekamthi, in the midst of a herd, was knocked from his horse and trampled. Ruddell said one of his legs—Shane said both—was broken. The other hunters carried Tekamthi across the Mississippi to the Missouri villages where the Shawnee who had migrated from the Miami River valley were still living. It seems likely that he was taken in and nursed by relatives, his sister or perhaps mother, but that is not directly mentioned. (After leaving Ohio, Methoastaske disappears from records and tales.) By the spring, Tekamthi had somewhat healed but was still gimpy. Cheesekau suggested that he remain in Missouri, but the younger man insisted he was able to go on, and he did, the travelers moving southeast into the Cherokee country.

Since 1776 when Cornstalk had gone south seeking their aid, the Cherokee—or at least the unsubdued Chickamauga division of them—had maintained a close and cooperative relationship with the Shawnee. By the late 1780s, warriors of those two nations were virtually the only reds still fighting against the Long Knives in Kentucky and northern Tennessee. Among other things, their persistent guerrilla activities had made a prophet of Dragging Canoe, still the leading Chickamauga war chief. Ten years previously, after more pacific Cherokee leaders had ceded some of their traditional hunting grounds to the whites, Dragging Canoe had warned Daniel Boone, "You have bought a fair land, but you will find its settlement dark and bloody."

In 1788 the fighting was heaviest, almost continuous, in the middle basin of the Cumberland River. After settling in among the Chickamauga, the six Shawnee volunteered to join one of their war parties in an attack on a fortified station. While the raid was being organized, Cheesekau had a vision, so Stephen Ruddell was told. Cheesekau foresaw the day and time when the attack would be made. The fighting would be bloody, but the warriors would take the fort if they persevered. He himself would be shot in the head and die at midday. The others urged Cheesekau to stay behind after receiving such a terrible warning. He refused on the grounds that, if this was a true vision, then trying to escape his ordained fate would be cowardly.

A double log cabin guarded the entrance to the station. Unable to surprise the settlers, the Cherokee and Shawnee attempted to force their way into this building. One of them, having pried out enough chinking, was able to insert his gun between the logs and kill a defender with a blind shot. While the whites were so distracted, Cheesekau, staying low, came beneath a window and split the planks which barred it with his hatchet. As he was hoisting himself over the sill, one of the whites inside shot him directly in the face. Mortally wounded, Cheesekau was carried out of firing range. Despite his agony, he told Tekamthi that he was honored to die in battle as their father had. He said he did not want to be buried like an old squaw and instructed that his body be left in the open so that the "birds of the air could pick his bones." He died at noontime.

The little that is known of him suggests that Cheesekau had a full measure of the unusual quality—charismatic and mystic—which was so prominent in this family. While he lived he was his younger brother's chief mentor and role model, and it is reasonable to think that thereafter the memory of Cheesekau continued to influence Tekamthi.

In the heroic tradition, Tekamthi's reaction to Cheesekau's death was to seek to avenge it before mourning him. The events of the morning demonstrated beyond doubt that his brother's vision had been a true one. Tekamthi reminded the members of the war party that it had also been prophesied that they would take the fort if they endured. However, the Cherokee found the happenings too spooky and refused to continue the ill-omened engagement. Without them, there was no hope of overcoming these particular whites, so Tekamthi led the remaining Shawnee to a smaller, less secure, nearby settlement (probably one established by a family named Montgomery) on Drake Creek. They killed and scalped three men and made prisoners of several of their women and children. There were various accounts of this raid, which offered different casualty totals, but all agreed that Tekamthi went to Drake Creek to satisfy his honor in the mortal world, and that of Cheesekau, wherever he was.

For two years after Cheesekau's death, Tekamthi roamed the south with both the Cherokee and the Creek, raiding the Long Knives from Kentucky to Alabama and Florida. There are only wispy accounts of these actions, but the gist of them is that he took scalps and prisoners and came to be accepted as a young brave who had obviously listened attentively to the discourses of the aged. There were stories that he was preternaturally a night person, able to see and interpret small sounds in the dark as few other men could, that he was one who seemed always to sleep with one eye and ear open. It was said that on at least three occasions, Long Knives attempted surprise attacks against him at night, but in each instance, Tekamthi sensed their presence. Another time along the Tennessee River, he and his party were surrounded by thirty white rangers, but before the trap could be sprung, it was broken. Taking advantage of the terrain, Tekamthi led his men on a fierce charge through the would-be ambushers, killing two of them and escaping without loss.

According to what is remembered of them, the warriors of the woodland nations customarily regarded sex as they did hunger, fatigue, and fear—that is, something to be heroically controlled and sublimated. Hunting, war, and trade often separated them from women, and when they were home there were traditions and taboos which restricted sexual relations. Prior to certain religious ceremonies, important athletic contests, or military actions, there were periods of days or even weeks in which respectable, serious-minded men did not touch women, carnally or otherwise. Even when they were free to act without restraint, men of the Ohio Valley nations generally treated women coldly and were an exceptionally unromantic, even prudish lot.

An instructive story was told by James Smith, who lived when a young man as a naturalized Wyandot, whose sexual customs were similar to those of the Shawnee. One summer, somewhere in Ohio, Smith along with a young red friend, Chinnohete, attended a large international social frolic which attracted, among others, members of the Ojibway nation. While picking cranberries, the two boys— they were both about eighteen—came into a glade occupied by three Ojibway girls, who immediately began giggling at the youths and advancing toward them. Chinnohete grabbed Smith and told him they must run from the place very quickly, which they did. After they caught their breath, Smith asked Chinnohete why he seemed to be so frightened. "He replied," recalled Smith, " 'did you not see those squaws?' I told him I did, and they appeared to be in a very good humor. He said the Jibewa were very bad women and had a very ugly custom among them . . . that when two or three of them could catch a young lad that was betwixt a man and a boy out by himself, if they could overpower him, they would strip him by force, in order to see whether he was coming on to be a man or not. He said that was what they intended when they crawled up." Chinnohete said that they were very fortunate to have escaped such a fate and, a bit uncertainly, Smith agreed.

Among the Shawnee whose communities were often overstocked with widows and other unattached females—because of the violent pursuits of the males—polygamy was permissible but seldom practiced. Men married late, often it seems reluctantly and more to get sons than for pleasure. Their mothers and other old women not

only arranged the formal unions but directly supervised the con-
summation of them. The nature and reasons for these traditions was
described in intimate detail to a white recorder.

> When a man is twenty-five years old, at the time he is custom-
> arily married off, he doesn't know a thing about the way to have
> intercourse with his wife. At the time they must marry, there-
> fore, young men are given personal instruction in the way each
> one should try to act when having intercourse with his wife. It
> seems that once a woman helped her son learn the way he
> should try to act. "You must pull over your clothes like this," she
> said to her daughter-in-law, "and you must lie still," she told
> her. She helped her son get an erection. When he had an
> erection, he got on top. "Crawl off," she told him. Properly she
> directed his penis to the woman's vaginal orifice. "Now, if you
> get it to go in, say "all right" to me, and I'll turn the two of you
> loose."

Tekamthi seems to have been thoroughly acquainted with the
facts of life well before he was twenty-five. (Perhaps it was because
he had no mother to guide him.) Anthony Shane described an
incident which sounds convincing because the circumstances and
subject are so universal—a group of young bucks gathered around a
campfire after a day in the woods, talking about girls. Tekamthi told
the others "that he would only marry a handsome woman, because
handsome women wanted to be with him and he did not want to
disappoint them." ("Marry" was no doubt a euphemism supplied
by the transcriber of Shane's oral history.)

Stephen Ruddell delicately said that "the women were very fond
of Tekamthi." Then he added primly that his hero, though he
treated them in polite, courtly fashion, generally spurned their
advances and "never evinced any great regard for the female sex."

When Ruddell came to write his memoir, he was a Baptist
minister and intent on showing that his boyhood companion had
always been pure and perfect, a kind of red Galahad. Shane, a much
earthier man, probably knew more about this side of Tekamthi than
Ruddell did—or than Ruddell thought it proper to admit to knowing. In any event, Shane's recollections are different and livelier.
He said that after Tekamthi had distinguished himself in the south
as a promising young warrior, he had several "overtures of marriage" from Creek women but turned them down because he did
not want to be "burdened" with a wife. However, during this same
period there was a beautiful Cherokee girl who shared Tekamthi's
cabin when he was in her part of the world. The liaison was known
to others and in time led to the rumor that the Cherokee bore
Tekamthi a daughter, sometime before he was twenty-one. Perhaps

she did, but if this was the case, the daughter never appeared or was recognized later in Tekamthi's life. The stories about her circulated after he was famous, when many were claiming to be better acquainted with him than they probably were.

To have taken a woman hunting with him, to war or on political missions would have, according to the ancient taboos, amounted to going out of one's way to court misfortune. There is no mention that Tekamthi did so. But Shane went on to say with a touch of envy that throughout his life Tekamthi, wherever he settled, usually had a young, attractive woman with him "in the capacity of a wife." He seems to have found them easily and frequently changed these companions. (Ruddell said tersely that Tekamthi "had at different times a wife whom he did not keep long before he parted provoked.")

Shane thought that one of the best-looking of Tekamthi's paramours was a Shawnee girl who lived with him for several years around 1800. One day, planning to entertain an important friend at dinner, Tekamthi went out hunting in the morning and returned with a large turkey, which he gave to the girl to dress and cook. When the bird was served, he found that it had been improperly boned. Nothing was said at the time, but when the guest left, Tekamthi told the girl that her slovenly behavior showed a lack of respect and had disgraced him. Therefore she must immediately gather her belongings and leave, permanently. Shane says that after pleading to be permitted to stay, the girl regretfully did as ordered.

As is the case with so many areas of Tekamthi's life, the facts in regard to this private part of it are too flimsy to support heavy conclusions. Yet there is an impression that he had both the appetites and the aphrodisiac qualities which commonly, in many cultures, are associated with exceptionally confident, competent, and powerful men.

Like Tekamthi and the companions who had come out with him in 1787, there were other young Shawnee warriors adventuring in the south, collecting experiences and scalps. Cherokee braves were doing the same above the Ohio, living for long periods and fighting against Long Knives with the Shawnee and Miami. Furthermore, British agents continued to circulate among the nations, attempting to control and coordinate their activities. In consequence there was a regular exchange of information between the northern and southern centers of red resistance. In late October of 1790 a courier from the north arrived in middle Tennessee bringing very good news. Several weeks before, Little Turtle and Blue Jacket, the war chiefs of the Miami and Shawnee, with their own and allied warriors, had ambushed an American force led by Gen. Josiah Harmar. At a great battle on the outskirts of Kekionga, Little Turtle's and Blue Jacket's men had overwhelmed Harmar's and completely routed the United States Army. The prospects for winning more victories were excellent, but the Shawnee and Miami needed every available warrior.

Tekamthi and his band must have left almost immediately upon learning of these events. They traveled north through western Virginia, taking, it was said, a few white scalps as they passed through the mountains. Shortly before winter set in, they were back in the Shawnee villages along the Maumee in Ohio.

VII. Made to Smart

George Washington and other officials of the early United States envisioned an orderly westward migration of Americans, which would end the civil war in the trans-Appalachian country. Dotted with communities of responsible Revolutionary War veterans, the frontier would advance at a rate that promoted the overall national interest as determined by the President and Congress. The Indians, dependent on the wilderness, and the British, needing Indian hunters and warriors, would be displaced without undue expense or distress.

All of which was reasonable as a long-term projection. However, as policy planners are apt to be, those of the Washington administration were overly optimistic about others accepting their assessments of reality. By 1790 it had become clear that neither the Indians nor British had any intention of surrendering to the Americans and voluntarily leaving the Ohio and Great Lakes country. As for the pioneers, they came as expected, but in torrents which poured across the mountains more like a flash flood than a stream from a spigot controlled by political engineers. A United States Army officer stationed on the Ohio with the responsibility—but small means—for regulating the traffic, noted with astonishment, "From the 10th of October 1786 until the 12th of May 1787, 177 boats, 2689 souls, 1333 horses, 766 cattle and 102 wagons have passed Muskingum, bound for Limestone and the Rapids [central Kentucky]." The rate of immigration was sustained and in the 1785–90 period, some 20,000 new souls came into the Ohio Valley.

Most of these pioneers were, one way or another, dissidents who had left the east because they were not satisfied with the economic or social arrangements that prevailed there. They were white and generically Americans, but their ties to the United States were tenuous. In fact, for the next thirty years there were occasional plots and a great deal of talk about the western settlers establishing their own nations or joining the British in the north or Spanish in the southwest. Contrary to the first expectations of Washington and the other leaders, the frontier people did not solve the Western Question but, rather, became like the British and Indians a major problem for the United States. Henry Knox, the first Secretary of War, grimly advised the Congress that the "whole western territory is liable to be wrested out of the hands of the Union by lawless [white] adventurers or by the savages."

The first difficulty was that the numbers and racial belligerency of the pioneers doomed plans for getting rid of the Indians peacefully. After the more vulnerable reds were disposed of in 1785–86, the Shawnee, Miami, and other wild nations showed little inclination to negotiate. Rather, in response to the hordes of new pioneers, they became truculent, killing 1,500–2,000 Americans during the 1780s, after the Revolution. The response of the settlers—along with retaliating as best they could—was to put increasing pressure on the United States to start a general Indian war of the sort Washington thought would be so disastrous.

After becoming Secretary of War, Henry Knox did some calculations which confirmed Washington's opinion. Knox estimated that it would require 2,500 men and $200,000 to fight the Ohio Valley natives but only $15,000 to pay for a "conciliatory" system of small subsidies and bribes. The Secretary of War recommended that manipulating and intimidating the Indians was not only the cheapest but the best way to get their land since it avoided the "blood and injustice [of a race war] which would stain the character of the nation."

Other federal officials reckoned as Washington and Knox did. Requests for massive military assistance were turned down, and the westerners were told that they should stay out of Indian country for the time being. This response naturally angered frontier whites. Had their distress been the only issue, the President and his men—who had little sympathy for this class—might have borne it for some time. But the settlers created another problem which the Washington administration felt had to be dealt with immediately and forcefully.

In its first years the United States was close to bankruptcy. Minor tariffs and excise taxes provided the only source of income, and the government was burdened with large Revolutionary War debts, including back pay and bonuses owed to veterans. Selling or giving away—to satisfy the claims of the ex-soldier—the virgin western lands was the only way of quickly raising substantial new revenues. In this regard the Indians presented obvious difficulties, but the behavior of frontier whites was almost as vexing to federal officials. From their standpoint the thousands of unruly pioneers who took choice properties simply by squatting on them were stealing government property in such quantities as to threaten the solvency and therefore existence of the nation.

In 1787, to correct this situation and satisfy a formidable lobby of land speculators, the Congress passed the Northwest Ordinance. The act federalized most of the country west of the mountains, north of the Ohio, and east of the Mississippi, what is now Ohio, Indiana, Michigan, Illinois, Wisconsin, and upper Minnesota. All previous colonial and state claims in this region were quashed. Until such time as parts of it became populous enough to be organized into states, the sprawling Northwest territory would be administered by a federal governor. He and three federal judges were to establish and maintain law, and oversee the surveying and sale of public lands. Arthur St. Clair, one of Washington's former officers and president of the Congress, was named as the first governor. St. Clair made no bones about why he took the job. He had a large family and would be well positioned to get rich in the real-estate business when not occupied by his public duties.

The most immediate beneficiaries of the Northwest Ordinance were land speculators. Two months after the legislation was passed, the Ohio Land Company (in which a combine of New England financiers, Gen. Rufus Putnam, a Revolutionary War hero, and Arthur St. Clair were interested) arranged to buy 1.5 million acres along the Muskingum River, north of Marietta. To sweeten the deal the Congress threw in, for free, 300,000 additional acres, which were to be given to settlers already in the area and to deserving war veterans. As it turned out, these bonus acres were not distributed as designated but were appropriated and disposed of by officials of the land company. The price for the tract was set at $1.00 per acre but the Ohio Company asked for and got discounts. Eventually it paid the federal government only nine cents an acre. Other real-estate operators were granted similar tracts of public lands, in some cases under even more liberal terms.

The Northwest Ordinance tidied up the western land situation in a bureaucratic way. However, it did not deal with the crucial problem of the United States, which was that in regard to white settlers, the Indians, and the British, it had no way of enforcing its policies or claims in the region. Washington continued to believe that major confrontations should be avoided but recognized that no one would pay much attention to a nation which did not have some sort of a military presence. Obtaining one, immediately after the Revolution, was tricky business, since a standing army was repugnant in principle to many of the republican-minded states and their citizens. The best Congress could do was to approve a 700-man army, made up of state militiamen more or less lent to the central government. The commander of this makeshift force, the 1st American Regiment, was Josiah Harmar, an undistinguished Revolutionary War brigadier general. He got his new position principally because he was a resident of Pennsylvania, which had contributed the largest number of men, 260, to the contingent. In 1785 Harmar took the regiment to the Ohio. Too few and badly equipped to do much about the Indians, the troops occupied themselves for the next several years trying to keep white squatters off unsold public lands on the north side of the river. They had indifferent success with this work but did intensify the secessionist sentiments of civilians in the region.

After he was inaugurated in 1789 as the first President of the new constitutional republic, Washington turned his attention toward beefing up the military so that it would at least appear to be a force in readiness on the frontier. In 1790 Congress established a genuinely federal army of 1,216 men and officers. Most of the men who were recruited during the first summer were sent directly to the west. Washington also notified St. Clair and Harmar (who became the first commander of the U.S. Army) that because of the raids of a few Indian "bandits" they were authorized to raise 1,500 additional militiamen from Kentucky and Pennsylvania for temporary frontier duty. The President made it clear to his two western representatives that they were not to engage in a major war and should use the army only for police actions and to intimidate the natives.

Unfortunately St. Clair and Harmar were bellicose by temperament and had felt humiliated because they had not been able to deal forcefully with the savages. Therefore, they followed the letter but not the spirit of Washington's instructions. Perfunctory peace overtures—a series of take-it-or-leave-it ultimatums—were made and, predictably, rejected by the Indians. Simultaneously, the two federal leaders began to raise the militia army that Washington had authorized. Their plan was to take it to Kekionga on the Maumee and there confront the Miami, Shawnee, and other bandits they might find. How they then intended to impress them was made clear by St. Clair, who advised Harmar that he had noted a spirit of "savage ferocity about the militiamen," which it would be "unnecessary and perhaps improper" to restrain. At Kekionga, the savages "should be made to smart."

Though fully agreeing with these sentiments in principle, General Harmar was less sanguine than the governor about the temper and abilities of newly recruited civilians, remarking, "No one can have a more contemptible opinion of the militia in general than I do."

When they began to arrive at the staging area, the newly built Fort Washington (Cincinnati) on the Ohio, the militia did nothing to change Harmar's mind. The first to come in were the Kentuckians—800 of them rather than a promised 1,000. One of Harmar's regular officers reported that they appeared to be "unused to guns or the woods." As to the fighting spirit which had impressed St. Clair, "Their whole object seemed nothing more than to see the country without rendering any service whatever."

When the Pennsylvanians—300 rather than 500 as expected— turned up, they were even worse. The second in command of this outfit, Maj. James Paul, confessed that most of his troops were substitutes, hired to serve as replacements for richer men; that because of poverty many of them had never owned a gun, did not know how to fix a flint in the hammer, or even oil a musket.

It is a tenet of American folklore that all men of that time were much like Daniel Boone was supposed to be: dead shots, crafty woodsmen, each one worth half a dozen or so Indians, perhaps twice that number of French or English men. They might be too free spirited to please elitist professional soldiers, but if turned loose, they made superb, irregular fighting men. In the two hundred years since, this fiction has evolved and spawned many associated myths. The most pervasive one is that the nature of Americans is such that at a moment's notice they can take up a long rifle or its equivalent—providing subversive bureaucrats have not denied them the right to bear arms—and like their pioneer forebears rather easily whip anybody in the world.

The facts are contrary. The condition and later performance of the men who assembled at Fort Washington in 1790, as the first army organized by the constitutional republic, was not unusual. This and similar expeditions had very little success against the Indians. Subsequent American military triumphs have been fewer and less spectacular than is popularly credited. Invariably they have been achieved, after civilian recruits were partially transformed into professional soldiers, at the expense of opponents much inferior in numbers and resources. Most particularly, Americans from the time of these first frontier campaigns have shown little aptitude for free-form, guerrilla-type wars and have regularly been humbled by improbable people who do.

During September of 1790, using his regulars as instructors, Harmar tried to teach the Kentucky and Pennsylvania civilians the rudiments of soldiering. At the same time he was quarreling with profiteering suppliers and responding to a deluge of advice from St. Clair, President Washington, and the War Department. Among many other things, Harmar was told that his army should make "quick movements . . . to astonish the savages," but proceed cautiously so as to avoid a surprise attack, should deal very firmly with the Indians but not antagonize any of them who might be thinking about making peace in the near future. As he was contemplating these instructions, Harmar received a personal note from Henry Knox, who wrote that it had come to his attention that "You are too apt to indulge yourself to excess with a convivial glass." (This was quite true.) Knox warned that Harmar must control himself and that if there was any trouble in this regard, his military career and reputation "would be blasted forever."

All in all, it was not a happy command—1,133 militia and 320 regulars—which left Fort Washington on September 30 1790. However, during the first two weeks as it marched up the Miami and then into the Maumee drainage system, the army had no difficulties other than those presented by inadequate rations, interminable forests, and constant bickering between militia and regulars. Advanced units arrived at Kekionga on October 15 and were pleased but surprised to find the villages deserted. While the men began to burn and loot, Harmar and his officers decided that the savages had fled in panic. This was not the case.

Unobserved by the Americans, scouts sent out by Little Turtle and Blue Jacket had followed Harmar's army closely. Furthermore, the two war chiefs had accurate information about the plan of campaign before it began. This intelligence was from a very reliable source, Henry Knox, the Secretary of War. As Harmar was making his preparations, Knox had become nervous about what the British would think of the American strike. He therefore directed St. Clair to inform Maj. Patrick Murray, the commandant at Detroit, that Harmar had been sent out with "the sole design of humbling and chastising some of the savage tribes." It was hoped that this would not alarm or offend the British. St. Clair relayed the message and asked that it be kept secret. Murray promptly informed his Indian agents, the Miami and Shawnee, of the planned invasion. So forewarned, Little Turtle and Blue Jacket sent messengers to their western allies asking for help. The first of these reinforcements, some 200 Ottawa warriors, arrived at Kekionga shortly before Harmar did. Then the villages were evacuated while the war chiefs deployed their men.

On the morning of October 19, hoping to catch a few stragglers, Harmar sent out thirty regulars and 150 mounted militia under the command of a Kentucky politician, John Hardin. Hardin paused in a swampy meadow to get his bearings. As he was doing so, Little Turtle charged out of the surrounding thickets with his Miami warriors. Immediately the mounted militia cut and ran, colliding, literally, with an infantry company which had been sent out to support them. One of the terrified horsemen screamed, "For God's sakes retreat. You will all be killed. There are Indians enough to eat you up." The infantry did not need a second invitation to join the flight. Singly and in disorganized groups, the men continued to straggle into Harmar's main camp until after nightfall.

Back in the wet meadow the thirty regulars, supported by only nine militia men, dug in and attempted to hold the ground. These were the first soldiers of the United States army to see serious action. They gave a good account of themselves, killing a dozen or so warriors before they were overwhelmed. Only eight of these thirty-nine survived—by pretending to be dead and wriggling away into the thickets. When they returned to the camp, they were ready to fight again—against the "dastardly" militia who had abandoned them and their dead comrades.

The next day Harmar began to withdraw but on the morning of the twenty-first he ordered a detachment back toward Kekionga to act as a rear guard. His first intention was to use the remaining regulars for this work, but he found he could spare only sixty of them, the rest being needed to calm the militia and keep them together on the road. Finally Harmar selected 400 of what seemed the best of the civilian-soldiers and under Hardin, who was anxious to redeem himself, sent them off with the regulars.

To make a bloody story short, this detachment was also ambushed, Blue Jacket and his Shawnee closing the trap. Again the militia fled while the regulars stood and for the most part died. In the two days of fighting, seventy-five soldiers and 108 militia were killed. Not many were wounded because of the nimbleness of the civilians, but an unspecified number were rounded up in the woods and taken prisoner by the warriors. Chiefly because of the work of the regulars, the Indian losses were relatively high, about 100 of the braves falling in the action.

After the second ambush, the inclination of the remaining militia was to run, every man for himself, back toward the Ohio River. Harmar, using his surviving regulars with loaded muskets and mounted bayonets, bullied them into staying together in some semblance of military order. At about the same time, the allied Indians held a council. As a first order of business they interrogated three American prisoners. After learning as much as these men knew about Harmar's situation, they killed them. Blue Jacket, elated by his success, pointed out that the Americans were in such confusion that a series of vigorous attacks might wipe out most of them. (The same thought occurred to Ebenezer Denny, Harmar's adjutant, who feared if the Indians came again, "the sick and wounded, and all the stores, artillery, etc. would have fallen, a prey to the savages.")

Other chiefs were more cautious than Blue Jacket, arguing that the warriors had not eaten in three days. They were also concerned about their hungry families still hiding as refugees from Kekionga. Some Fox and Sauk who had arrived from the west too late to take part in the battles supported the Shawnee, advising that for a few days they could get along by eating Americans, who were in good supply.

Then there was a curious happening, one which constituted the only bit of luck Harmar had and probably saved the lives of many in his army. The night was a clear, bright one. As the talks continued, a dark shadow suddenly appeared on and, for a time, obscured the face of the full moon. This greatly alarmed the Ottawa. An Ottawa shaman said that the darkening of the moon was an evil omen for his people and, if they fought further in this place, they would lose many warriors. Blue Jacket railed at them for being overly superstitious, but the Ottawa were not convinced. The next day they left for home, reducing the Indian force by half. With only a hundred or so of his own warriors left, Blue Jacket was "obliged," as he told a British agent a few days later, "to suffer the Americans to retreat without further molestation."

"A hored savage war Stairs us in the face," Rufus Putnam, the former general and Ohio land developer, predicted after Harmar's defeat. The Indians were much elated with their success and threatened "there should not remain a Smoak [made by whites] on the Ohio by the time the leaves put out."

This was the mood of his people when Tekamthi returned to the Maumee in the late fall of 1790. However, satisfying as the rout of the Americans had been, it had also caused considerable hardship, since Harmar's men, before they were beaten, had destroyed 20,000 bushels of corn standing in the field along the Maumee. Food supplies were further reduced because red traditions obligated the people of Kekionga to feed, even feast, the allied warriors whom Little Turtle and Blue Jacket had called in from the west. Also, most of the cabins in Kekionga had been burned or demolished. After the Americans had been driven off, the people came out of the woods and repaired their homes sufficiently to get through the winter. In the spring when the weather improved, many of them (including virtually all the Shawnee and the Canadian traders) moved forty miles down the Maumee to its confluence with the Auglaize River and built new villages there, which were more convenient to the Lake Erie supply routes.

British Indian agents supplied some food, clothing, and ammunition to the Kekionga people. This enabled the warriors to fan out to hunt, as they usually did during the winter, but also, as was not customary in this season, to strike white settlements, which were in great disarray because of Harmar's defeat. So far as the raiding went, the warriors were to keep it up throughout the year.

Whites said that, commencing in 1791, no warrior gave them more trouble than did the young Tekamthi; but this was a deductive opinion arrived at after his name became well known. Only bits of anecdote describe what he did and where he was during the following year, but very probably he went with Blue Jacket, with whom he was increasingly associated, on one of the first raids of 1791.

In early January, Blue Jacket and 200 warriors came south from the Maumee. On the Ohio they first killed one surveyor and captured another, Abner Hunt. With him they moved on to surround Dunlap's Station, a fortified community near Cincinnati, which was occupied by about seventy-five settlers and a thirteen-man garrison of regulars, commanded by Lt. Jacob Kingsbury. Blue Jacket's men began firing at the blockhouse, and Kingsbury was told that, unless he surrendered, they would take the place and kill all the whites. Kingsbury refused, deciding that surrender would not improve their chances of survival. Thereupon, Abner Hunt was brought out, stripped, and tied down on the frozen ground in view of the fort. A fire was kindled and coals from it were inserted into knife slits made in Hunt's body. Throughout the night as he screamed in agony, the warriors taunted the defenders. However, Kingsbury and the others held out for a week, until they were relieved by a company of ninety-six regulars from Fort Washington, where news of the attack had been received from a passing white hunter who had heard the firing from Dunlap's Station.

At about the same time a smaller war party had easier hunting at Big Boulder, one of the Ohio Land Company's smaller outpost communities on the Muskingum River. Surprising the settlers, of whom there were twenty-one, before they could hole up in their blockhouse, the raiders killed fourteen and made prisoners of four others. Only three escaped. The next week Rufus Putnam wrote his old comrade-in-arms, George Washington, reporting the attacks and advising that "unless the government speedily sends a body of troops for our protection we are a ruined people."

Another land speculator, John Cleveland Symmes, formerly a New Jersey congressman and supreme court judge, was involved in developing and selling portions of a million-acre tract around Cincinnati. Symmes was also worried about being ruined, at least financially, by the Indians. Writing to an associate, he reported that business was bad:

> I should have had several new stations advanced further into the purchase by next spring but now I shall be very happy if we are able to maintain the three advanced stations. The settlers at them are very much alarmed. . . . Moreover, I expect that the panic running through this country will reach Jersey and deter many prospective settlers.

Along with attacking the outposts, the warriors routinely bushwhacked river boats which brought in new pioneers and supplied the ones already in the country. In the years following, whites were also to say that Tekamthi had been the most active of all these pirates. Whether or not this was the case, he did take part in some of these actions, according to Ruddell and Shane, and probably in many of them, since hijacking flatboats was something of a Shawnee specialty.

The river raiders were out early in the spring of 1791. Immediately after the ice broke and the traffic began to move, they took two boats, killing twenty-four whites. Then they made what the warriors probably considered the best catch of the season, ambushing a boat and making prisoners of the twelve whites aboard. Among the captives they found Michael Greathouse, who, with his brother Daniel, had been a leader of the drunken party which had killed the family of Logan, the Mingo chief. These murders had led directly to the great battle at Point Pleasant, where Puckeshinwa and so many others had died. The boat was taken by a mixed band of Shawnee and Mingo, and they immediately recognized Greathouse, who had been infamous among them for two decades. The other whites were spared and later taken back to the Maumee. On the spot, Greathouse and his wife were stripped and each loosely tied to a sapling. Cuts were made in their bellies and pieces of their intestines lashed to the trees. Then, prodded with clubs and hatchets, the Greathouses were forced to walk in circles around the saplings, winding their guts around them. So they died and were left as a sign to other whites, some of whom discovered the bodies a few days later.

The Americans responded to this and other acts of hideous violence according to their own customs. Cabins and supply caches, ostensibly still in use, were booby-trapped with explosives and poisoned food. Settlers' associations and land companies offered up to $50 each for any Indian scalp. Collecting these bounties became a profitable sideline for former Long Hunters, the only whites able or willing to stay out in the woods. Soon after the Greathouses were gutted, one of these ranger parties led by Simon Kenton caught some Shawnee as they were disembarking from their canoes on the Ohio. After a sharp fight, five Indians were killed and all were of course scalped. One of them, a young boy, was also decapitated and his head mounted on a pole along the river as a white sign.

The Greathouse brothers were indisputably murderous villains. Had Kenton and his rangers not scalped and mutilated the five Shawnee, the same would have been done to them. However, other men, women, and children who had done nothing specifically to deserve them met similar fates so frequently that the incidents had begun to lose their power to shock and outrage. Though 1782 was called the Year of Blood, 1791 was much worse, the most atrocious time of this or perhaps any civil war. By then both races were so habituated to random, vicious killings, so accustomed to enduring the horrors as an intrinsic part of frontier living, that nobody bothered to give 1791 a special name.

Field agents of the British Indian service, men like McKee, Elliott, Caldwell, and the Girty brothers, were elated by the defeat of Harmar and what was done to Americans after it. However, for policy rather than humanitarian reasons, their superiors in Quebec and London were of a mixed mind about the red offensive. At the time, Sir Guy Carleton (the recently created first Baron Dorchester and during the Revolution commander of British forces in Canada) was serving as the governor-general of Canada. He was concerned that a drubbing such as had been given to Harmar might stir up the United States to launch a full-scale invasion of the Northwest, which would threaten Detroit and other posts retained by the British. These were commercially and strategically valuable properties, but royal ministers in London made it clear that because of larger international difficulties with France, they did not want to fight the Americans in the Great Lakes and Ohio Valley country at that time. The savages should be kept in readiness but not completely unleashed.

To comply with these directives, Dorchester, in 1791, resurrected a plan which had been discussed for more than a decade. It involved setting aside the Northwest as a permanent, neutral buffer zone in which the individual Indian nations or confederacies of them would remain sovereign in domestic matters but function internationally as British satellites. After Harmar's defeat, Dorchester dispatched McKee and other agents to suggest to the western natives that, since the Americans were clearly on the defensive, it might be a good time to talk about a general peace settlement. The British would undertake on behalf of their red friends to act as intermediaries in negotiating a boundary which would give the Indians, in perpetuity, all the lands north of the Ohio and west of the Muskingum. The Crown would guarantee such an arrangement—that is, come immediately to the defense of the Indians if the Americans crossed the treaty line. The Miami and Shawnee listened politely but made no commitments, since their warriors were then enthusiastically killing Americans along and south of the Ohio.

During the winter of 1791 Dorchester informally (using George Beckwith, a British agent in Philadelphia) put the same proposition to the United States government or at least to Alexander Hamilton, the de facto prime minister of the Washington administration. Hamilton rejected it out of hand, refusing to bring it to the attention of the President. He said it was insulting to suggest that his country treat with "vagrant Indian tribes" as though they were "great or respectable nations."

Hamilton's curt response reflected the fact that another element had been interjected into the struggle for the west. Almost immediately after learning of Harmar's defeat, President Washington altered his opinions about peacefully occupying the western territories and advised that, both to defend the frontier and the national honor, the savages must be punished severely.

So far as Josiah Harmar was concerned, a congressional committee began to investigate his actions. Eventually he was able to defend himself against charges of military incompetence, but there was little sympathy for him personally, and as Knox had warned, his career and reputation were ruined. After receiving news of the disaster on the Maumee, Washington told Knox that he was not surprised at the fate of the expedition, because "I expected little from it from the moment I heard he was a drunkard."

Within Washington's administration the consensus was that the strike against Kekionga had failed because of Harmar's personal flaws. Therefore the next move seemed obvious: Organize a similar campaign against the savages but put a better man in charge of it. Arthur St. Clair, the governor of the Northwest Territory, having good political connections with the Federalist party, was given the job.

St. Clair, born in Scotland, was commissioned in the British Army and had come to North America in 1758 as an aide to Lord Jeffrey Amherst. In the 1760s he married the daughter of a well-to-do merchant, retired from the army, and became a large Pennsylvania property owner and land speculator. He reluctantly joined the colonists at the outbreak of the Revolution, announcing that he considered himself a loyal subject of King George but that the incompetence of the King's ministers made the insurrection necessary and moral. He served throughout most of the Revolution as a member of Washington's staff and rose to the rank of major general. In his most notable action as a field commander he had abandoned Fort Ticonderoga when it was outflanked by the British.

After the war St. Clair expressed great contempt for the republican government of the United States and continued to hope that it would evolve into a monarchy, which he believed was "the only government that can be supported by God." (Like other unreconstructed American Tories, he thought that George Washington was the obvious choice to serve as the first King of the United States.) As the federal governor of the Northwest, St. Clair took it upon himself to investigate the political philosophies and loyalties of prominent citizens, sending back frequent reports to Washington that this or that man should not be considered for public office since he was "tainted with democracy." Personally, St. Clair had been a bold and energetic young man. But in 1791 when he was made commander in chief of the United States Army, he was fifty-seven years old and though still bold, or at least bellicose, had become a very fat man who suffered from gout, asthma, and choleric temper tantrums.

Washington, Knox, and St. Clair reckoned it would require a 3,000-man army—with regulars being the most important component—to punish and overawe the savages. However, when St. Clair began to assemble this force, he found that because of casualties and low reenlistment rates, there were fewer than 600 regulars on the frontier. (As a cost-saving measure, the wages of federal privates had been cut from four to two dollars per month.) Therefore to get the needed troops, Congress passed legislation so that 2,000 men could be recruited for six months' service on the frontier. In addition to these temporary soldiers, St. Clair was authorized to raise another 1,000 militia in Kentucky and Pennsylvania.

Fort Washington on the Ohio was again the staging area. His army being larger, St. Clair encountered somewhat larger organizational problems than Harmar had the preceding year. There were disputes between regulars and the temporary levies. Rival politicians serving as militia officers bickered about authority and perks. Private contractors swarmed around Fort Washington like rats in a corncrib, selling the army supplies of poor quality at outrageously inflated prices. The principal profiteer was William Duer, a former secretary of the Treasury, a crony of Alexander Hamilton, and, in 1791, a partner of the Secretary of War, Henry Knox, in a New England real-estate deal. Later his public thieveries were exposed, but this did St. Clair little good at the time when he was largely dependent on Duer to outfit his army.

So far as military potential was concerned, the men St. Clair assembled were no more than the equals of those Harmar had led the year before. John Cleves Symmes, the Cincinnati real-estate operator, got a chance to look at them and judged that they had been recruited "from the prisons, wheel barrows [impressed labor gangs] and brothels of the nation at two dollars a month [and] will never answer our purpose of fighting Indians."

St. Clair was less concerned about the quality of these troops than was Symmes and others who saw them. Though agreeing that these men were mostly scum, he was confident that, after he shaped them up a bit, they would prove far superior to the Indians he would lead them against. As the army was gathering, he issued a general order explaining how and why they would be victorious. "It has been proved that savages if violently attacked will always break and give away—and when once broke, for the want of discipline, will never rally." (Arthur St. Clair was not, in the usual sense, a bigot. But he was a ferocious snob. Except for a few American and British gentlemen whom he considered his social equals, he was contemptuous of the rest of humanity, regardless of race, color, creed, nationality, or sex.)

In early September an advance base, Fort Hamilton, was built on the Great Miami River about twenty miles upstream from the Ohio. While St. Clair remained in the Fort Washington–Cincinnati area, the logistics of assembling the army at this post were left to his second in command, Richard Butler, the former United States peace commissioner, who five years previously had intimidated Kekewepellethe and his bedraggled band of Shawnee. When all the units available had arrived, St. Clair and Butler had 2,300 men, half of them being the short-term federal conscripts. There were also about 200 women, whom the soldiers had collected through their own enterprise and brought along to Fort Hamilton. St. Clair, Butler, and the other officers shortly became convinced that the men would not march without them so, while officially ignored, these "cooks" went along when the army headed out into Indian country.

On October 4, 1791, the expedition left Fort Hamilton with the intention of finding and "violently attacking" the savages on the Maumee River, 150 miles to the north. As the men proceeded they cut roads for their supply wagons and the dozen pieces of field artillery. The work of hacking through the virgin forest was slow and exhausting at best and made more difficult in this case because William Duer's contractors initially had provided the expedition with only eighty axes and one crosscut saw. Flour and meat were in short supply and of a bad quality. The government-issue boots began to come apart at the seams after several days. Furthermore the men had to shoulder much heavier than usual packs after many of the mules and horses died or wandered off. The horsemaster sent along by Duer had little experience in this line of work.

On the nineteenth of October, having advanced less than five miles each day, the army halted at the upper end of the Miami Valley. There, though still nearly 100 miles from his objective on the Maumee, St. Clair built another post, Fort Jefferson. Doing so, occupied the fatigued troops for another ten days, during which the fall weather turned bad, first to cold rain and then to sleet. At this time it was found that the civilian contractors had not, as specified, waterproofed the tents. Under these conditions the men began slipping off individually or in small groups. St. Clair had three captured deserters shot and, when this did not correct the problem, sent 300 of his regulars back down the trail toward the Ohio to catch or turn back the soldiers who were attempting to escape.

St. Clair decided to push on to attack the savages before his army disappeared. Leaving behind a garrison at Fort Jefferson of 120 men who were too sick or mutinous to travel and the 300 regulars who were hunting deserters, St. Clair marched north with 1,400 troops, about 100 durable women, and eight pieces of field artillery. He himself was frequently carried in a litter because of gout and asthma attacks.

St. Clair's army might be compared to an exotic beast, an elephant or the last of the dinosaurs, which improbably appeared and tried to survive in the Ohio jungles. This was how the American force looked to the red warriors, as a clumsy thing with dull senses and slow reflexes, which presented a hunting rather than military problem. The obvious response was to watch the creature and wait until it stumbled into a position where it could be pulled down, as a wolf pack does a buffalo. By mid-October 1,000 warriors had gathered along the Maumee. There, Little Turtle and Blue Jacket studied reports from their scouts and planned when and where to make the kill.

As Josiah Harmar had been the previous fall, St. Clair was oblivious to the realities of his situation. Despite the hardships of the army and his poor health, he remained optimistic. On October 21 St. Clair sent off a dispatch to Henry Knox, reporting that except for a few "wandering hunters" no Indians had been encountered, that he thought most of the savages were fleeing ahead of him, but he still had hopes of luring a few of them into battle.

One of the "wandering hunters" lurking in the woods was Tekamthi. Sometime after the spring campaigns along the Ohio, he returned to the Maumee villages. Then in August he was sent by Blue Jacket, the commanding Shawnee war chief, back to the south as the leader of a detachment of scouts. In addition to keeping an eye on the Long Knives as they slowly assembled their army, the warriors were free, when circumstances permitted, to continue the harassment of white settlers.

In mid-September, Tekamthi's patrol crossed the Ohio in the vicinity of what is now Parkersburg, West Virginia, and started up the Little Kanawha River valley. There they rustled some horses being herded by Frank, a twelve-year-old black slave owned by James Neil. The boy was taken prisoner or perhaps simply decided to throw in with the Shawnee. He traveled with them for several weeks, then escaped or was left behind, was later picked up by whites, and told them about what happened.

Leaving the Little Kanawha, the scouts struck cross-country toward Marietta, the principal settlement of the Ohio Land Company, located at the mouth of the Muskingum River. While traveling they went hungry for several days, finding nothing to eat but a large turtle, which was divided equally, Frank getting the same portion as the others. Their fast was involuntary. The fall had been very dry, and not even Shawnee hunters were able to stalk game across the thick carpet of dead, rustling leaves. Also the area was unnaturally devoid of wildlife. For three years, warriors had not only been raiding settlements around Marietta but conducting a scorched-earth campaign, systematically killing game to prevent whites from having it.

Along the Ohio, six miles above Marietta, Tekamthi and his men picked up the trail of an intrepid drover, Nicholas Carpenter, who was attempting to bring a herd of cattle from Wheeling to the hard-pressed settlers on the Muskingum. At dawn, Tekamthi's raiders rushed the camp. Three of the herdsmen were killed immediately while two escaped, including one who had been answering a call of nature and fled bare-bottomed through the woods. The warriors found Carpenter, a lame man, and his young son trying to conceal themselves in the brush. Both were killed but neither was scalped or mutilated. This puzzled a party of rangers from Marietta who, a few days thereafter, found the bodies. Later, when whites were persuaded that Tekamthi had led this band, the incident contributed to the legends that he was one of the last old-fashioned honorable warriors, red or white, still fighting along the Ohio.

After the ambush of Carpenter (during which Frank ran away or became separated from the Shawnee), the scouts descended the Ohio, skirting Fort Washington and the Cincinnati settlements, and then turned north, up the Great Miami. In mid-October they were hidden on a small tributary, Nettle Creek, so said Anthony Shane—who avoided mentioning where he was and how he knew this. Working from the Nettle Creek camp, the scouts watched St. Clair's army as it lumbered along, and Tekamthi sent at least one messenger north to the Maumee to inform the war chiefs of what was happening.

Except that he stayed south of the American army, between it and the Ohio, Shane provided no details about Tekamthi's movements during the next several weeks. No doubt he and his scouts did what other small detachments of warriors were doing—rustled horses which Americans thought were straying and picked off straggling soldiers who their officers believed had deserted. Tekamthi was well-positioned for this work but did not, Shane and Ruddell agreed, take part in the main battle, which was shortly fought.

After a month in the field, St. Clair's army had advanced only about eighty miles north of Fort Hamilton. On November 3 the Americans came to a small river, which they thought was the St. Mary's, a branch of the Maumee, but was in fact the upper Wabash. On the east bank—close to the point where the stream crosses the present Indiana–Ohio state line—they found a height of land which was less heavily timbered than the surrounding country. St. Clair decided this would be a good place to halt for at least a day and set the men to making a camp in the middle of the low, six-acre plateau. About 200 Kentucky militiamen were stationed on the far side of the Wabash in the bottomland. They were placed there so that if they tried to desert, which was thought likely, the Kentuckians would have to slip through the rest of the army to reach the trail to the south.

On the same day, Little Turtle and Blue Jacket had 1,000 men within a mile or two of this clearing above the river. The surrounding swamps, creeks, and underbrush made it a natural corral, and the war chiefs decided this would be a good place to butcher the white army beast. During the night American pickets caught fleeting glimpses of a few of the warriors, but duty officers thought they were probably only free-lance thieves trying to steal horses. Consideration was given to telling St. Clair of this increased Indian activity, but no one thought it prudent to do so since the commanding general's gout was giving him all sorts of hell, and when he was so afflicted, his temper was savage.

Just before dawn on the fourth, the men were roused out of their thin, wet blankets and paraded. Then they were dismissed to build fires to cook and warm themselves, for it was a very raw, cold morning. While they were so occupied, Little Turtle and Blue Jacket turned loose the warriors. In a half-moon formation, they came against the camp from three directions, each man screeching as he ran. The war whoops alone (which some said sounded like the continuous ringing of 10,000 cow bells, and others likened to the howling of thousands of wolves) had an appalling effect on the Americans. According to a survivor, the noise so terrified many of them that they did not pick up their weapons but began running "helter skelter" about the camp, in some cases directly toward the advancing warriors.

The Kentucky militia on the far side of the Wabash fired one ragged volley, then broke and ran back through the stream to the main camp, where their panic infected the other troops awaiting the onslaught. It came almost immediately, remembered Ebenezer Denny, an eyewitness. The first wave of warriors "killed or cut off nearly all the guards," and then sprinting from tree to tree, "so that it is almost impossible to find them out or to know to direct your fire," broke into the main camp area. (Denny, a charmed young regular officer, survived both Harmar's and St. Clair's defeats.)

Some federal artillery men ran to their guns and commenced firing, but their elevation was too high. A detachment of Shawnee, with Blue Jacket leading, came in low under their shot and overran the batteries. Attempting to rescue the gunners, Richard Butler led a unit of the 2nd American Regiment (so newly organized that some of the men had not previously fired their muskets) in a bayonet charge. They were decimated. Within a few minutes the guns were silenced and literally buried under white corpses. While badly wounded, Butler was able to bring a few men back to the center of the camp, though all but three officers of the 2nd Regiment were killed. The warriors were well aware of the importance of rank in a white army, and their sharpshooters made it a first order of business to pick off officers who were recognizable by their insignia.

When the attack commenced, St. Clair was in his camp bed and in agony because of the gout. He put on a tricorn hat, a greatcoat over his underwear, and painfully stumbled out of his tent. With the help of several other soldiers, his orderly attempted to lift him into the saddle of his horse, but could not, because of the general's great weight and crippled condition. While he was struggling to mount, both the horse and orderly were shot and killed, and St. Clair hobbled off into the melee armed with only a pistol. Shortly he came upon a group of soldiers hiding among the officers' tents. At gun point he attempted to force them to turn back toward the enemy, but they did not, by this time being far more frightened of the warriors than they were of the commander in chief of the United States Army. St. Clair wandered off trying variously to organize a counterattack or to form the remaining troops into a defensive square. There were few officers left to take his orders and no organized units to execute them. Here and there small groups of regulars held out, but numbers of dazed men stumbled about the clearing or sat praying and crying. The wounded crawled among them like broken-backed snakes. There were no forward or rear positions. The warriors were everywhere, methodically cutting up Americans with their hatchets and knives.

After the fight around the artillery positions, Richard Butler dragged himself to a grove of trees. There he was found by his two brothers, Capt. Edward and Maj. Thomas, also badly wounded, and several other officers. They attempted to carry him with them but could not. (Obesity was prevalent in the upper echelons of the American military establishment. Henry Knox, the Secretary of War, weighed 325 pounds, St. Clair and Butler were comparably fleshy.) Butler told his brothers he was mortally wounded, to leave him and save themselves if they could. Having no other choice, they did as he asked. A few minutes later two Shawnee found Butler propped against an oak tree, bleeding profusely. They killed and scalped him. Then Simon Girty, and others who knew who this man had been, came by and identified the corpse. They cut out Butler's still warm heart and diced it into fourteen pieces so that representatives of all the nations fighting there that day could eat of it and taste revenge. Thus the ultimatum—that the Shawnee must either give up their lands to the Americans or be destroyed by their soldiers—which Butler had offered five years before at Fort Finney was remembered and answered according to the customs of this time and these people.

By nine in the morning, three hours after the first attack, the military action was finished. While the butchering continued, 500 Americans congregated on the south side of the plateau. Not as an army, but as a frightened "drove of bullocks," as one of them recalled, they fled down the road, so laboriously cut through the woods during the previous month. Shortly they were strung out for five miles. With those who still had mounts, mostly officers, in the lead, each man went as fast as he could ride, run, or hobble. St. Clair was toward the front of the rout, an aide having succeeded in getting him up and tied down on a pack horse. As he jolted down the trail, the pain in his gouty legs was such that he later said he would rather "die a thousand deaths" than experience it again.

Ebenezer Denny tried to form a rear guard but gave up, finding that "such a panic had seized the men" that it was impossible to make any of them stand and fight. Fortunately they did not have to, for victory had done to the red army what defeat had to the white one—that is, turned it into a disorderly mob. As he had after the rout of Harmar, Blue Jacket attempted to organize a pursuit, but only twenty of his Shawnee were willing to try, and after a few miles they returned to the main camp where the rest of the warriors were amusing themselves with still-living Americans and picking through the stores that had been abandoned. The military loot included 100 or so pack horses, 40 tents, 1,200 muskets, considerable powder and shot. Since the warriors could not haul them away, eight captured artillery pieces were eventually buried along the river for possible future use. The Americans naturally left all their personal baggage on the field, and that of the officers yielded some attractive trophies. Later, back on the Auglaize, one of the warriors who had sacked the camp strolled about the Shawnee village wearing the formal dress coat of an American captain, a tricorn hat, and two silver watches dangling from his ear lobes.

By and by some kegs of whiskey were found. The wild drunken victory celebration which followed ended any possibility of the warriors following and finishing off St. Clair's army. Knowing nothing of these developments, the Americans were driven on by their fear that the howling savages would come down on them again. Though many of them were wounded and all of them were virtually without food, the surviving soldiers got back to the Cincinnati area by the ninth of November. In this flight they covered in four days the same distance it had taken them five weeks to travel when they were marching north to punish the Indians.

After the last stragglers turned up at Fort Washington, the still-functioning officers assessed the magnitude of the disaster. Beyond the loss of all the expedition's supplies, they calculated that 623 officers and men, twenty-four civilian teamsters and sutlers had been killed, while 271 had been severely wounded. (Later it was learned from whites living in the Maumee villages that the Indian loss had been twenty-one killed and forty wounded.) Proportionate to the numbers involved, this still stands as the most one-sided defeat ever suffered by the United States army.

The American casualty figures did not include the "cooks," the women who had followed the soldiers, but it was thought that of the hundred or so who had gone as far as the Wabash, only three returned to the white settlements. Some were killed during the battle but more were taken home by the warriors. At least one couple, Polly Meadows and Henry Ball, was spared. They were among the few whites, other than supply contractors, whose fortunes were improved by the battle. Where they first came from or how they came to be on the Wabash is no longer remembered. All that is known of the pair is that after St. Clair's defeat, they were brought to the Shawnee village on the Auglaize River. There they became acquainted with Oliver Spencer, another American boy who after being captured on the Ohio River, had spent a few grand years living red. Later Spencer returned to the whites and, as did so many ex-captives, wrote a memoir about his experiences. In it he mentioned Ball and Meadows, who spoke of themselves as husband and wife. By the summer of 1792 the couple was well established among the Indians and prospering. Ball operated a flatboat, the management of which was not congenial work for the Shawnee, and was hauling freight up the river from British suppliers near what is now Toledo. Polly Meadows did well as a laundress and seamstress, since after the sack of St. Clair's camp, ruffled shirts, belted coats, and other items of white gentlemen's apparel were popular among fashion-conscious Shawnee.

In military terms the victory over St. Clair was a much grander, less costly accomplishment for the Indians than the defeat of Harmar the previous fall. On the other hand the hardships that followed in the winter were greater. As compared to 1790, nearly twice as many allied warriors had assembled to campaign in 1791. They had to eat, and very little food was found in the stores captured on the Wabash. The same unseasonably cold, wet weather which had made life so miserable for the American army greatly reduced the corn harvest of the women farming along the Maumee. In consequence the Miami and Shawnee again appealed to British Indian agents for emergency rations, and again, without having much time to enjoy the ruffled shirts and silver watches, the warriors dispersed, spreading out in small parties throughout Ohio and Indiana looking for game.

Wherever he had been on November 4, when St. Clair's army was annihilated, Tekamthi, before the end of the year, was hunting at the head of a small party in the Miami Valley. According to after-the-fact stories, he and his men, in December of '91, had a brief skirmish with some Kentucky rangers along the Ohio. Later they were with a larger party which took a passing swipe at Fort Jefferson, St. Clair's advance camp, which was still held by regular troops. However, in general there was very little fighting during the winter of 1791–92. As the warriors hunted for food, the Americans assessed and assigned blame for the defeat, buried their dead, and commenced to rebuild the United States army.

The bulk of the Kentucky militia rode or ran directly from the battle on the Wabash to their homes, but those from Maryland and Pennsylvania hung around Fort Washington–Cincinnati for a month or more. While trying to make arrangements to transport them back east, territorial authorities had small means for providing the survivors with food, quarters, or medical care. Under circumstances which were not much better than those they had endured in the field, these men survived as best they could, begging, sometimes stealing from the regular troops and civilians in Cincinnati. One thing seldom in short supply around frontier communities was raw corn whiskey. Almost as soon as they came in from the woods, many of the beaten men started drinking and kept it up for as long as they were around the settlement, unnerving local residents. In an attempt to do something about them, St. Clair withheld the back pay of the former soldiers on the grounds that they had done nothing on the Wabash to deserve it, and if they had money, would only spend it on more whiskey.

Both to control the remnants of his first army and to create a second one, St. Clair had an immediate need for new regular officers to replace those who had been lost in the fall campaign. Among the replacements sent out by the War Department was the eighteen-year-old William Henry Harrison, son of the late governor of Virginia. In the summer, his family having suffered financial reverses, Harrison had dropped out of medical school in Philadelphia and obtained a commission as an ensign in the 1st Regiment of the United States Army. Leading eighty new recruits, Harrison was ordered west. To further his military education, while on the road, he read Cicero.

Arriving at Fort Washington shortly after St. Clair's demoralized men streamed in from the woods, Harrison did not fit in well with his brother officers. They thought him a pampered, priggish youth who had received his commission only because of his family's political connections. Harrison thought that four fifths of the frontier officers were drunkards and that, even when sober, they spent too much time gambling, fighting, and whoring. Harrison kept to himself, continued his reading and studying, made few friends, and endured considerable mockery.

The shortage of junior officers was so critical that in January, Harrison was given his first field command, being sent out with twenty regulars to escort freight packers bringing supplies to Fort Jefferson, which had been more or less forgotten in the confusion following St. Clair's defeat. The first relief party that got through found the 116-man garrison eating their horses, leather harnesses, and boots.

January of 1792 was long remembered by those who lived through it as a terrible winter. Heavy snows alternating with rain and thaws left the Miami Valley country either flooded with slushy water or, when the temperatures dropped, covered by sheets of ice. On his first frontier assignment, Ensign Harrison proved to be a tougher man than many of those who taunted him at Fort Washington thought he was. He bore up at least as well as his troops while the detachment slogged ahead, eating short, sodden rations, sleeping in the slush, propped against their saddles, sometimes freezing to them during the night. Within ten days they reached Fort Jefferson, where Harrison waited while civilian scouts went ahead to the site of the battle on the Wabash. There they found, under telltale mounds of ice, hundreds of bodies or "scattered limbs and organs." To protect them from wolves, panthers, and smaller carnivores who had already done considerable scavenging, the remains were shoveled into a large pit in the frozen ground and covered as well as conditions permitted. After the burial party returned, Harrison marched his regulars back to Cincinnati. He missed the brief, inconsequential attack made by the Shawnee on Fort Jefferson and saw no other Indians, though signs of them were abundant. However, since both young men being abroad in that grim country, the paths of Harrison and Tekamthi may well have crossed during those weeks. An imaginative tableau comes to mind, of one standing studying the frozen moccasin or boot print of the other, considering the meaning of the sign, how it might influence what he could or should do. If such a happening occurred, it seems peculiarly fitting, considering how intricately knotted together they would become, that the lives of Tekamthi and Harrison first intersected sometime in the winter of 1792, somewhere in the cold, soggy Miami Valley.

VIII. The Black Snake

On an evening in November of 1791 an agitated army officer rode a tired horse up to the gate of the Philadelphia mansion then serving as the official residence of the President of the United States. The rider was told that President Washington was at home, but was entertaining at a private dinner party and could not be disturbed. The officer insisted that he must see the Chief Executive, and the gate porter summoned Tobias Lear, the President's confidential secretary. Lear said he would take whatever messages the courier had and pass them along when convenient. The dragoon officer remained adamant, telling Lear that he had come from the western army in Ohio with orders to deliver his dispatch personally to Washington and as soon as he arrived in Philadelphia. Impressed by his sense of urgency, Lear asked the man to wait in an anteroom. Then he went back to the dining room and in a whispered conversation explained the situation to the President. Washington excused himself, spent a few minutes alone with the messenger, and returned to the table without, according to Lear, remarking on the interruption or showing any change of manner.

The guests departed about ten o'clock, and after Martha Washington had retired, her husband asked Lear to join him in his private study. There the President paced back and forth in a distraught manner. He was silent for several minutes and then spoke in a voice strangled with emotion: "St. Clair's defeated—routed;—the officers nearly all killed, the men by wholesale; the rout complete—too shocking to think of—and a surprise into the bargain!"

The President flung himself on a sofa, then jumped up and began to pace again. His "wrath became terrible," recalled Lear. Shouting, he said:

> HERE on this very spot, I took leave of him [Arthur St. Clair]; I wished him success and honor; you have your instructions, I said, from the Secretary of War, I had a strict eye to them; and will add but one word—BEWARE OF A SURPRISE. I repeat it, BEWARE OF A SURPRISE—you know how the Indians fight us. He went off with that as my last solemn warning thrown into his ears. And yet!! to suffer that army to be cut to pieces, hack'd, butchered, tomahawk'd, by a surprise—the very thing I guarded him against!! O God, O God, he's worse than a murderer! how can he answer it to his country;—the blood of the slain is upon him—the curse of widows and orphans—the curse of Heaven!

After the tantrum, which left him shaking and Lear "awed into breathless silence," the President suddenly fell silent and "his warmth began to subside." Then he turned to Lear and in a composed, matter-of-fact voice, said, "This must not go beyond this room. [It did not for many years, Lear remaining silent about the incident until after Washington's death.] General St. Clair shall have justice; I looked hastily through the dispatches, saw the whole disaster but not all the particulars; I will receive him without displeasure; I will hear him without prejudice."

He did not explain his abrupt change of mood to Lear at the time or to anyone later. However, given Washington's reputation as the Great Pragmatist, it seems likely that after he vented his emotions, several realities occurred to him. Beyond being his own, hand-picked choice as leader of the expedition, St. Clair was a prominent member of Washington's Federalist party. Also the manner in which St. Clair's army had been supplied was beginning to be a scandal, one which would certainly grow and draw in administration officials if the President were to stir up the public about the "particulars" of the disaster.

For whatever reasons, when St. Clair came to Philadelphia later in the winter to make his personal report, he was politely received by the President, who used his influence to sidetrack a Congressional investigation into the unfortunate campaign. St. Clair resigned from the army but stayed as the governor of the Northwest Territory.

St. Clair's defeat had two contradictory political consequences. First, it changed Washington's mind, and that of his Federalist supporters, about the conciliatory policy which had been previously advocated. The President became convinced that, like it or not, the United States was at war with the Ohio Indians, that defeating them was imperative but would require a far more substantial military response than had been made. Secondly, the debacle on the Wabash brought home the true horrors and costs of an Indian war—against which Washington had warned for a decade—to many Americans in the eastern regions who had previously not taken a great interest in frontier affairs. Immediately there was an upwelling of public and congressional sentiment in favor of making peace with the western savages and at least temporarily halting the invasion of their lands.

This peace movement was substantial and vocal enough so that when Washington and Knox went to the Congress for the military appropriations they thought were needed, they were forced to make a deal to get them. The House authorized a bigger and better army, but with the understanding that it would not be used until a serious attempt was made—and had clearly failed—to arrange a general peace treaty. The agreement was compatible with the long-range plans of the President and his men who were skeptical about the chances of making a peace on their terms with the Indians. However, attempting to do so, beyond silencing domestic critics, might distract the savages and give the administration time to organize an attack against them. Such a respite was needed, for in 1792, what with the losses St. Clair had suffered, resignations, and desertions, there were only about 750 federal soldiers west of the mountains, barely enough to garrison the six forts which the United States still held there.

The American peace offensive began early in 1792. As a first step, Henry Knox, Alexander Hamilton, and Thomas Jefferson informally made it known to George Hammond, the British minister, that the United States had become interested in considering the proposition put forward by Lord Dorchester the year previous—for a negotiated western settlement. Upper-level British diplomats and politicians were receptive since it seemed that talking might well lead to what they had long wanted: the creation of an Indian buffer zone which would allow them to keep, without war, their forts, trade, and influence in the Northwest.

Bringing in the Indians, necessary third parties for any such discussions, proved to be a difficult and dangerous matter. Early in the spring of 1792, Knox began trying to get word to the Miami and Shawnee that the United States wanted to meet and talk peace with them. At various times six messengers were sent out, but before they reached the Maumee villages, all the men were caught and killed as spies. One of them was Col. John Hardin, the Kentucky politician, who while serving under Harmar had twice led his men into bloody ambushes.

Finally the Americans were able to employ several prominent Iroquois to make contact with the belligerent western nations at a grand council which was held in the summer of 1792 at the Shawnee villages on the Auglaize River. (Though no longer of sovereign consequence, the Iroquois still had many experienced and able diplomats, politicians, and warriors. After the Revolution and throughout much of the nineteenth century, they found work in the west as intermediaries between reds and whites, as interpreters, scouts, and mercenary soldiers.)

The Iroquois delegation to the Auglaize Conference was headed by Red Jacket, a Seneca sachem. He was coldly received but not physically abused, his safety having been guaranteed by the British Indian agents who paid—that is, supplied food and ceremonial gifts—for the council. It lasted several weeks and was attended by nearly a thousand representatives from a dozen western nations. When he was permitted to speak, the gist of Red Jacket's message was that the Americans were in a conciliatory frame of mind. In return for peace, they might be willing to agree to a boundary line along the Muskingum River which would leave everything west of it and north of the Ohio—except for tracts already settled by whites—in Indian hands. Red Jacket advised that, if the Americans were indeed to make such a generous offer, the western nations should not "be too proud-spirited and reject it lest the Great Spirit should be angry with you."

A scathing reply was given by Messquakenoe, a Shawnee orator. He pointed out that during the past five years, while the western nations were fighting against the Long Knives, warriors of the once great Six Nations had been notably absent, that the Iroquois had always been an untrustworthy people and seem to have grown more so since they had been intimidated and seduced by the Americans. As for the Long Knives, the Shawnee, Miami, and their allies had within the space of a year twice rather easily defeated large armies of them. In consequence they had no reason to accept terms from the Americans but, being reasonable people, might offer terms to them.

The chiefs of the western nations then convened privately and drafted an answer which they said the Iroquois could take back to the Americans. They did not want to talk about and would not accept a boundary along the Muskingum River. All of the land north of the Ohio was theirs. Americans already there must withdraw. The Shawnee, specifically, must be reimbursed for their former hunting grounds in Kentucky, which had been illegally occupied and ruined by white settlers. If the Americans wanted to accept these conditions and have peace, then the Miami, Shawnee, and their allies would be willing to receive official representatives of the United States at a council to be held the following summer.

Red Jacket, mindful of where he was, replied that now that it had been clearly explained, he understood and agreed with the position of his western brothers and would so inform the Americans. In fact, he and the other Iroquois were quite certain that returning with such an answer would reflect badly on their own diplomatic skills and influence. Therefore, in reporting to American agents they severely edited the message given to them on the Auglaize. No mention was made of settlers getting out of Ohio or the Shawnee being paid for Kentucky. Rather, Red Jacket said that he had been able to persuade the westerners to think seriously about peace and to talk formally about it the next year.

American and British authorities to the east may have been misled about the temper and intention of the western natives, but frontier whites were not. "The savages," Rufus Putnam, the Ohio land developer, reported, "believe them Selves invinsible and have much cause of triumph." Putnam would not have known his name at the time, but Tekamthi was one of the warriors who had led him to this conclusion, since in the year after St. Clair's defeat, he took at least four Shawnee patrols into actions against whites. The first of these encounters was typical of border skirmishes and the only one of Tekamthi's reported by an eyewitness on the Indian side. The engagement occurred in the early spring of 1792, and Stephen Ruddell admitted, perhaps because it was a straightforward fight without atrocities, that he was there as a Shawnee warrior.

After rustling some horses in Kentucky, Tekamthi, Big Fish (Ruddell), and eight other braves swam the animals across the Ohio a few miles upstream from Fort Washington—Cincinnati. Soon after the raid, their trail was picked up by a party of white rangers led by Simon Kenton, then reputed to be the most formidable of all Kentucky woodsmen and irregular Indian fighters. With twenty-eight men, Kenton began tracking the Shawnee. After they rafted across the Ohio, the Kentuckians found and killed one of Tekamthi's men, who had lagged behind looking for strayed horses. Then they caught up with the main Shawnee party, which was camped on the East Fork of the Little Miami River near what is now Withamsville, Ohio. Kenton decided to make a midnight surprise attack on the savages. What followed was described by Ruddell:

Tecumthe had laid down at night outside of the camp or tents [bark-covered lean-tos] alongside of the pine where we had been gherking some venison through the day. In the night the attack was made by firing into the tents. Tecumthe sprang to his feet with his war club in his hand, a weapon which he invariably carried both in peace and war, hunting and in battle, and calling to me asked Big Fish, where are you? Here I am says I. Then do you charge on that side and I will charge on this with that he rushed on those on his side, knocked one in the head with his club and drove the rest back. I on my side met a man as I came out of the tent, whom I afterward found out to be Kenton himself. I fired on him but my gun having gotten a little wet through the day it blowed considerably and at last just blowed out the ball without injuring Kenton who had taken to his heels. I raised the Indian yell and called that they were running, upon which the rest of the Indians in the tent who had till now remained silent, sprang out and raising the war-whoop we run them off the ground.

In the melee one of the Shawnee slid into the river. The commotion he made trying to climb out, up the steep, muddy bank, was heard by Kenton's rangers who thought the sounds signified the approach of another large band of warriors coming to the aid of Tekamthi. This greatly hastened their flight. Nevertheless the Kentuckians later claimed to have killed fourteen and wounded seventeen Indians. Ruddell thought the Shawnee lost only one man—the rear-guard horse herder who fell before the main attack began—and killed at least two whites.

At dawn the next day Tekamthi discovered the trail of a single white man, Alexander McIntire, who had fled in a different direction from that taken by most of Kenton's rangers. Tekamthi and four others began tracking him and caught up after a few miles. McIntire heard them coming and was waiting with his rifle ready. Before he could get off a shot, Tekamthi slipped through the brush, surprised and overpowered him. When they got back to camp, the prisoner was left with others while Big Fish and Tekamthi went out looking for more strayed horses. Again Ruddell: "On our return the rest of the Indians had killed McIntire, at which Tecumthe was very angry telling them that it was a cowardly act to kill a man who was tied and expressed in his strongest terms his disapprobation of their conduct."

A month later Tekamthi was in West Virginia, where he raided an isolated white station established by John Waggoner. Waggoner's wife and three of his children were killed while two other daughters and a son were taken back to the Shawnee villages as prisoners.

(The boy, Peter, lived with the Shawnee as one of them for more than ten years, eventually taking an Indian wife by whom he had several children. Later he was found by friends of his father and brought back, forcibly, to West Virginia. He was kept under guard for a time but "gradually," so said neighbors, "he became reconciled in a measure to his new surroundings but was ever melancholy, frequently lamenting that he had left his savage family.")

Since virtually all the Shawnee attended, Tekamthi presumedly went north in the summer for the great council on the Auglaize where Red Jacket presented the American peace overtures. However, though he had established himself as a successful young partisan commander, Tekamthi's age and rank did not entitle him to deliver public speeches or take part in the deliberations of the senior chiefs, except perhaps as an aide to Blue Jacket, the Shawnee commander.

After the council Tekamthi went back to hunting and scouting along the Miami. There, in early winter, his patrol had a skirmish with a party led by Robert McClelland, another well-known white ranger. A few months later he again met, fought, and seems to have gotten the best of Simon Kenton and his company.

The events of 1792—the difficulties in starting peace talks and the continued raids on whites by warriors such as Tekamthi—did not surprise and perhaps, in strategic terms, did not entirely displease President Washington. Strife on the frontier worked against the congressional peace advocates, allowing the administration to make its military preparations without having to endure much political sniping. With St. Clair's defeat still fresh, Congress appropriated $1,026,477.05, an enormous sum for the times, to pay and equip 5,000 regulars. The President was by then convinced that recruiting more civilians and sending them, as such, out under political generals to fight the warriors would only lead to new and greater disasters. His need was for a commander in chief, a military mechanic, who would take country and city boys of the sort the United States could afford to hire and convert them into passable Indian fighters. For several months Washington looked for such a man, drawing up a list of twenty names which were considered by his Cabinet. Serious objections were raised about all of the candidates. They were rejected, one by one, because they were variously too old, infirm, or drunk, had too little field experience, or belonged to the wrong political faction. How serious the flaws of the others were thought to be is indicated by the known deficiencies of the one who was finally selected, Anthony Wayne.

Wayne entered the Revolution commanding a Pennsylvania battalion. He fought at Brandywine, Paoli, Monmouth, Valley Forge, Stony Point, and Yorktown, rising to the rank of brigadier general. Though never an independent commander, he earned a reputation as a dependable officer and a ferocious disciplinarian. Aside from this good if not brilliant record, there were many unsettling things about Wayne which worried Washington and his advisers. He was another fat, gouty, drinking general, though somewhat less afflicted in these regards than Arthur St. Clair or Josiah Harmar. He was an irascible man who had a history of offending and feuding with other officers; he was a womanizer and notably vain. He had two nicknames, Dandy Tony and Mad Anthony, neither of which was affectionate or complimentary. As to the latter one, a Revolutionary soldier who had been a civilian neighbor of Wayne's deserted from the army and was caught. He told the military police to get in touch with his old and good friend General Wayne, who would quickly straighten out the matter. When Wayne refused to help or even recognize him, the deserter explained that Anthony must be mad. The name stuck, and as Mad Anthony, Wayne has come down through history as supposedly either a very crazy or rash officer. At least in military matters, however, he was an exceptionally rational and prudent man.

After the Revolution Wayne fell on hard times. He lost considerable amounts of money in business ventures in Pennsylvania and then, moving south to Georgia as a plantation owner, went bankrupt. In Georgia he ran for a seat in the U.S. House of Representatives, principally because he hoped that in this office he would be safe from creditors who were trying to put him in a debtor's prison. On the first canvass he won the seat but his election was overturned as fraudulent.

Despite all of this, Washington kept returning to this name as he searched for a new general. Finally, in April 1792, Wayne was offered and eagerly accepted the job as major general, commanding the United States Army. Even after the decision was made, Washington was not at all convinced that he had done the right thing, writing, "I was never more embarrassed making any appointment." Optimistically, the President thought that perhaps "time, reflection, good advice, and above all, a due sense of the importance of the trust which is committed to him will correct his foibles, or cast a shade over them."

Beyond hoping for the best Washington may have known something about the man or recognized hidden qualities in him that others did not. Whatever the reasons it was made, the appointment did not embarrass the President. Rather it enhanced his reputation for sagacity, since Wayne turned out to be far and away the most competent white military man who had served, or would serve, on the American frontier.

In the summer of 1792 Wayne set up his headquarters at Pittsburgh. There the Legion of the United States, as Henry Knox named the new army, began to assemble. The recruits were no more promising than those who had been made available to Harmar and St. Clair. However, Wayne enjoyed a considerable advantage over his predecessors, having made it clear to the President and Congress that he would not take these men into action against the savages until he was satisfied they could soldier.

The new legionnaires' training during their first months was basic and brutal. Using the small cadre of regulars, Wayne saw to it that the men were kept busy, "between manoeuvering & fatigue" from dawn to dusk. They were taught to dress, maintain their equipment and quarters, drill, march, shoot, and obey orders by the military book which Wayne did not hesitate to revise as it suited him. Flogging was the most common punishment; twenty lashes for minor offenses—being dirty, slothful, or improperly uniformed—100 lashes for such things as insubordination, drinking or sleeping on duty. Initially Wayne wanted to brand, with a hot iron—a C for coward—on the foreheads of soldiers who were overheard talking about desertion, as many were during the first month or so. Henry Knox dissuaded him, advising that "this is a punishment upon which some doubt may be entertained as to its legality."

Wayne had a free hand to deal with proved deserters, those who were caught and returned. Seven of them were shot. By early September the commanding general was able to report to the Secretary of War that there had been no defections during the preceding two weeks and the troops were showing marked improvement in close order drilling and marksmanship.

Though he did not flog or execute any of the regular officers, Wayne found many of them to be unsuitable and commenced to ship out those he could not shape up. A subaltern was discharged for talking out of the corner of his mouth while on parade. An ensign who wept while a deserter was being executed was charged with drunkenness and cashiered.

A spectacular case involved Capt. Ballard Smith, a frontier veteran with the 1st Regiment. One night military police found Polly Sprague, the wife of a sergeant, in Smith's quarters. So disturbed, she picked up the captain's sword, jumped onto his bed, and began swinging the weapon while shouting at the MP, "I'm a

THE BLACK SNAKE 165

little queen, who can whip you even if you are a sergeant." She was finally subdued, though in the process the arresting officer received a nasty cut. Thereafter Ballard Smith was suspended from the army for six months on the grounds that his conduct had caused "discontent to the sergeant [Polly Sprague's husband]." William Henry Harrison was promoted to take his place. Though there was never much affection between the lusty, fiery-tempered old man and the rather sedate young one, Harrison was the kind of orderly, sober officer Wayne needed, and he later made him an aide.

Late in the fall, to further their military education and to make it harder for them to get whiskey and venereal diseases, Wayne moved his troops, then numbering about 1,000, twenty miles downstream from Pittsburgh to a newly built camp, Legionville. In this raw, isolated place they endured a frontier winter and additional training. Guards and pickets were posted and expected to perform as though they were in the heart of Indian country. Companies were sent out, both night and day, on cold forced marches. Sham battles were fought in which some units were detailed to dress, howl, and try to behave like Indians. In their spare time the troops continued to practice at targets and with their bayonets.

During these first months, Wayne was occupied with improving himself as well as his men and officers. Specifically, as soon as he assumed command, he commenced to study subjects which had not much interested Harmar or St. Clair: the history, culture, economy, and military tactics of the western Indians. To better himself in this regard, Wayne interviewed, among other frontier experts, the Rev. John Heckewelder, then probably the best formal student of the Ohio natives. After mulling over the information he collected and analyzing the defeats of his predecessors, Wayne came to some insightful conclusions, which he incorporated into a report to the War Department. In his opinion the savages could be very formidable opponents if they were allowed to fight in places and at seasons of their own choosing. "In the *fall* of the year he's strong [the warrior], ferocious and full of spirits—corn is in plenty and venison and other game everywhere to be met with; in the Spring he is half-starved, weak and dispirited."

Wayne went on to pinpoint, as no American commander had before, the intrinsic weakness of the Indian nations and how to exploit it. They were not organized and could not afford to conduct long campaigns. The proper strategy was to draw them into wars of attrition instead of trying to respond to their hit-and-run attacks. Therefore Wayne proposed to Henry Knox:

Permit me to choose the season for operations. Give me time to manoeuver and discipline the army, so as to inspire them with a confidence in their own prowess, authorize me to direct ample and proper magazines of forage, stores and provisions to be thrown into the advanced posts at the most favorable and convenient periods. . . . Give me authority to make these arrangements and I will pledge my reputation as an officer to establish myself at the Miami villages, or at any other place that may be thought more proper, in the face of all the savages of the wilderness.

It was some time before Washington and Knox agreed to Wayne's ideas and occasionally in the heat of campaigning, he himself was to ignore them. However, generally during the next two years, Wayne followed the sound strategic plan he outlined in the fall of 1792 and was able to do as he had promised.

In the spring of 1793, Wayne moved the legion to Fort Washington at Cincinnati, but found this frontier community a worse hellhole than Pittsburgh. Therefore he built a new camp beyond the town and called it Hobson's Choice. As the name suggested, it had little to recommend it other than its being removed from the taverns and brothels that had grown up around Fort Washington. Once in position, Wayne informed the War Department that he thought the Legion was ready to do serious work against the hostiles and should be so employed that summer. He was told by Henry Knox that the Legion must remain at Hobson's Choice while another attempt—which would no doubt fail—was made at negotiating with the Indians. Knox explained that high matters of state and public relations were involved:

The sentiments of the great mass of Citizens of the United States are adverse in the extreme to an Indian War and although these sentiments would not be considered as sufficient cause for the Government to conclude an infamous peace, yet they are of such a nature as to render it advisable to embrace every expedient which may honorably terminate the conflict.

Knox went on with his lecture on realpolitik, adding:

the favorable opinion and pity of the world is easily excited in favor of the oppressed. The Indians are considered in a great degree of this description—If our modes of population and War destroy the tribes the disinterested part of mankind and posterity will be apt to class the effects of our Conduct and that of the Spaniards in Mexico and Peru together—.

As a good many generals have since, Wayne fumed that his hands were being tied by lily-livered politicians. However, he obeyed orders and spent the summer building roads and sending supplies to the advanced forts in the Miami Valley, preparing for the time when he would be allowed to attack. While he was so occupied, three prominent Americans, Benjamin Lincoln and Timothy Pickering of Massachusetts and Beverly Randolph of Virginia, were sent north as peace commissioners to represent the United States at the council of western Indians which, as promised, was convened on the Maumee. They went by the way of Niagara, where they were first received by John Simcoe, the governor of Upper Canada (Ontario) and Lord Dorchester's principal deputy. They were greeted warmly, for at the time the British government, being at war with France, was particularly eager to make a peace, which would maintain the status quo in North America.

The Canadians and the peace commissioners themselves were justifiably concerned about what might happen to the Americans if they appeared in person at the Indian council. Therefore Lincoln, Pickering, and Randolph got no closer to Maumee than Matthew Elliott's estate near the mouth of the Detroit River. They stayed there for nearly a month in midsummer, living comfortably and safely. However, they were unable to deal or even speak directly with Indians and depended on British and Iroquois agents as intermediaries and interpreters. (Their host, Matthew Elliott, his superior, Alexander McKee, and others of the Indian service had interests which were quite different from those of either the Americans or the British government. Because of business and personal ties, they were nearly as anxious as the Shawnee and Miami to humiliate the Americans and drive them out of Ohio. During the lengthy council they worked behind the scenes to forward their private policies.)

The talks opened on a sour note with the Shawnee asking why, if they were so eager for peace, had the Americans put a new and apparently formidable army on the Ohio River. Pickering and the other commissioners provided documents from the War Department, which they said proved that Wayne's Legion was at Hobson's Choice purely for defensive purposes and would take no offensive action so long as there was any possibility for making peace. The Shawnee warned that they would keep their own warriors along the Ohio and trusted their reports about Wayne's activities more than they did the written words of Americans. This matter being temporarily set aside, the peace commissioners put forward their government's proposals on the last day of July. First, the United States was willing to give way on a matter of principle and history which had been a sticking point in previous negotiations. The Americans conceded that they had been wrong in claiming that, because they had defeated the British in the Revolution, they had also defeated the western Indians and obtained title to their lands by right of conquest. It was now accepted that these nations were sovereign and unsubdued. Previous agreements made between Britain and the United States about Indian lands were no longer valid. Any new ones would be made directly with the original and rightful owners of the property. In keeping with this enlightened policy, the United States would withdraw all claims to lands north of the Ohio except for certain areas around Cincinnati, the Scioto, and Muskingum rivers. These tracts had already been sold to land developers and were occupied by so many settlers as to make removing them inconvenient and prohibitively expensive. As compensation for the territories, the United States would pay the nations who had lost them a lump sum of $50,000 and an annuity of $10,000. If in the future the United States required more land for its citizens, it would bargain honestly and pay liberally for it.

The Shawnee, with Alexander McKee acting as a translator and adviser, took the lead in framing a response to these proposals. After two weeks of discussions, representatives of sixteen nations (including the Cherokee and Creek) attending the council agreed to the formal answer. It was delivered to Lincoln, Pickering, and Randolph on August 15. In regard to the admission that the United States had been mistaken in treating the Indians as British subjects, the Council replied contemptuously:

> You agreed to do us justice, after having long, and injuriously, withheld it. We mean in the acknowledgment you now have made, that the King of England never did, nor ever had a right to give you our Country, by the Treaty of peace, and you want to make this act of Common Justice a great part of your concessions, and seem to expect that, because you have at last acknowledged our independence, we should for such a favor surrender to you our country.

There is a sense that Alexander McKee or somebody else familiar with European legal principles may have helped considerably with this passage. But another taunting, ironic statement was very Shawnee in style and substance.

> Money, to us is of no value . . . and as no consideration whatever can induce us to sell the lands on which we get sustenance for our women and children; we hope we may be allowed to point out a mode by which your settlers may be easily removed, and peace thereby obtained. . . . We know these settlers are poor, or they would never have ventured to live in a country which has been in continued trouble ever since they crossed the Ohio; divide, therefore, this large sum of

money, which you have offered to us, among these people . . . and we are persuaded, they would most readily accept of it, in lieu of the lands you sold them. . . . If you add also, the great sums you must expend in raising and paying Armies, with a view to force us to yield you our Country, you will certainly have more than sufficient for the purposes of repaying these settlers for all their labor and improvements.

After receiving the message from the council the Americans sent back a terse answer: that there was no point in continuing the talks. They added, "We sincerely regret, that peace is not the result; but knowing the upright and liberal views of the United States, which, as far as you gave us an opportunity, we have explained to you, we trust that impartial judges will not attribute the continuance of the war to them."

The commissioners may have been disappointed with the mission, but their superiors in Philadelphia seem to have been satisfied. There is much evidence that the peace offensive was something less than genuine, was conceived as a public relations exercise which would permit the United States, as a matter of diplomatic and historic record, to go to war as an "upright and liberal nation." Thomas Jefferson put the matter succinctly, remarking that the negotiations of the summer had been undertaken only "to prove to all our citizens that peace was unattainable on terms which any of them would admit."

Lincoln, Pickering, and Randolph had instructions to conclude the business with the Indians no later than the first of August, so as to give General Wayne three good camapigning months in 1793. Unable to deal directly with the savages, they had failed to meet this deadline. Not until the end of August were the commissioners able to send off a coded note, "We did not effect peace." As had been previously agreed to by Henry Knox, this message was an order to Wayne to commence "vigorous offensive action."

Couriers (including an Iroquois chief, Big Tree, hired by the Americans as a secret agent) bringing the news that the peace talks had ended did not reach Wayne at Hobson's Choice until September 11. He immediately commenced moving the Legion into the field, hell-bent on getting at the hostiles. As it turned out, he was prevented from doing so for almost a year by unforeseen happenings that enraged him at the time but in retrospect may have saved Wayne from making his one serious mistake on the frontier— ignoring his own studied opinion that the fall of the year was the worst possible time for a white army to try to catch or fight Indians.

Earlier in the summer Wayne had arranged, so he thought, to make Fort Jefferson, the most advanced American post built by St. Clair, into a major supply depot. His plan was that the Legion, unencumbered by slow baggage trains, would march to Fort Jefferson, pick up provisions there, and move on quickly to the Indian villages on the Maumee. When he arrived at the post, Wayne was astonished to find that only a quarter of the supplies had been delivered as ordered and was furious that he had not been told of this deficiency. In part the blame lay with corrupt, incompetent civilian contractors who continually plagued Wayne as they had his predecessors. Also, although it was not understood until much later, he had another unique and serious problem. A cabal of his officers with his second in command, Brig. James Wilkinson, as the ringleader, had intentionally sabotaged the supply services. Their hope was that a military debacle, or at least scandal, would result and embarrass Wayne.

James Wilkinson was a brilliant, seemingly reflexive conniver whose "influence everyone felt," remarked Humphrey Marshall, a contemporary Kentucky politician, but "which none would suspect or scrutinize." Wilkinson was already a secret agent in the pay of Spain and possibly the British. (These connections later led to the so-called conspiracy of Aaron Burr to detach the western territories from the United States.) In 1793 he was mainly scheming to get rid of and succeed Anthony Wayne, whose job as the commander of the U.S. Army he coveted, since it would further some of his commercial and espionage ventures. As Marshall indicated, Wilkinson was a master at covering his tracks, and in this case surreptitiously inveigled other bolder but less subtle officers into vilifying Wayne to the Congress and in the press as a brutal, slothful, dissolute tyrant. Meddling—or having others meddle—with the supply services was one of many subplots aimed at providing evidence that Wayne was stupid and unfit. That this particular game caused considerable hardships to soldiers of the Legion was of no concern to Wilkinson, who throughout his tangled career was consistently loyal only to himself. "He was," wrote the distinguished chronicler of the period Frederick Jackson Turner, "the most consummate artist in treason that the nation ever possessed." Marshall and Turner fairly represent the consensus of both Wilkinson's contemporaries and subsequent historians.

Ironically, the breakdown of the Legion's supply system had an opposite effect from the one Wilkinson intended. Such was Wayne's impatience that, had Fort Jefferson been provisioned as ordered, he would certainly have tried to campaign that fall as Harmar and St. Clair had. But because of Wilkinson, the supplies were not there, and Wayne came to his senses, giving up the idea of fighting in the cold November jungle with freezing, starving troops.

While waiting for a better season, Wayne occupied himself during the winter of 1793–94 by trying to solve his supply problems and advancing the line of American forts closer to the Maumee villages. Finding the location or facilities at Fort Jefferson inadequate, he built a new camp, Greenville, six miles to the north, on the location of the present Ohio town of the same name. In December, apparently bored by garrison life, Wayne rose from a sickbed—he was troubled by both gout and influenza—to lead eight companies of Legionnaires and some artillerymen on a winter march to the site of St. Clair's defeat on the Wabash river, twenty miles north of Greenville. Some more bones, the fleshless remains of St. Clair's soldiers, were found and buried. Thereafter Wayne put his men to work building still another fort, which he named Recovery. It consisted of four blockhouses connected with a fifteen-foot-high palisade around which the Legionnaires dug a six-foot trench in the frozen ground. To provide a clear field of fire the trees standing within a thousand yards of the fort were felled and burned. During the work, three of the artillery pieces that the victorious Indians had taken from St. Clair and cached on the site were found. These guns, cleaned and remounted, were used to give Wayne a nine-volley salute when he returned to Greenville on the last day of 1793. A 150-man garrison was left at the new Fort Recovery, which as the crow flies was only ninety miles south of the principal Miami and Shawnee villages.

Many of the warriors who attended the summer council on the Maumee remained there, and others who had left early returned as Wayne began to move the Legion north. They anticipated that he would do what other American generals had done—come against them in the fall—and that they would be able to treat him as they had the others. The war chiefs were perplexed and disappointed when Wayne halted and put his men behind stockade walls for the winter. Several moderately successful, probing raids were made against the Legion's supply lines. Had it been continued, this sort of work might have done considerable damage, for by then the string of forts which had to be provisioned by the Americans extended for 100 miles north of the Ohio. However, when it became apparent that no grand battles would be fought that fall or winter, many of the Indians left the Maumee Valley.

By then the allied nations had maintained more than a thousand warriors in the field for about six months, including the time they spent at the summer's peace council. During the period the men had done little hunting or otherwise produced income for their people. The British and to some extent their Shawnee and Miami hosts had supported the red army, but by late fall, rations were generally short. Also the force was a polygot one, made up of units from many nations who were at least as different from one another as were the French and British. After having been together for much of 1793 without the excitement of war, international prejudices and disagreements of ancient origin had begun to surface. Hungry, bored by waiting on Wayne, tired of putting up with foreigners, anxious to make their winter hunts, nearly all of the men from the west and Great Lakes had gone home to their families by the end of 1793. These defections verified Wayne's assessment that Indians were not politically or economically able to fight long wars.

On the Maumee the remaining Miami and Shawnee pondered the new tactics of the Americans and commenced to have doubts about their prospects for winning another quick victory. Events of the fall had demonstrated that Wayne's Legion was not such a slow, stupid thing as those of Harmar and St. Clair had been. On the move it covered a good ten miles or so a day. It was difficult to weaken or confuse this army by nipping at its flanks or tail, which were protected like those of an immense porcupine or armored reptile. The Legionnaires routinely put up log breastworks around their bivouacs and posted numerous, alert guards. Beyond the picket lines there was always a screen of woodsmen nearly as skillful as the warriors. Determined not to suffer as Harmar and St. Clair had for the lack of good intelligence, Wayne recruited a cadre of civilian scouts, spies, and informers. Some were veteran hunters and rangers like Robert McClelland against whom Tekamthi had fought. Others were men who had lived with the savages but had defected from them, as had William Wells, the son-in-law of Little Turtle. Wayne also had some birthright Indians of his own, a contingent of sixty Chickasaws who, as ancient enemies of the Shawnee, willingly came north to work for the Americans.

One frustrated Shawnee veteran said it had become hard "to steal even one horse" from the Americans, much less kill their guards or stragglers. Frustrated by this new enemy, the warriors began to speak of Wayne as Sukachgook—the Black Snake, naming him for an animal whose guile and wariness impressed them.

So far as frontier affairs were concerned, the most important happening of the winter of 1793 occurred not in Ohio, where Wayne, Little Turtle, and Blue Jacket waited for better weather, but in Quebec. There on February 10, Lord Dorchester delivered a remarkable speech to a delegation of Iroquois and other St. Lawrence—area Indians. At some length he berated the United States as a greedy, untrustworthy nation, which had persistently encroached on Indian lands and threatened British interests in the Northwest. The governor of Canada concluded with a stunning comment, that it might soon be necessary for His Majesty's Government to teach the insolent Americans a hard lesson, and "I shall not be surprized if we are at war with them in the course of the present year."

Dorchester's provocative statement had not been authorized by his superiors in London and did not reflect their views. (Eventually he was reprimanded but such were communications then that the rebuke was not received until five months later, well after the damage from the speech had been done.) It appears that Dorchester said what he did because he was personally irritated by the United States: for bringing Wayne's army so close to British posts, for the pro-French sentiments of many of its politicians, and because of disputes between the two nations about maritime rights. If he spoke in a fit of pique, it was one which lasted for some time. After giving the speech he directed his lieutenant governor, John Simcoe, to have Indian agents circulate it among the Miami, Shawnee, and their allies. Then to emphasize the belligerent words, he ordered Simcoe to build, garrison, and find artillery for a new British fort near the rapids of the Maumee, on the southwestern outskirts of the present Toledo, Ohio.

The effect of this on British—U.S.—Indian relations was somewhat like throwing grease on a fire, since the natives, both red and white, assumed that Dorchester, as its highest ranking North American representative, was speaking for his government. Among other things, he had said that when war came, as he thought it would, boundary lines in the Northwest "must then be drawn by the Warriors." The Indians were thus naturally encouraged to believe that, if they needed them, they would not only be given supplies but soldiers and artillery by the English king—in short, that the good old days of the Revolution were about to return. In the United States public and political opinion was outraged by what Dorchester had said and particularly by what he did, since the fort on the Maumee, called Miamis, was the first the British had built in the region in more than a decade. The pro-French position of Thomas Jefferson and his Democrats was strengthened. Peace advocates were confounded, and the military preparations of the Washington administration suddenly became popular.

As for Anthony Wayne, Dorchester's outburst did not much

surprise or alarm him. Rather it confirmed his long-standing view that British and Indian problems were all of one piece. If he could thrash the savages, the British, having no substantial military forces of their own in the area, would have to abandon the Northwest. If they were no longer there to agitate and supply the Indians, the warriors could not continue to fight. From Wayne's standpoint, Dorchester's belligerent behavior relieved him of any obligation to pussyfoot with the redcoats. If they got in his way as he was going after Indians, he was confident that it was his Legion which would teach the hard lessons.

Wayne hoped to start north with the army no later than April 15, 1794. However, on this date he was still at his headquarters in Greenville, fighting not Indians but civilian suppliers and—though he had yet to identify him as a principal enemy—Brig. Gen. James Wilkinson. As the delays lenthened, Wayne's temper shortened. At one point he sent troops back to Cincinnati to commandeer military stores from haggling contractors, saying that, "I will no longer be imposed upon or trifled with, nor shall the army be starved to death." Even so, the spring passed and summer commenced as Wayne struggled to stockpile sufficient supplies at his forward bases so that he could use them as a springboard for his attack.

The reports of their scouts made it apparent to the war chiefs on the Maumee that sooner or later the Black Snake would strike. They decided to throw him off balance by making the first move. In May the call for allies went out, and warriors from the north and west again began gathering in the Miami and Shawnee communities. Convinced that there was little they could do to the Americans so long as they remained holed up in their forts, Little Turtle and Blue Jacket concluded that the most promising plan was to try to cut the supply lines of the strung-out Legion. The hope was that, so harassed, Wayne would have to use many of his soldiers to defend the roads and baggage trains. Drawn out from the forts, enough of these escorts could be ambushed to halt the American advance and perhaps to send the Black Snake slithering home. In principle the tactics were sound, but they were not practiced in the field.

Late in June, Blue Jacket, with Tekamthi at his side, came south from the Maumee with about 1,200 allied warriors. The first objective was to blockade and isolate Fort Recovery, Wayne's most forward position. Matthew Elliott, the British agent, went with them and noted that, though he had contributed 300 bushels of corn to the expedition, the Indian army was very short of food and depended chiefly on its hunters, who were bringing in about 200 deer and an equal number of turkeys each day. The observation is instructive in regard to a fundamental aspect of red-white warfare. Having to carry everything it needed, Wayne's army was slow to get into the field and, once there, not very agile. On the other hand, the wealth of the Americans was such that the Legion could campaign indefinitely—or at least as long as it pleased the President, Congress, and taxpayers—if it protected and did not get too far away from its supply trains. Blue Jacket's warriors were able, in fact had, to move quickly because their 400-a-day deer/turkey supply system did not allow them to occupy or fight in one place for long.

On the afternoon of June 29, a pack train, escorted by 140 Legionnaires, arrived at Fort Recovery carrying 1,200 barrels of flour. A few hours later the first of Blue Jacket's men moved into the woods near the post. They were observed by a Chickasaw scout, who raced back to the fort with this intelligence. However, the man had very little English. Capt. Alexander Gibson, the Legion officer in command, did not have a Chickasaw interpreter and apparently did not understand sign. Therefore the scout's work served no purpose.

The next morning while the escorts were finishing breakfast, the pack animals and herders started down the road, returning to Greenville. A mile beyond the stockade they were attacked, the horses stampeded and the drovers killed by a small party of Indian scouts. Immediately fifty dragoons galloped out of the fort to the rescue and into an ambush arranged by Blue Jacket. They fled, running into 100 infantrymen coming to their aid. Before the Legionnaires could get back inside the stockade, about half of them were killed.

At this point, Blue Jacket and Tekamthi tried to draw off the warriors on grounds that, having done what they had come to do, they should continue south looking for more opportunities along the supply roads. The Ottawa and others from the Great Lakes (who made up more than half of the army) objected. Elated by this first easy action, they were determined to capture Fort Recovery. Blue Jacket argued that this was foolish and contrary to what had been planned. The Ottawa were not convinced and began to storm the palisade walls. Reluctantly, the Shawnee followed them. Using the artillery recovered from where the Indians had cached it after St. Clair's defeat, the garrison beat off the attack, killing twenty or thirty of the exposed warriors. By nightfall the Ottawa had had enough. The next morning, charging that the Shawnee had failed to support them vigorously, they left for home, taking along many other men from the Great Lakes. (Another characteristic of the hit-and-run style of the Indians was that they tended to be easily discouraged by rather small—according to white military standards—setbacks. Actions which began badly were often abandoned as ill-omened, a belief which reflected the fact that it was difficult for them to hang on in one place and eat.)

Blue Jacket was left with only about 400 warriors, insufficient, he thought, for raiding further south against the Americans. Returning home, the Shawnee found that some of their women farmers had been robbed and several raped by the Lakes Indians who had passed through the Auglaize villages on their way north. This was the first time during the long, brutal war that any warriors were accused by others of this crime.

During the next several weeks, cooler heads prevailed. Emissaries were dispatched, gifts were exchanged, and apologies of a sort made. By the end of July war parties, which had retired after the failure at Fort Recovery, began to return to the Maumee, where they and the Shawnee agreed to suspend the quarrel and continue joint operations. While the alliance was being patched up, Little Turtle made a visit to the military commander at Detroit, Col. Richard England, to find out exactly how, after all of their fine talk of the winter, the British planned to help the Indians against the Black Snake.

Specifically, the Miami war chief wanted twenty British regulars and two pieces of field artillery, with which he thought it might still be possible to take Fort Recovery and greatly delay or halt Wayne's invasion. Colonel England, who said Little Turtle was the "most decent, modest, sensible Indian" he had ever met, listened sympathetically but was evasive about lending soldiers or cannon. Reporting on the meeting, he assured Lt. Gov. John Simcoe, "I of course talked him over for two or three days and dismissed him seemingly contented." (By then Dorchester, Simcoe, and other Canadian officials had given thought to their own weak military position and to their standing orders from London—which were to keep the natives restless without getting drawn directly into their wars—and had become less truculent than they had been in the winter.)

Colonel England was mistaken in thinking that Little Turtle was "contented" with their talks. To the contrary, he left Detroit convinced that the British were neither able nor inclined to give genuine military assistance. Therefore when Wayne finally started his Legion marching north, Little Turtle advised that it would be impossible to defend the open villages along the Maumee and Auglaize. Miami and Shawnee noncombatants began evacuating their farms and homes.

The American army—2,200 regular infantry and 1,500 militia cavalry from Kentucky—arrived at Fort Recovery on July 28 and picked up supplies at the post. The next day, engineers laying road and throwing up bridges in front of them, the Legionnaires advanced to the headwaters of the St. Mary's River, where they paused for two days to build another fort, Adams. During its construction Wayne was very nearly killed when timber cutters felled a great beech tree so close to him that the branches knocked him to the ground. He was badly bruised and, for several days, suffered from internal bleeding. Later, Wayne became convinced that this had been no accident but was rather an attempt on his life arranged by James Wilkinson. As with so many others, he could not prove these suspicions but, Wilkinson being what he was, they were not necessarily paranoid ones.

Leaving Fort Adams, the Legion reached the upper Auglaize River and on August 8 marched down it through what had been the heartland of the Shawnee nation.

> This place far excels in beauty any in the western country, and believed equalled by none in the Atlantic States [observed a journal-keeping trooper]. Here are vegetables of every kind in abundance, and we have marched four or five miles in cornfields down the Oglaize and there are not less than 1000 acres of corn round the town. The land in general of the fair nature . . . and the river navigable, not more than sixty miles from Lake Erie.

Trampling the crops, burning deserted cabins, the Legionnaires came to the abandoned Shawnee–Miami community at the confluence of the Auglaize and Maumee, which Wayne called "the grand emporium of the hostile Indians of the West." There, as was their standard practice, the Americans built a fort, Defiance, and settled down for a week to see what the warriors would do next. Though increasingly gouty and still aching from being brushed by the falling tree, Wayne was in an optimistic mood, convinced, as he explained to his officers, that the west was already won. If the Indians did not fight, they would have to change their life-style or leave the country, which was now studded from the Ohio River almost to the Great Lakes with well-garrisoned forts. If they chose to fight, Wayne was certain the Legion would overwhelm them.

Downstream from Fort Defiance where the allied warriors, then some 1,500 strong, were discussing their plans, Little Turtle was saying much the same: that to meet Wayne in open battle without substantial British assistance would be very foolish. He warned the council:

> We have beaten the enemy twice under different commanders. We cannot expect the same good fortune to attend us

always. The Americans are now led by a chief who never sleeps. The night and the days are alike to him, and during all the time that he has been marching on our villages, notwithstanding the watchfulness of our young men, we have never been able to surprise him. Think well of it. There is something whispers to me it would be prudent to listen to his offers of peace.

These were not words the warriors wanted to hear. Responding, Blue Jacket, supported by Tekamthi and the other young fighting men, asked if his old comrade, the Little Turtle, had listened too much to the lies of the Americans? Had he become a coward? Blue Jacket pledged that if the braves were resolute, they could defend their lands, women, and children, scotch the Black Snake, and force him to leave a bloody trail behind as he writhed out of Ohio. Turkey Foot, the Ottawa war chief, and other speakers from the Lakes nations expressed similar views. Then Little Turtle spoke again with great dignity, saying that he had "heard the words of the Ottawas, Potawatomis, and Shawnees. They are young men and their arms are strong." As for himself, said Little Turtle, he was now an old man waiting for the Great Spirit to take him. If the young men wanted to fight once more, he would go into battle with them, but not as an allied commander, only as a leader of his own Miami, who by then could muster only about 250 warriors.

Little Turtle's resignation was accepted, and Blue Jacket became the ranking war chief of the Indian army, thus ending the long and successful partnership between the Miami and Shawnee leaders. Formally they had been coequals, but their abilities were quite different. Blue Jacket, a traditional push-ahead, blood-and-guts warrior, was a terror in battle and a great inspiration to his men. In this regard he served Little Turtle, the planner and diplomat of the red coalition, somewhat as George Patton would serve Dwight Eisenhower.

Blue Jacket, the tactician, was immediately concerned with where to fight—not, as the strategist Little Turtle had been, with the question of whether to fight. After learning from his scouts that Wayne had left Fort Defiance and was marching down the north bank of the Maumee, Blue Jacket moved his army to intercept the Americans at what he considered a good battle site. It was located opposite the head of the Maumee rapids in an area cut by sharp ravines and littered with trees which had been blown down by a tornado. Not only was the terrain and cover favorable, but Fallen Timbers, as the place came to be remembered, was only five miles upstream from Fort Miamis. Blue Jacket reasoned that if a retreat became necessary, his warriors could find protection under the big guns of the British post, which Alexander McKee, still wanting a war, had led him to believe had been built for this specific purpose. To further encourage Blue Jacket, whom he regarded as a less astute but more manageable Indian than Little Turtle, McKee brought to the council seventy white Canadian militiamen led by his long-time deputy, William Caldwell. McKee suggested that this unit, which was in fact a paramilitary one raised by the Indian service, gave tangible proof that the English King intended to stand by his red friends. Blue Jacket accepted the Canadians' and McKee's explanations without asking, as Little Turtle might have, why, if they were there as a formal token of British support, were Caldwell's rangers dressed and painted to look like Indians.

Blue Jacket's men were already at Fallen Timbers when, on August 17, Wayne brought up the Legion and halted it several miles west of the Indian position. Surprise was no longer a factor, scouts having kept each commander well informed about what his opponent was doing. Wayne waited for two days and built his last fort, one called Deposit, at which he cached all the baggage not needed in combat. On the evening of the nineteenth, he ordered the Legionnaires to be ready to go into the woods against the savages at dawn the next day. Whether by design or accident, the delay at Fort Deposit gave the Americans an important advantage. Traditionally, the Shawnee and warriors from many of the allied nations did not eat on the day before a battle. The notion was that a little hunger sharpened their wits and reflexes and improved their courage. Having expected to fight on the eighteenth, they entered Fallen Timbers on the seventeenth without rations and, because of the proximity of the Americans, had had to wait there. By the morning of the twentieth, they had fasted for nearly three days. A few of the less self-controlled warriors slipped away looking for food, and many of those who remained in position were weak and giddy from hunger.

The red army was hidden in the woods about a mile inland from the Maumee, parallel to the shoreline trail, which provided Wayne with the only good passage into Fallen Timbers. Blue Jacket arranged his men in a favorite Indian formation, the one which had worked so well against St. Clair, a long half-moon-shaped line. In the center were the Ottawa, Potawatomi, and men from the other Great Lakes nations. Along the left horn of the arc were the Miami and Delaware; on the right, in a swampy area between two small ponds, were Caldwell's Canadian partisans disguised as Indians, the Wyandot, and Blue Jacket's own Shawnee with Tekamthi as, in white terms, a company commander.

The Indian center faced a small open meadow, through which it logically seemed Wayne would try to force his way into the woods. It was Blue Jacket's hope that there the warriors from the Lakes nations would engage the Americans and draw them further into the trees. When they were well within the semicircle, his trusted veterans would charge their flanks, divide the Legion, and cut down its forward units in the heavy underbrush. Wayne did as Blue Jacket anticipated, but the Ottawa did not.

The early morning of August 20 was very rainy, and the Legionnaires were slow getting started but by 9 A.M. they were in position, facing Fallen Timbers with their backs against the river. Wayne knew that there were Indians waiting in the jungle ahead but not exactly where they were deployed. However, it seems that by then he did not much care. Having grown tired of cautious preparations, he simply wanted to have at the savages. He drew up his four regiments, two commanded by Wilkinson, two by Col. John Hamtramck, and sent them toward the woods. They were preceded by 150 militia cavalrymen from Kentucky.

At this point the course of the battle was altered by the bold but unruly Ottawa. Rather than wait for the Americans to come to them, as Blue Jacket had directed, their warriors, just as the cavalrymen entered the meadow, burst out of their hiding place and charged across the clearing in a howling attack. With the Lakes Indians all about them, the cavalry and then the front infantry lines began to flee in panic and confusion. For a few chaotic moments there was a distinct possibility that another American army would be annihilated. But this did not happen because during the previous two years the Legionnaires had been changed from civilians into soldiers by the Black Snake. In a kind of déjà vu incident, Wayne, limping on gouty legs, had to be boosted onto his horse. Thereafter he remained in the saddle and in control of his army. Pushing into the milling men, he bellowed at his officers to remember their standing orders to shoot any soldier who started to run from the hostiles. Several of these executions and Wayne's wrath were enough to halt the retreat. The Legionnaires re-formed their front lines sufficiently to halt the Ottawa charge. These warriors paused to consider what to do next, but they had advanced so far that they were out of touch with their allies on the left and right. Because of this gap left by the Ottawas, Blue Jacket's original line was broken into three separate segments. The location of each became known to the Americans as warriors on the flanks, not understanding what the Ottawa were doing, commenced firing.

Wayne firmly believed that the Indians were most dangerous when attacking, far less so on the defensive. He ordered Wilkinson and Hamtramck to form their regiments into tight double columns and immediately go on the attack to take advantage of the enemy's confusion. Wilkinson either did not receive—as he later claimed— or more likely ignored the order and held back his regiments so as to protect against another ambush. Hamtramck moved ahead smartly with Wayne himself in the midst of the Legionnaires. Fearing that his excited general would get himself killed, his aide, William Henry Harrison, tried to distract him by asking what further orders he should pass along to Hamtramck. "Charge the damned rascals with the bayonet," screamed Mad Anthony.

The Legionnaires did. Their hatchets proving inferior to the bayonets of the tightly ranked Americans, the Ottawa fell back. Turkey Foot, their war chief, stood on an outcrop and tried to rally them, shouting that if they were brave, the Great Spirit would favor their cause. An American sharpshooter felled Turkey Foot who sang his death song and died at the base of the rock. Belatedly Wilkinson's regiments joined those of Hamtramck, and the Legionnaires began an encircling movement of their own. Unable to recover Turkey Foot's body, the Ottawa broke and fled, taking with them most of the other warriors on the Indian left. "We could not stand against the sharp end of their guns," said Kinjoino, an Ottawa chief of the second rank, "and we ran to the river, swamps, thickets, and to the islands in the river covered with corn. Our moccasins trickled blood in the sand, and the water was red in the river."

Blue Jacket might have suffered a defeat comparable to the one he had inflicted on St. Clair had not Caldwell's Canadians, the Wyandot, and the Shawnee on the right fought stubbornly and slowed down the Americans. Positioned on the extreme end of the original line, Tekamthi and his warriors were among the first to engage Hamtramck's men. They held their ground against the first American assault but were flushed out from behind the logs by succeeding waves of Legionnaires. His own gun having failed, Tekamthi picked up a "fowling piece," collected some Shawnee stragglers, and organized a second stand in a dense thicket. There, his eldest surviving brother, Sauwauseekau, was killed. Tekamthi held his warriors together until they were surrounded by Americans and then made a last desperate counterattack which enabled his rear guard to cut through and escape from Hamtramck's Legionnaires.

The fighting at Fallen Timbers, from the time the Ottawa made their first untimely charge until Tekamthi and the last of the warriors were driven from the woods, lasted only about an hour. In comparison to those of Harmar and St. Clair the casualties were light. Of the Americans thirty-one were killed and 100 or so were wounded. Indian losses were probably greater but only forty of their dead and severely wounded were actually counted. Despite being the only clear-cut American victory in the first twenty years of the wars, the battle itself was less important, so far as the next twenty years were concerned, than what happened in the few hours immediately following it.

Blue Jacket and the other surviving chiefs and warriors ran in bloody moccasins from Fallen Timbers to Fort Miamis, where they expected to find sanctuary. Contrary to the promises of Alexander McKee, the commandant there, a Capt. William Campbell, had explicit orders that he was to defend his post against the natives, either red or white, but otherwise not get involved with them. Campbell did as directed. When the first of the Indians approached the British fort, he barred its gates against them and had his men stand by their guns in case any of the savages should try to get in over the palisades. For a time the warriors milled about outside Fort Miamis. Then Tekamthi and others of the rear guard appeared and reported that the Americans were coming. The warriors ran on down the Maumee, convinced that Little Turtle had been right in saying that it was foolish to count on the British.

During the afternoon the Americans arrived and formed up just beyond the gates of Fort Miamis. There, gleefully, as one of the Legionnaires recalled, "We beat our drums. Blowed our trumpets." The next morning Campbell sent a messenger to Wayne asking what these men were doing prancing about "almost within reach of the Guns of this Fort, being a Post belonging to His Majesty, the King of Great Britain."

Wayne answered that he was there, on what was legally American territory, to make certain that no savages were lurking about the premises. He added with heavy sarcasm that had he found any, "the post and Guns you mention—they would not have much impeded the progress of the Victorious Army under my command. . . ."

Wayne and Campbell spent the next two days lobbing insults at each other, but both realized they could easily start a war between their two countries and avoided getting into a shooting match. On the morning of August 23, the Legion of the United States paraded in front of Fort Miamis, then turned around and started back up the Maumee. The Americans followed the river, destroying Indian farms and dwellings that they had missed on the way down, until they came to Kekionga, the Glorious Gate of the Miami. There they built a permanent fort to serve as an administrative headquarters for the newly occupied territory and named it for Wayne.

On the second day of the march up the Maumee valley, the Legionnaires found eight warriors hanging around one of their camps looking for food. One of them was killed and scalped, the others ran off. Beyond this, nothing was seen of the Indians. Writing to his son Isaac, Wayne speculated that their mood "must naturally be gloomy and unpleasant." It was.

. By the middle of September, more than 2,500 Indians, defeated and wounded warriors along with their families who had fled from their villages in front of the Black Snake, gathered along the swampy eastern shore of Lake Erie between the mouth of the Maumee and the River Raisin. There they survived, barely and badly, largely because of the efforts of Alexander McKee and Matthew Elliott. Despite their self-serving attempts to manipulate the Indians, these veteran British agents had many relatives and friends among these people. To their credit they did not abandon them after Fallen Timbers. McKee, particularly, was a skillful bureaucratic infighter. He badgered Canadian civilian and military officials (most of whom had suddenly become very uninterested in the affairs of savages) to provide food, clothing, and shelter for the refugees.

Since Blue Jacket and the other Shawnee went to the Lake Erie camps, presumedly Tekamthi did likewise, and there was reunited with those who were left among his family and friends. However, after fighting his way out of Fallen Timbers and being turned away from Fort Miamis he disappeared, so far as records or even tales go, until early the next spring. He turned up in the Scioto River valley of southern Ohio near where he had spent his early boyhood in the secure years before his father was killed at Point Pleasant. With him was a young woman, Mamate (who though she had a white father was said to be one of the most beautiful of Shawnee women), his younger brother Lalawethika, also with a wife, and a dozen or so other Shawnee whose names and circumstances are no longer remembered.

IX. We Shall All Be Americans

During the fall of 1794 the Indian refugees in the camps along Lake Erie took what aid Alexander McKee and other Canadians could give. But the memory of Fort Miamis being closed against them was fresh, and they rejected suggestions that they regroup and try to go on fighting the Americans. Among the Shawnee there was some talk about migrating to Missouri or farther and obtaining Spanish supplies and munitions. These vague plans were abandoned after American agents circulated among them bringing an offer from Anthony Wayne—that if they laid down their arms, they could return to Ohio.

In January of 1795 Blue Jacket, with an escort of fifty warriors, traveled to Wayne's headquarters at Greenville. The Shawnee war chief told the Black Snake that his heart and those of his people had changed; that they wanted to make an immediate truce and would return in the summer to negotiate a permanent peace treaty. Emissaries from other nations came in and gave similar pledges. When the ground thawed, refugees began to return to Ohio where, though not molested, they were carefully watched by federal troops. The Miami resettled in the vicinity of old Kekionga and the new Fort Wayne. Most of the Shawnee followed Black Hoof, by then their principal civil chief, to the upper Auglaize River. Above Fort Defiance they built Wapekoneta, the main community in a complex of settlements which were sometimes called the Tawa villages.

After the planting season 1,100 chiefs and warriors from the nations of the defeated coalition went to Greenville to receive Wayne's peace terms. As the Indians were gathering, they heard that late in the previous year, the English and Americans had signed their own treaty in London. In regard to the frontier, the critical provision of it was that the British agreed to evacuate, by 1796, Detroit and the other posts in the Northwest and to retire peacefully to Ontario. Many other issues were considered at the London talks, and by no means all of them were resolved. However, John Jay, the special American envoy, found that even before Fallen Timbers, the British were agreeable to drawing back in the Northwest. An underlying reason for this was that after more than a century of overharvesting the wild animals, the fur trade was petering out in this area and shifting to virgin lands west and north of the Mississippi. By 1794 accountants calculated that the Canadian-based fur trade was bringing in some £200,000 a year, a very tidy sum. But only about £40,000 of the business was generated in the Ohio, Indiana, and Michigan country. In consequence there was no compelling reason for the British government to go on deferring to the traders left in this area or to continue to pay for maintaining the posts and extensive network of Indian agents which served them.

The grand council at Greenville was organized and catered by the Americans who provided the victuals, small gifts, and gaudy souvenir medals as party favors. Whiskey, rum, and wine flowed so that, as Wayne said, "We will on this happy occasion, be merry, but without passing the bounds of temperance and sobriety."

Wayne was not a reflexive Indian hater, but he kept his Legionnaires on the alert to impress his guests and restrain any of them who might be inclined to violence. Otherwise the chiefs and warriors were treated respectfully as brave but defeated men. However, the United States government did not conceive of the Greenville council as an occasion for serious negotiations. Rather it was convened to remind the savages, ceremonially, that during the previous year they had been beaten at Fallen Timbers, their lands had been occupied, and they had been abandoned by the British. The red delegates were well aware of these realities. Speaking to the point of whether agreements made at Greenville would be respected thereafter, a pragmatic Potawatomi chief remarked, "You may depend on our sincerity. We cannot be but sincere, as your forts are planted thick among us."

Nevertheless the western natives continued to worry and, to some extent, frighten the Americans. Despite Jay's treaty the Washington administration remained suspicious about the intentions of the British in the Northwest. A particular concern was that, if large numbers of Indians found the American peace terms too harsh, they might relocate in Canada and there be used by Alexander McKee and his agents in guerrilla actions against Americans. In consequence United States officials wanted what was left of the savages to remain within their territories, so as to keep them under surveillance and out of the clutches of the British. On the other hand Americans did not want to go on fighting the western nations or to conduct police actions against small bands of unsubdued warriors. Wayne had demonstrated how the savages could be beaten—by keeping a sizable professional army in the field for several years—but also how expensive this method was. Even as the Greenville council was proceeding, the Legion of the United States was being disbanded because the President, Congress, and taxpayers did not feel they could afford it any longer.

With these considerations in mind, Timothy Pickering (the peace commissioner of 1793 who in 1795 succeeded Henry Knox as the Secretary of War) sent Wayne his instructions for the Greenville council. He should obtain title to most of the Ohio country but should not press so hard that the savages became belligerent or British. "*Peace* and not *increase* of *territory* has been the object of this expensive War," he cautioned his general.

Pickering, an astute entrepreneur, understood that being somewhat magnanimous in territorial demands was economically as well as politically advantageous. The sale of western lands was a principal source of income for the United States government, as speculating in them was for many good Federalist supporters of the administration. If Wayne were to obtain enormous tracts from the Indians, this sudden new supply of land would depress property values throughout the west and be bad for the business of many public and private real-estate agents. Pickering recognized that eastern and southern Ohio would shortly be sold and settled, thus creating demands for new lands to the west but, as he pointed out in his dispatch to Wayne, when this time came, arrangements made at Greenville would be revised so as to acquire more Indian territories.

In short, the victory at Fallen Timbers and the withdrawal of the British allowed the United States government to return to the conciliatory policy of the 1780s, i.e., depending on the advancing tide of white settlement to dislodge the Indians. Pickering was a strong advocate of this cheap, natural approach and succinctly explained why:

> At any future period, Indians having no ideas of wealth, and
> their numbers always lessening in the neighborhood of our

Settlements, their claims for compensations will likewise be diminished; and besides that, fewer will remain to be gratified, the game will be greatly reduced, and lands destitute of game will, by hunters, be lightly esteemed.

For the moment, Wayne's mission was to get enough good land in Ohio to satisfy the immediate needs of the pioneer classes but at the same time to stroke the Indians a bit so that they would leave the council in a pacific frame of mind. Therefore the central provision of the treaty offered at Greenville called for a firm boundary, dividing in perpetuity, the Indians were led to believe, their lands from those of the whites. This line ran up the Cuyahoga River from Lake Erie (Cleveland) south for about fifty miles. Near what is now Canton, it made a right angle turn to the west to Fort Recovery, then veered southwest taking in a sliver of eastern Indiana and striking the Ohio River opposite the mouth of the Kentucky.

Everything south and east of this boundary—that is, about two thirds of the present state of Ohio plus the slice of Indiana—would henceforth be the exclusive property of the Americans. North of the boundary to the Canadian border and west for an indefinite distance was to be Indian country, but with some important reservations. The United States retained the military posts it already held west of the Greenville line at Fort Wayne and elsewhere, and those such as Detroit which it would shortly get from the British. Americans had the right to establish new bases at the southern tip of Lake Michigan (Fort Dearborn) and in other strategic locations. The Indians must allow the Americans to pass freely through their lands to these posts, build connecting roads, control fords and portages. In addition, west of the boundary in Indiana and Illinois, four tracts each of several hundred thousand acres were set aside for white use.

The United States promised that, aside from these reserved sections, it would attempt to keep its citizens out of the Indian country. Federal agents would also license and try to control traders doing business with the natives. (In accordance with the agreement made by John Jay in London, British–Canadian fur buyers were permitted to go on trading in the United States territories of the Northwest.) A minor clause of the Greenville treaty directed the Indians to return all "prisoners," but this exchange was a voluntary one. Whites who had been living with the natives were free to go on doing so if they chose. Many found the prospect of remaining with their defeated, adopted people unattractive and took the opportunity to rejoin white society. Among those who came into Wayne's headquarters from the woods were Stephen and Abraham Ruddell. Abraham, while with the Shawnee, had turned into an obnoxious alcoholic. He hung around white settlements drinking, doing odd jobs, and generally leading a worthless existence. Stephen returned for a time to his family in Kentucky but made frequent visits to his Shawnee friends. In time he was ordained as a Baptist minister and also found occasional employment as an interpreter and consultant on Indian affairs. Anthony Shane, the half-breed, went on living both red and white. He operated a public ferry across the upper Wabash, sometimes hunted and traded with the Shawnee but also spied and informed on them for the Americans.

In return for agreeing to the terms offered by Anthony Wayne, the Indians, in addition to perpetual peace, were to get, immediately at Greenville, $20,000 and $9,500 each year thereafter. The benefits were to be paid not in cash but in goods of equivalent value—as determined by the Americans—and prorated among the twelve nations which were represented at the council. Initially $25,000 was appropriated for the first, lump-sum settlement. However, Wayne decided that his red guests should pay for the American party and deducted $5,000 to cover the expense of the council.

To facilitate negotiations, certain private, informal arrangements were made with individual native leaders. The Americans agreed to set aside a plot of ground near Fort Wayne and build a good house on it for Little Turtle. Blue Jacket got an honorary commission in the United States army and, secretly, a $300-a-year annuity. This retainer had been arranged for the previous winter when he brought the first Shawnee into Greenville to make an armistice with Wayne.

Blue Jacket, the bluff, direct man of war, apparently decided that, having fought and lost at Fallen Timbers, there was little else he could or wanted to do. At Greenville he accepted the American terms as offered and in fact became a shill for their treaty. Thereafter he used his new wealth to indulge his appetites for fancy clothes, strong drink, and the social high life. The more politically astute Little Turtle behaved differently. The year before, he had been scorned as a coward for advising that it was more prudent to negotiate with Wayne, while the allied army remained intact, than to try to fight him at Fallen Timbers. But at Greenville Little Turtle was one of the few red leaders who publicly objected to the concessions which Wayne demanded. In particular he argued that putting the strip of Indiana (called the Gore) on the white side of the boundary deprived his people of good hunting grounds, trade and travel routes. Wayne, having included the Gore for precisely these reasons, refused to alter the treaty. Since the other chiefs failed to see the strategic significance of the matter, Little Turtle reluctantly dropped the issue.

In early August of 1795, after torrents of ceremonial oratory, ninety-one chiefs representing twelve nations of the Ohio Valley and lower Great Lakes region put their marks on the Treaty of Greenville. The last to sign was Little Turtle, who vowed that he would also be the last to break the agreement. The Miami warrior-statesman was good as his word. During the last fifteen years of his life, he urged his people to keep the peace with the whites and try to adjust to their ways. In consequence he lost the respect of many reds who came to regard him as an American collaborator. He also continued to complain to United States officials about their failure to respect the promises made at Greenville in regard to keeping white squatters, unscrupulous traders, and whiskey merchants out of supposedly Indian lands. Therefore the Americans came to think of him as an annoying troublemaker and a potential security threat. Blue Jacket, on the other hand, made no public protests after the Greenville accord, went on enjoying his pension and perks, and came to be accepted as a good old pro-American redskin. Yet he remained at heart an unreconstructed Shawnee warrior who privately despised the Long Knives and surreptitiously used what small influence he still had against them.

At Greenville the Americans took less than they might have, being confident that by the time there was a demand for more western lands, the Indian populations in them would be much reduced by disease, poverty, and whiskey. Despite misgivings of men like Little Turtle, the reds accepted what was offered, being resigned that their only choice was to make the best of a bad bargain in the country which was left to them. There was, however, one influential man who was not at Greenville that summer, did not accept the premises on which the treaty was based, and in time effectively challenged them. This was Tekamthi. Largely because of him the council did not, as many established white and red leaders thought, finally end the twenty-five years of fighting. Rather it created a longish truce which preceded the last decade of the civil war in the west.

Both Ruddell and Shane noted that Tekamthi did not attend the Greenville council but gave no explanation of why. Perhaps he was simply uninterested in the proceedings or, being an abstinent, self-controlled man, did not fancy sitting around drinking American whiskey for a month. However, several happenings of the summer suggest that he may have been absent for political reasons. Though he had not been a prominent leader of the former coalition, he was an aide to Blue Jacket with more military experience and reknown than many of the warriors and chiefs who came in for the talks.

Certainly he would have been welcomed at Greenville and probably was specifically asked to attend the meetings. Not wanting any of the nations or even factions within them to be able to argue later that they were not aware of or therefore bound by the treaty, Wayne made attendance at the council more or less obligatory. During the forepart of the summer, American Indian agents circulated throughout the northwest extending invitations to the Greenville party. They made it clear that not appearing would be regarded as an unfriendly act. Wayne was especially concerned about the Shawnee, whom he considered the most recalcitrant people. Though he himself had then not heard of Tekamthi, some of his scouts and spies certainly had.

Late in July, Red Pole, a Shawnee subchief, came to Greenville with about a hundred followers. To make amends for his tardiness (Red Pole had remained around Detroit with the British) he offered to go out and bring in a small Shawnee band led by "young men, uncontrolled by their other chiefs," who were hunting in the Ohio woods and who, he had heard, had "fallen into bad practices." Red Pole went on to tell Wayne that "to convince you that we will never permit such practices, I now offer to leave with you my aged father, as a hostage, and proceed immediately, myself, to call home those people, and take measures to prevent their future misconduct."

Wayne replied that Red Pole had behaved "like a candid, honest man in acknowledging the errors of his people." He said it would not be necessary for him to leave his father as a hostage, that he knew as a man of honor, Red Pole would do his duty in this matter. There is no record that Red Pole brought in the mischief makers or, in fact, that he actually went looking for them. The band in question was not specifically identified, but there were not many Shawnee, other than Tekamthi and his people, roaming about southern Ohio during the summer of 1795.

To demonstrate his new friendship for the Americans, Blue Jacket went out at least three times to gather up Shawnee stragglers and bring them to Greenville. If he did not meet with Tekamthi, it was not because he did not know where to find him. Immediately after the council adjourned, Blue Jacket traveled to Deer Creek, stayed there for a time with his former aide, and told him about the newly signed treaty. What else passed between them is unknown, but that, contrary to Shawnee tradition, the older man visited the younger one suggests that Tekamthi had come to have some special importance.

An explanation which plausibly connects these happenings is this: Tekamthi was well aware of the significance of the Greenville council and refused to attend as a matter of principle. Blue Jacket, Red Pole, and others too prominent and vulnerable to do likewise understood his motives and approved of his behavior as a small act of protest aimed at the Americans.

In years to come the fact that Tekamthi, virtually alone among the men who had been much engaged in the campaigns of the 1780s and 90s, had not formally surrendered to Wayne and had taken no part in making the Greenville treaty, enhanced his influence among the western Indians. However, there is no reason to believe that in 1795 he was already thinking about organizing and leading a red resistance movement. If his absence from Greenville was a gesture of defiance it was most likely the personal one of a proud, stubborn young man.

After he left Fallen Timbers and returned to southern Ohio, Tekamthi's circumstances were comparable to those which many Confederate officers—say, a major coming back to his Georgia home after having served four years in the Army of Northern Virginia—found themselves in seventy years later. He did much as many of them were to do: set to work under difficult conditions to support his family and less fortunate friends, reestablish, as best a soldier from a defeated army could, his prewar style of life.

Tekamthi and the people with him must have arrived at Deer Creek by at least May of 1795, for they cleared the overgrown fields, planted and harvested corn, staying on there during the fall and early winter. Whatever else he was to this band, Tekamthi was its most proficient hunter according to a story told by Anthony Shane, who kept in touch with his Shawnee kin. In addition to Tekamthi and Lalawethika, there were at least two other able-bodied men with the Deer Creek group. One of them bet that he could take the most deer during the fall hunt. The challenge was accepted. When the final tally was made, Tekamthi had thirty hides, more than the combined total of the other three.

Their hunt in 1795 was successful enough, but generally game populations were so reduced—by white settlement, war, and trade—that not even a small band could live for long in one place. Tekamthi and his people moved on in the spring of 1796 to another of his boyhood haunts, the upper Miami Valley. They made a camp near the ruins of Piqua, the former Shawnee town which had been abandoned after being sacked by whites in 1786. In 1797 they migrated again, settling and staying for several years along the White Water River in eastern Indiana. About 1800 they received an invitation from a group of displaced Delaware living on the White River (above the present Indianapolis) to join them there. The offer was accepted, and the Shawnee built their community adjacent to the Delaware villages. This remained their base of operations for the next five years.

During this time his wife, Mamate, died or was replaced after bearing a son, Pachetha. (Tekamthi gave this boy to his sister Tecumpease to rear.) On the White River he lived for several years with the girl who, as noted, eventually displeased him because of her failure to dress a turkey properly. She was replaced, according to the always interested Anthony Shane, by another beautiful woman, who remained with him for five years. After separating from her in 1807, Tekamthi, by then much involved in large public affairs, apparently did not make another lasting liaison with a woman.

By the time he settled on the White River with the Delaware, Tekamthi was the leader of a hundred or so people. Black Hoof and other established chiefs of the main body of Shawnee—then located around Wapekoneta on the Auglaize—were contemptuous of this band and charged that Tekamthi was an upstart without legitimate authority. Their annoyance was understandable, since the existence of this independent community threatened their position with the Americans as the official representatives of the entire nation. Black Hoof and his counselors refused to acknowledge Tekamthi as a de jure chief, but there was little they could do about him becoming a de facto one—that is, to stop others, including their own people, from joining and following him. Throughout their history, the tradition of the pragmatic Shawnee had been, in times of crisis, to abandon large, established groups and form new, smaller ones around men they thought to be especially competent.

Both Stephen Ruddell and Anthony Shane were emphatic about Tekamthi having been a youth whom all others were eager to follow and please. After studying him, twenty some years later, William Henry Harrison wrote to the Secretary of War that he seemed to be a "bold, active, sensible man daring in the extreme and capable of any undertaking." No doubt the dispossessed, demoralized people who made Tekamthi an acting chief in the late 1790s found in him the qualities which Ruddell, Shane, and Harrison had noted.

* * *

Within a week or so after Tekamthi and his band left the ruins of Piqua for the White Water River in Indiana, one Job Guard, who had been a sutler in Wayne's army, moved onto the campsite they vacated and began building fences and a cabin. Guard was among the first of the whites who pioneered into central Ohio, up the Muskingum, Scioto, and Miami valleys after the Greenville settlement. (By 1803 when the territory became the seventeenth state of the American union, it had a white population of nearly 60,000.) The advancing settlements may have hastened the departure of these Shawnee by further depleting the game but there is no indication that Guard or other whites directly forced them to leave. As for Tekamthi himself, after relocating his people in Indiana, he often returned to Ohio to hunt, trade, and increasingly, after 1800, to politic. There are no reports that he had personal difficulties while openly traveling and living among the whites. Rather, it seems he got along quite well with the new settlers and was regarded by many of them as an interesting, agreeable man.

The brothers John and William Conner operated trading posts on the White Water and White rivers in Indiana. They had been acquainted with Tekamthi most of their lives, continued to see him frequently during the early 1800s and to think highly of him. The Conners were members of one of the first white families of the frontier. Their father, Richard, had voluntarily come into the Ohio country directly after the French and Indian wars. There he met and married their mother, Margaret Boyer, who as a very young girl had been captured, naturalized, and reared by the Shawnee. When the Rev. David Jones visited the Shawnee villages along the Scioto in 1773, the senior Conner was living there as a fur buyer and merchant. John and William Conner were born, a few years after Tekamthi, among the Indians and lived all their lives with them. They were fluent in several native languages and both had Delaware wives. After Greenville, John Conner received a federal license to operate a post on the White Water, a few miles to the east of the Greenville treaty line. There he prospered and earned a reputation as an unusually honest trader. Tekamthi often stopped by to do business and socialize. John Conner remembered him as an intelligent, articulate, "magnetic" man whose powerful words "never failed to move his hearers, red or white."

John Johnston, another veteran of Wayne's campaign, also became a certified federal trader. He developed an especially close rapport with the Shawnee who followed Black Hoof, but knew

Tekamthi. Like Conner, Johnston had a very good opinion of him, recalling:

> He was sober and abstemious; never indulging in the use of liquors, nor catering to excess; fluent in conversation and a great public speaker. He despised dress, and all effeminacy of manners; was disinterested, hospitable, generous and humane—the resolute and indefatigable advocate of the rights and independence of the Indians.

Abner Barrett, an early Ohio pioneer, settled on Mad Creek, a tributary of the Miami, and there became acquainted with Tekamthi. One evening Barrett was entertaining a party of neighbors and a very fat visitor from Kentucky who was in the area looking for land investments. Unexpectedly Tekamthi, dressed and armed for a hunt, appeared at the farm. After staring silently and impassively at him for a few moments, he stepped forward and tapped the cringing Kentuckian on the shoulders, saying "a big baby, a big baby." Then Tekamthi, Barrett, and the others in the room who had a taste for red humor began howling with laughter at the cowering real-estate speculator who had imagined a massacre was imminent.

There were also the Galloways. Whatever the true relationship of this family to the mortal Tekamthi, members of it contributed substantially to the reputation of the mythic Tecumseh. The first of them to come to Ohio was James Galloway, who fought and raided against the Shawnee with George Rogers Clark. A man of strong antislavery sentiments, he left Kentucky in 1797 and settled near the present Xenia, within a few miles of the place where Tekamthi was born. There he and his family met the Shawnee leader and became very friendly with him, or so wrote a great-grandson, William, born sixty years later. William Galloway was a respected Xenia physician and, avocationally, an avid local folklorist, archaeologist, and all-around antiquarian. In time he published a book, *Old Chillicothe—Shawnee and Pioneer History—Conflicts and Romances in the Northwest Territory*. It is a volume of some merit since in many passages Galloway demonstrated that he was an industrious student of the old days in Ohio. However, most professional historians now dismiss him and his works because of one of the romances with which Galloway dealt at length as if it were absolutely factual. It had to do with his grandmother, Rebecca, and Tekamthi. William Galloway's account, which he says was based on stories told to him as true by older members of his family, runs as follows.

When Tekamthi began stopping by her father's place, Rebecca was fifteen or sixteen years old. According to her grandson, she possessed "auburn hair, blue eyes, a fair, clear complexion . . . a wonderful character but she was essentially feminine." It also seems she was a high-minded girl who spent a lot of time reading in the library of the Rev. Robert Armstrong, Presbyterian pastor practicing in the neighborhood.

Having come initially to visit with her father and brothers, Tekamthi met and fell in love with this beautiful, accomplished nymph. For some time the innocent Rebecca was not aware of the passions which she had aroused in this savage's breast. However, she enjoyed his company and began reading to—later with—him from worthwhile books so as to improve his knowledge of English, literature, and history. (Hamlet, said Rebecca, was a character who particularly appealed to Tekamthi.) On fine days they would sometimes break off their pursuit of culture to go canoeing on the Little Miami River. Often they picked wildflowers, Rebecca having a keen interest in botanical science and beauty. The girl sometimes called her companion, "Mr. Tikomfa Chief," which according to William Galloway, "always pleased him." The kittenish Rebecca also teased her companion to be less taciturn and more forthcoming about the secret lore—especially as it had to do with medicine and natural history—of his people.

Tekamthi visited and mooned about the Galloway place until at last he got up nerve to ask James, the ex–Indian fighter, for his daughter's hand in marriage. James said that while he was much honored by the proposal of such a distinguished man, Rebecca must decide for herself. Upon being told of his intentions, Rebecca said she too was flattered but needed time to make up her mind. Tekamthi said he would come back for her answer at the next full moon. He did. By then Rebecca had decided, after much soul-searching, that he was not only an attractive and gentle man but one of exceptional powers who if properly directed by the right woman could do great good for both reds and whites. However, the level-headed girl also believed that she could not fulfill herself living as an Indian. On the evening when Tekamthi reappeared, she took him canoeing on the river and explained these things, saying if he would be willing to dress, work, and generally act as a white man, she would become his wife and was certain that together they could have happy and important lives. With great regret and equal tact, Tekamthi rejected her counterproposal, saying that "to do as she required would lose him the respect and leadership of his people." He added that they must part forever but assured the girl that he was leaving with great love in his heart, that neither she nor her family need ever fear him or his people. William Galloway was of the opinion that, had Tekamthi done as

Rebecca asked, much racial turmoil and bloodshed would have been avoided, since "her notable patriotism would then have found its best expression in directing his great abilities into the realm of peace-making statesmanship."

All of which has understandably outraged serious-minded modern students of those times as an awful example of a ridiculous fiction being treated as fact. Certainly it is difficult to make a case for the Rebecca-Tekamthi tale being a true one. Beyond the interior absurdities ("Mr. Tikomfa Chief," alone, makes it hard to swallow) there are no records of anybody making public mention of Tekamthi being smitten by Rebecca until long after he was dead and gone. It is inconceivable that Anthony Shane, who took a lively interest in Tekamthi's love life, or other contemporaries would not have said a good bit about this romance had it occurred.

William Galloway may have added a few flourishes, but there is no reason to suppose that he did not repeat the story more or less as he heard it from his grandmother. As for Rebecca, a lady of eighty when she told the story to her grandson, her childhood was so spent that one day there could have been a glimpse of, even a few shy words of conversation with, an impressive red man dressed in hunter's buckskin, leaning against a fence, talking with James Galloway about bears, guns, or the weather. "Now, Becky, you've seen a genuine Shawnee chief. That fellow down by the crib, they call him Tecumseh. For a heathen he's a fine man, seven or eight notches above most of them red niggers. There's not a better shot in this country than him, and Abner Barrett says he fought like a panther agin Mad Anthony but you can't rightly blame him for that."

From less than this—a dreamy sixteen-year-old girl on a backwoods farm, a stalwart, exotic warrior whose name was shortly to be famous—have come fantasies about how things might have been which are more vivid sixty-five years later than memories of how things really were.

However the tale got started, it was told and retold, in American histories until the midpart of the twentieth century. The manner in which it persisted is thought-provoking. The creation and acceptance of the Romance of Rebecca adds to the sense that there were qualities about Tekamthi which others found obvious but difficult to describe in purely factual ways. To get at what was remarkable, they turned to fanciful analogies, apocryphal anecdotes, and fictions. So it was said: Tekamthi could see in the darkest nights, caused earthquakes, was a British general and such a Noble Savage that a Scotch-Irish frontiersman was willing for him to marry his beautiful daughter.

*   *   *

According to the terms of the Greenville Treaty, Tekamthi and the Shawnee were illegal aliens in southern Ohio, but territorial authorities, hoping to keep the frontier quiet, overlooked the scattered bands so long as they remained small and on the move. However, some of the new white immigrants were made uneasy by the continued presence of savages in the country. In the fall of 1799 settlers along the Mad River became alarmed about Shawnee hunting and camping in the area. Abner Barrett, James Galloway, or someone acquainted with Tekamthi asked him to talk with the whites. He did and was able to calm the settlers, even though the interpreter confessed that he had great difficulty translating the "lofty flights" of Tekamthi's language.

(Ruddell, Shane, Conner, and others testified that Tekamthi had a reasonably good command of English, but when treating formally with whites, he refused to use their language.)

A more serious incident occurred in April of 1803 in the Scioto valley near Chillicothe, the white capital of Ohio, which had been built on the site of the former Shawnee town. Thomas Herrod who had taken up an outlying homestead was found dead and scalped. Indians were immediately suspected of committing the murder. A former frontier ranger from Kentucky, David Wolf, then settled along the Scioto, vowed to avenge Herrod privately. Employing two local men who were at liberty, a Ferguson and a Williams, he went into the woods looking for an Indian. The first one he found was an elderly Shawnee, Wawwilaway, who had been living in the area for some time and was thought by his white neighbors to be a good-natured, harmless man. When they met, Wawwilaway shook hands with the three whites and inquired about the health of their families. While small talk was being made and under the pretext of admiring the gun, Wolf was able to jimmy Wawwilaway's rifle. Then he asked the Shawnee why the Indians had killed Thomas Herrod. Wawwilaway said this was news to him and suggested that perhaps some bad white man had done the deed but made it look like the work of red men. Then he excused himself but only got about ten paces away before Wolf shot him in the back. Despite a terrible wound and his advanced years, Wawwilaway, using his rifle as a club, killed Williams and beat Ferguson and Wolf insensible before he himself bled to death.

When word of this encounter was received, whites around Chillicothe assumed that the Shawnee—of whom there were probably fewer than 100 in the area—would soon seek revenge. The militia was called up, and panicky settlers began to abandon their farms, fleeing to the town. In the midst of this scare, Edward Tiffin, the very new governor of Ohio, sent for Tekamthi, who was then living in Indiana. He agreed to come to Ohio as a peacemaker and, when he arrived, spoke for several hours to the whites assembled in Chillicothe. On this occasion he had a skillful interpreter, Stephen Ruddell, and a summary of his oration was preserved. Tekamthi told the settlers that none of his people had killed Thomas Herrod, and he did not know who had. As for the bushwhacking which followed, it was regrettable but Wawwilaway had ably defended his honor and was now no doubt being welcomed as a hero in a better place than Ohio. So far as the Shawnee were concerned, the matter should be ended, enough blood having already been spilled.

In the crowd that day was a militia colonel, John M'Donald. He recollected:

> When Tecumseh rose to speak, as he cast his gaze over the vast multitude [the population of Chillicothe was then about 500] which the interesting occasion had drawn together, he appeared one of the most dignified men I ever beheld. While this orator of nature was speaking, the vast crowd preserved the most profound silence. From the confident manner in which he spoke of the intentions of the Indians . . . he dispelled as if by magic the apprehensions of the whites—the settlers returned to their deserted farms and business generally was resumed throughout that region.

This was the first public indication of the extent to which Tekamthi, who had returned from Fallen Timbers as no more than a competent warrior and deer hunter, had become a politician. Governor Tiffin, Colonel M'Donald, and the other whites were so pleased with his declaration that he and his people did not intend to molest whites who had settled in Ohio east of the Greenville Treaty line, that they tended to overlook a qualification of this promise—that whites must, as they had agreed at Greenville, leave the Indians alone in their lands west of the boundary.

In 1797 John Adams replaced George Washington as the President of the United States; Adams did not have and was not required to take much interest in frontier affairs. During the final four years of the eighteenth century, following Fallen Timbers, the red natives were in great disarray, and the whites were busy settling and developing new lands in Ohio. In consequence it was an era of, if not good feeling, at least of greatly reduced tension.

This began to change in 1801 when Adams was succeeded by Thomas Jefferson who as a naturalist, anthropologist, social philosopher, and a pragmatic politician, took a keen interest in the western lands and people.

During Jefferson's first term of office, the Ohio country filled up rapidly with settlers thus creating a demand to open new territories for pioneering. Also the President purchased, in 1803 from France, the vast Lousiana country beyond the Mississippi. Under these circumstances the remaining pockets of Indians immediately blocked new settlement in the northwest and stood in the way of the future expansion into the far west which Jefferson felt was the manifest destiny of the nation. Therefore he was even more determined than his predecessors to remove the savages from the strategic Ohio Valley and Great Lakes regions. For reasons of need and temperament Jefferson was less inclined than Washington and his advisers had been to let nature take its course in this matter. An inveterate social engineer, he had many creative ideas about how the process could be speeded up and directed.

As a first administrative step in forwarding his policies, Jefferson fired Arthur St. Clair—who opposed frontier development for reasons of antidemocratic principle—as governor of the Northwest Territory. In fact, though not in title, he was succeeded by William Henry Harrison, who became governor of the Indiana Territory, which, after Ohio was admitted as a state, included most of the lands still administered by the federal government. Harrison had resigned from the Army, married well to the daughter of John Cleves Symmes, the Cincinnati real-estate tycoon, bought an interest in a distillery, and become the first representative of the Northwest Territory to the United States Congress. He was, like St. Clair, originally a Federalist, but was not an ideologically inclined man. Jefferson spotted him, as Wayne had, as a competent bureaucrat, willing to adjust his own beliefs to suit those of whoever employed him.

Early in 1803 Jefferson sent Harrison a long letter, to give him an "extensive view of our policy respecting the Indians." The communication was private since, Jefferson pointed out, official correspondence had a way of falling into the hands of unsympathetic members of the public. The President made it clear that he expected Harrison, as the principal federal agent in the western territories, to treat the informal memo as a firm directive and "conduct yourself in unison with it in cases where you are obligated to act without instruction."

Basically Jefferson wanted to convince or force the Indians to give up their nomadic, communal ways and settle down on plots which they owned (and therefore could sell) as individuals, not as members of an independent nation. Jefferson told Harrison:

> We wish to draw them to agriculture, to spinning and weaving. . . . When they withdraw themselves to the culture of a small piece of land, they will perceive how useless to them are their extensive forests, and will be willing to pare them off from time to time in exchange for necessaries for their farms and families. To promote this disposition to exchange lands which they have to spare and we want for necessaries . . . we shall push our trading houses, and be glad to see the good and influential individuals among them run in debt, because we observe that when these debts get beyond what the individuals can pay, they become willing to lop them off by a cession of lands.

Harrison was an obedient public servant. During the next three years he obtained legal title, at least to the satisfaction of the United States government, to about 70 million acres of land west of the Greenville Treaty line, in northern Ohio, southern Michigan, Indiana, Illinois, Missouri, and Wisconsin. The acquisitions were made piecemeal, through treaties with small, impoverished bands of natives. For example, in August of 1803 the Kaskaskia, a small almost extinct nation of about 100 people (who Harrison thought were probably the "most depraved on earth") and one chief, gave up their claims to 8 million acres in central Illinois. For it they received the promise that they would be allowed to retain several small village sites and be protected by the United States. This transaction, which did not require the expenditure of federal funds, was announced with considerable satisfaction by Jefferson in his message to the Congress in 1803:

> The friendly tribe of Kaskaskia Indians, with which we have never had a difference, reduced by the wars and wants of a savage life to a few individuals unable to defend themselves against the neighboring tribes, has transferred its country to the United States, reserving only for its members what is sufficient to maintain them in an agricultural way.

Not all of the new acquisitions were immediately opened to white settlement. Some were so far to the west as to be temporarily inaccessible for pioneers. In other cases the natives actually in possession of the lands were contemptuous of the claims of such pathetic people as the Kaskaskia and refused to vacate the territories. Nevertheless, the treaties negotiated by Harrison gave the Americans legal titles, so they judged, which could be exploited when they were ready to move farther west. Perhaps most importantly, from the standpoint of the President, the creation of new white enclaves speeded up the process of exposing the savages to civilization.

Jefferson thought very well of the Indians becoming civilized. The President seldom lost an opportunity to endorse this course of action to delegations of western natives whom he often invited to visit him in Washington. On one such occassion he advised a group of chiefs from the Delaware:

> Let me entreat you therefore on the lands now given you to begin to give every man a farm, let him enclose it, build a warm house on it, and when he dies let it belong to his wife and children after him. You shall unite yourself with us, and we shall all be Americans.

All of which was intellectually, morally, and politically very appealing to Jefferson. If appreciable numbers of the savages embraced civilization, they would in effect cease to be red and a problem for the United States government. Unfortunately, the racial realities of the time were quite contrary to Jefferson's vision of a harmonious mestizo society.

Many red people in the Northwest regarded living white as a fate somewhat similar to death. Those others who were inclined to adopt white ways—having concluded that further physical resistance was suicidal—did not have the knowledge, skills, or capital to do so. The most prominent leader in this latter group was Little Turtle. The Miami chief agreed in theory that the sort of vocational training Jefferson advocated offered the only alternative to extermination. But he was not optimistic that enough could be accomplished to relieve the immediate distress of his people, particularly of those who had lived when and as he himself had. On a ceremonial visit to the east he was given a tour of Philadelphia and afterward sadly observed:

> Here I am deaf and dumb. When I walk through the streets, I see every person in his shop employed about something. One makes shoes, another hats, a third sells cloth, and everyone lives by his labor. I say to myself, which of all these things can you do. Not one. I can make a bow or an arrow, catch fish, kill game, and go to war, but not one of these is of any use here. I should be a piece of furniture, useless to my nation, useless to the whites, and useless to myself.

Jefferson's solution involved transforming, within a few years, thousands of people who had been for centuries seminomadic hunters, foragers, and heroes into small farmers, artisans, and entrepreneurs. It is doubtful that such a massive reeducation program could have succeeded even had it been a matter of top priority for the United States government. In fact little effort was made to implement these ideas. Occasionally Jefferson, who was more interested in principles than practices, encouraged federal agents and religious missionaries to think about teaching the reds how to be white. The work actually done for this purpose was sporadic and never involved more than a very few people or federal dollars. None of the pilot projects lasted long or were successful.

There was another critical factor. Even if the Indians had been able and willing to live like and with Americans, there was very little chance that they would have been permitted to do so except perhaps on the grounds of the White House or Monticello. On the real frontier there were many more rabid Indian haters than there were enlightened humanists. The most tolerant of the settlers might put up with an impressive, useful redskin such as Tekamthi, but even they did not want many savages near them for long. Both in Ohio and to the west of the Greenville boundary, where numbers of whites regularly trespassed on Indian lands, incidents such as that involving David Wolf and old Wawwilaway were frequent. If there was a hint that Indians had committed crimes or caused minor mischief, whites were quick to turn to vigilantes. Where any sort of due process was followed, it was thought proper that reds be tried in American courts and that other reds, to demonstrate their goodwill, apprehend the suspects and turn them over to white lawmen. St. Clair and Harrison, neither of whom were notable bleeding hearts, reported to the War Department that these appalling illegal and legal atrocities were a principal reason why the savages resisted civilization. Their complaints accomplished nothing, since the federal government, outside its own posts and military bases, had little control over white civilians.

In passing along his thoughts about savages, Jefferson advised Harrison:

> In the whole of this it is essential to cultivate their love. As to their fear, we presume that our strength and their weakness is now so visible that they must see we have only to shut our hand to crush them, and that all our liberalities to them proceed from motives of pure humanity.

Compared to previous officials who had wrestled with the native problem, Jefferson spoke oftener and perhaps thought better of acting out of motives of pure humanity. Even so his basic assumptions were similar to those of his predecessors. The savages were culturally and economically obsolete. They either had to bow gracefully to civilization or go quietly elsewhere to escape it. Paying them something for their land or setting aside small reservations for them was comparable to a good-hearted, up-to-date plantation owner offering to buy out an impoverished, inefficient neighbor (rather than wait for the inevitable sheriff's sale) and allowing him to remain temporarily on the property in a tenant house. Like Washington and Knox, Jefferson was ultimately frustrated by the failure of the natives to appreciate the liberalities of the United States and by their irrational determination to remain where and what they had always been. By the end of Jefferson's administration, there were more natives in the Northwest who despised civilization and had been debilitated by it than there had been when he took office. Almost none of them had learned to love Americans.

The Indians who remained at large, as did Tekamthi and his band, grew steadily more impoverished as game declined, and it became difficult to find secure places in which to raise corn and escape white posses. Those who came into American posts seeking food and protection fared no better. Unable and unwilling to work in the manner of whites, they did what fur trading they still could. However, they largely survived on their treaty annuities and credit, which, in accordance with Jefferson's instructions, was at first given liberally to their leaders. Later when these sources of income proved inadequate, they became, as Jefferson had predicted, much more agreeable about selling their land.

In the shanty towns which sprang up around the government posts, the refugees were weakened and died from smallpox, whooping cough, influenza, and, most commonly, from the effects of alcoholism. Venereal diseases were rampant as a result of Indian girls and women selling themselves, often with their men acting as pimps, to white Indian agents, soldiers, and traders. Ironically the nations and bands who tried the hardest to keep the Greenville peace fared the worst. The Miami, whose warriors a decade before had been the shock troops of the red army, followed Little Turtle to Fort Wayne and for the most part accepted his counsel that they had no choice but to bow to the authority of whites. By 1810 they were reduced to a thousand diseased, drunken, demoralized people. Little Turtle himself died in 1812 in his government house. In his last years he suffered severely from gout, the same malady which had tormented his old foes, Arthur St. Clair and Anthony Wayne.

The Shawnee who went with Black Hoof to the Auglaize also made some ineffectual attempts to master "agriculture, spinning, and weaving," but generally they declined as the Miami did. Black

Hoof himself lived much longer and better than did any of the other chiefs who had campaigned against the Americans in the eighteenth century. He died peacefully on his own land in 1832 at an immense age—some claimed he was 105 years old—and probably collected more in pension money and goods from the United States government than did any other red man in the Northwest.

The behavior of the exhausted, dispirited followers of Little Turtle and Black Hoof may have been unheroic, but it was not irrational. Making themselves as comfortable as possible, they waited passively for the end like victims of an incurable disease. However, others continued to struggle against the afflictions of civilization and to hope that there might be some strong, as yet undiscovered, medicine that could save them. Nearly all of those of this mind-set eventually turned away from their old allegiances and leaders and became constituents of Tekamthi.

By the time civilization created a desperate need for a red resistance leader, Tekamthi was specially positioned to be one. He came from a family which traditionally produced chiefs and had been a protégé of some of the greatest men of his nation. When he went to Chillicothe in 1803 to conduct his first major negotiations with whites, he was thirty-five, just old enough to be judged fully mature by the standards of his people, to have known the good old days from personal experience, to have demonstrated his abilities and won glory as a warrior. Yet he was still a man of youthful vigor and passion, whereas Little Turtle, Black Hoof, Blue Jacket, and the other surviving heroes suffered from the infirmities and doubts of age. Also, Fallen Timbers and the Greenville council had tarnished the reputations of the old leaders and made them timid about opposing the Americans. Tekamthi, in contrast, had fought valiantly against Wayne's Legionnaires. But he bore no responsibility for that defeat and had not agreed to the humiliating peace treaty that followed. He returned from the wars formally unsubdued, not beholden to the whites or apparently intimidated by them. The confident, sometimes imperious manner with which he dealt with American farmers, traders, soldiers, and politicians, could scarcely have failed to impress his own people who often saw their established chiefs acting like cringing supplicants.

As for his own generation, it had supplied the commandos and junior field officers of the red alliance and therefore had been prematurely thinned by twenty-five years of war. Cheesekau, Sauwauseekau, Turkey Foot, and many others who might have led nations or coalitions of them had fallen in Tennessee, Kentucky, and Ohio. There may have been a few others in the prime of life as well endowed as Tekamthi to rally their people but for whatever reasons none came forward as an alternative or rival to him. Within his own race, his opponents were always older men who feared that he would steal what authority remained to them and would bring down the wrath of the Americans.

Given his attributes and their situation, it now seems all but inevitable that still defiant reds turned to Tekamthi for inspiration and direction. But he was by no means a reluctant political activist. During the last decade of his life he responded willingly to those who looked to him for leadership and openly tried to persuade others to join him. Many whites concluded that he was obsessed by the desire to revenge himself on their race, but there is little indication that Tekamthi had an uncontrollable hatred for all pale faces. Throughout his life he associated rather easily with whites and apparently took a certain amount of pleasure from the company of a few of them.

Black Hoof, Little Turtle, and other members of what might be called the red establishment charged that Tekamthi was driven solely by prideful, selfish ambition to be thought a great chief. No doubt there were some factors of ego involved, for commonly men who so naturally attract followers as he did seem to have abnormally strong psychic needs for them. Yet the simplest and most inclusive explanation for his motives was the one which Tekamthi himself made repeatedly after he became a public figure—that he was moved by the plight of red people and the desire to improve their circumstances.

X. The Brotherhood

Tekamthi's address to the nervous residents of Chillicothe in 1803 was a prototype for a series of orations which he delivered during the next decade. Traveling between the Great Lakes and Gulf coast, he appeared before both red and white audiences to speak about race relations. As a political campaigner, Tekamthi changed his words to fit local circumstances but the substance of his message was everywhere much the same.

With Americans his approach was legalistic, akin to that of a prosecuting attorney specifying the charges against a defendant. At length, he reviewed the manner in which whites had cheated and bullied his people, broken their own promises solemnly made while negotiating treaties. He dramatized the history lesson by telling and retelling atrocity stories: of the unarmed Delaware who as they knelt praying at the Gnadenhutten mission had been clubbed to death by Charles Builderback; of the aged Shawnee chief, Moluntha, standing confidently in front of the flag of the United States and there being struck down and scalped by Hugh McGary.

After sitting uncomfortably through Tekamthi's lecture, William Henry Harrison reported to the War Department: "Every instance of injustice and injury which have been committed by our citizens upon the Indians from the commencement of the revolutionary war (There are unfortunately too many of them) was brought forward and exaggerated. . . ."

Whether intuitively or from study of their behavior, Tekamthi apparently concluded that, since the whites put such a great stock in appearing to be morally right, it was possible to manipulate them by pointing out how they had violated their own codes of conduct. At least for negotiating purposes, it was a technique which usually succeeded in putting American officials on the defensive.

To red audiences Tekamthi's readings of history were hotter, designed to raise their passions and strengthen their determination to resist being further victimized.

To the Osage in Missouri he said:

> Brothers—The white men are not friends to the Indians: at first they only asked for land sufficient for a wigwam; now, nothing will satisfy them but the whole of our hunting grounds, from the rising to the setting sun.
>
> Brothers—The white men despise and cheat the Indians; they abuse and insult them; they do not think the red men sufficiently good to live.

To the Creek in Alabama, Tekamthi said:

> Accursed be the race that has seized our country and made women of our warriors! Our fathers, from their tombs, reproach us as slaves and cowards; I hear them now in the wailing winds. They seize your land; they corrupt your women; they trample on the ashes of your dead.

For the living the lessons of the past were clear, argued Tekamthi. It was foolish for red people to think that they could live peaceably or at all with whites as close neighbors. Bluntly he told the Osage, "Red men all wish for peace: but where white people are, there is no peace for them, except in the bosom of our mother [the earth]."

He expanded on the subject with the Choctaw:

> Before the pale-faces came among us we enjoyed the happiness of unbounded freedom, and were acquainted with neither riches, wants, nor oppression. How is it now? Wants and oppressions are our lot; for are we not controlled in everything, and dare we move without asking, by your leave? Are we not being stripped day by day of the little that remains of our ancient liberty? Do they not even now kick and strike us as they do their black-faces? How long will it be before they will tie us to a post and whip us and make us work for them in their corn fields as they do them?

He went on to warn the Choctaw: "The white usurpation of our common country must be stopped, or we, its rightful owners, be forever destroyed and wiped out as a race of people."

Among both races he made the point that, as the original inhabitants of it, the Indians had good legal and moral title to all of the country. Nevertheless, as he conceded in his first oration at

Chillicothe and on later occasions, in the lands to the east whites were too numerous to be dispossessed. As a practical matter, the usurpers must be stopped at the line agreed to at the Greenville council in 1795. Any settlers further to the north or west were, and would be treated as, illegal trespassers. As for the territories in Indiana, Illinois, Michigan, and Wisconsin—supposedly purchased by Governor Harrison in the first years of the nineteenth century—the claims of the United States to them were invalid, the so-called treaties having been made with ragtag bands who had no rights to sell the lands.

"I want," Tekamthi was to tell Harrison, "the present boundary line continued. . . ." He blandly added that maintaining the Greenville boundary would provide a simple, peaceful solution to most of the racial problems and was one that the Americans would no doubt find agreeable since their own General Wayne had made this arrangement and promised that the United States would eternally honor it. Tekamthi seemed well aware that while this approach offered a way to have a bit of intellectual sport with the Americans, legal and ethical arguments were not going to halt their westward movement. As he told the Choctaw:

> Have we not for years had before our eyes a sample of their designs, and are they not sufficient harbingers of their future determination? . . . They are a people fond of innovations, quick to contrive and quick to put their schemes into effectual execution no matter how great the wrong and injury to us; while we are content to preserve what we already have. Their designs are to enlarge their possessions by taking yours in turn.

Tekamthi reasoned that such were the designs of the whites that reds could keep only those rights or lands which they were willing and able to defend forcefully. But history also clearly demonstrated that none of the western nations alone was strong enough to hold off the Long Knives. Therefore, as he told the Osage: "If you do not unite with us, they will first destroy us, and then you will fall easy prey to them. They have destroyed many nations of red men because they were not united, because they were not friends to each other."

The old style of international cooperation—alliances such as Little Turtle and Blue Jacket had put together in the 1790s and Pontiac had formed thirty years before them—had failed. What was needed was a new federation of red people who owed their primary allegiance to their race, not to small, separate nations. He urged the Choctaw: "Let us form one body, one heart and defend to the last warrior our country, our homes, our liberty and the graves of our

fathers." What he proposed was a "consanguinity of blood."
Once created, the red union was to be sovereign in regard to
negotiating, making war or peace with the Americans.

> The facts avowed by Tecumseh in the broadest manner are
> [Harrison reported to the Secretary of War], that it was the
> object to form a combination of all the Indian tribes in this
> quarter to put a stop to the encroachments of the white people
> and to establish a principle that the lands should be considered
> common property and none sold without the consent of all, that
> it was their intention to put to death all the chiefs who were
> parties to the late Treaty [one which Harrison had recently
> made with the remnants of the Miami], and never more suffer
> any village chiefs to manage the affairs of the Indians, but that
> everything should be put into the hands of the warriors. That
> the Americans had driven them from the sea coast, and would
> shortly if not stopped, push them into the Lakes, that they were
> determined to make a stand, where they were.

Tekamthi also told Harrison that there were many others, everywhere in the west, who accepted these principles and that "I am
the head of them." Beyond saying that all power would belong to
the people (that is the warriors rather than the established chiefs)
he did not explain how the red federation would function. Given
the nature of his constituency it was neither possible nor necessary
to pay much attention to constitutional details. Traditional red
political philosophy was based on the premise that all cooperative
ventures should be voluntary ones, that once individuals judged a
course of action to be wise and necessary, they would pursue it
without being supervised or coerced.

It now seems unlikely that a political organization so lacking in
structure as the one Tekamthi conceived could have matured into
and survived as a genuine (that is white-style) nation. On the other
hand, since no governmental hierarchy or infrastructure had to be
established, his movement could be formed quickly and easily. As
he traveled through the west delivering his stirring orations,
Tekamthi not only described the need for a racial union but
instantly created one, among listeners who accepted his ideas. In
consequence the established authorities—red and white—could
prevent Tekamthi from recruiting followers only by keeping prospective ones away from him or exposing the fallacies of his
arguments. Given the grim conditions of the time, his energy,
persuasiveness, and intellect, it was difficult for them to do either.

The Tekamthi issue—whether or not to become citizens of the
union he proposed—divided reds more along generational and
class lines than ethnic ones. By 1810 or so he had, as he told

Harrison, supporters in virtually all of the nations between the Great Lakes and the Gulf of Mexico and as far west as the prairie country of the Iowa and Sioux. Most of them were younger than he and did not then hold high rank in their own communities but were true believers in his cause. ("The implicit obedience and respect which the followers of Tecumseh pay to him, is really astonishing," observed Harrison.)

As he did not mention to Harrison, Tekamthi also had detractors and opponents in all of the nations. Village chiefs whom he promised to eliminate, by execution if necessary, clearly had no reason to wish him well. Among the more prominent national leaders, there were those like Black Hoof who, if they did not fear for their lives, saw him as a threat to their positions, the pensions and perks they were receiving from the Americans. Also there were those who stood against Tekamthi because they thought him a foreign agitator who, to satisfy his private ambitions, counseled gullible men to take actions which would prove disastrous. Of this persuasion was Pushmataha, a principal chief of the Choctaw. After Tekamthi addressed his people, Pushmataha rose to answer him, saying among many other things:

> Halt, Tecumseh! Listen to me. You have come here as you have often gone elsewhere, with a purpose to involve a peaceful people in unnecessary trouble with their neighbors. Our people have had no undue friction with the whites. Why? Because we have had no leaders stirring up strife to serve their selfish, personal ambitions. . . . In that regard they have nothing in common with you. I know your history well. You are a disturber. You have ever been a trouble maker. . . . Not only that, you are a monarch and unyielding tyrant within your own domain; every Shawnee man, woman, and child must bow in humble submission to your imperious will.

Though neither man lived to know of it, Tekamthi's vision of the future proved to be more accurate than that of Pushmataha's. After the northern Indians were defeated and Tekamthi killed, the Americans drove the Choctaw off their native lands in Alabama and Mississippi, forcing them to relocate in the Oklahoma territory. Attempting to stay this expulsion through negotiation, Pushmataha traveled to Washington. He died and was buried there, reportedly succumbing after a heroic drinking bout in which he and his aides were supplied with $349.75 worth of whiskey and oysters by American agents.

*   *   *

From the first days of the Washington administration, a fundamental objective of American frontier policy had been to keep the savages divided and to deal with them in the smallest possible lots. Therefore federal officials were greatly disturbed when they learned that Tekamthi was proposing a racial union on a scale never before contemplated. After first hearing of the plan, Harrison informed the War Department: "A step of this sort would be of infinite prejudice to the United States." The scheme of Tekamthi alarmed Harrison for two essential reasons. First: "It would shut the door against any further extinguishment of Indian title upon the valuable tract of country south of the Wabash." (This was a property he was then trying to acquire from the Miami and Delaware.) Secondly and more seriously: "The establishment of tranquility between the neighboring tribes will always be a sure indication of a war against us."

Harrison attempted to convince "government chiefs" of the tamer nations that collective bargaining was contrary to their best interest, since the Americans could better respond to their needs if they were presented separately as had been the case in the past. The establishment of a red federation was unnecessary, contrary not only to their ancient tradition but natural and divine laws as well. Had it been the intention of the Great Spirit that the red men belong to a single nation, "He would not have put different tongues into their heads, but have taught them all to speak the same language," said Harrison.

Tekamthi's response was again clever and exasperating. He advised the governor that he should calm himself, saying, reported Harrison:

> That the White people were unnecessarily alarmed at his measures . . . the U. States had set him the example of forming a strict union amongst all the fires [states] that compose their confederacy. That the Indians did not complain of it—nor should his white brothers complain of him for doing the same thing in regard to the Indian Tribes.

As for trusting in the good intentions of the Americans, this was addressed on another occasion. Exercising his talent for framing difficult rhetorical questions, Tekamthi asked Harrison:

> How can we have confidence in the white people when Jesus Christ came upon the earth you kill'd him and nail'd him on a cross, you thought he was dead but you were mistaken? You have shaken among you and you laugh and make light of their worship.

The "shaken" referred to Shakers whose missionaries had visited Greenville and declared that the Indians there were pious rural reformers. Harrison later expressed his great displeasure with these woolly-headed innocents and the theological ammuniton which they had given to Tekamthi.

Tekamthi's admiration for the government of the United States and his disillusionment with Christianity was clearly disingenuous and an ironic, adversarial thrust. On these and other occasions his insight about the workings of white society and the manner in which he contemptuously probed at the pretensions and paradoxes of it confounded the American and later British officials who had to contend with him. At the same time they were invariably, if grudgingly, impressed with Tekamthi's improbable knowledge and intellectual prowess. After trying to match wits with him, Harrison concluded that the Shawnee leader was a genius. Others thought he was even more freakish. A nineteenth-century Ohio historian, E. G. Randall, remarked: "Tecumseh, though a savage of the forest, evidenced in his character a rare combination of Italian craft, Spanish revengefulness, German patience and Anglo-Saxon fortitude."

Randall's observation that Tecumseh thought, talked, and acted like a very able white man was a common one. Not surprisingly it led many to claim that in fact he was mostly or all white but had concealed his ancestry to advance his political career. Though often and easily exposed as a fiction, the rumor persisted for a century or more among race-conscious Americans, because it seemed to be the only plausible explanation for the gifts of this formidable man.

Whether red, white, or hybrid, the genius of Tekamthi was perhaps best displayed by the manner in which he dealt with the issue around which all others revolved—that of war and peace.

After Fallen Timbers, most of the old, so-called government chiefs came to agree with Little Turtle that reds could no longer oppose the whites. Tekamthi formulated an equation which led him to different conclusions. As in so many matters, there is no direct testimony as to what his private thoughts were but, on the basis of what he was to say and do publicly, they may have evolved along the following lines:

Passively accepting a dictated peace and attempting to become civilized would destroy his people as surely as war, and the process would be more painful and humiliating. No matter how much Americans might talk about treating Indians fairly, they did not want to live near reds and were determined to eliminate them collectively from the Northwest.

The potential strength of the United States was indisputable, but it was to a considerable degree latent. Only after lengthy preparations, of the sort which Wayne had made, were the Americans able to get themselves in a position where they could crush the Indians. Despite their great superiority in numbers and resources, they seemed curiously reluctant to make such an effort. Tekamthi and other reds did not fully appreciate the extent to which whites dreaded war because of the expense, loss of property, and disruption of business which it entailed. They therefore assumed that whites feared it more than reds did because they were of a naturally timid race and cared very little about honor.

From such assessments Tekamthi concluded—again as indicated by his actions—that although his people could not long survive either a total peace or war, the threat of war might at least temporarily halt the advance of the Americans and buy some time in which other solutions, perhaps a united red state, could be explored. It was a risky plan which depended on escalating, rather than reducing racial tensions but it probably was the only one which offered the Indians of the Northwest an alternative to immediate elimination.

With whites, the persuasive mission of Tekamthi was to convince them that, if they did not mend their ways, a terrible war—which reds of all nations, united behind him, were determined to pursue to the last man—would inevitably follow. However, while thus playing on their fears, it was also necessary to avoid arousing the Americans to the point where they would organize themselves to make preemptive military strikes. Walking this narrow path, he presented himself as a reasonable and peace-loving man but an unsubdued one who kept close at hand an awful club of war. Thus Tekamthi said to Harrison that if his demand that the Greenville boundary be maintained was not met, it would be "difficult to remain friends of the United States" and if the Americans by continuing to usurp the lands of his people rejected their friendship, "I assure you it will be productive of bad consequences."

He spoke differently among his own people, telling them that their cause was just, that they should unite and prepare for war, should not fear but embrace it as a better thing than living at wretched peace.

Tekamthi asked the Osage:

> Who are the white people, that we should fear them? They cannot run fast, and are good marks to shoot at: they are only men; our fathers have killed many of them; we are not squaws and we will stain the earth red with their blood.

In regard to the white menace, he asked the Choctaw:

> Shall we calmly wait until they become so numerous that we will no longer be able to resist oppression? Will we wait to be destroyed in our turn, without making an effort worthy of our race? Shall we give up our homes, our country, bequeathed to us by the Great Spirit, the graves of our dead, and everything that is dear and sacred to us, without a struggle? I know you will cry with me: Never! Never! Then let us by unity of action destroy them all, which we can now do, or drive them back whence they came. War or extermination is now our only choice.

As Tekamthi was traveling the continental midlands, speaking in this fashion to people of his own race, the Americans had little good information about what he was doing and saying. "For four years he has been in constant motion," Harrison advised the War Department in 1811. "You see him to-day on the Wabash, and in a short time hear of him on the shores of lake Erie or Michigan, or on the banks of the Mississippi; and wherever he goes, he makes an impression favorable to his purposes."

But there were enough rumors, which became larger and wilder the further they traveled, about the purposes of Tekamthi to convince many frontier whites that the red resistance movement was already menacing and was bound to become more so. In retrospect this may have been Tekamthi's most impressive accomplishment. For five years he sparred skillfully with American officials while threatening war. But he kept the peace by creating a balance of terror. Not until the bitter end, when all other hopes had failed, did he call out the warriors for a racial jihad.

The red natives of eastern North America were an especially religious-minded people. There were theological differences among them, but generally they were deists who believed that a Great Spirit, or the Maker of Life, ultimately controlled the fate of all living creatures. However He (or in some nations She) remained rather remote from routine temporal affairs and delegated authority for ordering them to a host of lesser noncorporeal beings. Some of these spiritual administrators had special responsibility for particular phenomena—bodies of water, topographic features, the wind, rain, trees, and especially the various species of animals. Others were direct and obedient messengers and servants of the Maker of Life. A sizable cadre of these agents specialized in the affairs of humans, who remained the apple of the Maker's eye. Yet as was the case among Europeans of the time, many red people believed that there were devilish, witchlike beings among them. These wicked wights were eager to tempt mortals into error and impiety, seduce and possess them so as to make men and women instruments of evil.

Once they appeared, the metaphysical position of whites was a matter of great curiosity to the reds. Many thought that, because of their unnatural color and behavior, they might be hybrids, the products of unfortunate matings between nasty spirits—of the werewolf or snake sort—and corrupted humans. Later as they became more intimately acquainted by doing business, fighting, and mating with whites, it became evident that they were mortals. However, the suspicion continued that these aliens had special and dangerous supernatural connections, had been sent either by the Maker of Life to punish the red people or by wicked rogue spirits over whom He had little or no control. In consequence, as whites multiplied and advanced westward, the psychic certainty of the red people declined.

Kinjoino, the Ottawa, tried later to explain why, after they had won so many great victories in previous years, the warriors, clearly the superior men, had been so badly beaten at Fallen Timbers. He said: "The Great Spirit was angry and had turned his face away from his Red Children." After the Treaty of Greenville this pessimistic notion became general among the natives of the Northwest.

Little is known of Tekamthi's private religious beliefs. In his public addresses he occasionally mentioned the Great Spirit. However, these were passing pro forma references, comparable in style and substance to those made by white politicians to indicate that God agreed with their policies. There is a sense that, like most of the founding fathers and early officials of the United States, Tekamthi was a secular humanist, more interested in worldly than heavenly affairs. However, he obviously had to and did pay attention to the spiritual condition of his racial compatriots. Whatever his own convictions, it would have been difficult to rally a people who believed that either their gods had deserted them or had been overpowered by those of the white man. In 1805 Tekamthi received assistance and perhaps instruction in this matter from an improbable source, his younger brother Lalawethika.

Had he lived a century or so later, capsule biographies of Lalawethika might well have appeared in psychiatric literature to illustrate the connection between abnormal childhood experiences and adult behavior. First of all he was one of a set of triplets. To people as sensitive to portents as the Shawnee, this rare phenomenon seemed to presage some momentous happening. When he grew to be a man, it was frequently said that this fact of birth was enough to make him, inevitably, odd and specially endowed.

He did not know his father, Puckeshinwa, who was killed when the triplets were infants or, according to some tales, while they were still in the womb. His mother, Methoastaske, left the family and went to live permanently in Missouri when Lalawethika was a toddler. His much older brother, Cheesekau, and sister, Tecumpease, dutifully cared for him but Tekamthi, then six or seven years old, enjoyed most of their affection. Lalawethika compared very unfavorably to his paragon of a brother. He was a fat, clumsy, timid child, not good at sports or the mock hunting and war games which were so important in the Shawnee educational system. His physical shortcomings were accidentally compounded. Sometime in his midchildhood, while playing with a bow and arrow, his right eye was pierced and blinded, leaving that side of his face permanently and hideously twisted.

Lalawethika did not bear his afflictions stoically or at least in a manner which gained him much sympathy or respect. Rather he was the Rattler, a loud, boastful, obnoxious youth. By his own admission he became a drunkard while still in his teens. By Shawnee standards the most disgraceful thing about Lalawethika—who was at least thirty years old in 1805—was that he had never taken part in a battle or even skirmish against the enemies of his nation. (There were tales that he had gone into Fallen Timbers with his two older brothers but had fled before the fighting began.)

There seems to have been only one socially respectable calling which attracted Lalawethika. In most Shawnee communities there was a prophet. Lesser ones had various skills and specialties, but the most renowned were practitioners of both material and magical medicine who treated the bodies and minds of their patients, interpreted dreams, and gave advice about the future. The prophet in the community which first congregated around Tekamthi was the elderly Penagushea, or Changing Feathers. After the band settled near the Delaware on the White River in Indiana, Lalawethika began hanging about the old shaman. At first Penagushea had no great liking for this unprepossessing youth, but in time decided he had a natural bent for these sciences and arts and took him on as an apprentice. Late in 1804 Penagushea died. There being no one else available Lalawethika, though incompletely trained, succeeded him at least as a physician. His first attempt as an independent practitioner turned out badly. During the winter of 1805 people in the village began to sicken from some sort of infectious disease, quite possibly a virulent strain of influenza brought to them by whites. Lalawethika prescribed medicines, magical remedies, and prayers. However, none worked. The epidemic worsened, and some of his patients died.

By early spring the disease ran its course, but Lalawethika was depressed, and began to drink heavily. One evening in April while sitting before the fire in his cabin on the White River, Lalawethika collapsed and fell to the floor in a coma, which appeared to his wife, and then to neighbors whom she called in, to be much more serious than an ordinary alcoholic stupor. They watched him through the night during which he did not seem to breathe or show other vital signs. In the morning it was decided that he was dead, and funeral preparations were commenced. Whereupon Lalawethika stirred, regained consciousness, and said haltingly that he had undergone an experience similar to but more extraordinary than death. His soul had been taken from his body and presented to the Master of Life, who in a long conversation had told Lalawethika what red people must do to regain His favor and better themselves. Lalawethika was returned to life, specifically to bring the Master's message to other mortals.

During the next month or so Lalawethika entered into similar trances and returned from them with additional divine advice. The Shawnee in his own village, then the Delaware from adjacent ones, gathered to listen to the accounts of his mystical experiences. Soon travelers from the Ottawa, Potawatomi, and other nations came to investigate them. There were few skeptics among the first pilgrims. They returned to their people saying that miraculously Lalawethika, the former incompetent Shawnee sot, had been transformed into Tenskwatawa, the Open Door, a mighty prophet. By the end of the year the news about Tenskwatawa and his hopeful revelations had spread throughout the Northwest and greatly excited many of its natives.

Before and after Tenskwatawa, there were a number of North American Indians who claimed they had experiences and bore divine messages very similar to his. Among the most notable were Pope, a Hopi revivalist who preached in the Spanish-occupied territories of the Southwest in the 1680s; the Delaware Prophet, who advised Pontiac following the French and Indian wars; Wovoka, the Paiute founder of the Ghost Dance religion which swept through the defeated nations of the Great Plains during the 1880s.

Contemporary ethnohistorians, cultural anthropologists, and comparative theologians interested in such phenomena believe that these individuals were products of social not sacred forces. The opinion is based on the observation that throughout the world members of disintegrating cultures have often turned to saviors and miracle workers of the sort who in better times would be dismissed as deluded eccentrics or self-serving charlatans. According to this theory, the Indians of the Northwest, under fierce pressure from the whites, were ripe in the early 1800s for a messiah. Tenskwatawa appeared at the right time with the right temperament and ambition to fill this community need. Nowadays serious-minded students put no stock in the explanation he himself and the other native prophets gave—that he was directly ordained by the Great Spirit who had taken pity on the plight of His red children.

Tenskwatawa did not, so far as is remembered, describe his epiphanic experiences in chronological order or give a single, comprehensive account of them. Details were added, subtracted, and altered according to the occasion and audience. However, on the basis of what he himself and his closest apostles reportedly said, the spiritual travels of Tenskwatawa and the gospel which flowed from them can be summarized as follows.

A pair of handsome, immortal warriors came to Tenskwatawa's cabin on the White River. They escorted his soul to the gates of heaven, where he was met by the greatest of spirits. Since he was to return to the temporal world, Tenskwatawa was not permitted to pass through the gates, but on his first trip he was allowed to peer through them for a brief glimpse of paradise, a "rich, fertile country abounding in game, full of pleasant hunting grounds and fertile corn fields." It was inhabited by red people who had led virtuous lives on earth and therefore were able to spend eternity enjoying the best of their mortal pursuits.

Though He did not show it to him directly, the Master warned Tenskwatawa that there was also a Hell. It somewhat resembled an enormous fire ring or gauntlet of the sort which the Shawnee used for the torture of prisoners. Within it were contained and tormented the wicked and impious. The Master pointedly told Tenskwatawa that special punishments were reserved for drunkards. Molten lead, for example, might be poured down their throats until they were left writhing and breathing flame. The greatest and most unrepentant sinners after long tortures were turned into ash and smoke, and disappeared as humans or any other sort of beings. Lesser and contrite offenders after suitable torments would finally be removed to paradise but would not be permitted to enjoy, as did truly good men and women, all of its rewards and pleasures.

The Master went on to tell Tenskwatawa that he was sorrowed because in recent years many of His red children had fallen into evil ways and were headed toward Hell. However, He had made a compassionate decision: to instruct them—using Tenskwatawa as his messenger—as to how they might live better lives on earth and in consequence improve their prospects for entering paradise directly after their death. Most importantly, red people had become corrupted, in many cases very willingly, by white men whom, the Master told Tenskwatawa, "I did not make and hate."

As to the creation of whites, at least two versions were offered in the gospel of Tenskwatawa. Both suggested that this race was of unclean, marine origins. One explanation had it that the whites had been made by evil spirits from the scum on the surface of the ocean, driven east and piled on the North American coast by a magic and malicious east wind. Alternatively, it was said that whites were descendants of an enormous, foul werecrab, which had first crawled out of the sea in the vicinity of Boston, Massachusetts. Along the New England shore it spawned white, humanlike creatures which began crawling westward.

Both to protect themselves against those aliens and to regain His esteem, reds must cleanse themselves of the white influences which had tainted so many of them. The Master provided Tenskwatawa with a lengthy list of taboos. It was headed by alcohol, which all pious reds must forswear. They should not eat white man's foods, particularly wheat bread, the flesh of cattle, hogs, and other domestic animals. They should feed as their ancestors had on native plants and animals, use their fibers and skins, rather than the woven cloth of white men. They should no longer covet white baubles and adornments, but dress and decorate themselves in the traditional fashion. Warriors must shave their heads, leaving only honorable scalp locks such as their forefathers had worn. It was permissable to fight against the whites with guns, but hunting should be done with bows and stone-tipped arrows or other traditional devices. Bow drills and natural tinder should be used rather than flint and steel when starting fires. As a sign of respect for Him, a blaze should be kept burning perpetually in each lodge or cabin. Dogs were unclean animals, which should not be eaten, kept as pets, or used for hunting.

Seduced by white ways, red people had become lax about observing their own good, old customs, and this process must be reversed, the Master told Tenskwatawa. They must stop coveting and accumulating personal property, return to the tradition that all wealth was communal. Wives should once again become obedient to their husbands and willingly bear their children. Husbands should stop beating their wives and embrace their obligations as providers. Divorce and polygamy must be eliminated or greatly curtailed. The respect of the young for the elderly must be reestablished, and members of families, villages, and nations should treat each other with greater kindness and love. Also there was, among the reds, a class of witches, sorcerers, and false prophets who had become far too prevalent. They were agents or captives of evil spirits who caused dissension among decent people, corrupted their morals, and made them less able to resist whites. It was necessary to identify and eliminate these twisted individuals.

Once He was satisfied that they had purified their lives, the Master would aid His red children against the alien whites. Tenskwatawa and his apostles said that He would either cause a series of upheavals, which would overturn the surface of the earth or shroud it for two or more days in a magical darkness. The consequences of either happening would be the same. Whites and their works would be destroyed. Thereafter the forest would regenerate, streams and lakes clear, the animals would return and multiply.

From the beginning, the close connection between Tekamthi's political visions and the religious one of Tenskwatawa was so apparent that it raised questions about which of the brothers was the prime mover, who was in charge. The two men who left records and were in the best position to know about this had completely different opinions on the subject.

Like many others, Stephen Ruddell never liked Lalawethika, the Rattler, and after he became Tenskwatawa, the Open Door, still thought him to be a liar and hypocrite—"anything but lovely either in looks or conduct." Furthermore, after his own religious transformation into a Baptist preacher, Ruddell thought the gospel of Tenskwatawa was a blasphemous abomination. So convinced, Ruddell was troubled about why his boyhood idol, the heroic Tekamthi, readily accepted his worthless younger brother as a true and great prophet. Since it seemed to him that Tekamthi "was much the smarter man in every respect," Ruddell could only think that unholy, devilish devices had been used to dupe or brainwash Tekamthi. This explanation undercut Ruddell's contention that Tenskwatawa was a ridiculous charlatan.

By nature Anthony Shane was a less idealistic man than Ruddell. Also he probably saw more than Ruddell did of the two brothers during the first years of their respective ministries, since he visited their villages as a courier, interpreter, and spy employed by agents of the United States government. Shane said that initially

"Tecumseh disbelieved" in the prophecy of his brother but "found that most of the Indians believed in him [Tenskwatawa], and as a matter of policy he assented and after that made use of him to further his own designs."

Shane is more plausible than Ruddell, who seems to have been mainly concerned with defending what he considered to be the nobility and innocence of Tekamthi. Yet even if, as Shane suggested, Tekamthi was himself a skeptic, there is no evidence that he invented his brother as a useful tool, made him think or claim that he was divinely inspired.

A better explanation than that one of the brothers was a creature of the other, is that their relationship was symbiotic. For reasons of breeding or formative experience, both possessed exceptional abilities and desires to influence others but did so in keeping with their separate natures. Tekamthi, a competent, popular man, already established as a warrior and politician, was especially equipped to be a secular leader. Tenskwatawa was not, but as it turned out he had a genius of his own for sacred affairs. What is clear is that the red political and religious revival could not have grown as quickly and substantially as it did—perhaps not at all—without both of these remarkably endowed brothers. It is difficult to imagine that they did not recognize how greatly they complemented and needed each other.

XI. Witches and Spies, Chiefs and Governors

Neither Tekamthi nor Tenskwatawa elaborated on their relationship, at least to anyone who left records. Whatever the arrangements between them, the brothers, in 1805, acted jointly to advertise their secular and sacred intentions.

In midsummer of that year, they left the village on the White River in Indiana and returned with their people to Ohio. There members of the band began putting up cabins and planting late gardens on the overgrown grounds of Fort Greenville, which the Americans had decommissioned and abandoned after the treaty of 1795. The symbolic significance of moving to the former headquarters of Anthony Wayne, the late Black Snake, was immediately obvious to both reds and whites.

Later in the year Tenskwatawa went to Wapekoneta, Black Hoof's stronghold on the Auglaize where there was a gathering of travelers from the western nations. Before he was forced to leave by Black Hoof and his henchmen, Tenskwatawa preached several rousing sermons and, as it developed, made a number of converts. Among other things, he said that those who spoke or acted against him were almost certainly possessed by evil spirits, were the witches whom the Master of Life had explicitly advised must be reeducated or eliminated.

The Delaware, living on the White River where Tenskwatawa had first spoken of his visions, were impressed by this message. In the winter of 1806 they asked Tenskwatawa to return to the White

River and help them purify their communities. He came and conducted a successful witch hunt, catching and punishing five of these abominable creatures. The first to be apprehended was an old woman, Coltos. She was roasted over a slow fire for four days and before expiring confessed that she possessed a sorcerer's medicine bag in which there was paraphernalia which enabled her to fly secretly for long distances through the air. After Coltos had been disposed of, Joshua, a Christianized Mohican who was living with the Delaware and sometimes served as an interpreter for whites, was found to have a magical familiar, a giant man-eating bird. Joshua was clubbed and burned. Then two Christian Delawares, Teteboxti and his nephew, Billy Patterson, both subchiefs, were indicted for trafficking with evil powers and met the same fate as Joshua. Finally, Patterson's wife was accused and convicted. As she was being tied to the fire stake, her brother, a youth of only twenty, suddenly appeared, freed his sister, and led her by the hand out of the council building. Returning he said scornfully, "The devil has come among us, and we are killing each other." This bold action flummoxed the tribunal, and the inquisition among the Delaware was suspended.

Tenskwatawa moved on to the Sandusky River at the request of some of his converts of the Porcupine clan of the Wyandot. Again witches were found, but no executions took place because the proceedings were halted by Tarhe (the Crane), a veteran, propeace, government chief who retained considerable authority among his people.

Later white apologists claimed that the noble Tekamthi had thoroughly disapproved of Tenskwatawa's witch work. Anthony Shane went so far as to say that he threatened to kill his younger brother. This is not convincing. If a Delaware stripling and an aged Wyandot peace chief could put a stop to these trials it is hard to imagine that Tekamthi, if he had wanted to, could not have halted them even before they started.

All of the Delaware victims and Tarhe the Wyandot as well were people who had taken to the religion and ways of whites. Judging from his actions at the time and later, Tekamthi regarded the trials, whatever his attitude about their supernatural significance, as a politically useful way of sending a message to American lackeys. He may, as Shane claimed, have been angry at Tenskwatawa but for the way he had botched things. Allowing himself to be faced down and timidly withdrawing was not calculated to impress either potential followers or opponents. Whatever the disagreement, it was a minor one. In the following months, the brothers cooperated closely, and there are no reports that their relations were strained.

As for Americans, when they learned of them, the inquisition in the Delaware villages was a source of righteous, gratifying indignation. Since the terrible business was entirely the work of the savages, it dramatically confirmed the common opinion that they were an innately vicious and ignorant people. There was an additional moral bonus accruing from this affair. Out of it, Tenskwatawa first emerged as a kind of red archfiend, a role he would fill for the rest of his life and thereafter in histories of the period.

Whereas Tekamthi made many whites feel uncomfortable, even inferior because of his personal virtues and patriotic defense of his people's rights, Tenskwatawa presented no such problems. Here was a bestial torturer, a blatant racist, and religious loony. He made such a satisfying villain that few of the accounts of frontier events by contemporary whites failed to catalog and deplore some of the many depravities attributed to the Shawnee Prophet.

He was, said John Johnston, the trader then licensed to do business with the Shawnee, "a man devoid of talent or merit, a brawling, mischievous Indian demagogue." Even Thomas McKenney, the gentle Quaker ethnologist and the first federal superintendent of Indian affairs, had no use for Tenskwatawa. He was, in McKenney's opinion, a malicious mountebank who preyed on his superstitious followers, deluded and intimidated them so that he could live in luxurious idleness while, among other things, enjoying the sexual favors of many women. "An imposter in everything, he seems to have exhibited neither honesty nor dignity of character in any relation of life."

As governor of the Indiana Territory in which this scoundrel appeared, William Henry Harrison heard about the witch trials shortly after they occurred. He was not then aware that larger political, antiwhite issues were involved, but in the interests of public law, order, and morals, he did not think that it was good for the savages to become orgiastically excited. In mid-April he sent one Capt. William Prince, bearing a message, to the Delaware. In it he chastised them for being so weak and foolish as to listen to "this pretended prophet who dares to speak in the name of the Great Creator." Then Harrison counseled, "Drive him from your town and let peace and harmony once more prevail amongst you. . . . I charge you to stop your bloody career; and if you wish the friendship of good opinion of the Seventeen Fires [states of the Union], let me hear, by the return of the bearer, that you have determined to follow my advice."

The Delaware were unrepentant and told Prince to tell Harrison that, "You white people also try your criminals, and when they are found guilty, you hang them or kill them, and we do the same among ourselves."

Much worse consequences, from Harrison's standpoint, were to follow. In his message Harrison had advised the Delaware to investigate the credentials of the pretended prophet: "demand of him some proofs at least of his being the messenger of the Deity. If God has really employed him he has doubtless authorized him," Harrison suggested sarcastically, "to perform some miracles, that he may be known and received as a prophet. If he is really a prophet, ask of him to cause the sun to stand still—the moon to alter its course—the rivers to cease to flow—or the dead to rise from their graves."

Harrison intended all of this to be a logical crusher which would expose the charlatan, but Tenskwatawa accepted the challenge, announcing that indeed he had been given divine authority to do miracles and intended to perform one. On June 16, 1806, he would, at Greenville, cause the sun to stand still and for good measure darken it, turning the day temporarily into night. On the appointed day, before a large crowd he did as he promised.

Immediately, and for years thereafter, Americans attempted to explain to the superstitious savages that, appearances aside, their prophet had simply obtained advance information about an eclipse, a natural phenomenon, and made use of it for his own purposes. Whites did not accept Tenskwatawa's own explanation that he was guided by the Great Spirit, and there were various theories about how he had come by this information. One had it that Tekamthi, while talking with white acquaintances who had an almanac, learned of the impending eclipse, told his brother of it, and with him stage-managed the miracle.

Whatever lay behind the performance, many of the red people at Greenville were convinced that Tenskwatawa could make the sun do his bidding. Word of this spread quickly. Throughout the summer of 1806 and well into the winter, pilgrims traveled to Greenville to see this extraordinary holy man. They learned either from him or his leading apostles that the miracle performed in June was no more than a minor demonstration of the powers which he had been granted. Among other things, it was said he could feed hosts of men with only twelve ears of corn, heal the wounds and diseases of his followers, protect them when they were attending him from death itself and make them invisible to their enemies.

Though it was said that he continued to receive clarifying messages from the spirit world, Tenskwatawa apparently made no major out-of-body journeys during this period. Rather, during

1806–7 he codified his previous mystical experiences and established formal religious practices. Followers of the Prophet were taught (in accordance with ancient customs or the new revelations) to chant and dance, paint their bodies, decorate their clothes and belongings so as to express their piety and identify themselves to one another. They were expected to pray around the perpetually burning fires in their lodges twice daily, beseeching the Master to protect them and hasten the apocalypse that would cleanse the earth of whites and other nonbelievers. Both as talismans and as missals of a sort they carried small sticks intricately carved with sacred symbols. Apostles traveling among distant nations brought strings of sacred beans, consecrated by the Prophet. Converts, while praying, fondled these necklaces to signify that they accepted the teachings of Tenskwatawa. This symbolic act came to be called "shaking hands with the Prophet."

Confessional was also part of the new religion, as Tenskwatawa explained to three Shakers who visited him at Greenville in the winter of 1806. Initiates were expected to seek out either him or one of his authorized ministers and recount all the bad things they had done since they were seven years old. "They cry and tremble when they come to confess," Tenskwatawa observed.

The Shaker clergy asked why this papist practice had been adopted. Tenskwatawa admitted that he had first heard of confession from a Wyandot who had been schooled by priests in Detroit. But, he explained, "Roman Catholics confess their sins, but go and do bad again. Our people forsake their bad ways when they have confessed."

The three Shakers, members of a newly organized, charismatic sect which was widely despised by other Christians, were virtually the only whites to have sympathetic dealings with Tenskwatawa. He responded by talking to them for most of a day, setting aside his own edict that holy matters should not be discussed with Americans. The three men returned to their church in Kentucky and reported that the Prophet and his people seemed to them to be genuinely pious people. "We felt as if we were among the tribes of Israel on their march to Canaan. Their simplicity and unaffected zeal for the increase of the work of the Good Spirit . . . were considerations truly affecting."

The visiting Shakers were also impressed by the sobriety of the people living in Greenville. Others elsewhere observed that while many of the Prophet's followers, like he himself, had previously been drunkards, they almost always became teetotalers after their conversion. The other taboos against using white things, which Tenskwatawa had first announced, were less faithfully obeyed than the one against alcohol. Some of the original zealots made a show of practicing with bows, arrows, and other traditional Stone Age tools, but few went so far as to throw away their guns, hatchets, or iron utensils.

John Tanner, who had been captured as a child in Kentucky and lived nearly forty years in Wisconsin among the Ojibwa, was another white man who eventually wrote an instructive memoir about his experiences. He recalled that when the first missionaries from Tenskwatawa returned, many of his neighbors took up the sacred beans, enthusiastically shook hands with the Prophet, and began putting aside white ways and things. Not because of race— by then he was for practical purposes a red man—but because he was a natural skeptic, Tanner objected. He argued that he did not think that giving up useful, inanimate objects honored the Great Spirit. Nevertheless, the peer pressure was such that even Tanner for a time stopped using flint and steel and started his fires by rubbing together sticks. But he absolutely refused to get rid of his hunting dogs, saying that they were also creatures of God, "and can you believe he wishes now to deprive us of their service?"

A year or two later another apostle from the Prophet came to Tanner's community and announced that many of the more "troublesome" taboos had been withdrawn. The prohibition against alcohol remained, and people were instructed to continue treating each other with love and respect. However, they could, with good conscience, go back to using such things as steel fire starters and dogs.

Even when the excitement about the Prophet was most intense, there were many throughout the Northwest who rejected his teachings either for pragmatic reasons, as did Tanner, or for spiritual ones. Also he made few converts among the nations most dependent on the Americans. Theology aside, Tenskwatawa, like Tekamthi, threatened the secular authority of the government chiefs such as Little Turtle, Black Hoof, and the Crane. They made strenuous efforts to keep their followers from being seduced by the Shawnee brothers.

Generally the new religious and political doctrines were most popular in the Great Lakes and prairie regions, among the Kickapoo, Ojibwa, Ottawa, Potawatomi, and Winnebago, well removed from the white settlements. By midspring of 1807 some 1,500 pilgrims, mostly from the backwoods country, had passed through the Fort Wayne area on their way to Greenville. Not only their numbers but the fact that they were well armed and in an insolent, anti-American mood alarmed William Wells, the chief federal Indian agent at Fort Wayne. In addition to sending reports to

Harrison about this suspicious movement, Wells began making plans of his own to put a spoke or two in the wheels of Tekamthi and Tenskwatawa.

Of the many who lived both as a red and white, Wells was one of the few who rose to positions of prominence among both peoples. Two years younger than Tekamthi, he had been captured when he was fourteen, in Kentucky, by a Miami raiding party. He took to their ways quickly and completely. Named by the Miami Apekonit (the Wild Carrot) because of his orangish hair, he at first served them, willingly, by dressing up as a white boy and acting as one of the decoys who lured flatboat crews into ambushes along the Ohio. Later as a precociously successful warrior, he became a favorite of Little Turtle and while still in his teens married the great war chief's daughter, Sweet Breeze. Wells fought valiantly alongside the Miami in their great victories over Harmar and St. Clair. While he was engaged in the latter campaign, Sweet Breeze, visiting relatives on the lower Wabash, was among the women and children taken captive by American militiamen who raided an undefended village.

After St. Clair was routed, Wells with the blessing of his father-in-law, Little Turtle, went to Cincinnati to arrange for the release of Sweet Breeze. He did so and then spent some time visiting his natural family in Kentucky. There he decided to switch sides, to leave the Miami and rejoin white society. Later he explained himself to a traveling French journalist, the Comte de Volney. Wells told Volney that, having reflected on the two cultures, he had concluded that he had no future, literally, if he continued to live as a red man.

> All your pleasures [as an Indian] consist of eating and drinking, and these are not always to be had, and hunting. The upmost flight of ambition is to be a great warrior, of some repute among five or six hundred men. Old age comes on with speed, your strength fails, your influence is no more . . . and the only boon you can beg for is the stroke that puts an end to your existence.

This being the case, Wells said he had decided to become a white man again in order to "get a comfortable living for the present, lay up something for old age . . . establish a farm, bring up children, who when we are worn out with age, will close our eyes."

So far as prosperity was concerned, Wells was able to achieve his ambition. Recognizing his special experience, Anthony Wayne employed him, at what were then very handsome wages, as his chief of scouts and an adviser on Indian affairs. It was a shrewd move for, largely on account of Wells, Wayne was the first American frontier commander whose intelligence service was equal to the savages'. (That Little Turtle never denounced his son-in-law contributed to his removal as a commander of the allied red forces.)

At the Greenville council, Wells continued to serve as an interpreter and consultant. Then with fine recommendations from Wayne and a federal pension—he was wounded in the campaign—Wells went into partnership with Col. John Hamtramck, a principal American hero at Fallen Timbers. The two men took up a large tract of land near Fort Wayne. They worked it profitably, using black slaves purchased in Kentucky to raise apples, corn, and hogs. Also, in 1802, Wells was appointed by Thomas Jefferson as the supervising federal Indian agent in the area, responsible for distributing treaty annuities to and keeping an eye on the Miami and other adjacent tribes. This put Wells in an influential but odd position, since at Fort Wayne he was reunited with his father-in-law, Little Turtle, and became a de facto prime minister to the ranking chief of what was left of the Miami. Understandably, conflict of interest charges, both formal and informal, were brought against Wells. Reds from many nations and rival traders complained that portions of the annuity payments found their way into Wells's pocket, that he favored the Miami and used his connections with them to advance his real-estate interests. There were also doubts about the political loyalties of Wells. Red dissidents such as Tekamthi came to believe that he had made a puppet of the venerable Little Turtle and was working through the old chief to make new treaties and take more Indian lands in the west. Harrison and other white officials had suspicions that Wells encouraged Little Turtle to raise awkward questions (going twice to Washington to do so) about the failure of Americans to keep promises made at Greenville.

Wells almost certainly profited privately from his government job. However, in this respect he was not much different from many federal officials who dealt with the Indians. In other matters, as a man of two cultures, he had far more sympathy for the natives than did most of his white colleagues. Like his father-in-law, Wells was certain that renewal of warfare would be a disaster for the Indians remaining in the Northwest, that compromise, conciliation, and pressing the Americans to respect their treaties was the only practical alternative that remained for them. In consequence, both whites who wanted the country cleared of reds and reds who wanted to continue their resistance tended to mistrust Wells and Little Turtle.

Before other federal agents began seriously worrying about them, Wells became convinced that Tekamthi and Tenskwatawa were threats to his authority and that of Little Turtle. In April of 1807 he sent a messenger to the outlaws at Greenville, employing Anthony Shane who he thought was well enough connected to carry out or at least survive this mission. Shane expected to talk with the Prophet, whom he knew and had little regard for, but was nonplused to be received by Tekamthi. While a good many whites in southern Ohio were acquainted with Tekamthi as a reasonable, congenial Indian, Wells and Shane were probably the only American agents who then appreciated what a formidable and potentially dangerous man he was.

(Though never more than a hanger-on with either reds or whites, Shane was well connected, having married a kinswoman of Tekamthi. Wells and Tekamthi had served in the allied red army during the early 1790s. Neither mentioned how they had gotten along in their youth when they were aides to their national commanders, Little Turtle and Blue Jacket. But the one-time Wild Carrot of the Miami had changed both his allegiance and name to become Capt. William Wells of the United States. After 1807 he and the Crouching Panther and Shooting Star of the Shawnee were openly hostile. The animosity continued during what remained of the lives of the two men.)

With some trepidation Shane delivered the message from Wells. The gist of it was that Tekamthi, Tenskwatawa, and their people by settling illegally at Greenville had demonstrated disrespect for the United States government. They must vacate this place immediately and furthermore must send emissaries to Fort Wayne where Wells would read them a letter from Thomas Jefferson, which would explain how they must in the future love and obey the Americans.

Shane, well aware of what often happened to those who carried disagreeable messages, was understandably nervous. However, Tekamthi only treated him to "an impassioned and glowing harangue." First he gave him a short version of The Speech, reviewing the ways in which whites had mistreated the reds and why they could not be trusted. He concluded by saying that he and his people were at Greenville because the Master of Life "has appointed this place for us to light our fires, and here we will remain. The Master of Life knows no boundaries, nor will his red people acknowledge any."

As Shane was leaving, Tekamthi got in a parting shot, warning him that if indeed the President of the United States wanted to continue negotiating with him, he should send a man of "note," for he "would hold no more intercourse with Captain Wells."

Later in the summer Tekamthi treated with a number of other Americans, but in the spring when Shane met him, he was largely engaged in trying to accommodate the hundreds of visitors who were arriving at Greenville. His brother was little help in this logistical work, for never a practically competent man, Tenskwatawa had become fully occupied as a holy one. Most of the pilgrims of the year came to be instructed by the Prophet. Many left at least as true believers, and some became important missionaries. One of the most effective was an Ottawa, the Trout. When he returned to his home territory in northern Michigan, he began evangelizing, adding some doctrinal flourishes of his own. Among other things, he warned the Ottawa and later the Ojibwa, that doomsday was near. When it occurred, only the faithful followers of the Prophet and such good dead men as he chose to raise from their graves would be spared. The manner in which the savages of the western Great Lakes region were excited by the sermons of the Trout alarmed American agents and especially annoyed traders at Michilimackinac, who reported that the initiates of the new religion were refusing to accept whiskey in exchange for their furs.

While Tenskwatawa was clearly the main attraction at Greenville, Tekamthi was also busy among the visitors. During 1807 he recruited a number of men who in the future were to be his principal political and military lieutenants. Included in this cadre were four young men from the west, rising chiefs and orators among their people: Metea, of the Potawatomi; Shabbona (Burly Shoulders), an Ottawa; and from the Winnebago, Wakawn (the Snake). The most important was Stiahta, a Wyandot whom whites came to know and fear as Roundhead. Stiahta had first come to Greenville in 1806 and became the equivalent of Tekamthi's chief of staff. Little is known of his earlier history except that after Fallen Timbers he had done as Tekamthi had—gone back to the Wyandot home territories in southern Michigan and gathered a band of still defiant people who accepted him as their chief. The Wyandot, though not numerous, were still influential, having traditionally been respected by other nations of the Northwest for their valor and wisdom. By joining Tekamthi early and remaining so steadfast, Stiahta lent important credibility to the resistance movement.

There were at least two interesting young recruits, one of mixed blood and the other white. Billy Caldwell was the son of William

Caldwell, an Anglo-Irish soldier of fortune who had become one of Alexander McKee's first and most energetic Indian agents in the Northwest. Though he had married a Potawatomi woman, Caldwell senior had been closely associated with the Shawnee since the early days of the American Revolution. He had fought with them against the Long Knives at the Blue Licks ambush in Kentucky and at numerous engagements thereafter, including Fallen Timbers where he disguised his Canadian militia as Indians. He sent his half-Potawatomi son to a Jesuit school in Detroit. There Billy Caldwell did well, leaving with a good civilized education and manners. An attractive youth, he mingled easily with prominent Canadians, but remained proud of his Indian blood. Too white and Catholic to be much moved by the Prophet, Billy Caldwell found a secular idol in Tekamthi when he came to Greenville in 1807.

Tekamthi may have first met Billy when he was a small child in the Shawnee camps but if not, knew of him through his father. He received the boy warmly and made good use of him, even though culturally he was perhaps more of a white man than William Wells. Later, when he was an old man, living permanently with the Potawatomi, who had been sent to reservations west of the Mississippi, Caldwell continued to brag of his connection with the great and good Tekamthi and claimed that he acted as his chief's "private secretary." This was an exaggeration, but at times in the years immediately following 1807 Caldwell served as an interpreter and courier.

Andrew Clark was all white by blood, but red by experience. His mother, Margaret McKenzie, had been captured in what is now West Virginia in 1774 just before the battle of Point Pleasant. She grew up with the Shawnee and was, she said, well acquainted with Tekamthi and his family. She married a trader and bore three children while living as an Indian. Margaret and others of the family eventually went back to live with the whites, but the youngest son, Andrew, did not. Little else is remembered about him except that he remained with Tekamthi to the end and was also sometimes employed as an interpreter.

Mixed in among the youths were a few veterans. One of them was Blue Jacket. After he had looked up Tekamthi in 1795 to tell him about the Greenville treaty, the former Shawnee war chief had largely retired from public life. Though he did nothing openly that would jeopardize the pension he received from the Americans, he remained in touch with Tekamthi and was, at the very least, covertly in sympathy with the resistance movement which his former protégé organized. With his two sons, Blue Jacket visited

Greenville in 1807 and was able to do the community a considerable service during the summer.

Since the Prophet did not see fit to provide magical rations,
feeding the pilgrims who poured into Greenville was a continuing
problem. It was compounded by the animosity of Black Hoof, the
government chief of the large Shawnee faction at Wapekoneta on
the Auglaize. Black Hoof argued, and Wells immediately agreed,
that the rabble of Greenville who had been duped into following
Tekamthi and Tenskwatawa should not receive any of the supplies
which the United States was obliged by treaty to pay annually to
the Shawnee. Blue Jacket was able to frustrate these maneuvers.
Doing so presumedly gave him a good bit of personal satisfaction
since he had little love for Black Hoof, who had replaced him as the
principal Shawnee chief. William Wells distributed the annuities
which the United States owed the Indians but his superior was
William Hull, the federal governor of the Michigan territory, who
made his headquarters at Detroit. Understanding this, Blue Jacket
traveled to Michigan in midsummer to make medicine with Hull.
Though no longer having much authority with his own people,
Blue Jacket's name was still a famous one among the Americans.
Hull, not well acquainted with local politics in Ohio and Indiana,
listened to him respectfully and agreed to give half the Shawnee
annuity to the people at Greenville. Later the decision was revised,
but the influx of supplies from Detroit temporarily eased the food
crisis for Tekamthi and his people.

The most important established red leader who early on allied
himself with the dissident Shawnee brothers was Main Poc of the
Potawatomi. He was a contemporary of Blue Jacket but unlike him
remained an active, vigorous chief, the most powerful one so
William Wells thought, within his nation. Main Poc was a bluff,
bloody-minded man of the old school, who had spent much of his
life, happily, on the warpath, often against the Osage, hereditary
enemies of the Potawatomi. Also he was a renowned shaman,
having been born with a withered hand which he said—and others
came to believe—was a sure sign that he possessed supernatural
powers. When this formidable old man arrived with his entourage
at Greenville, he was not overly impressed with Tenskwatawa's
new religion, because he himself had conversed directly with the
Great Spirit. As for the political designs of Tekamthi, Main Poc
agreed with the overall objective, since he too thought the Americans were disgusting and dangerous, but he put little stock in
newfangled ideas about creating a single red union, in which the
nations would put aside their traditional rivalries. Main Poc told

the Shawnee brothers that they could count on him to campaign against the whites, but he had no intention of changing his personal life-style. The Great Spirit had advised him, he said, that "if he refrained from going to war [particularly against the Osage] and drinking spiritous liquor he would become a common man."

Through his informers, William Wells kept the Greenville situation under surveillance and repeatedly warned Harrison that it was becoming a dangerous one. During the forepart of 1807, his reports were largely ignored because there were suspicions that he was exaggerating the problem in the hope that he would be given greater authority and means to deal with it. However, in midsummer Harrison and other higher authorities became greatly, almost hysterically, alarmed by the Red Menace. The sudden change in attitude had less to do with the intelligence supplied by Wells than with a happening which occurred in the Atlantic off Hampton Roads along the Virginia coast.

There on June 22 the British warship *Leopard* came alongside the *Chesapeake,* a frigate of the United States navy, and ordered her to heave to so that a boarding party could search the vessel for deserters from the Royal Navy. The captain of the *Chesapeake,* Commander James Barron, refused. Thereupon the *Leopard* fired three broadsides into the American frigate. The *Chesapeake* was so newly commissioned that not all its guns were yet in place, and Barron struck his colors. The British came abroad, searched the ship, and took off four alleged deserters, three of whom later proved to be lawful citizens of the United States. Previously in the course of the Napoleonic wars His Majesty's navy had conducted similar "impressment" exercises but against merchant vessels and with somewhat more excuse. These and other high-handed British maritime policies had already caused much indignation among the Americans. After the unforgivable insult given to Old Glory on June 22 resentment burst into a blaze of patriotic anger and belligerence. Thereafter diplomatic relations between the two countries deteriorated until they were broken off by the War of 1812.

During the summer of 1807, in response to the public rage, American politicians vied with each other in lambasting Perfidious Albion. William Henry Harrison was among them. Addressing the Indiana territorial legislature in August he thundered:

> The blood rises to my cheek when I reflect on the humiliating, the disgraceful scene, of the crew of an American ship of war mustered on its own deck by a British lieutenant for the

purpose of selecting the innocent victims of their own tyranny! . . . The unheard of outrage has made a deep impression upon the American mind; citizens of every political denomination are rallying around the standard of their country, and pledging their lives and fortunes in support of her rights.

Though far from salt water, the patriotic frenzy was in some ways more intense in the Ohio Valley than elsewhere. Westerners had strong reasons, the *Chesapeake* incident aside, for wanting to revenge themselves on the British. The principal one was noted by Harrison in his speech to the legislature:

> We are, indeed, from our situation, peculiarly interested in the contest which is likely to ensue [a war against the British]; for who does not know that the tomahawk and scalping knife of the savage are always employed as the instruments of British vengeance. At this moment, fellow citizens, as I sincerely believe, their agents are organizing a combination amongst the Indians within our limits, for the purposes of assassination and murder. . . .

Harrison was expressing what most American settlers took to be a truism, that redcoats and redskins went together like powder and shot. That summer the memories and hates from the years of blood before Fallen Timbers were resurrected and began to work powerfully on the white imagination. As for the contemporary assassins and murderers, they were clearly the witch-burning, religious lunatics gathered at Greenville. Their savage Prophet was not a holy man of any sort but rather, as Harrison advised the War Department, "an engine set to work by the British for some bad purpose."

For the next five years American policies in the west reflected these sentiments. There would and should be a war. The primary aim of it was to finish the good work commenced by Anthony Wayne—clearing the country of the British and their savage minions. Later Henry Clay, the Golden Voice of Kentucky, and others of the so-called War Hawks were to expand this objective to include the conquest and permanent occupation of Canada.

In keeping with the consensus among his constituents, Harrison was tempted, as William Wells had been advising, to march into Greenville and wipe out that nest of terrorists. However, his martial enthusiasm cooled rapidly when he considered the means he had for doing this job. The quality of the frontier militia had not greatly improved in the fifteen years since the disastrous defeats of Harmar and St. Clair. Reviewing the men at his disposal, Harrison decided that they were so poorly disciplined and armed that a mob "bearing sticks" could probably do as much harm to the enemy.

As a safer, cheaper displacement activity, Harrison began hiring spies at a great rate. His intent was to collect information about the Indians and also to catch some of the numerous British agents who, he felt certain, were secretly operating in the Northwest. This he reasoned would at least buy some time for military preparations, since it seemed unlikely that without foreign aid and supervision the savages could organize major massacres.

There is no convincing evidence to support the contention that Tekamthi and Tenskwatawa were tools of purely British design. To the extent that the red resistance and revival were anything but a native phenomenon, they were the product of American policies and behavior on the frontier. Harrison and the others were, however, correct in assuming that in any confrontation, the British would again try to make use of the Indians and especially such defiant ones as those who followed the Shawnee brothers. Though not to the extent that Harrison thought, military and intelligence officers in Canada had indeed begun in 1807 to make arrangements which would allow them to pursue this course of action. By way of brief summary:

Much occupied by Napoleon and no longer vitally concerned with the fur trade in the Ohio Valley and lower Great Lakes, the British, during the decade after Fallen Timbers, took little official interest in the affairs of the natives of those territories. Alexander McKee, the long-time head of the western Indian service, died in 1799 of natural causes. For a time he was replaced by Matthew Elliott, but Elliott was shortly charged with misusing government funds and dismissed. Thereafter the Indian department was for practical purposes disbanded, though many of its former members remained in touch with their long-time red allies and clients. Also Canadian traders continued to visit the American Indians—as they were permitted to under the provisions of Jay's treaty—and to receive them at their posts in Ontario. Many like Elliott and William Caldwell had Indian wives and by then grown sons who entered the business of their fathers and continued to associate with the people of their mothers.

The belligerent reaction of the Americans to the *Chesapeake* affair at first seemed for some reason to surprise the British. However, the continued saber rattling in the United States shortly convinced them that they might have to fight again in North America.

A new governor of Canada, James Craig, was appointed in October of 1807. A month or so later he passed on his views—and instructions from home—about Indians to his deputy, Francis

Gore, then the chief royal administrator in Ontario. Craig told Gore that, if war came, "we must employ them [the savages]." Then he added delicately:

> I would avoid coming to any explanation with them as long as possible, at least to any public explanation, yet when ever the subject is averted to, I think it would be advisable always to insinuate that as a matter of course we shall look for assistance of our Brothers. It should be done with delicacy, but still in such a way not to be misunderstood.

Gore translated this bureaucratic gobbledygook without difficulty. The Indian service was reorganized and strengthened under William Claus, a part-Mohawk grandson of the late Sir William Johnson, the one-time viceroy to the Iroquois. Though nearly seventy years old, Matthew Elliott was brought back as a deputy to Claus and the chief of field operations in the Northwest. Elliott's reappointment was more or less mandatory because in his instructions to Gore, Governor Craig specifically stated:

> I shall be very glad to receive some information as to the history of the Prophet, as he is called, and the extent of his influence among the Indians; if this is great and some of our Indian Department can enter into intercourse with him, it might be worthwhile to purchase it though at what might be a high price upon other circumstances.

Gore replied that Matthew Elliott was just the man for this tricky work since he "is personally acquainted with the Prophet, having been in service with his Nation (the Shawneese)."

Beyond having known Tekamthi and Tenskwatawa since they were boys, Elliott had good sources of contemporary information. Among the best was Frederick Fisher, a trading partner and former government subordinate of Elliott, who had gone, purely it seems for business reasons, to Greenville in 1806 when the community was first organized. He stayed on permanently to trade and to pass along bits of intelligence about their activities to Canadian officials.

Though Fisher was a paid, if part-time, agent and his British connections were fairly obvious, Harrison's counterintelligence operatives overlooked him. But in October they did manage to catch what they and the governor thought was a genuine and dangerous spy. The man—who was never named in the official reports which followed—insisted that he was a loyal American who had been living with the Indians. Harrison was not fooled by this cover story. After apparently a very close examination, he concluded: "He is evidently not what he claims to be. A prisoner for two years among the Indians would not have such clean underwear beneath his buckskin suit. Then his hair has recently been cut by a barber."

After being interrogated, the man was sent to a military prison in Cincinnati. He may have languished there for the rest of his life, since there are no further records regarding his case. Though he continued to warn against them, this was the only British spy Harrison found. The work of his espionage service continued to be poor to ludicrous.

In 1807 the political situation in the Northwest was similar to the one which had prevailed just prior to the American Revolution. The British were once again seeking mercenaries among the savages and the United States was trying to frustrate them. However, during the course of the intervening thirty years, the strength of the Indians in comparison to that of the United States had greatly declined. By then there were about 50,000 Indians and more than 700,000 American settlers in the Ohio Valley and Great Lakes regions. (According to the census of 1810, the count of whites was Kentucky, 407,000, Ohio, 262,000, Indiana, 25,000, Illinois, 12,000, and Michigan, 5,000.) Also disease, poverty, and war had undermined the morale of all the western nations and splintered what had been the most powerful of them, the Miami and Shawnee, into small, hostile factions. During the next five years, as they prepared to fight each other again, both American and British strategists concluded that the only Indian force of consequence was the international following of the two Shawnee brothers.

Tenskwatawa continued to preach to his congregations that the Great Spirit favored their cause and would give miraculous assistance if they were sufficiently pious. Tekamthi, on the other hand, indicated by his actions that he was well aware of the temporal weakness of the red coalition and of the need to buy time in which to strengthen it. To this end he was much occupied during the summer of 1807 trying to calm American settlers, who after the *Chesapeake* incident were inclined to see war parties and British agents behind every bush. In midsummer a white man named Myers was killed in the woods. The signs indicated he had been done in by Indians. To talk over the matter, Tekamthi with sixty or seventy men and Black Hoof with a similar entourage from Wapekoneta met with a gathering of whites at Springfield, Ohio. The inquiry degenerated into a shouting match between Tekamthi and Black Hoof, both claiming that they knew nothing about the murder of Myers but that the other did. In the course of things, Tekamthi put his hand on Black Hoof's shoulder in an insulting way and announced to the settlers, "This is the man who killed your white brother." Though well over seventy and a peace rather than war chief, Black Hoof went for his hatchet, as did the men with him. Alarmed whites, fearing they might be caught up as innocent bystanders in a savage battle, separated them. A compromise agreement was hastily reached to the effect that somebody else other than Shawnee had no doubt killed Myer. (This was probably true. The most likely culprits were some wandering Potawatomi warriors of old Main Poc.)

Black Hoof and his men left immediately after the no-fault settlement was made, but to demonstrate their good intentions, Tekamthi and his party remained with the whites at Springfield for three days. There, according to a Dr. Hunt who mingled with them, they "amused themselves by engaging in various games and other athletic exercises, in which Temuseh generally proved himself victorious. His strength, and power of muscular action were remarkably great, and in the opinion of those who attended the council corresponded with the high order of his moral and intellectual character."

The frolic at Springfield did not entirely dissipate the settlers' anxiety about the savages at Greenville. Therefore, Thomas Kirker, the governor of Ohio, sent two prominent citizens, Thomas Worthington and Duncan McArthur, to the village. They were accompanied by Stephen Ruddell, as an interpreter, and instructed to inquire about the intentions of these Indians, particularly how they stood in regard to the British. Blue Jacket, recently returned from his successful supply-gathering mission in Detroit, was put forward as the principal Shawnee speaker. Since he was remembered by the Americans as a great war chief, he was a shrewd choice for talking peace to them. During the course of a two-or-three hour oration, Blue Jacket said that he had heard that there might again be war between the English and "our white brethren, the Americans." As he had learned by the bitter experience of Fallen Timbers, the English were treacherous, and no good would come to red people if they sided with them in a war. Therefore, promised Blue Jacket, the people at Greenville were determined to remain neutral. "It is not that they are afraid of their white brethren but that they desire peace and harmony. . . ."

When Blue Jacket finished, Tenskwatawa could no longer restrain himself and gave a passionate impromptu harangue. After getting in a few digs at how untrustworthy and impious Black Hoof and the people with him were, the Prophet explained, much as Tekamthi had earlier to Shane, why he and his people had located at Greenville. Basically, it was the will of God. According to Ruddell's interpretation, Tenskwatawa said:

> They did not remove to this place because it was a pretty place, or very valuable for it was neither; but because it was revealed to him that the place was a proper one to establish his doctrines; that he meant to adhere to them while he lived; they were not his own, nor were they taught to him by man, but by the Supreme Ruler of the universe; that his future life should prove to his white brethren the sincerity of his professions.

Tenskwatawa concluded by saying that, if the whites so desired, important men from Greenville would travel to Chillicothe, the capital of Ohio, and there explain things further. McArthur and Worthington thought this was a good idea. Tekamthi, whose ability to sway white crowds was well established, headed the delegation which accompanied the Americans when they returned home. With him went Blue Jacket, Roundhead, the Wyandot, and the Panther, a Delaware who had come to Greenville that summer.

Tekamthi spoke at Chillicothe for three hours, his "utterance" being, said witnesses, "rapid and vehement, his manner bold and commanding." He said that if whites respected the Greenville treaties he and his people would keep the peace no matter how strongly the English might urge them to make war. This address, like the one he had previously made at Chillicothe, had a good effect on the whites. They were spellbound by his oratory and sufficiently reassured by the substance of his remarks that Governer Kirker dismissed the militia units he had mobilized. However, again they were so relieved by his promise not to bring his warriors east of the Greenville boundary that they paid little attention to his warnings about what would happen if the Americans did not halt their invasion of the lands west of it.

Sometime during the course of this conference, the four red emissaries were guests at a formal dinner hosted by one of the peace commissioners, Thomas Worthington and his wife. (Worthington was a large landowner, real-estate speculator, and general of the militia. He was reputed to be one of the wealthiest men in Ohio.) The couple gave the banquet at Adena, their newly built mansion, the size and splendor of which had become the talk of the frontier. The Worthingtons put themselves out considerably on this occasion. Exotic victuals were shipped in from the east. Fancy china and the best silver were brought out, and the table was arranged in the intricate pyramid style then thought very fashionable. Also the guests and servants were briefed by Stephen Ruddell on how to deport themselves with the savage dignitaries. "We were strictly charged," recalled a Worthington daughter who attended, "to take no notice of their eccentricities and to manifest no displeasure at any accident."

At this distance in time, the scene as it comes to the imagination is exceedingly bizarre, a party of aliens as disparate as mad hatters and giant rabbits. Not much is known about the previous history of Roundhead and the Panther, but assuming it was similar to that of Blue Jacket and Tekamthi, these four men had between them probably cut down, bashed in the heads, and lifted the scalps of more than a hundred white people. Yet here they stood in a room designed and decorated in the heights of provincial elegance, balancing cups, making small talk with the crème de la crème of the backwoods gentry.

Inevitably an accident did occur, something so odd that even Ruddell did not understand at first what was involved. When the servants passed around the coffee cups, one of the savages, the Panther it seems most likely, was inadvertently overlooked. Immediately the other three began to gibber excitedly at him and he to respond with growing heat and apparent anger. What was actually happening was that they were making an *umsoma* joke, ribbing him about having a totem animal so slow and stupid that it could not find coffee. Understanding nothing of this, the white guests imagined that they had seriously insulted the chiefs and that soon the pyramid table might be drenched with blood.

Thereupon Tekamthi displayed his social skills somewhat as he had exhibited his athletic prowess at Springfield a few months earlier. Noticing the consternation of the whites as the *umsoma* banter was heating up and understanding the reasons for it, he explained to the Worthingtons that he and his men were making jokes which were hard to explain to outsiders. Relieved, the whites fell all over themselves to keep the cups of the savages filled. Years later, when he came across an account of the dinner at Adena, Gaynwah, the Shawnee historian and great-grandson of Tekamthi, was vastly amused, commenting: "I have no doubt these quantities of extra coffee was another great joke followed up after they returned to Greenville. I could not help laughing when I read about the chief, knowing what followed."

Before the party broke up, Stephen Ruddell had a chance to take the four chiefs aside and talk to them. After they left, he told the Worthingtons that the savages had been "well-pleased with their entertainment." After the remarkable dinner at Adena, there were no other accounts of Tekamthi being in a social situation where he could or wanted to charm Americans. His subsequent dealings with them were either confrontational or violent.

XII. To the Mid Day

Early in the spring of 1808, Tekamthi and Tenskwatawa began making preparations to abandon the base at Greenville. Their intention was to resettle with their followers in Indiana on a tract which had been offered to them by the Kickapoo and Potawatomi. It was located at the confluence of the Wabash River and Tippecanoe Creek. Tenskwatawa again said that the move was directed by the Great Spirit. There were also some compelling secular considerations. Occupying Anthony Wayne's old fort at Greenville had effectively called attention to the brothers and their designs. But the location was deficient for several tactical and logistical reasons. Tippecanoe was in better farming and hunting country, closer to the western nations from whom the brothers drew most of their followers and further removed from the white settlements.

In April Tekamthi left Greenville, leading a packtrain and many of the warriors overland toward the new town site. Tenskwatawa and the remainder of the people brought the heavier baggage by water, paddling down Mississinewa River to the Wabash. On the Mississinewa they were intercepted by Little Turtle and a party of his Miami warriors. Alarmed that if the upstart Shawnee established themselves at Tippecanoe, they would soon cause dissension among his own people at Fort Wayne, less than a hundred miles away, Little Turtle forbade Tenskwatawa to settle anyplace in the upper Wabash Valley. If they tried, warned Little Turtle, he and the other government chiefs would "cut him [Tenskwatawa] off" and his scalp would hang in his, Little Turtle's, lodge. In effect Tenskwatawa laughed in the old man's face. He said he was going on, as directed by the Great Spirit, to Tippecanoe. There, after the

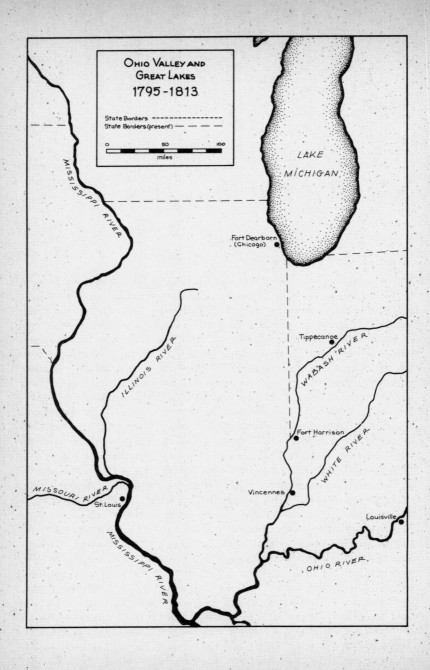

OHIO VALLEY AND
GREAT LAKES
1795-1813

State Borders ------------
State Borders (present) — —

0   50   100
miles

LAKE
MICHIGAN

MISSISSIPPI RIVER

Fort Dearborn
(Chicago)

Tippecanoe

ILLINOIS RIVER

WABASH RIVER

Fort Harrison

WHITE RIVER

MISSOURI RIVER

St. Louis

Vincennes

Louisville

MISSISSIPPI RIVER

OHIO RIVER

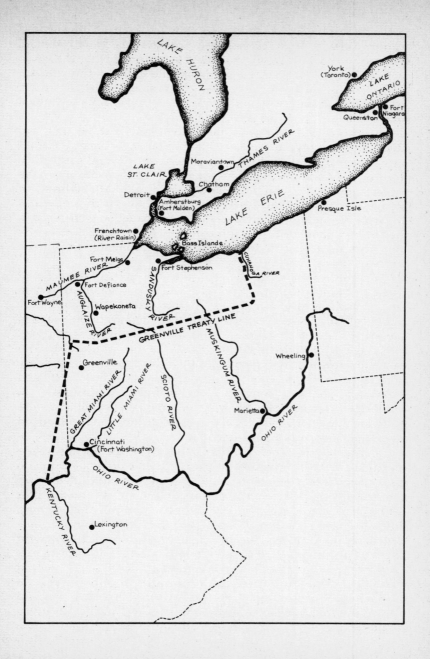

new community was built, representatives from all the nations would assemble. From this vantage point they would jointly defend the territories which rightly belonged to all red people. If a white man crossed into them, "the warriors could easily put him back." Little Turtle, the once great war chief of the west, departed, humbled by a youth who until a few years previously was known only as a cowardly drunk and braggart.

Tippecanoe was laid out differently from most villages and obviously for a special purpose. The individual cabins were built on symmetrically spaced lots along the river. Beyond them were three public buildings: a large council hall, a tabernacle where the Prophet preached, and a sizable hostel called the House of Strangers which provided accommodations for visiting pilgrims. Tekamthi was not much involved in the construction work since in the late spring he traveled north to negotiate, formally, for the first time, with the British at Amherstburg, their stronghold in Ontario, opposite Detroit.

Under orders from Sir James Craig, the governor-general of Canada, and his deputy, Francis Gore, the revitalized Indian Department had dispatched couriers throughout the Ohio Valley and Great Lakes regions. They brought invitations to the western nations to come to Fort Malden, at Amherstburg, in the spring. There agents of their friend, the English King, would distribute gifts and supplies, make medicine about the political and military situation. During May and June of 1808, some 1,500 chiefs and warriors responded. Many of them, including emissaries from Black Hoof's faction of the Shawnee, represented people who were settled within the boundaries of the United States and had pledged their allegiance to that government.

The situation was a delicate one for the Canadian officials. While seeking to reenlist the natives as partisans, they did not want to do it so openly as to precipitate a confrontation with the United States before the British government chose to have one. Therefore, after wining and dining the red leaders who came to Amherstburg, William Claus, Matthew Elliott, and the other British agents diplomatically suggested that it was possible that their government might again make war on the United States. If so, the redcoats would come in great force and with their big guns. Should their old allies, the valiant warriors, join them they might together sweep the treacherous Americans from the Northwest. Thereafter the land would be restored to the red people who owned it and their rights would be perpetually guaranteed by their true British friends. The chiefs and warriors were asked to think on these matters and, if they had grown rusty from disuse, resharpen their hatchets.

Canadian authorities were especially eager to get in touch with the Prophet and sent him—through Frederick Fisher, the Greenville trader—a flattering message. However, it was Tekamthi who came to Amherstburg, arriving on June 8 with a guard of five young warriors. There he was met by Claus and Elliott. They were advised that he was not simply another local village or small war chief but the head of something new, an international federation representing all the free red people of the west. Because of his position, it was beneath him to take part in conferences with men, white or red, of lesser importance. Most particularly he refused to enter into any negotiations which also involved Black Hoof or his followers who, though Shawnee themselves, had become American dogs.

The haughty, imperious style of Tekamthi impressed Claus and Elliott as it did many white officials. They told him that they would arrange a meeting with their own superior, Francis Gore, the governor of Upper Canada, who was expected shortly to make an official visit to Amherstburg. Accepting Gore as a man of sufficient rank for him to deal with, Tekamthi said he would wait but not in Ontario with the crowd of other Indians who were camped around Amherstburg. He and his guardsmen crossed the Detroit River and spent the next month in Michigan, probably with Roundhead and the Wyandot.

Gore arrived during the first week of July and on the eleventh of that month made a speech to a thousand gathered Indians. He expressed, in a guarded way, the friendship and sympathy his government had for the red people and the hope that they would stand together in the dark days which might soon come. Thereafter Gore met privately with Tekamthi. No official record of their conversations was preserved, but Gore later summarized them in a letter to Sir James Craig, the governor-general of Canada. Tekamthi (who struck Gore as a "very shrewd and intelligent man") agreed that the Americans were a mutual threat. But he was not at all certain that the British would make effective, trustworthy allies. Thereupon he reviewed the events of the Fallen Timbers campaign of 1794, which had ended with British troops barring the doors of Fort Miamis against the warriors who were trying to regroup. Many of his former companions, great chiefs and warriors who had died there, might well, said Tekamthi, still be among the living had the British kept the promises they had made before that battle. Tekamthi went on to explain the scope and strength of the red federation he was in the process of creating. Shortly he would have at his disposal a force sufficient to stop the Americans from advancing any farther to the west. This being the case, Tekamthi told Gore, it would be best for him and his people to remain neutral in any war between the English and Americans. Only if the British government made major commitments of troops, artillery, and supplies would he and his warriors consider joint operations against the Americans.

All of which Gore swallowed, like a game fish rising eagerly to an attractive, well-placed lure. According to the report he made to James Craig, he left the meeting persuaded that Tekamthi with the Prophet led a powerful coalition, the only red one which would be of much use if it came to shooting, that the Shawnee brothers could not be bought in the customary way but, because of their implacable hatred of the Americans, could be drawn into a war providing they received substantial military assistance.

While Tekamthi, at Amherstburg, was hooking Gore—and through him most of the other important Canadian officials—Tenskwatawa, back in Indiana, was casting peace bait at William Henry Harrison. After Tippecanoe was built, he sent an obsequious message to Harrison whose headquarters were at Vincennes, the capital of the Indiana Territory. Tenskwatawa said that he and his followers had moved to Tippecanoe so as to be closer to Governor Harrison, to demonstrate their loyalty and enjoy his protection. Despite what he may have heard from malicious men, they were a poor, harmless people who wished only to practice their religion without disturbing any of their neighbors. The Great Spirit had specifically instructed them, the Prophet told Harrison, "Do not take up the tomahawk. . . . Do not meddle with anything that does not belong to you, but mind your own business, and cultivate the ground, that your women and your children may have enough to live on."

In August Tenskwatawa appeared in person at Vincennes with several hundred men, women, and children. They stayed for two weeks, and Harrison was obliged to feed the party, an act which helped solve one of Tenskwatawa's most pressing problems. (Tippecanoe had been settled so late in the season that there had not been time to put in a good crop.) At Vincennes Tenskwatawa preached openly to his own people, sermons which whites were welcome to and did attend. Also he had a series of conversations with Harrison and left him greatly impressed. Reporting to Henry Dearborn, then the Secretary of War, Harrison wrote:

> The celebrated Shawnese Prophet is rather possessed of considerable talents. . . . I was not able to ascertain whether he is, as I at first supposed, a tool of the British or not. His denial of being under any such influence was strong and apparently candid. . . . He frequently harangued his followers in my presence and the evils attendant upon war and the use of ardent

spirits was his constant theme. . . . Upon the whole Sir I am inclined to think that the influence which the Prophet has acquired will prove rather advantageous than otherwise to the United States.

Tenskwatawa left Vincennes toward the beginning of September with the best wishes of Governor Harrison, several pack loads of corn, gardening utensils, powder, shot, and other supplies which were given to him by the Americans and helped the people at Tippecanoe survive the winter.

Shortly after Tenskwatawa departed, Harrison—in part because of the testimony of William Wells, Little Turtle, and other government chiefs—reverted to his original belief that the Prophet was a scoundrel and a British tool. Thereafter he held to the opinion that the Shawnee brothers were at least putative enemies of the United States but changed his mind frequently about exactly how dangerous they were. At times during the next two years Harrison was persuaded that thousands of warriors, heavily armed by the British, were about to assemble at Tippecanoe and sweep down on the white settlements in Ohio and Indiana. On other occasions he was convinced that the Prophet's following had been greatly reduced by starvation, disease, and internal dissension, that Tenskwatawa had lost the allegiance of the western Indians and would shortly be exiled or assassinated by them.

The confusion in the governor's mind and therefore policies reflected the conflicting information he received from his spies. To some extent Harrison, like many public officials before and after him, became a prisoner of the intelligence service which he created. Enthralled with espionage, he employed and listened to numerous secret agents, nearly all of whom were either untrustworthy (having their own axes to grind) or spectacularly incompetent. His agents who were able to get into the Tippecanoe community were invariably spotted for what they were and either sent packing or used to supply American officials with misinformation. Mesmerized by the Prophet, the informers and therefore Harrison himself remained ignorant of the most important happening of 1808, Tekamthi's negotiations with Francis Gore in Canada.

James Madison became the President of the United States in 1809. Much occupied with maritime matters and increasing British-American tensions elsewhere, he gave Harrison a freer hand than had Jefferson in managing western affairs. In that year Harrison was persuaded by selected reports from spies that the Prophet's movement was all but defunct, and it was therefore safe to set about obtaining title to 3 million acres which were still held by Indians in the central Wabash Valley. This acquisition, the governor reasoned, would stimulate immigration and forward his ambition of leading Indiana into the union as a state, something which could not be accomplished until there were 60,000 white residents in the territory. Also he had his own real-estate interests, which he expected would benefit from new people and lands.

His once-affluent family had gone bankrupt in his youth. Thereafter supporting his wife, Anna, and their ten children was a lifelong concern for Harrison. As he sought and took increasingly more important government jobs, the salary they offered was at least as much of an inducement as the opportunity to gain power and prestige. When a federal employee, he regularly entered into private business ventures in hopes of augmenting his income. Whether because of his ethics or lack of entrepreneurial skill, none of them made much money. Compared to colleagues whose opportunities to line their pockets as public servants were no better than his, Harrison remained a remarkably impecunious man. He also retained his reputation, as many contemporary politicians did not, as an honest man.

In the spring of 1809 messengers were sent to the Miami, Delaware, and Potawatomi who had various claims along the Wabash, asking them to meet with the governor at Fort Wayne. Only bands and chiefs who were being subsidized by and beholden to the United States were asked to attend. The Prophet was pointedly not invited. Tekamthi spent the summer along the Mississippi seeking support among the Fox, Sauk, and Winnebago. Most of the warriors either went with him or elsewhere on recruiting missions, leaving Tenskwatawa at Tippecanoe with the women, children, and pilgrims.

Harrison came to Fort Wayne in early September with a military escort. William Wells, John Conner, and Joseph Barron, a trader who had become Harrison's chief adviser on Indian affairs, acted as interpreters. The Americans were met by about a thousand government Indians. The aged and ill Little Turtle arrived wearing a pair of elegantly inscribed pistols, which had been presented to him during the course of a visit he had made twelve years previously to George Washington. The other principal red man, Winamac, the leader of a faction of the Potawatomi, was the most enterprising of all the government chiefs when it came to working the Americans for subsidies and bribes.

In summary Harrison told the assembled Indians: The lands in

question were no longer of much value to them, the game on them
having already been greatly reduced; there were many Americans
in the area and more would soon arrive; the warriors no longer had
reason or means to defend these territories; to try would be suicidal
and if the British had told them they would or could help, they had
lied; while they still could get a decent price, it was clearly in the
best interests of his red children to accept, before he changed his
mind, the generous offer of their father in Washington. Presents
were then given to selected chiefs and whiskey was provided.

Little Turtle made some objections, saying that he needed to
confer further with his people, since land was their only remaining
possession of value. However, the old chief was browbeaten and
intimidated by Winamac and others. There followed some haggling
about how the sale price would be divided among the bands. After
this was settled, the Indians present signed the treaty Harrison
offered, exchanging title to a bit more than 3 million acres for an
immediate payment, in goods, of $7,000 and an annual subsidy, to
be split up among the sellers, of $1,750.

The short-term results of the Treaty of Fort Wayne were quite
contrary to what the Americans and government chiefs had expected. When word of the agreement spread, other red people were
enraged, either for reasons of principle or because they had not
received a share of the purchase price. Immediately warriors,
mostly Main Poc's Potawatomi, began to raid outlying white farms
and communities. After fifteen years of relative peace, the frontier
once again became a dark and bloody place. Instead of pressing
forward into the lands Harrison had obtained in the fall, some
settlers that winter began to flee eastward to save their movable
property and scalps.

Of more long-term consequence was the fact that the Fort Wayne
treaty plainly confirmed the predictions of Tekamthi and Tenskwatawa: that whatever the Americans may have promised at Greenville and elsewhere, they would, when it suited them, commence
dealing with tame, corrupt chiefs to take more Indian lands.
Throughout the winter emissaries from distant nations came to
Tippecanoe. There the implications of the treaty were discussed.
Fortuitously, Tenskwatawa and his people had been able to harvest
a bumper corn crop in the fall. Furthermore their material circumstances and morale were greatly improved by the arrival of supplies
from Canada, smuggled in by British Indian agents. These were the
first tangible rewards of Tekamthi's dealings with Francis Gore.

Tekamthi remained at Tippecanoe for only a few months. When
the weather broke, he recommenced his recruiting, which was
made easier by the Fort Wayne treaty. First he met again with the

Fox and Sauk, who reaffirmed their loyalty. Then he moved eastward. On the upper Maumee he found that nearly half of the remaining Miami, including most of the young men, were disgusted with Little Turtle because of the part he had played in the treaty council. They said that they were ready when the time came to join the red resistance. From there he traveled to his own people on the Auglaize, visiting Wapekoneta. Such was the temper of the residents, or perhaps the strength of Tekamthi's guardsmen, that Black Hoof and his counselor were unable to stop him from talking to their people. Later they reported to American agents that Tekamthi had little success among the Shawnee at Wapekoneta. Another, somewhat more objective observer told a different story.

John Norton was the son of a Cherokee woman and a British army officer. As the result of a string of odd coincidences, he spent his boyhood with the Iroquois on the Canadian side of the St. Lawrence. Then he was sent to England, where he received an excellent formal education and made the acquaintance of a number of prominent Englishmen. Returning to North America, he became an important Iroquois sachem. In 1809 he began a long journey through southern and western portions of the United States, exploring the possibility of an Iroquois migration in this direction. Well connected in many red and white communities, a witty and observant man, he kept a journal in which appears some of the best—insightful and stylish—travel writing and political commentary from this period. Norton intended to publish this work but for various reasons did not. It remained in manuscript until found and privately printed in 1970.

Norton, who had been in the Ohio country in the 1790s, had come to know a number of Shawnee and fought with them briefly during the campaign against Anthony Wayne. In June of 1810 he stopped by Wapekoneta to visit some of his old acquaintances. On his first night with them, Norton's Shawnee friends told him that the great Tekamthi had been there only a few days before. They described him as a "very sensible man, and brave Warrior, of an independent spirit, and enthusiastic to preserve the territory and independence of his brethren." Norton added that during the visit Tekamthi "had persuaded the greater part of this village to join him [in the fall] at the Wabache, where a number of other Nations adjoin the Shawanon Settlement . . . only a small number remain here with the Old Chiefs."

The next day there was a meeting at the council house in Wapekoneta, and Norton, as a political journalist, attended. There he met Stephen Ruddell, who told Norton that he still thought his old friend Tekamthi was an admirable and able man, but had been misled by his wicked brother, the Prophet. Ruddell himself had come to Wapekoneta as a man of God to advise his Shawnee friends that it would be suicidal for them to join the red resistance. Norton dryly observed that Ruddell should be "cautious about interfering in politics [because] the people would suspect him of being an aider and abettor of those who are more earnest in their endeavors to deprive them of their earthly domain than to direct them on the road to a Heavenly Kingdom." Ruddell remained determined to preach.

> When all were seated [reported Norton], he rose with a Bible in his hand, which he began to explain. Considering the extent and grandeur of the subject he dwelt too long on the minutiae of the miracles performed by Moses in Egypt—such as lice and frogs, etc. While he spoke the congregation listed with that gravity and decent attention, which reasonable men will or ought always to show to the word of God.

The meeting broke up without controversy but according to Norton, Ruddell did not change the minds of any of those who favored Tekamthi.

In 1809 Tekamthi had visited among the Wyandot, seeking the support of these steady, well-respected people. However, except for the followers of the Roundhead, he did not have much success, mainly because of the opposition of the Crane (who had put a stop to Tenskwatawa's first witch trials) and of an even more pro-American old man whom whites called Leather Lips. The treaty of Fort Wayne and the resentment it caused changed the situation dramatically. While Tekamthi was among the Shawnee, messengers came in from the Wyandot saying that many of that nation were now ready to join the Shawnee brothers. As a token of earnestness, some of these dissidents executed Leather Lips, cutting him down with a hatchet while several of his American friends looked on helplessly. Then a hundred or so Wyandot warriors left Ohio for Tippecanoe. On their way they stopped by the Miami villages in the Fort Wayne area, where they talked against the old chiefs and persuaded some of the young Miami men to go with them to the Shawnee brothers.

Leather Lips was ostensibly killed as a witch, but the political implications of the executions were obvious to other uneasy government chiefs, several of whom immediately got in touch with Harrison. He took the defection of the Wyandot seriously and, as his dispatches to the War Department indicated, once again changed his mind about the red peril. Whereas during the early spring, he had dismissed the Prophet and his followers as a minor problem, Harrison by July was warning that a general Indian uprising was imminent. As usual some of the governor's informants were able to confirm this assessment. Traders reported that many of the warriors from the west who were traveling to Tippecanoe were armed with new rifles and plentifully supplied with powder and shot. Some had insolently told Americans that they no longer planned to do business with them because their British friends in Canada were offering much better bargains, in some cases simply giving them the supplies they needed.   .

One of Harrison's favorite spies was a French-Canadian, Michael Brouillette, whom the governor engaged at the exceptionally high salary of twelve dollars a month to work as an undercover operative in and around Tippecanoe. Harrison took a personal interest in outfitting him with trade goods so as "to disguise his real character." Brouillette was sent to Tippecanoe about the first of June. He was allowed to stay two weeks, just long enough to collect—or more probably be given—and pass along a spectacular piece of misinformation. Brouillette said that, shortly after he arrived, he had engaged the Prophet himself in a conversation and was told that there were 3,000 well-armed warriors within thirty miles of Tippecanoe. Included was a large contingent of Creek, the first party from the deep south. (Later reports suggested that there were probably 600 or so warriors, among them thirty Creeks.)

Brouillette's brief career as a spy, and very nearly his life, came to an end in mid-June. In light of the unrest caused by the negotiations at Fort Wayne, the Americans that summer were taking pains to pay what was owed the Indians, according to previous treaties, fully and promptly. On the tenth of June a flatboat, carrying salt and other supplies which were part of the annuity for the Kickapoos, came up the Wabash. At Tippecanoe it was intercepted by Tenskwatawa, who held but did not harm the crew. He told them they would have to wait there until his brother returned and made a decision in the matter. A day or so later Tekamthi appeared, having completed his recruiting work among the Ohio Shawnee. He flew into a rage, seized several of the boatmen by the hair, and shook them violently, asking if they were American spies. The terrified freighters assured him that they were French-Canadians (as they were) and were released. They were told that they must take their salt back to Vincennes, for accepting it would be tantamount to agreeing to provisions of the hateful treaties which the Americans had forced on them. When Tekamthi had settled the salt question, Tenskwatawa turned on Brouillette, saying that he had always known he was a spy. Calling him "an American dog," Tenskwatawa ordered Brouillette to leave Tippecanoe immediately, which he did.

Following so many other alarming ones, the salt-boat incident convinced Harrison that the warriors, stirred up and armed by British agents, were poised to make a preemptive strike. He began making emergency appeals for federal assistance and to look to his own militia. However, as in 1808, the wretched condition of the local troops considerably dampened his martial enthusiasm. Therefore, as a temporary expedient, he invited the Prophet to come to Vincennes so as to better ascertain his plans and perhaps somehow to intimidate him.

Harrison in his message to Tenskwatawa said that his heart was saddened that his red friends had misunderstood the Treaty of Fort Wayne. In his opinion, said Harrison, this agreement was not only legal but in the long turn would benefit the Indians. He would be glad to elaborate on these matters if the Prophet visited Vincennes. If he did not find satisfaction there, Harrison would arrange for him to make a state visit to the Great White Father, President Madison, in Washington.

As a courier Harrison chose Joseph Barron, his principal interpreter and Indian consultant. As soon as he entered Tippecanoe, Barron was confronted by Tenskwatawa, who told him that he was tired of having American spies lurking about his town. Then he ordered Barron to look at the ground on which he was standing "for this would be his grave." Before any action was taken, Tekamthi appeared. He waved his brother aside, promised Barron he would not be harmed, and took him off to his own cabin for a long conversation. The incident was later to be cited as evidence that Tekamthi was the noble, reasonable brother and Tenskwatawa the vicious one. However, there is also the possibility that the two Shawnee had hit on the good-cop–bad-cop routine as a form of psychological karate.

Barron spent the night with Tekamthi and had, he reported, a friendly talk. Tekamthi began by telling him that he, not his younger brother, would travel to Vincennes to make medicine with the governor. Then he added casually that in fact he had met, or at least seen, Harrison once before. When he was a young officer attending his General Wayne, Tekamthi as a young warrior had watched him, just out of rifle range, from the spot where he had lain hidden in the Fallen Timbers on the morning of that battle.

As for the substance of Harrison's message, Tekamthi said he would be glad to talk and try to work out their difficulties, for he was eager to have peace. However, he warned there was one nonnegotiable issue. The Treaty of Fort Wayne must be set aside. The land involved belonged to all the red people, not to the few cowardly old chiefs who had signed the agreement.

Barron, on his return, gave such a glowing account of Tekamthi that Harrison decided that this elder brother must be "the really efficient man—the Moses of the family," and a reasonable savage with whom it might be possible to do business in a civilized way. Only one part of the exchange bothered him. Tekamthi had told Barron that, since it was to be a peace mission, he planned to bring only his usual honor guard of thirty or so warriors. Then he added blandly "that young men were fond of attending such occasions" and therefore perhaps a hundred or more of them might also come along for the excitement.

Harrison immediately sent another message to Tippecanoe saying that he would be pleased to welcome Tekamthi and a *few* of his young men. There was no further communication until, on the twelfth of August, Tekamthi arrived in Vincennes with 400 of his people, who paddled down the Wabash in a flotilla of eighty canoes. An army captain stationed with the small garrison there noted that the warriors "were all painted in the most terrific manner . . . and well prepared for war." Tekamthi was in the lead canoe and was, said the soldier, "one of the finest-looking men I ever saw—about six feet high, straight, with large fine features, and altogether a daring, bold-looking fellow." When the formal talks commenced three days later, Tekamthi left the bulk of his men camped outside the town and, as he had promised, brought only his personal guardsmen to the council. Even so the general effect was that the citizens of Vincennes, not the savages, were overawed.

On the morning of the fifteenth, Harrison arranged to receive the Indians on the portico of the governor's mansion. Waiting at the steps with him were a number of prominent civilians, several justices of the territorial supreme court, and a squad of a dozen soldiers. Tekamthi brought his party within forty yards of the mansion and then halted. Joseph Barron, the interpreter, was sent forward to ask his pleasure. Tekamthi told Barron that he did not care to talk within the confines of the white chief's house. He preferred the council to be held in an adjacent grove of trees. Barron went back with the message, and Harrison affably agreed to the change. Then he came forward with his people to meet Tekamthi, saying that he thought talking in the open would be pleasant. Since it was the explicit wish of his own chief, the Great White Father in Washington, that the mighty Shawnee be shown every courtesy, he would order chairs and benches brought into the grove so that he could offer proper seats to his honored guests.

Tekamthi quickly made use of the circumstances to do what he did frequently and skillfully—make white men feel a bit awkward and foolish in his presence. Raising his arm and dramatically pointing to the sky, he spoke for the first time directly to Harrison: "My father? The Great Spirit is my father—the earth is my mother—and on her bosom I will recline." So saying, he and his men arranged themselves comfortably on the grass, leaving Harrison and his escort to squat and stand around them as the meeting proceeded.

Tekamthi spoke first and apparently for several hours, according to a summary transcript of his remarks which one of Harrison's interpreters recorded. He reviewed ("at unfortunate length," as Harrison later remarked) the history of relations between the two races and how, in his opinion, whites had mistreated reds. Turning to contemporary events Tekamthi said that despite these abuses his people, after Fallen Timbers, had agreed to live at peace with the Americans on the lands which were left to them by the Greenville treaty. It was his own true wish to live harmoniously. But this had proved difficult to do for, contrary to their solemn promises, the Americans had continued to press westward, trespassing on red lands, taking them by force and through fraudulent treaties. "You are," Tekamthi told Harrison, "continually driving the red people [and will] at last drive them into the great lake where they can't either stand or work." Furthermore the American policies were obviously intended to be divisive.

> You want by your distinctions of Indian tribes in alloting to each a particular track of land to make war with each other. You never see an Indian come and endeavor to make the white people do so. Perhaps it is by the direction of the President to make these distinctions. It is a very bad thing and we do not like it.

He and his brother, said Tekamthi, had organized a great coalition to stop further encroachments by the Americans. Their followers came from throughout the Northwest. They had put aside the former national "distinctions," and now were determined to act as one people. The lands left to red people were the common property of all of them and could not be disposed of by individual chiefs, clans, or nations. He and his warriors stood ready to defend this proposition, with their lives if necessary.

As for the Treaty of Fort Wayne, if there was to be peace this must be rescinded, for he and his people would never accept the hateful provisions of this transaction. It had been made by a few greedy, cowardly village chiefs, who, if the agreement were allowed to stand, would shortly be disposed of by him and his warriors. "I now wish you to listen to me," Tekamthi demanded of Harrison. "If you do not [nullify the Fort Wayne treaty] it will appear as if you wished me to kill all the chiefs that sold you this land. I tell you so because I am authorized by all the tribes to do so. I am the head of them all."

Then Tekamthi dramatically pointed out Winamac, the venal Potawatomi whom Harrison had brought to Vincennes. This man, shouted Tekamthi, was a traitor to his race, had tricked old and confused men into signing the Fort Wayne treaty. He went on to berate Winamac so rapidly and roundly that Harrison's translators could not render the abuse into English. The Potawatomi chief plainly understood what was being said. He ducked behind the Americans and started to load his pistol, but was disarmed and hurried away by some of the whites before he used it. As a distraction, Harrison stepped forward to defend the legality of the Fort Wayne treaty, saying that Tekamthi's theory about reds being all one people who communally owned the land was nonsense. Whereupon Tekamthi wheeled on the governor and began to harangue him, again in terms which the interpreters could or did not care to repeat. The general nature of his remarks was made clear as Tekamthi's warriors rose and put their hands menacingly on their weapons. Harrison's soldiers gathered protectively around him, and several of the civilians slipped away to get guns.

Harrison was sometimes a fatuous man but he was no coward. Stepping forward, using gestures which reinforced the translation of his words, he faced Tekamthi and told him that he was a "bad man" for so interrupting their deliberations. He would, said Harrison, talk no further under these conditions. He turned on his heel and left the grove with the other Americans, his exit somewhat balancing the powerful entrance which Tekamthi had made.

By the next morning tempers had cooled, and the council was reconvened. It was a brief one since neither side had new proposals or concessions to offer. There was a round of polite speeches in which Tekamthi apologized for his outburst of the previous day, saying that he had been temporarily and uncharacteristically overcome by a fit of anger. However, in response to a direct question from Harrison—would the Indians allow white surveyors to enter the 3 million acres which had been obtained through the Fort Wayne treaty—Tekamthi gave an unequivocal answer. "I want the present boundary line to continue," he said. "Should you cross it, I assure you it will be productive of bad consequences."

The Indians stayed for several more days around Vincennes, and on the day before they departed, Harrison paid an informal visit to

Tekamthi at his camp. Though they were no closer to agreeing than they had been when the meetings began, there is a sense that during the confrontational public sessions they had developed a certain amount of mutual respect. Harrison said that he would be happy to send forward Tekamthi's objections to American policies to President Madison. He added that in all honesty there was very little chance that the United States would accept the premise that red lands were communal property or withdraw the Fort Wayne treaty. Tekamthi answered reflectively: "As the great chief [Madison] is to determine the matter, I hope the Great Spirit will put sense enough into his head to induce him to give up this land: it is true, he is so far off he will not be injured by the war; he may sit still in his town and drink his wine, whilst you and I will have to fight it out."

During the course of the Vincennes talks, Tekamthi told Harrison that, after they were finished, he would go to a council of the western nations, where he expected to increase his following substantially. Thereafter he might well visit Canada to make medicine with the British. Since until that time he had been very secretive about his activities, it is difficult to imagine that Tekamthi's disclosure of his immediate plans was not intentional, a tactic calculated to give the Americans something to chew on in case they began thinking about making an offensive move against his people at Tippecanoe.

By September Tekamthi, with Shabbona the Ottawa and Billy Caldwell as aides, was in western Illinois among the Potawatomi and Kickapoo. He then went north into Wisconsin, holding a series of rallies among the Fox, Menominee, Sauk, and Winnebago. He was met enthusiastically and received many pledges of allegiance. The western mission would have been an unqualified success except for the activities of Main Poc, the grim old shaman/soldier. Having little interest in diplomacy or strategic planing, the Potawatomi chief spent the late summer, as he had most of his life, on the warpath. He and his men made sporadic raids against the whites in Illinois, stealing their stock, looting their farms, and killing six of them. Then while Tekamthi was recruiting in Wisconsin, Main Poc, apparently for no better reason than that it was his pleasure, crossed the Mississippi with some of his braves and ambushed and scalped a few Osage. The raid understandably cooled the enthusiasm of the Osage for joining Tekamthi's coalition, of which Main Poc was a charter member.

In November, accompanied by his own guard and more than a hundred western warriors, Tekamthi met with Matthew Elliott and other agents at Amherstburg. If anything, his manner was more imperious than it had been the year before. He told the British officials that whereas for many years his people had been like children to the English, requiring their advice and protection, the situation had changed. "We are now Men, and think ourselves capable of defending our Country." He went on to explain that his support was general throughout the Great Lakes and Ohio Valley. During the next year he intended to travel to the south and bring in the powerful nations of that quarter. He expected that by early 1812 he would have led his people into the "Mid Day," a metaphoric code expression used to indicate the time when the great red federation would be completed. After Mid Day the Indians would have no need for English soldiers and advisers. If war came between the whites, he and his warriors would defend themselves and probably, as an independent army, aid the English. However, he told Elliott, "after raising you on your feet we will leave you behind but expecting you will push forwards toward us what may be necessary to supply our wants."

In his report, Matthew Elliott said that Tekamthi "fully convinces me that Our Neighbors [the Americans] are on the eve of an Indian War, and I have no doubt that the Confederacy is almost general." Therefore he provided a considerable quantity of supplies which were packed back to Tippecanoe.

More senior Canadian military and political officials were uneasy about Tekamthi's plans, since they had no intention of being drawn into a western war until and unless it suited their purposes. On the other hand they needed the warriors as a force—and threat-in-waiting. In consequence Elliott's superiors waffled, ordering him and the other agents to be circumspect so as not to antagonize the Americans, but at the same time to cultivate the friendship of the Shawnee who seemed to have become the "King of the Savages."

For the Americans and the Indians, 1811 was a repeat of the previous year. What with the provisions Tekamthi brought back from Canada and another good fall harvest in 1810, the winter was fairly easy at Tippecanoe. Religious pilgrims and political couriers continued to come and go, but generally Tenskwatawa and Tekamthi were quiet, and by spring Harrison had again decided that their movement was waning. So encouraged, he began sending surveyors and scouts into the Fort Wayne treaty lands. None were killed, but all were driven out by warriors from Tippecanoe. Then having laid up all winter in the Illinois country, Main Poc (who had been wounded in his fall skirmish with the Osage) emerged refreshed and in his usual pugnacious mood. He and his Potawatomi commenced raiding and scalping white settlers.

As panic increased among his constituents, Harrison, in April, dispatched another agent, this time William Wells (who was back in the governor's favor), to Tippecanoe to inquire specifically about the depredations of the Potawatomi. Tekamthi told Wells that, although these raiders had not acted under his direct orders, they were indeed among his supporters. Several of the warriors who had killed white settlers had visited Tippecanoe, but they had departed. But even if they had still been in his town, he would not, Tekamthi said, have turned them over to the Americans. Whereupon Wells, a brave, hot-tempered man, and Tekamthi got into a shouting match. Wells told his former companion-in-arms that his plans for a red federation were foolish and would never be realized. Tekamthi replied ominously that if by chance Wells lived much longer he would "see the contrary."

Finally in June another flatboat, loaded with salt and other goods for the Kickapoo, started up the Wabash. Tekamthi himself was gone, recruiting among the Ottawa in Michigan, but at Tippecanoe Tenskwatawa stopped the boat, and this time seized the cargo. He sent the crew back to Vincennes with a message for the governor: He needed the supplies since he had 2,000 warriors to feed and was momentarily expecting his brother to return from Michigan with many more.

Enraged by the insolence and alarmed by the misinformation, Harrison, as he had the summer before, sent a message asking Tekamthi to come to Vincennes for a conference. On this occasion he mentioned in his first invitation that it would be inappropriate to bring a large number of warriors. The Shawnee arrived at Vincennes on July 27 with 300 men. Harrison, having learned something of how Tekamthi operated, was able to greet him with 800 regulars and militiamen hastily collected from posts along the Ohio. There was some preliminary bickering about how many soldiers each leader would keep at his side, but a compromise was reached, and the talks began two days later.

Harrison said that the United States remained determined to occupy lands to which it held good title, that he was saddened to hear that Tekamthi continued to oppose this course of action but if he brought on a war, the consequences would be terrible for the Indians. Tekamthi agreed that war would be unfortunate and was unnecessary but whether or not there would be one was up to the Americans. If they did not invade Indian lands, then there would be no reason for reds and whites to fight.

Since neither man had changed his mind about the basic questions, they turned to some specific and immediate issues. In regard to the latest flatboat incident, Tekamthi remarked that it seemed difficult to please Harrison. The year before he had been angry because the salt annuity had been refused, now "was equally so because it was taken." As to the killing of Americans in Illinois, he admitted that some of his people had done so. Though he would not give them over to white judges or juries, he would, when he returned, look into the matter and perhaps pay reparations for their misdeeds.

On the final day of the talks, Harrison again broached the subject of Tekamthi and Tenskwatawa meeting President Madison in Washington. Tekamthi said he was more favorably inclined toward this proposal than he had been but could not make such a state visit until the next spring or summer. He then proceeded to explain Mid Day in even more detail than he had to the British. According to the report which Harrison sent to the War Department:

> He said that after much trouble and difficulty he had at length brought all the northern Tribes to be united and place themselves under his direction. . . . As soon as the council was over he was to set out on a visit to the Southern Tribes to get them to unite with those of the North. After having visited the Creek and Choctaw he is to visit the Osages and return by the Missouri . . . that he wished everything to remain in its present condition until his return—our settlements not to progress further. . . . That the affairs of all the tribes in this quarter were in his hands and that nothing would be done without him—that he would dispatch messengers in every direction to prevent them from doing any more mischief . . . that he would [upon his return] then go and see the President and settle everything with him.

The formal talks at Vincennes lasted five days. After they were finished, Tekamthi paid a private visit to Harrison who said he "labored hard to convince me that he had no other intention by this journey [to the south] than to prevail on all the Tribes to unite in bonds of peace." The next morning, while most of his followers returned upstream to Tippecanoe, Tekamthi with a guard of twenty picked young warriors started down the Wabash, traveling south toward the Mid Day.

XIII. Red Sticks and Big Knives

By the beginning of the nineteenth century the Cherokee in the southern Appalachians had suffered defeats comparable to Fallen Timbers and been fragmented as were the Miami and Shawnee to the north of the Ohio. However, to the south and west of them, the Chickasaw, Choctaw, and Creek were still independent and relatively unscathed by battles fought and treaties made elsewhere. With a collective population of about 50,000, these three nations constituted the largest enclave of free reds remaining east of the Mississippi. Tekamthi promised the British and warned the Americans that he would easily obtain the support of these important people during his fall recruiting trip. When this was accomplished, all reds would stand in the Mid Day. In part these claims may have been advanced as another misinformation exercise.

The Chickasaw, Choctaw, and Creek were mainly farmers—and frequently slaveholders—living in permanent villages. In comparison to the northern natives, they were less dependent on game and immense hunting territories for their food and foreign exchange. One consequence of this was that, contrary to the situation north of the Ohio, the Europeans who came into the country southwest of the Appalachians did not greatly antagonize the natives or disrupt their culture and economy. There had been red-white disputes over land and other matters but not, as in the north, fifty years of bitter warfare to stir up racial passions. Therefore, in 1811 the Chickasaw, Choctaw, and Creek did not feel particularly threatened by whites and had reasonably amicable relations with most of the traders and settlers. In fact, so far as the Chickasaw and Choctaw were concerned, the Shawnee had traditionally been more troublesome than the Americans. The wisdom of forming a political union with the northern nations was, to say the least, not then obvious to most of the southerners.

Tekamthi left Vincennes by canoe on the fifth of August. He was escorted by twenty-one men, six each from the Shawnee, Kickapoo, and Potawatomi nations, two Creek, and as his personal prophet, Seekabo. Seekabo, who was also Tekamthi's maternal cousin, may have been part Creek. Even if not, he had grown up among those people. As an adult he had apparently traveled throughout the deep south and was able to act as an interpreter for the Shawnee when they were among the Chickasaw and Choctaw.

No literate reporter went with Tekamthi in the fall of 1811. Accounts of the trip are sketchy, based on the recollections—often reported years later—of men who said they saw, talked, or listened briefly to the northern visitors. The stories vary greatly in detail but agree about the general itinerary, the nature, and results of the mission.

Below the Ohio they traded for or stole horses. Later some said that all of the men were mounted on splendid coal-black animals, a touch in keeping with Tekamthi's flair for creating dramatic impressions. They stopped first among the Chickasaw in what is now northern Mississippi, even though these people were ancient enemies of the Shawnee and Kickapoo. They remained a week in this nation, and Tekamthi spoke at several public meetings but obtained no promises of support or recruits. Either to show him respect or to keep him under surveillance, he was escorted south to the Choctaw by a band of Chickasaw warriors.

In August the party crossed over a tributary of the Yazoo River and were met by a minor village chief of the Choctaw, Red Pepper, who lived near the present West Point, Mississippi. Having heard of "this strange chief from the north," Red Pepper hospitably arranged a campsite for Tekamthi's men and the Chickasaw escort. During the night the latter found enough whiskey to become belligerently drunk. In this condition they recalled old grievances against the Choctaw and began to threaten Red Pepper's people. Before a brawl started, Tekamthi had his guards subdue the Chickasaw. They were tied up with rawhide and left to spend the night so immobilized.

Tekamthi then held a long conversation with Red Pepper, inquiring about local politics and race relations. He was "guarded" about his specific plans, but told the Choctaw that his ambition was to bring together all the red people, from the Great Lakes to the Gulf, so that they could resist the whites. Red Pepper, who described this meeting much later to Americans, said that he was alarmed by the talk of war since he was always a man of peace but thought it best not to argue with the formidable Shawnee. The next morning the Chickasaw were untied, and they rode off toward their homes, presumedly cramped and crapulent. Much relieved, Red Pepper provided Tekamthi with guides and sent him off south into the heartland of the Choctaw nation.

Near the present community of Macon, the northerners came to the village of Mashuletubbe, a Choctaw war chief. A more important and bolder man than Red Pepper, he was initially enthusiastic about the idea of a red coalition. He supplied escorts so that Tekamthi and Seekabo could visit and speak in nearby Choctaw towns. Mashuletubbe also dispatched messengers throughout his nation calling on the chiefs and warriors to attend a great council at his camp to listen to Tekamthi.

The Choctaw gathered during the early part of September. Their principal man was Pushmataha, renowned as a war and peace chief. Some claimed that as a public speaker he was Tekamthi's equal. The debate which occurred between the two men has ever since been cited as a classic duel between red orators. Possibly it was, but contrary to the inferences of later published reports, there was no verbatim recording of the speeches. However, at least in the case of Tekamthi the style and substance of the remarks he purportedly made are similar to addresses he gave elsewhere.

It was said that Tekamthi and his party kept to themselves until hundreds of Choctaw gathered. Then he and his men made their entrance into the council ring. Each was naked except for a breech clout. Their heads were close shaven, leaving only a high, thick scalp lock ending in a braided cue which hung down between their shoulders and was plaited with hawk feathers. Their faces were marked with a single slash of vermilion war paint under each eye. On each arm they wore a silver bracelet around the biceps. Tekamthi was outfitted as his guards were except that he wore a forehead band of blood red cloth overlaid with silver. (On many other occasions both reds and whites noted that by the standards of his time and people, Tekamthi dressed very plainly and seemed to have contempt for those who went in for cocked hats, fancy feather arrangements, watches worn as earrings, and other gaudy accessories.)

Tekamthi tailored The Speech to suit the Choctaw. No nation, he told them, had a more beautiful country than theirs. Would, he asked, they be willing for this country, "the gift of the Great Spirit, to become the possession of the pale face?" Inevitably this would occur unless the Americans were stopped by the combined forces of the red federation which he proposed. Those who recalled the oration emphasized the most warlike passages in which Tekamthi spoke eloquently of what the warriors could and would do to the Americans, how they would drench the land with their blood. But, as usual, the gist of the message was that if they joined together as one people, the peace and their lands could be kept because the whites would fear to make war on them.

Pushmataha responded, in essence, that the Choctaw and the Americans were already at peace and that "our people have no undue friction with the whites." It would be madness to bring war to their own country by sending young men to fight the battles of distant, northern people. As for Tekamthi, Pushmataha said: "I know your history well. You are a disturber. You have ever been a trouble maker. When you have found yourself unable to pick a quarrel with the white man, you have stirred up strife between different tribes of your own race."

Pushmataha concluded by saying that Tekamthi could expect no support or sympathy from the Choctaw. Then speaking directly to the eager young warriors of Mashuletubbe, Pushmataha warned that if any of them foolishly went off to join this northern agitator, they would be traitors to their own nation and executed if they attempted to rejoin it. Not even Mashuletubbe opposed Pushmataha at the open council.

Some said that the Tekamthi was threatened with death if he stayed longer among the Choctaw. Whether or not this was true, there was clearly no point in talking further to these people. Tekamthi and his guard left, riding toward Alabama and the Creek. (The effort to recruit Choctaw was not entirely abandoned. Later, messengers from Tekamthi secretly returned for further discussions with Mashuletubbe, the most belligerent-minded of the Choctaw chiefs. There were also reports that the next year a few young Choctaw attempted to slip away to join the war against the Americans, but before they were able to do so were tracked down and killed, as Pushmataha had promised they would be.)

It seems that from the beginning, Tekamthi judged the Creek to be the southern people most likely to support him. For more than a century they had good relations with the Shawnee, often allowing them (including Tekamthi's father and mother) to take sanctuary in their territories. Furthermore, as the easternmost of the three southern nations, the Creek were experiencing the most trouble with white settlers and treaty makers. Though their difficulties were not yet as great as those of Indians north of the Ohio, they were sufficient to have created an anti-American faction. These potential resisters were most numerous in what was called the Upper Towns along the northern tributaries of the Alabama River.

Commencing on September 20, the Creeks held a general national council at the centrally located community of Tuckabatchee at the confluence of the Alabama and Tallapoosa rivers. Tekamthi and his escort came there and waited several days while the Creek took care of domestic business. Then he addressed them and again was challenged by old-line, established chiefs who spoke against him as a dangerous and even demented man bent on leading their nation into entangling, very likely suicidal, foreign alliances. However, as had not been the case with the Choctaw, there were a sizable number of the Creek who were impressed with both the political propositions of Tekamthi and the religion of his brother, the Prophet. (Several Creek, most notably a Josiah Francis, a mixed blood whose father operated a trading post, became evangelists, preaching the gospel according to Tenskwatawa.) The pro-Tekamthi faction, though a minority, was strong enough to arrange a compromise. While not promising national support, the Creek agreed to send a party of warriors north to assess the situation.

Tekamthi spent several weeks traveling about Alabama, speaking to and increasing his following among the Creek. In the course of things he—or Seekabo, his prophet—initiated his supporters into the mysteries of the Dance of the Lakes. Among other things it required the ceremonial preparation of supernaturally endowed wands painted with the colors and symbols of war. Properly used, they would indicate the location of enemies, how to surprise and confound them. Thereafter the anti-American faction of the Creek were known as Red Sticks. Toward the end of his stay, Tekamthi attended another general council. On this occasion, irritated by the opposition of older chiefs, he allegedly told his listeners that he would, upon returning to his home, stamp his foot and cause the earth to shake. Wherever he was, Tekamthi was not at Tippecanoe when the New Madrid, Missouri, earthquake occurred on December 16. (This was the first in a series of major seismic upheavals which continued throughout the next year, causing much property damage and panic in the Mississippi Valley.)

In late October Tekamthi and his men left the Creek nation, crossed the Mississippi, and traveled north. In Arkansas or southern Missouri, they stopped to address a council of the Osage, who received them respectfully but made no pledges of assistance.

From there, according to one account, Tekamthi's party headed into the open prairie country to talk with the Iowa and Sioux. It is also possible that, somewhere in the sheltered breaks of the

Missouri, they found a good campsite, laid up, hunted geese on the river, elk and bear in the bottomlands, and rested. Whatever they did, it was done well off the beaten track. The red courier system still was a rapid, efficient one. It is most improbable that had their whereabouts been known, messengers would not have come to Tekamthi and his men and told them of the pitched battle fought at Tippecanoe on the seventh of November between the forces of Harrison and Tenskwatawa. The alternative, that Tekamthi, someplace in Missouri or Iowa, did learn about the battle of Tippecanoe and ignored it for six weeks or so, is implausible.

Early in 1811, Tekamthi's support among the nations of the Ohio Valley and the Great Lakes was widespread, and he possessed more real political power than he had before or would again. But in the late summer of that year he made the two most serious mistakes of his public career. First he misjudged the temper of the Chickasaw, Choctaw, and Creek and his ability to sway them. This might have been correctible; that is, in time he might have made more headway with these nations or at least factions among them. However, he also overestimated his influence on Harrison and his brother Tenskwatawa. This miscalculation was to have irrevocable consequences.

Before he left Indiana in August of 1811, Tekamthi had worked out what he thought was a truce. Tenskwatawa had been directed to keep their people from making any "mischief." Harrison had been assured that there would be peace until he returned. Then he would talk further, perhaps with President Madison, in hopes of arranging a general settlement. In fact, both the governor and the Prophet saw the absence of Tekamthi as providing a golden opportunity to advance their own belligerent policies.

Harrison's reasoning was straightforward and, as it proved, sound. He reported to the War Department that he had become convinced that whatever the Shawnee brothers might say in council meetings, they were virulently anti-American. It must be made plain to the savages, Harrison advised, that if any of them "should dare to take up the tomahawk . . . they would be absolutely exterminated or driven beyond the Mississippi." This could not be done unless the influence and power of the Shawnee brothers was destroyed.

Harrison suggested to William Eustis, Madison's Secretary of War, that Tekamthi's departure

> affords a most favorable opportunity for breaking up his Con-
> federacy . . . . He [Tekamthi] is now upon the last round to put

a finishing stroke to his work. I hope, however, before his return that that part of the fabrick, which he considered complete [the coalition of northern nations] will be demolished and even its foundations rooted up.

What Harrison had in mind was to demand that Tenskwatawa turn over any of his people who might have taken part in frontier raids, so that they could be judged and punished by Americans. If the Prophet refused to do so, as Harrison thought likely, then a strike should be made against Tippecanoe to wipe out this nest of revolutionaries and demonstrate the power of the United States to all the savages in the Northwest. Harrison advised that a sufficient military force must be gathered to ensure absolute success of the operation, for if it failed, the opposite message would be sent, that, as Tekamthi said, the Americans could be beaten. Thereupon the warriors from all the nations might immediately commence raiding the frontier.

Eustis agreed that it was a good idea to teach the hostiles a lesson and that United States regulars could be employed for this purpose. However, he cautioned that, what with the delicate international situation in regards to the British, he and President Madison wanted no general frontier war. Perhaps a sizable gathering of troops would be sufficient to overawe the Prophet and discredit him. Only as a last resort should Harrison use force, and if it came to that, the operation, said Eustis, should be "surgical," a very quick, local one.

Harrison took these vague instructions to mean that he had been given a free hand to campaign as he saw fit in the Wabash valley. His interpretation was not corrected or criticized by any of the authorities in Washington. Toward the end of September with an advance contingent Harrison proceeded to a point about a hundred miles south of Tippecanoe (near the present Terre Haute). There he built a new fort, which he named for himself, and waited throughout much of October while additional troops advanced to the front. Eventually he assembled about 1,000 men, of which 350 were regulars of the 4th Regiment, U.S. Army, and the remainder militiamen from Kentucky and Indiana. He also employed a small band of loyal (to their government chiefs) Delaware and Miami who acted as scouts. Throughout October, in addition to drilling his raw troops, Harrison exchanged ultimatums and other messages with Tenskwatawa at Tippecanoe. As they waited at Camp Harrison, the Americans became increasingly and understandably jittery.

So far as quality was concerned, the men whom Harrison led were quite similar to those who had gone out and died with Harmar and St. Clair, twenty years before. They were hastily armed civilians who had little experience at or taste for soldiering. Beyond what they may have learned hunting small game around their farms or villages, they had little woodcraft. Except for a handful of old-timers, none had even seen or heard, much less fought, against a hostile warrior. Yet from boyhood on they had listened to yarns about the prowess and ferocity of the savages. As for their general, Harrison's wartime service had been very limited, and he had not commanded as much as a company in action. On the other hand he was a younger, more vigorous, and sober man than Harmar or St. Clair had been.

Though it was not appreciated at the time, Harrison's army did enjoy one considerable advantage over its predecessors. The hostiles arrayed against them in 1811 were far less formidable than those of the 1790s. Little Turtle and Blue Jacket had been served by men like Tekamthi, who had been instructed since childhood in the arts of war and were veterans of dozens of skirmishes. The 500 warriors who were then gathered at Tippecanoe were young men who, somewhat like the Americans with Harrison, had for the most part only heard about the battles of twenty years before from their elders. Tenskwatawa who led them was a preacher and prophet who had never raised a hatchet against the Long Knives.

As Harrison's army lumbered up the Wabash in the fall of 1811, it was in a situation almost identical to that of Harmar's and St. Clair's. What to do about this beast—stay out of its way or nip at the flanks until it was lured to a place where it could be ambushed and butchered—would no doubt have been obvious to a Little Turtle, Blue Jacket, or Tekamthi. But Tenskwatawa had neither the training nor the instincts of a warrior. If there were others around him who understood these things, he ignored their counsel. While Harrison advanced, Tenskwatawa vacillated, sometimes sending conciliatory messages offering to parlay but also making bombastic threats about what would be done to the Americans if they did not go home. Throughout October he remained very visibly at Tippecanoe, in effect, offering a stationary target.

On November 6, the Americans camped about two miles from Tippecanoe. Tenskwatawa first sent a messenger suggesting that they talk on the following day about a truce, but in the evening, he began to harangue the warriors to stand and fight a pitched battle in the morning. Victory was guaranteed by the Great Spirit. His Master had come to him, Tenskwatawa assured his people, and promised that He would cover the field with a magical fog. It would enhance the vision of the warriors while at the same time blinding the Big Knives. It was the specific wish of the Great Spirit that

Harrison be killed. After this was accomplished, the surviving Americans "would run and hide in the grass like young quails."

Nearly all of those who listened to this prophecy on the night of November 6 believed it to be another true one, and so quite possibly did Tenskwatawa himself. However, it is interesting to imagine what other things may have been working on his mind. He had grown up awkward and disfigured, incompetent at traditional manly pursuits. Then, miraculously, he had emerged as a messenger and confidant of the gods. But after only a few years of prominence, he had returned to a position where he received and was expected to obey the orders of Tekamthi, the brilliant older brother in whose long shadow he had spent most of his life. Tenskwatawa was a man who might very well have listened attentively for inner voices, which whispered that he could and should be a hero in his own right.

Before dawn on November 7, Tenskwatawa turned loose the warriors on a wild charge. Initially the Americans fell back, but rallied and held their ground largely because of the firmness and personal example of Harrison. Harrison's greatest virtue as a commander was his rapport with the frontier troops he led. The men were his political constituents, in many cases friends and neighbors. To a far greater degree than had patronizing eastern generals, he enjoyed their confidence, understood what they could and would do.

The fighting at Tippecanoe was fierce but essentially involved two armed mobs having at each other among the trees in the half light of morning. The Americans suffered 180 casualties, including fifty men killed. Afterwards they found forty dead Indians on the field and more were known to have been carried or walked away with severe wounds. After about two hours, their ammunition running low, it became apparent to the warriors that they could not rout the Americans. They broke off the fighting and retreated, filing past Tippecanoe and their Prophet.

Whatever Tenskwatawa's visions had been, they did not include him personally going against the Americans with a hatchet or gun. He had remained literally above the battle, standing on a small knoll beyond the town, beseeching the advice and assistance of his Master. As they were passing by, it was later said that the warriors mocked and reviled him, that a party of Winnebago considered killing him on the spot for telling them that "the white people were dead or crazy when [in fact] they were all in their senses and fought like the Devil." Tenskwatawa pleaded that the fault had not been his but that of his wife, who had failed to tell him that she was menstruating, a condition which interfered with his power to hear and interpret divine messages. Hard-pressed as they were, the Winnebago and others spared Tenskwatawa. Pausing to pick up what possessions they could carry, most of the men who had fought at Tippecanoe left for their homes in the west. There they spread stories that Tenskwatawa was a false prophet and a cowardly man.

Later in the day Tenskwatawa gathered his wits and what few people remained with him, some 200, and evacuated Tippecanoe. They retreated ten miles and made a bad winter camp in the thickets along Wildcat Creek. On the eighth of November, having buried their dead and treated the wounded, Harrison's men entered Tippecanoe and partially destroyed it. They left hastily for Vincennes when rumors began to circulate that Tekamthi was approaching with 1,000 warriors whom he had recruited in the south.

Americans came to speak of Tippecanoe as the first battle of the War of 1812. More accurately it was the final confrontation—in which red and white residents of the Northwest were the sole antagonists—of the long civil war in that region.

Wherever he had been, Tekamthi, with an escort of only eight men, came to the camp of the Tippecanoe refugees early in January of 1812. According to Anthony Shane, his rage was so great that, while Tenskwatawa was attempting to explain the disastrous battle, Tekamthi seized him by the hair, drew back his head, and said he would kill him were it not that they were blood brothers. On the spot Tenskwatawa was in effect defrocked and demoted. After Tippecanoe, he never again was accepted as, or apparently claimed to be, a holy man. In outlying districts some of his disciples continued to preach, but within a year or so the religion of the Shawnee prophet had disappeared. As for secular matters, during the next two years, after his initial anger had passed, Tekamthi was to employ his brother as a minor aide, but did not turn to him for advice or give him large responsibilities.

The rage of Tekamthi when he returned to the Wabash country was understandable. During the previous five years he had created a resistance movement, the strength of which largely depended on the fears of his enemies and hopes of his followers about what might happen. The battle of Tippecanoe, which his fool of a brother could have easily avoided, in effect called Tekamthi's bluff. The fighting itself had been a draw. But that Harrison had not been defeated was enough to raise doubts about Tekamthi's red union being inevitable and irresistible. Also Tenskwatawa had undercut the mystical foundation of the movement. Thereafter it was difficult for even the most credulous to believe that divine authorities specially favored and protected the Shawnee brothers.

After dressing down and dismissing Tenskwatawa, Tekamthi was faced with the immediate, if homely, problem of getting the Tippecanoe refugees through the winter. A few warriors returned to the ruined townsite to scavenge for caches of food which the Americans had not burned. Hunters were sent east of the Wabash. Tekamthi himself made a winter journey to Canada to appeal to Matthew Elliott and other British agents for supplies. At Amherstburg he ate considerable crow.

On his previous visit he had dealt imperiously with the British, telling them that the Mid Day was nigh, that after it arrived, he and his people would be perfectly capable of handling the Americans by themselves. In the bad winter of 1812, Tekamthi could not take such a high tone. Addressing Elliott politely as "father," he said that as he had previously told him, he had traveled south leaving specific instructions that his people should avoid any trouble with the Americans while he was gone. However, mistakes had regrettably been made.

> On my return lately I found great destruction and havoc—the fruits of our labor destroyed—the bodies of my friends laying in the dust, and our village burnt to the ground and all our kettles carried off. . . . We are truly poor, in want of the common necessities of life both for ourselves and our women and chidren, everything having been destroyed by the Big Knives.

Elliott was able to supply some provisions, which helped the Tippecanoe people to survive the winter. In the spring the refugees at Wildcat Creek moved back to Tippecanoe and commenced planting gardens. After they were settled, Tekamthi started another round of travel for the purpose of repairing as best he could the holes in what Harrison had called the "fabrick" of his political designs. Among the other red nations, as with the British, Tippecanoe had changed the balance of things and necessitated a less authoritarian approach. In the spring of 1812 he appeared not as the "head of them all," seeking recruits for a single red nation, but as a war chief attempting to arrange alliances among equals. That during the next several months he was able to patch together a substantial coalition testified to his abilities and reputation.

Though their warriors had done most of the fighting and dying at Tippecanoe, the western nations—the Potawatomi, Winnebago, Fox, and Sauk—remained generally loyal and anti-American. In the east it was a different story. Roundhead kept his Wyandot faction in line, but among the Delaware, Miami, and Shawnee there were defections, and the influence of the old-line government chiefs increased. John Johnston, the principal American agent to Black Hoof's Shawnee, wrote to the Secretary of War that these people were so opposed to the troublemakers and anxious to demonstrate their friendship to the United States that "If it was agreeable to the Government the Indians could be easily prevailed on to kill the Prophet and his Brother." Johnston added delicately, "I have been much embarrassed to know what to say to them on this head. I have however on reflection deferred the matter until Governor Harrison could be consulted."

The assassination scheme was not pursued, and Tekamthi continued to circulate among the eastern nations while placating the Americans sufficiently to keep them from making any sudden offensive moves. There was an exchange of messages with Harrison, in which the governor again suggested that Tekamthi and Tenskwatawa should visit President Madison in Washington, not so much, as they had talked about previously, to settle differences between their two people, but to demonstrate their peaceful intentions. Tekamthi replied that he would carefully consider the invitation but for the moment was occupied with other business.

As the spring wore on, Tekamthi's missionary work began to show results, as warriors from Illinois and the western Great Lakes reassembled at Tippecanoe. When they became aware of this gathering, Harrison, John Johnston, and William Wells increased their efforts to obtain pledges from the eastern Indians that they would oppose Tekamthi or at least remain neutral if trouble occurred. For this purpose, late in May a council was arranged on the Mississinewa River in eastern Indiana. Wells invited factions of the Delaware, Miami, Potawatomi, Shawnee, and Wyandot who were thought most friendly to the Americans. Unexpectedly Tekamthi himself appeared. In the open council, he reaffirmed that it was the intention of him and his people to keep the peace, that they would take up arms only to defend themselves. This was what they had been trying to do the fall before at Tippecanoe. The battle there had been an "unfortunate transaction that took place between the white people and a few of our younger men at our village. . . . Had I been home there would have been no blood shed at that time."

Though the Big Knives had clearly been the aggressor, Tekamthi said, he was not of a mind to avenge the incident at Tippecanoe. Emboldened by his conciliatory manner and eager to make a good impression on Harrison's agents, other speakers then rebuked Tekamthi as a troublemaker and demanded that he cease agitating among their people. A leader in this verbal attack was Isadore

Chaine, a Wyandot of mixed blood from the Detroit area, who spoke at the council as a representative of the peace party among his people. Following his speech he arranged to hold a meeting with Tekamthi, ostensibly to instruct him further about the error of his ways. The Americans were pleased with Chaine's public performance and hoped that in private he might bring even more pressure on the Shawnee.

In fact, Chaine was a British agent, under orders from Matthew Elliott to come to the council and ingratiate himself sufficiently with the Americans so as to be able to give Tekamthi an important message. Chaine brought from Elliott a black wampum belt signifying war, and the warning that hostilities were imminent. Elliott suggested Tekamthi inform the warriors but take pains to conceal their military preparations from the Americans so as to retain the advantage of surprise. Tekamthi should come to Amherstburg to obtain guns and ammunition for distribution throughout the northwest.

Tekamthi returned to Tippecanoe in early June to pass along this intelligence. He departed shortly, leaving instructions that the people there should at all costs avoid antagonizing the Americans for the moment. Thereafter in separate bands the warriors began to travel northward to Ontario. Tekamthi and his small escort arrived at Fort Wayne on June 17, and spent several days there. He openly told the American agent, Benjamin Stickney—who had replaced William Wells as the officer in charge—that he was going to Canada to attend a council being convened by the British. He added soothingly that his purpose was to persuade the red people who would be there to remain at peace with the United States. Stickney was suspicious, but reported to Harrison that he had not thought it "prudent" to try to detain him. A week or so later Tekamthi arrived in Amherstburg and learned that the United States had declared war on the British. The formal proclamation had actually been issued on June 18 while he was at Fort Wayne, but it took some days for word of it to reach the frontier outposts.

XIV. What Will I Do with These Women and Children?

Ostensibly the United States went to war in reaction to the high-handed maritime policies—impressment and interference with sea trade with Europe—of the British. Yet, paradoxically, the Americans most directly concerned with shipping were the ones who found the British practices the easiest to bear. Having profited handsomely during the Napoleonic wars as both legitimate and contraband shippers, the merchant classes saw little reason to begin a conflict that might upset the lucrative status quo. Generally the war was least popular in the coastal cities, and in New England there was sufficient opposition to stir up fairly serious talk about seceding from the union.

Though far from the salt waters, it was the citizens and politicians living beyond the Appalachians who were most ferocious in their demands for "Free Trade and Sailors' Rights." The patriotic outrage was no doubt genuine, but it also served to bring pressure on the federal government to embark on a venture which was closer to the hearts of the westerners than were oceanic ones. "On to Canada," was the slogan that mightily aroused the backwoods audiences of Henry Clay and the other War Hawk orators.

The clamor to conquer Canada reflected the widespread opinion that this was the only way to eliminate the Red Menace once and for all. The reasoning was that the lives and prosperity of citizens in the western regions of the United States were in constant jeopardy so long as the savages were being given sanctuary, supplies, and munitions in the north. Starting a full-scale war with the British as a means of controlling a few thousand impoverished Indians seems, in retrospect, somewhat like taking up a sledge hammer to drive tacks. But at that time many settlers were genuinely terrified by the prospect of hordes of warriors, well-armed from Canadian arsenals, ravaging the frontier districts as they had in the past. To a considerable degree these fears remained strong and general because of the artful manner in which Tekamthi and Tenskwatawa had played with the collective white imagination. The battle at Tippecanoe had not served—as it logically might have—to convince Americans that the Indian problem could be settled by a series of small, brisk police actions. It simply made westerners more optimistic than they had been about succeeding in an open war against the British and Indians. Since the chances of winning seemed greater, the enthusiasm for a military solution naturally increased.

There was another large consideration—revenge. Thrashing the redcoats and redskins in Canada would at least partially pay them back for Ruddell's Station and Blue Licks, for the defeats of Crawford, Harmar, and St. Clair. Far more than reports of sailors lobbing cannonballs on the high and distant seas, it was fresh memories of cabins burned, prisoners taken, and scalps lifted that inspired bellicose sentiments in the west.

The War Hawks from beyond the mountains were by no means solely responsible for the War of 1812, but their passions largely dictated how American military operations were initially conducted. Canada, in terms of attacking or defending it, was somewhat like a tree. The roots through which flowed the vital sap—commerce and military stores from the motherland—were along the Atlantic seaboard. A number of eastern strategists pointed out that if the supply arrangements were disrupted, Upper Canada (Ontario) would wither and fall as will the branches of an oak after the trunk is girdled. This approach was insufficiently direct and dramatic for the politicians, militiamen, and voters of the Northwest. Their immediate concern was to stop, by driving them out, the British from agitating and arming the Indians in the western Great Lakes region.

Because the War Hawk spokesmen were persuasive and their constituents were enthusiastic about answering the national call to arms, the westerners had their way. The first major American military operation was launched with the intention of invading Ontario from Michigan and capturing Fort Malden at Amherstburg, the base at the mouth of the Detroit River which had long been the center of British activities in the west. After Fort Malden and Amherstburg fell, the invaders planned to lop off other branches in Upper Canada.

Several months before the actual declaration of war, President Madison authorized the mobilization of 100,000 militiamen and had begun to organize the Army of the Northwest. This force was to be sent to Detroit to protect the settlers against Indian raids but also to be in a position, if needed, to move into Canada. Command of this army was offered to William Hull, who since 1805 had been the territorial governor of Michigan but in the spring of 1812 was back in his native Massachusetts on leave. Hull was then sixty years old and in the years following the Revolutionary War had prospered as a lawyer and politician. Age, good living, and again an over-fondness for the bottle had dissipated whatever ambitions Hull may once have had to be a hero. Initially he turned down the military command, saying he was well satisfied to remain a civil servant. However, William Eustis, the Secretary of War, was persistent, reasoning that Hull was at least familiar with local conditions. He upped the offer, proposing to Hull that if he accepted a commission as a brigadier general, he could also retain his rank and salary as the federal governor of Michigan. The veteran accepted and headed toward Ohio to organize the Army of the Northwest.

Hull did not learn that war had been declared until July 2, two weeks after the fact. (The message had been sent from Washington by regular mail.) He was then in southern Michigan on the River Raisin, near the present Monroe, with about 2,200 men. Some 400 of them were regulars gathered from forts along the Ohio River while the remainder were militia from Ohio and Michigan. Hull arrived at Detroit four days later, waited another week, and then crossed the river into Ontario on July 12. The invading forces were not opposed and entered the first Canadian community, Sandwich (now Windsor), without a shot being fired on either side. After proceeding a few miles downstream along the Detroit River, toward Fort Malden, Hull halted and waited just inside Canada during the remainder of July.

Even at the time, many of Hull's subordinates thought he was excessively cautious. Despite its many deficiencies, the Army of the Northwest, was much superior to the British forces directly opposing it. Col. Thomas St. George, the commander at Amherstburg, had about 300 regulars, who were mostly deployed to defend Fort Malden. Also some 800 militiamen had been mobi-lized, but they were no more warlike than their American counter-parts and shortly became even less so. The most effective measure

Hull took during his first weeks in Canada was to issue a proclamation in which he promised amnesty to any white Ontario
residents (many of whom had emigrated from the United States)
who did not bear arms against him. He added the threat that any of
them who were caught fighting alongside the savage warriors
would be executed. Once circulated through Ontario, this announcement had, from the American standpoint, an excellent
effect. Immediately about half of the militia disbanded and returned to their civilian pursuits.

As his proclamation indicated, it was the Indians who most
concerned Hull. Because of faulty intelligence reports and many
wild rumors, he formed the impression that thousands of warriors
were gathering both ahead of him in Canada and in the rear along
his supply lines. In fact, there were at the time about 1,500 Indians
in southern Michigan and Ontario. Many were noncombatants,
women and children who had followed their men northward
seeking sanctuary in Canada. Also some of the warriors were still
debating about whether or not to fight and if so on which side. For
example, there was Walk-on-the-Water, a thoughtful if not valiant
Wyandot, who led a hundred or so warriors from the River Raisin
area. Three times during the summer he crossed the Detroit River,
offering his allegiance—depending on the signs of the day—
alternatively to both the Americans and British. To the south,
surrounded by whites, the Shawnee of Black Hoof and Miami of
Little Turtle stayed on their reservations and promised at least
neutrality. (A few Shawnee and Miami agreed to join Hull as
scouts.)

Despite Hull's exaggerated fears, the only effective Indian—or
for that matter Canadian—force between him and Amherstburg
was a party of 300 warriors led by Tekamthi. On July 25, Hull sent
out 120 men on a tentative probe toward Amherstburg, twenty
miles to the south. Tekamthi and 150 of his men ambushed these
scouts on the Canard River, killing several of them. The Americans,
certain that they were surrounded by hordes of savages, fled back to
Sandwich. However Capt. William McCulloch, chief of Hull's
rangers, was able to bring down a single Indian and take his scalp,
the first one lifted in the War of 1812. In retaliation, Tekamthi's
men killed several of their American prisoners.

In terms of potential strength the United States was enormously
superior at the outbreak of the war. The nation then had a population of more than 7 million, a militia pool of 700,000 men, and a
regular army of 7,000. In contrast there were about a half million

white Canadians who at the most could provide 50–70,000 militia.
A good many of these citizens were of French descent and had little
enthusiasm for serving with the English. There were fewer than
8,000 British regulars in the colony, and most of them were in the
port areas to the east.

Nevertheless the British enjoyed several tactical advantages in
the west. They had the only naval forces on the Great Lakes and
therefore could shift men and supplies speedily and without risk by
water. Also they were led by Maj. Gen. Isaac Brock. Though at the
time he was serving as both the military commander and governor
of Upper Canada, Brock, unlike Hull, the politican-general, was a
professional soldier, the best the British were ever to have in the
Northwest. Having served brilliantly in the Napoleonic wars before
being posted to Canada, Brock was forty-three years old in 1812. He
was an imposing man of massive frame who stood several inches
over six feet, an inspirational as well as aggressive and imaginative
commander.

Brock had much more sympathy for the Indians than did most of
his colleagues and became an advocate of the plan for establishing
a neutral Indian nation in the Northwest. British policy-makers had
been teasing North American natives of both races with this idea
since the end of the Revolution. Brock believed that red demands
for an independent homeland were legitimate, and that guarantee-
ing them a territory of their own was a reasonable price to pay for
their assistance in the war. As for using Indian allies, which the
Americans were piously claiming was immoral and uncivilized,
Brock replied shortly to the proclamation which Hull issued when
he invaded Canada: "If their warfare [that of the reds] from being
different from that of white people is more terror to the enemy
[Hull] let him retrace his steps."

In June of 1812 Brock concentrated most of his forces, about a
thousand dependable militia and regulars, near York (Toronto) to
defend the heartland of Upper Canada against an American army
which was being slowly gathered in the vicinity of Niagara by Gen.
Henry Dearborn, another Revolutionary War veteran. However,
during July the British commander became increasingly concerned
about Hull's invasion from Detroit. A paramount consideration was
the effect it was having on Indians. Matthew Elliott and other
agents in Amherstburg were warning that if Hull should take Fort
Malden and lumber on eastward into Ontario, most of the warriors
would melt away, convinced that it was foolish to join the British.
Brock concurred with this opinion, but initially the risks of divert-
ing any of his small force from the Niagara frontier, seemed
prohibitive.

In mid-July Brock's dilemma was fortuitously solved. To the north the old trading post of Fort Michilimackinac, near the junction of Lakes Huron and Michigan, was held by a token garrison of sixty Americans. The nearest British post was forty miles to the east on St. Joseph's Island. The commanding officer there, Capt. Charles Roberts, heard about the outbreak of war on July 8. He then set out with his fifty regulars,some local traders, and about 400 Indians for Michilimackinac. They arrived early on the morning of July 17. The American garrison was completely surprised, having not previously been informed that their country was at war. Unprepared and outnumbered, they surrendered without firing a shot. The strategic importance of Michilimackinac was minimal since it was essentially only a wilderness trading post. But the psychological impact of its capture was considerable on the Great Lakes Indians and upon William Hull. The former suddenly became optimistic about the British chances and started making preparations to join Tekamthi in the south. As for Hull, his already substantial fears about the savages were magnified by visions of a canoe flotilla full of warriors descending on him from the north.

Receiving intelligence about Hull's jitters and noting that the Americans at Niagara were taking an inordinate amount of time to get themselves organized, Issac Brock decided that something immediately could be done about Hull's Army of the Northwest. In a week of furious activity Brock collected 300 militia, about 100 regulars, and sixty Iroquois from the St. Lawrence, including John Norton, the warrior/journalist. They were loaded into ten small boats and on August 8 set off on Lake Erie, headed for Amherstburg. The departure of these men left central Ontario virtually defenseless, but Brock reasoned, correctly as it turned out, that he might be able to rout the timid Hull with one quick strike and then return to the Niagara front before the disorganized Americans to the south became aware of his absence.

Even before Brock's tiny expeditionary force arrived in the west, the prospects for its success had been greatly improved by Tekamthi who, weary of watching the immobile Americans, organized an offensive sortie of his own. On August 2 with twenty-four picked warriors he crossed the Detroit River by canoe. On the Michigan side, on August 5, they ambushed 150 Ohio militiamen who had been sent south from Detroit to meet and serve as an escort for a supply train. Having inexplicably wandered away from the well-traveled main road and become lost in the rural countryside, the Americans attempted to ford Brownstown Creek. While they were so engaged, Tekamthi and his men came screaming out of the underbrush on the far side. Milling about in the middle of the stream, seventeen of the whites were killed, two were captured, and a dozen or so wounded before they extricated themselves and fled toward Detroit. (Upon arriving there, the commanding officer of the detachment, Maj. Thomas Van Horne, reported that he had been waylaid by at least 200 savages.) Among the dead was William McCulloch who, two weeks before on the Canadian side, had proudly taken the first red scalp of the war. Only one of Tekamthi's men, a young Shawnee, was killed. To give him an honorable sendoff on his journey to the next world, the two American prisoners were executed on the spot.

The engagement at Brownstown was repeated four days later in the same vicinity though on a much larger scale. On this occasion, Hull sent out 600 men to meet the supply train. Tekamthi in the meantime had received reinforcements from Amherstburg. The faithful Roundhead arrived with 200 warriors, and encouraged by Tekamthi's success, the British added 150 men to the party. This first mixed offensive was not a success. Tekamthi laid out another ambush, but before it was fully sprung, British troops, under the impression they had been attacked by the Americans, began firing on their Indian allies. The warriors naturally returned the fire, and during the confusion, the Americans were able to drive off the hostiles. In this odd, three-way fracas, Tekamthi received a painful but not disabling leg wound.

Hull's men took fairly heavy casualties, fifty wounded and twenty dead (those of the British and Indians were about the same) but since the Americans had held their ground, they counted the action as a notable victory. Their commander in chief was much less optimistic about the significance of this action. A week previously, camped south of Sandwich barely within the border of Canada, Hull had talked confidently to his staff about taking Fort Malden with a brisk bayonet charge. The news from Michilimackinac, the two strikes against his supply lines by Tekamthi, and reports that Brock was on his way from the east with a large army halted all discussion about offensive operations. Convinced that he was surrounded by vastly superior forces, Hull called off the invasion of Canada. On the twelfth of August he brought the Army of the Northwest back to Detroit and began to make plans to leave Michigan and retreat further south into Ohio.

The following day, Brock with his troops from Niagara and Tekamthi and his Michigan raiders arrived in Amherstburg. The place was also rapidly filling up with odd lots of Indians who had been judiciously waiting elsewhere, but, after the American setbacks, came in to join what appeared would be the winning side. All told there were more than 500 warriors on hand when Brock disembarked. They began wildly firing their pieces in welcome. Brock turned to Matthew Elliott, saying that while he was flattered by the demonstration, it was a waste of precious ammunition. Elliott went off and after the firing ceased, he returned with Tekamthi who, though still sore and limping, had brought the warriors under control. He told Brock that he agreed about the need to conserve powder and lead and would see that his men did not behave so foolishly in the future.

Introduced under these circumstances, Brock and Tekamthi took an immediate liking to each other. The former was impressed, as so many whites had been, with how the famous Shawnee dressed, carried himself, spoke, and thought. In an official report sent to the Colonial secretary in London, Brock commented about Tekamthi: "A more sagacious or more gallant Warrior does not I believe exist." To his own staff he spoke of him as "the Wellington of the Indians," the highest of praise from a veteran British officer of the Napoleonic campaigns. As for Tekamthi, after first meeting Brock, he turned to a bystander and said in English, which he rarely used on such occasions: "Ho-o-o-e. This is a man."

Brock gave a formal speech to the assembled Indians, saying that he had been sent by their great, good Father, the English King, to help them to drive the Long Knives from Detroit and thereafter as much farther south as was necessary. Tekamthi gave the Indian answer, replying he and his people were elated that the English King had "at length awoke from his long sleep and permitted his warriors to come to the assistance of his red children."

On the following day, the fourteenth of August, Brock, Tekamthi, and a few of their staff people met privately. Tekamthi first spoke of his ambition to establish a permanent, unified red nation in the northwest and his need for British help in doing so. Brock agreed that this was a reasonable war aim which he could support whole-heartedly. (He did so in the reports and recommendations he sent back to London.) Then they took up the immediate military situation. During his probes in Michigan during the preceding week, Tekamthi had captured several American couriers and the official dispatches—from and to Hull—which they carried. Brock had had a chance to look over these documents. It was his impression that Hull was in such a funk that, despite his sizable army, he might cave in if given or even threatened with a sharp blow. Tekamthi concurred and gave Brock his estimate of the American forces. Taking a scroll of fresh-cut elm bark from his belt, he drew, with the point of his scalping knife, a map of the village and fort at Detroit.

Brock raised a delicate subject. Could he trust the warriors to remain sober and, if Detroit was taken, refrain from a general massacre? (In addition to Hull's men at the fort, there were some 700 civilians in the town surrounding it.) Tekamthi said that he had made his men pledge that they would not taste "pernicious" liquor until the Big Knives were beaten. As for casually abusing prisoners for sport, he said imperiously, "No. I despise them too much to meddle with them."

Brock and Tekamthi immediately began to implement their offensive plan, moving their men to Sandwich, which faced Detroit and had been evacuated by Hull three days earlier. Early on the afternoon of the fifteenth, Brock sent Hull a message, saying that his forces were such that the Americans must immediately surrender Detroit. He added: "It is far from my intention to join in a war of extermination, but you must be aware, that the numerous body of Indians who have attached themselves to my troops, will be beyond control the moment the contest commences."

Though his panic was increasing by the hour, Hull replied bravely saying that he would not surrender and was "prepared to meet any force which may be at your disposal, and any consequences which may result from any exertion of it you may think proper to make."

Late in the day, to indicate that his intentions were serious, Brock had his artillerymen lob a few balls into Detroit. After night fell, Tekamthi collected his warriors. By then there were about 700 of them. They put on their war paint, stripped down to their breech clouts, and between midnight and dawn slipped across the river. At daylight they were very visible on the western and northern perimeters of Detroit, not shooting but making breakfast from gardens and cabins deserted by white settlers who had fled into the center of town.

Brock had about 600 of his own men in Sandwich, and at dawn on the sixteenth sent them across the river, where they established their position and six pieces of light field artillery south of Detroit. Hull had 1,500 men inside Detroit. The Americans had more and heavier artillery, but some of their pieces were immobile, and ammunition was very short. Also though he was not fully aware of it, some of Hull's militia officers (including Lewis Cass, the future governor of Michigan, and Duncan MacArthur from Ohio) were in the midst of spinning a mutinous plot aimed at removing Hull from his command. These officers had an additional 600 men a few miles south of Detroit, but either because they were not aware of what was happening or did not want to help Hull, they took no part in the action. More important than the condition of his defenses was the state of Hull's mind. There were many rumors later that he had been drinking heavily on the night of the fifteenth–sixteenth. Whether this was the case, he was clearly befuddled by his fear of the savages. Hull thought they were "numerous beyond example," and "more greedy of violence . . . than the Vikings or Huns."

As Hull and his staff were assessing their position, a lucky British cannonball hit his personal quarters. Several officers were killed and his own daughter and grandchildren were narrowly missed. Immediately Hull ran up a white bed sheet on the flagpole above Detroit and sent a messenger to Brock, surrendering all the 2,000 men of the Army of the Northwest. (The total included the mutinous units south of the Fort who had taken no part in the defense of it.)

At noon on the sixteenth, Brock with Tekamthi at his side rode into Detroit to accept the formal capitulation. As Americans lining the streets later remembered, the two grim men were impressive figures. Both were in field uniforms, Brock of a British regular and Tekamthi in the plain buckskins of a warrior. His only special adornment was a wide red sash—Brock's own formal one, which he had given to the Shawnee chief in gratitude for his services. (The next day when they met, Tekamthi no longer had the sash and Brock, fearful that he had somehow given offense, asked about it. Tekamthi told him that he had been greatly honored by the gift, so much so that he had passed it along to Roundhead, the Wyandot who during the campaign had performed more notably than he himself had.)

Nothing more was reported about what Tekamthi did, said, or thought on the day Detroit fell. But unless this man was so alien as to be absolutely unimaginable, it must have been a moment of delicious triumph as he walked his horse through the streets of this place which had been the center of white power—first the French, then the British and Americans—for a century in the west.

It is not remembered as such because it was such an easy, bloodless thing but the capture of Detroit and an entire army of the United States was the most strategically significant red accomplishment during the nearly 300 years of conflict in North America. In a chronological sense it was a collective, racial victory. Hull's dispatches made it plain that Detroit was taken, or more accurately given, principally because of the Indians. When he heard that they were on the outskirts of the town with the militia fleeing in front of them, he cried to an aide, "My God, what will I do with these women and children?"

Hull—as many of his critics were soon to point out—very possibly could have resisted Brock and Tekamthi. But he was overcome by a generalized fear of savages, one fed by hundreds of the hordes-from-hell stories which had been circulating among western whites for three generations. If they were in a place and condition to be still interested in worldly affairs, Cornstalk, Puckeshinwa, Cheesekau, Black Fish, Little Turtle, and Blue Jacket no doubt took considerable satisfaction from the fall of Detroit and their contributions to the enterprise.

Within ten days after Detroit was taken, Brock was back on the Niagara frontier, having won his gamble, since the Americans south of that border had taken no offensive action in his absence. Tekamthi, Roundhead, and their warriors remained in Michigan for a few days, raiding south toward the Maumee, destroying American supply caches. Then they returned to Amherstburg to regroup for further offensive actions within the United States.

Before the fall of Detroit, Tekamthi sent runners to the west, telling his followers to take up their war hatchets. The first to respond were the Potawatomi in northern Illinois, who began gathering for an attack on Fort Dearborn (Chicago) under the direction of a war chief, Black Bird. (Main Poc was with Tekamthi around Detroit.) Dearborn was garrisoned by fifty-four regulars of the 1st Regiment. The commander there, Capt. Nathan Heald, had also received a courier from the east bearing a dispatch sent in late July by Hull, who ordered Heald to evacuate the post and come to Detroit. Hull's messenger passed through Fort Wayne, where William Wells learned of his mission. Wells, still the American officer most knowledgeable about the Indians, collected thirty Miami warriors and set off for Fort Dearborn. (He had a personal interest in the post, his niece, Rebecca, being there as the wife of Heald.) Wells arrived on the thirteenth of August and bluffed his way through the Potawatomi who had begun to invest the fort. Inside he found, in addition to the soldiers, some forty civilians, nearby settlers who had come in for protection. Heald, in obedience to his orders, was preparing to leave. Wells protested vehemently that he should remain where he was, that it still might be possible to defend the fort against the Potawatomi, but once the Americans left their palisades they would be cut to pieces. Heald, a young, by-the-book regular officer, said that orders were orders. On the morning of the fifteenth the Americans marched out of Fort Dearborn, the soldiers flanking the settlers and their wagons. They traveled about two miles and then, in a sandy field, were overwhelmed by the Potawatomi. Over half of the Americans, including twenty-six of the regulars and fourteen of the women and children, were killed immediately. Heald, his wife Rebecca, and the rest were taken prisoner. William Wells, before leaving the fort, had painted his face black, as the Miami traditionally did when they reckoned the day had come that they would die in battle. Then he had ridden out with Heald. When the Potawatomi struck, the thirty Miami who came with Wells turned and fled without putting up any resistance. (Some switched sides and joined the Potawatomi.) Wells stood his ground and killed at least two of his attackers before he was chopped to bits. At the end of the brief skirmish, the Potawatomi cut open his chest and ate pieces of his warm heart. It was a complimentary gesture made in recognition of his valor and in the hopes that they could ingest some of it. Then they cut off his head. Mounted on the tip of a spear, it was displayed to the terrified American prisoners. Thus ended the brave, brilliant Wild Carrot, the man of two races. As Tekamthi had predicted when they had last met two years before, Wells lived just long enough to understand fully the true nature of the red resistance movement.

After taking Fort Dearborn the Potawatomi moved through northern Illinois and Indiana, picking up additional warriors as they went. Some outlying farms were looted and burned, but few scalps were taken, since the white settlers were by then fleeing eastward. On September 5, the Potawatomi reached the outskirts of Fort Wayne. There they began exchanging shots with the American pickets and waylaying military couriers but could not breach the main defenses of the post which was commanded by a future President, Zachary Taylor.

Meanwhile other war parties, answering Tekamthi's call, simultaneously attacked both Fort Madison near St. Louis and Fort Harrison on the Wabash. Here the Americans, including many civilians who had come in from the countryside, stayed behind their palisades and were able to hold off the raiders. In the same week Missilimetaw, a minor war chief from the Tekamthi faction among the Shawnee, led a band into the open settlement of Pigeon Roost in southern Indiana, burned the community, and killed twenty whites who were still there. By the end of the summer the warriors controlled most of the original Northwest Territory, except for Ohio south of the Maumee. Elsewhere, whites hung on in fortified strong points between which they could travel only in large armed parties during the daylight.

The American response to the red resurgence was initially confused and ineffective. The obvious first need was to replace the army that had been lost at Detroit. While the manpower was available—there were 50,000 potential militia west of the Appalachians—organizational efforts were hampered by the usual logistics problems and a considerable wrangle about who would lead the second Army of the Northwest. The Madison administration, like several of its predecessors, showed a great knack for selecting frontier generals whose unpromising credentials were fully validated by their wretched field performances. In this case, James Winchester was appointed to command the new army. His only previous military experience had been as a captain during the Revolutionary War, but during the thirty years following it, he had done well in business and politics. Though at the time Winchester was a resident of Tennessee, he remained in attitude and manners a member of the seaboard establishment. He had the customary disdain of his class for westerners who made up most of his troops. The feeling was mutual. It turned out that Winchester was not a ferocious enough disciplinarian to frighten the Kentucky and Ohio volunteers into obedience and too stiff and snobbish to win their affection. Junior officers and enlisted men obeyed his orders indifferently or not at all, mocked and played frontier-type practical jokes on the pompous old general. One evening pranksters, who were never caught, nailed a porcupine skin onto the seat of his private latrine.

In the west public consensus favored William Henry Harrison, the hero of Tippecanoe, as the man best suited to defend the territory still held and then launch a second invasion of Canada. Harrison fully agreed with these sentiments. By way of a bureaucratic counteroffensive, Harrison visited Kentucky, where he was named the commander of that state's militia with the rank of major general. In an attempt at compromise, William Eustis, the Secretary of War, offered to make Harrison a brigadier general of regulars, as was Winchester, and put him in charge of operations in Indiana and Illinois. Since this would have made him a subordinate to Winchester, whose commission had been given earlier, Harrison refused but did not abandon his hopes for military glory. During the fall he, Winchester, and assorted federal and state politicians contended with each other for rank, authority, and public support.

As between the two would-be commanders of the western army, Harrison was clearly the more energetic and popular man. When he learned from Zachary Taylor that the savages were gathering around Fort Wayne, Harrison more or less commandeered the 2,000 man force that Winchester had gathered at Cincinnati and marched it north. The first of his men arrived in time to discourage the Potawatomi. The Indians withdrew a safe distance and waited for assistance, which messengers told them was coming from Canada.

Throughout August parties of warriors from the northern Great Lakes region arrived in Amherstburg. A month after the fall of

Detroit, Tekamthi, Roundhead, and Main Poc had nearly 1,000 men gathered there, all of whom were eager for action against the Americans who seemed in such disarray. Their immediate objective was to take Fort Wayne, but they thought that to do so, field artillery was imperative. To get it, they had to deal for the first time with Col. Henry Procter, whom Isaac Brock had left in charge at Fort Malden.

Procter was a veteran professional soldier who, though lacking field experience, had been a competent aide and administrator. However, if Brock was comparable to Anthony Wayne, Procter as an independent commander proved to be more similar to William Hull. Unlike Brock, Procter had small regard either for the character or military abilities of the Indians. Since he could not get them to drill and obey like real soldiers, he saw little use in them, was constantly vexed and even a bit frightened by the savages. That he had to feed the warriors and their families from government supplies, which were not abundant, also greatly bothered this orderly minded, unimaginative man.

Mainly, it seems, to get the Indians away from Amherstburg for a time, Procter agreed to a joint expedition against Fort Wayne. About 200 British regulars and three cannons were ferried across from Amherstburg to the mouth of the Maumee in Ohio where they joined Tekamthi, Roundhead, and 800 of their warriors. By September 25 they had traveled upriver to the site of the former Shawnee community located at the junction of the Maumee and Auglaize. There it was learned that Harrison had reached Fort Wayne and with 2,000 men was moving slowly downstream toward them. (In fact, James Winchester had hurried north from Cincinnati and by virtue of his federal authority had recaptured the army from Harrison.) The ranking British officer with the expedition was Capt. Adam Muir, who was unenthusiastic about soldiering with Indians. On learning of the American advance, Muir began worrying about losing his cannons and defending his supply lines. He demanded that the advance be halted and that the expeditionary force dig in and prepare to defend itself. Tekamthi and Roundhead argued that the American army appeared to be a typically weak and disorganized one, which was ripe for ambushing, but that the place where Muir wanted to make a stand was not suitable for this purpose. Muir, as he later reported to Procter, decided the savages did not understand modern warfare. Therefore he loaded his cannons on flatboats and went back to Amherstburg. Convinced that it would be impossible to take Fort Wayne without artillery support, the Indians dispersed, many of the warriors returning directly to their homes on the northern shores of the Great Lakes. Tekamthi and

Roundhead with their own warriors returned to Amherstburg in early October. There they learned of a happening which was to have far worse consequences for them than the failed attempt on Fort Wayne. On October 13, at Queenston, on the Niagara Peninsula, Isaac Brock was killed in a sharp engagement, during which the long-awaited American invasion in that sector was thrown back. Thereafter as a brevet major general, Henry Procter became the commander of British military operations in western Ontario.

Beyond defending Fort Wayne, the Americans had two small, though not strictly speaking military, successes during the remainder of 1812. While at Fort Wayne in September, Harrison ordered his troops to destroy the nearby Miami villages and farms so that they could not serve to supply hostiles. In fact, the remaining Miami in these communities, followers of Little Turtle (who had died in July), had been making great and genuine efforts to keep the peace. But because of the temper of the times their homes and standing crops were burned. As refugees the Miami moved westward, and near the present Peru, Indiana, built several temporary villages. Harrison was still not satisfied about their loyalty and directed that they turn over some of their chiefs as hostages to ensure their good behavior. This was too much for the Miami who refused. In December 600 militiamen were sent to the refugee camps to enforce the order. There, though they had few weapons, the remnant of the Miami made their last stand. Some fifty of the 100 warriors there were killed while trying to defend their families. About an equal number of the women and children were taken prisoners. For practical purposes this was the end of the once-great nation, the only one which after Fallen Timbers had made a real attempt to live at peace on American terms.

In November a militia posse came up the Wabash to burn and level Tippecanoe, which, a few weeks earlier, had been abandoned for the last time by Tenskwatawa and his people. As the Americans were milling about the former capital of the red resistance movement, a few warriors returned and killed twenty of them who had strayed too far into the woods.

After Tekamthi left for Canada early in the summer, Tenskwatawa had remained behind on the Wabash, where he was responsible for several hundred women, children, and other noncombatants. He did his best to obey his orders to make no trouble and continued to profess his peaceful intentions to various American authorities. It was generally believed that he was lying, but the once-feared Prophet had become such an unthreatening figure that no great efforts were made to do anything about him. After the outbreak of the war, Tippecanoe served as a staging area for warriors who were raiding the frontier, but Tenskwatawa played a minor and, as always, unmilitant role in those operations. After leaving Tippecanoe, hungry and perhaps weary of making independent decisions, he turned east and joined Tekamthi at Amherstburg. With him, among others, was their sister Tecumpease and the thirteen-year-old Pachetha, Tekamthi's son, whom she was raising.

Tenskwatawa was not able to stay long out of the cold at Amherstburg. Almost immediately he was required to return with his brother to the United States on a winter recruiting trip. Later there were rumors that Tekamthi, toward the beginning of 1813, went south again seeking to raise Creek warriors. There is also some circumstantial evidence from offhand British reports that the wound he had received in August was slow to heal and continued to trouble him for some months thereafter. If so, he may not have gone far but laid up through the winter in a village in Illinois to recover his strength and plan for the spring campaign.

XV. American Groundhogs and Fat British Dogs

The disastrous fall campaign of 1812 made it clear to the Madison administration that, all matters of competence aside, James Winchester was simply too unpopular to lead an army of volunteers from Kentucky and Ohio. Direction of the war in the Northwest was turned over to Harrison, with Winchester remaining on as the second-ranking officer.

Despite unifying the military command, the United States continued to suffer reverses during the forepart of 1813. As much for political as strategic reasons—western citizens were still outraged by the manner in which Detroit had been lost and loud in their demands for a gesture of retaliation—Harrison considered mounting a winter counteroffensive. The plan called for Winchester to take 1,000 men and advance to the mouth of the Maumee and then turn north into Michigan. Simultaneously Harrison with an equal force would march from Fort Wayne to western Michigan, swing east, reclaiming the southern part of the territory, and meet Winchester near or at Detroit. Though he was eager to establish his reputation as an energetic commander, Harrison was also a prudent man who had been schooled by Anthony Wayne and understood the realities of winter weather and logistics in the Northwest. After thinking further about the risks involved, he gave up the idea of this campaign. Beyond not marching into Michigan, Harrison made another good decision in the winter of 1813. He began to apply political pressure on the War Department to construct some sort of naval force on the Great Lakes, which could threaten over-the-water British supply lines.

James Winchester was as interested as Harrison in gaining glory but a less foresighted man. Early in January he received a messenger from members of a community of Americans and French-Canadians who were living at Frenchtown (near what is now Monroe, Michigan) on the River Raisin. Pro-American, so they said, these people had not for some reason, been molested by raiding warriors. However, they feared they soon would be and asked Winchester for immediate help. He responded quickly, moving forward from the Maumee with his army to relieve Frenchtown. Though he did not consult with Harrison, by then his superior, Winchester did, just as he was leaving, send word to his commander in chief about where he was going.

Winchester arrived at Frenchtown on January 21 and found the place quiet. Tired and cold, his men built large fires and retired early. Scouts were not sent out, since Winchester had learned from a persuasive local resident that there were no hostiles in the vicinity. This informant was a British agent, one of several who along with a number of warriors had been keeping a close watch on the Americans.

The unwary Winchester presented an opportunity which Henry Procter, the British commander at Amherstburg across the Detroit River, could not ignore. By the time Winchester's army made camp, Procter had 500 of his own troops and some 600 Indians, led by Roundhead, hidden around Frenchtown. At four o'clock on the morning of January 22, they fell on the sleeping Americans and within an hour killed 400 and captured 500 of them, including the befuddled Winchester. Only thirty-three of his 960 men managed to escape and carry the bad news back to Ohio.

Though he had no intelligence to that effect, Procter became fearful that another American army might soon appear. As soon as the fighting at Frenchtown was finished, he took most of his British regulars and militia back across the river to Fort Malden. (After belatedly learning about Winchester's plans, and having a premonition of what might happen, Harrison had hastily gathered another 900 men at Fort Wayne and started down the Maumee to give what assistance he could. However, when the survivors from Frenchtown appeared, he decided that the British and Indians would be close behind them. Harrison therefore took his men and rapidly retreated to Fort Wayne.)

Procter, when he returned to Amherstburg, took some of the captured Americans, including Winchester, with him, but left a hundred or so prisoners and most of the Indians behind at

Frenchtown. After finding several barrels of whiskey, the latter began torturing and killing the former. Not until much later that night were Roundhead and a few remaining British officers able to halt the orgy in which eighty Americans were murdered. When news of it reached the United States, the slaughter of the unarmed prisoners understandably increased the Americans' fear of the Indians. However, in a cold, objective way, the atrocity had an invigorating effect on the national war effort. Thereafter the western settlers did not have to refer to old massacres which had occurred in the 1780s and 90s. They had one of their own which needed to be revenged and which morally justified more or less anything they might be able to do to the savages. "Remember the River Raisin" stirred Americans in 1813, as slogans having to do with the Alamo, the battleship *Maine*, and Pearl Harbor would their descendants.

By February Harrison had collected another army of some 1,800 men. Many of them were from Virginia and Pennsylvania, since the Kentucky and Ohio militias were in temporary disarray after Frenchtown. With them, he started down the Maumee, building forts as he went. At the rapids of the Maumee, within a mile or so of the Fallen Timber battle site, he commenced constructing an advanced base, which was named Fort Meigs in honor of the then governor of Ohio.

Meanwhile Tekamthi returned to Amherstburg. Whatever the state of his health, wherever he had been, he had had a good recruiting winter for by April nearly 1,500 warriors were congregated around the British post. Nearby there was also an ever-larger number of noncombatants, including Tenskwatawa, Tecumpease, and Pachetha, who were in Canada to be near their men and draw rations.

Still very short of troops of his own, Henry Procter, the British commander, had come to recognize his need for red allies and received them more accommodatingly than he had during the previous fall. The great assembly of Indians outside Amherstburg and Fort Malden presented him with two considerable problems. The first was finding provisions for these people. Secondly, as Tekamthi, Matthew Elliott, and other Indian agents explained, the warriors had to be employed soon or they would grow bored and drift away to hunt or conduct small raids of their own. About half of the fighting men were in a sense regulars, veterans of the international brigade committed to Tekamthi, Roundhead, and their cause. The remainder, mostly from the nations above and beyond the

Great Lakes, had come south for traditional heroic excitement—a few quick, wild fights, American scalps, and loot. They were willing enough to follow such renowned chiefs as Tekamthi and Roundhead into battle but the men from the north and west had little interest in garrison duty or taking part in tedious campaigns of maneuver. They had come as—and literally to have—war parties.

The nearest available Americans were those who were trying to dig themselves in at the Maumee rapids, just across the narrow end of Lake Erie from Amherstburg. Henry Procter thought taking Fort Meigs was a reasonable objective and made a major commitment of his own forces to the offensive. If Harrison could be driven away from the Maumee, the Americans would be denied access to Lake Erie and might be sufficiently discouraged to abandon, permanently, their attempts to reclaim northern Ohio and Michigan. In April of 1813 the prospects of accomplishing this seemed good, since Harrison was still in the process of constructing and garrisoning the new fort. At Amherstburg as preparations for the campaign progressed, there was a general air of confidence. During their enforced alliance of necessity, these were the only few weeks in which Procter and Tekamthi seemed to have enjoyed an amicable relationship. Though the conversation was never committed to paper, British aides later recalled that Procter made an informal agreement with Tekamthi about a postwar settlement. If things worked out as was hoped, the country north of the Maumee, including all of Michigan, would be set aside permanently and guaranteed by the British as a red homeland. Also, if they were able to capture William Henry Harrison, he would become Tekamthi's personal prisoner to be used as a hostage or in any other way.

The British-Indian expeditionary force left Amherstburg on April 24. Procter went by water in a flotilla of small boats which carried about 1,000 men (half of whom were regulars, the rest Canadian militia) and nine pieces of artillery. Also in the tiny fleet there were two gunboats of shallow enough draft to navigate the Maumee as far as the rapids. Tekamthi and Roundhead crossed the Detroit River directly into Michigan. There on the River Raisin they smoked war pipes with their men, painted themselves for battle, and prayed to their gods. When the ceremonies were completed, they marched overland around the tip of Lake Erie toward the Maumee. On the twenty-eighth of April, Procter and Tekamthi rendezvoused at the ruins of the former British Fort Miamis, where the warriors had been denied entrance after the battle of Fallen Timbers. The next day they moved upstream along the north bank to place their artillery within range of Fort Meigs on the opposite shore. While the artillerymen were mounting their guns, Tekamthi's braves gave them some protection by scaling trees and peppering the Americans within their palisades.

To defend the position against some 2,000 Indians and British, Harrison had about 1,200 men within the still-incomplete fort. He had about the same number of cannon as Procter, but his guns were of shorter range. Also, at the beginning of the siege the Americans had only 390 rounds for their eleven artillery pieces. (Harrison paid a bonus to soldiers who could retrieve spent British cannonballs for reuse.)

Despite the disparity in forces, the battle for Fort Meigs turned out to be the most substantial one fought during the war in the west and the only action in which both sides performed with what might be called military smartness. When the British and Indians appeared, Harrison called together his men and encouraged them with a rousing stemwinder of a before-the-battle speech. He pointed out that they were looking across the river at the site of the famous Fallen Timbers. He reminded them that he himself had been there and was now confident that they could win as great a victory as Mad Anthony Wayne and his men had. Harrison admitted that the savages outside the fort appeared to be numerous, but this should not cause panic since the inability and disinclination of the warriors to conduct siege operations had been repeatedly demonstrated. (One of the important consequences of Harrison's minor campaign against Tippecanoe two years before was that it made him credible, to the men who listened to him on May Day of 1813, as a general and Indian fighter.)

Two other factors worked in Harrison's favor. First he had at Fort Meigs a company of energetic regular army engineers. As the British placed their artillery, the engineers within Fort Meigs constructed a network of earthworks and slit trenches, which as it turned out provided effective cover against cannonballs. Secondly, before coming to Fort Meigs Harrison used his political influence to ensure that he would have reinforcements. As the siege began, a Kentucky militia general, Green Clay, was within four days of Harrison, marching to his assistance with 1,200 men.

Commencing on April 30 and continuing for the next three days, the British artillery and gunboats bombarded Fort Meigs. At the same time Tekamthi, who had encouraged his warriors by telling them that the Americans were so timid that they could only hide in their tunnels like groundhogs, sent his men on sorties against the perimeter of the fort. However, the British gunners and the braves inflicted only minor casualties on the Americans and were unable to force or bait them out of the holes they had dug for themselves.

Late in the evening of May 4, the garrison at Fort Meigs received the welcome news. Clay and his Kentuckians, floating down the Maumee on eighteen flatboats, were only two or three hours upstream. Shortly after midnight, a veteran woodsman, John Hamilton, slipped through the Indian lines with a message for the relief force. Harrison ordered Clay to divide his column, sending 800 men up the left (north) bank of the river to attack and destroy the British guns. The remainder were to stay on the south bank and go directly to Fort Meigs. This was done. With orders to return to Fort Meigs as soon as the guns were spiked, Col. William Dudley led the 800 men through the woods on the north bank. The maneuver surprised Tekamthi and Procter who, though they knew that Clay's relief force was approaching, had expected it to proceed directly to the fort. Therefore, Dudley was able to take the main British batteries, driving away the small contingent of regulars and Indian guards. Then Dudley ignored his orders and got into trouble. Thinking they had the whole British-Indian army on the run, the Kentuckians left a few men to dismantle the captured guns and started chasing the hostiles through the fallen timbers. When they were sufficiently strung out, Tekamthi and his warriors turned and within a few minutes killed about 100—including Dudley—and captured 500 more of the Americans. (Only 150 of Dudley's 800 men escaped across the river to Fort Meigs.) The prisoners, guarded by a detachment of warriors, were sent back to the site of old Fort Miamis, near to Procter's field headquarters. Tekamthi and Adam Muir gathered some of their men and went back upstream, where they recaptured the artillery batteries before the Americans were able to spike them.

Back at the prisoner compound some of the warriors began to attack the dazed, unarmed Americans, just as had been done at the massacre on the River Raisin four months earlier. On this occasion the butchery was brought to an abrupt halt. A runner having brought word of what was happening, Tekamthi, lashing his horse, galloped to the stockade. There he physically drove the murderously excited warriors from the prisoners—but not before forty of them had died. This documented incident, more than any other one, was responsible for Tekamthi being elevated, by whites, to the rank of the Noblest Savage. Most of the stories about how chivalrous he was, even as a youth, began to circulate only after he saved the prisoners during the battle of Fort Meigs.

The basic account offered by many eyewitnesses was that he arrived in a rage, put a stop to the massacre, and then berated nearby British officers who he said could have halted it sooner. Within a day or so, and for years to come, other stories were circulated which greatly embellished the incident.

It was said:

. . . Tekamthi swung down from his great black horse into the middle of the terrible melee in the stockade, took his war hatchet from his belt, and with it split the skulls of two Chippewa (Ojibwa) warriors who were dismembering helpless Americans.

. . . Having cowed the warriors, Tekamthi looked on his men who were left in a demented stupor, like drunks, after the bloody orgy and cried out, literally with tears in his eyes: "Oh! what will become of my Indians."

. . . Then Tekamthi strode into Procter's headquarters a few hundred yards away and demanded why the British general had not sent his officers to stop the slaughter. Procter replied, "Sir, your Indians cannot be commanded." "Begone!" shouted the infuriated Tekamthi. "You are unfit to command; go and put on petticoats."

. . . Matthew Elliott, the veteran British Indian agent, found in the mob of prisoners four Shawnee from Black Hoof's faction, who had been employed by Harrison as scouts. Knowing the enmity between Black Hoof and Tekamthi, Elliott pointed out the Shawnee to Tekamthi, saying, "Yonder are four of your nation who have been taken prisoner . . . dispose of them as you think proper." Tekamthi took the four men, two of whom had been friends in better days, and talked companionably to them, saying that they had no reason to fear. "I will send you back to your nation [Black Hoof's] with a talk to your people."

Despite the loss of more than half of Clay's relief force, the overall effect of the fighting on May 5 was to strengthen the Americans, since 550 of the Kentuckians had managed to reach Fort Meigs. After Procter made a pro forma demand that he surrender, Harrison replied in the high bravado style of Anthony Wayne, telling the British messengers to tell Procter "that he will never have this post surrendered to him upon any terms. Should it fall into his hands, it will be in a manner calculated to do him more honor than any capitulation could possibly do."

At a meeting with Procter two days later, Tekamthi urged that the siege be continued, saying that, if the Americans were going to act like groundhogs, he and his men would "work like beavers," tunneling under the walls of the fort. Whether even he could have organized such a project is doubtful. By then some of the auxiliary warriors from the upper Great Lakes had left and others were talking about doing so. Running down Dudley's troops in the woods had been exciting, but, staying on to fight Americans who hid in holes would not be. In somewhat the same mood, many

Canadian militiamen slipped away, returning to Ontario in time for their spring plowing. Procter decided to break off the engagement. Loading his men and guns on the boats he sailed back to Amherstburg. Without British supplies and artillery and with only his own veterans willing to continue the siege, Tekamthi had little choice but to follow. Harrison, once he was certain that the Indians and British had withdrawn, departed for the south to get on with the business of recruiting and organizing a new army of the Northwest. Green Clay was left in charge at Fort Meigs.

In late July of 1813 the events of early May were more or less repeated. While the first attack on Fort Meigs was being planned and conducted, warriors from as far away as the western prairies, including some Sioux, were traveling east to join the war. By late June, 2,000 of them, in addition to the loyalists of Tekamthi's international brigade, had assembled at Amherstburg. This was the largest red army which ever had been or would be mobilized in North America. Had the warriors been turned loose to campaign in their traditional style, making hit-and-run raids against white settlements, they almost certainly would have kept the Americans on the defensive throughout the summer. Quite possibly they could have realized the long-time ambition of driving the Long Knives back to the Ohio. But they were not employed in this way perhaps because Tekamthi's pride was stung by the failure at Fort Meigs in May. Even though the Indians had never done well in seige operations, they made another attempt to take Meigs in July. The decision to send the warriors against the fort a second time stands as the most serious error of military judgment in Tekamthi's career. It was apparently made because he allowed passion—his anger and desire for revenge—to overcome cool reason. This was the kind of behavior which he often warned his followers against.

The Americans under Green Clay remained in their holes at Fort Meigs. But in the three months following the first siege, they had increased the garrison to 1,500 men, improved their artillery, and generally become much more formidable groundhogs. Tekamthi and Roundhead brought 2,500 warriors overland through Michigan against them. (Though he was unenthusiastic about the expedition, Procter again came across Lake Erie by boat to the Maumee, but this time with only 500 of his own troops and four light artillery pieces. The British took little part in the second action, at which Procter was essentially an observer.)

Tekamthi arrived at Fort Meigs with a preconceived stratagem. His prideful determination to test the ruse reflected the uncharacteristic hubris which inspired this unfortunate campaign. The Indians and British arrived on the Maumee on July 21, surprising and killing a few outlying Americans on picket duty. For the next five days the warriors made themselves very visible, harassing the defenders with sporadic but not particularly effective rifle fire. On the twenty-sixth, Tekamthi paraded 1,000 men in plain view of the fort, then marched off with them, moving up the Maumee. A few miles back in the woods they staged a sham battle with much screaming and shooting. The purpose of it was to make the garrison believe that a column of reinforcements, which was thought to be approaching, was under attack. Tekamthi reasoned that in this way he might trick Clay into charging out of his hole to aid the nonexistent relief party. Once outside the fort the Americans could be ambushed and butchered in the customary way. Initially some officers in the garrison wanted to do just as Tekamthi hoped they would but scouts said that they doubted that reinforcements were nearby. Clay, having learned in the spring what could happen to his Kentucky militia when they were caught out in the woods, decided to remain where he was. After several hours Tekamthi halted the demonstration. Two days later the second siege, such as it was, of Fort Meigs was abandoned.

Tekamthi's stratagem having failed, Procter suggested that the expeditionary force move east to attack a much smaller and less well-defended American position, Fort Stephenson, on the Sandusky River. He argued that this position might be overwhelmed by numbers alone. If it fell, the effect would be to outflank the Americans on the Maumee and discourage them from making any moves toward Michigan or his own base at Amherstburg. Tekamthi had come to his senses in regard to assaulting forts and was not eager to try another one. However, he and his warriors went along to the Sandusky with Procter since, as always, the British were supplying the ammunition and food for the war parties.

Fort Stephenson had been built hastily the year before as a simple log stockade surrounded by several acres of cleared ground. It was garrisoned by 170 men and commanded by George Croghan, a twenty-three-year-old major of the 17th Infantry, U.S. Army. Harrison shared Procter's opinion that Fort Stephenson could not resist a serious attack. Therefore, when word was received that the large British-Indian force was approaching, he ordered Croghan to abandon the post. The young major simply refused to obey his commanding general.

Procter and Tekamthi showed up at Fort Stephenson on the first day of August, began to bombard it and make probing sorties against the palisades. Croghan and his regulars beat them off. They continued to do so for a day and a half, whereupon Procter sent Croghan a demand that he surrender. In the message he attempted to do what Brock had done at Detroit—that is, to intimidate the Americans by telling them that, when they fort fell, he could not control Tekamthi's savages or guarantee the safety of any survivors. Croghan refused with a sarcastic flourish, saying that, if Fort Stephenson was taken, there would be no survivors.

Late in the afternoon of August 2, Procter launched a furious frontal assault. As it was his idea, his troops were in the lead. Within an hour the British suffered a hundred casualties. Indian losses were less, since the warriors displayed their traditional aversion to climbing log walls while people were shooting in their faces. Only ten Americans were killed or wounded. At nightfall Procter and Tekamthi took their wounded and withdrew permanently. So far as the Americans were concerned, the defense of Fort Stephenson was the most gallant action of the western war. The disparity in forces made it comparable to the Alamo, but it has not been remembered in the same way because Croghan and his men kept, rather than lost, their fort and lives.

The Indian-British army returned for the last time to Amherstburg, where relations between the allies continued to sour. The inability and unwillingness of the warriors to conduct European-style operations confirmed Henry Procter's already low opinions about their military worth and character. Yet, gallingly, he found it increasingly necessary to placate and defer to them since his superiors in the east had turned down his requests for substantial reinforcements on the grounds that he should make do with the Indians. For their part, Tekamthi, Roundhead, and the other chiefs viewed Procter with mounting contempt as a man who lacked the brains and stomach to take the offensive against the Americans himself and would not provide sufficient support for them to do so. That the English King had failed to send more of his soldiers and left them dependent on the timid, foolish Procter raised suspicions that once again the British had lied about being able and willing to aid the red people.

Finally because of the great congregation of Indians and poor local harvests, the supply situation at Amherstburg worsened throughout the summer and was a source of chronic aggravation. To Procter, an instinctive bureaucrat, the warriors themselves seemed slothful and excessively greedy. But it was the thousands of women, children, and old people who followed them who drove Procter to distraction. Regularly he complained to Matthew Elliott, his Indian wallah, about the manner and rate at which these useless human locusts were gobbling up government stores. To Tekamthi and his men, it appeared that Procter was not only a fool and coward but an ungrateful niggard. Hiding behind his big guns, he expected them to fight his battles while their own stomachs and those of their families were empty.

After they returned to Amherstburg, Tekamthi and Procter got into a heated dispute over a matter which was small in itself but indicative of the tensions which were growing between them and of how little they liked and trusted each other. Somewhere in Ohio or Michigan, Procter's men had come by an American captive, a Captain LeCroix, who was then being held on a ship at Amherstburg, preparatory to being sent to Montreal. Tekamthi, it seems, had known and come to like LeCroix in the days before the war. Hearing of his capture, he went to Procter to make inquiries, saying that he wanted this particular American paroled and sent home. Procter was at first evasive about the status of LeCroix. Tekamthi lashed out saying that if he ever caught Procter telling him a direct lie, "I, with my Indians, will immediately abandon you." Procter did not think it safe or politic to force the issue. He admitted that LeCroix was a prisoner and promised he would be released immediately. Afterward, attempting to make the best of the humiliating situation, Procter explained to an aide that the thing had to be done because Tekamthi, whom he scathingly referred to as "the king of the woods," had to be humored.

During the forty some years of the intermittent war in the west, the Americans had suffered reverses in hundreds of small skirmishes and in a dozen or more major actions. But despite the defeats they had continued to advance, exterminating and dispossessing the original inhabitants of the region. In consequence, the frequent victories of the Indians were invariably pyrrhic ones, since even the greatest of them entailed some losses of men and resources, which they could not replace as the whites did. Moreover, the few engagements where the casualties had been about equal and the warriors had been forced to withdraw (Point Pleasant, Fallen Timbers, and Tippecanoe) had a worse psychological effect on them than the loss of entire armies did for the Americans. When the valor of the warriors failed to give quick, complete triumphs, doubts inevitably began to surface that perhaps the whites were so numerous, rich, and evil—or blessed—that it was impossible to beat them once and for all. Such thoughts led to dissension and defections from the red resistance movement.

These long-standing realities continued to operate during the first year of the War of 1812. In the twelve-month period the military forces of the United States were driven out of Ontario and Michigan, surrendered Detroit and Chicago, lost two entire armies,

Hull's and Winchester's, and about 4,000 men who had either been captured or killed. (Indian and British casualties were fewer than 500.) During the fall of 1812 the warriors had regained control of much of the open countryside in northern Ohio, Indiana, Illinois, Wisconsin, and Missouri. About the best the Long Knives could claim was that they had not lost more, specifically the forts Meigs, Stephenson, and Wayne. Nevertheless, at the end of this year of defeats and humiliations the Americans were stronger—and the Indians weaker—than they had been at the beginning of it.

. . . By August of 1813, white settlements throughout most of the Northwest were more secure than they had been, because the warriors who had swept down on them in 1812 had been drawn north to join Tekamthi. Winchester had blundered into the terrible ambush on the River Raisin. Harrison and Clay at Fort Meigs, the bold young Croghan at Fort Stephenson had barely held on by digging themselves in like groundhogs. However between them they had occupied and pinned down most of the red army.

. . . After the first siege of Fort Meigs was lifted, Harrison had continued to collect reinforcements. By the end of August he had 8,000 regulars and militia in varying states of readiness. This was the largest force the United States had ever gathered in the Northwest. In contrast Tekamthi was losing men. Discouraged by their inability to chase the Long Knives out of their burrows, insulted by the manner in which they were treated by Procter and other British officers, about 1,000 warriors, including the Sioux and most of the others from the prairies, went back to their homes. At Amherstburg, Tekamthi and Roundhead were left with fewer than 2,500 men (many of whom had serious doubts about staying there) and an almost equal number of their dependents.

. . . By at least not losing northern Ohio, Harrison had bought time and secured a place in which the United States could create a naval force to challenge the British and threaten their supply lines on the Great Lakes.

This latter work commenced in the early spring of 1813 when the Navy Department ordered a young lieutenant, Oliver Hazard Perry, to the south shore of Lake Erie. At Presque Isle (the present Erie, Pennsylvania), he organized a small company of military and civilian workers and cobbled together a crude shipyard. Using green timber and ironworks carted in from Pittsburgh, a four-day haul to the south, they built two brigs, three smaller gunboats, and armed five merchant vessels for light naval service.

While this work was going on, Perry was constantly fearful that the enemy might swoop down and destroy his shipyards, which were guarded by only a skeleton force of soldiers and marines.

Since the British had the resources, at least in the early part of the summer, for such a preemptive strike, the question of why it was not carried out has puzzled military analysts ever since. Perhaps the best explanation is that the principal Canadian decision makers, including the governor-general, George Prevost, and his military commander in Upper Canada, Francis de Rottenburg, appeared to suffer from what might be called a priori lassitude. In regard to Perry and the small navy he was building, their reasoning seems to have been that British control of the seas, of which the Great Lakes were an extension, was an incontestable fact. For the Americans to threaten them on Lake Erie was unthinkable. If Perry attempted to make mischief, he would be disposed of by some unspecified means.

On August 5, unopposed, Perry worked his vessels out from behind the sandspits at Presque Isle and sailed along the south shore of the lake to the mouth of the Sandusky River. There he met with Harrison, who was camped upstream at Fort Seneca with 5,000 men of his new army. Between them the two officers had come by some interesting and, for once, accurate intelligence about the enemy. Perry knew that the bulk of the British lake fleet was concentrated in the Detroit River off Fort Malden but it was not prepared for action. Harrison had learned about Procter's supply problems, that many of the warriors had already left and others might be encouraged to do so. Therefore it was decided that Perry should sail north across Lake Erie to reconnoiter the situation around Amherstburg and perhaps lure out the British squadron before it was ready. If Perry was able to gain control of the lake and sever the principal British supply line, Harrison would immediately commence the second invasion of Canada.

Perry appeared off Amherstburg on August 24 and with taunting intent maneuvered for several days. There were then six British ships anchored under the protective batteries of Fort Malden, but the tiny squadron was still in such poor condition that its commodore, Lieutenant Robert Barclay, made no attempt to respond to the challenge which Perry offered. The twenty-seven-year-old Barclay, who had lost an arm at Trafalgar, had become the ranking British naval officer in the area only four months previously. Neither he nor Henry Procter were as optimistic as their superiors that Perry's fleet could be more or less wished out of the water. During the summer these two officers, who were the furthest out on the limbs in western Ontario, had sent urgent requests back east asking for the men and materials needed to make Barclay's ships combat-ready. Their appeals were largely ignored. When Perry arrived, Barclay was in the process of converting soldiers into sailors and jury-rigging the vessels, only two of which, the brigs *Detroit* and *Queen Charlotte*, had been originally built for naval duty. Scrounging among local stores, mounting cannon from the fort on his decks, Barclay was in a desperate hurry, for he understood that ready or not he would soon have to come out and fight. Each day that Perry remained loose on the lake, blockading Amherstburg, worsened the supply situation and diminished the possibility that anything could be done about the Americans on either the land or water.

Among those watching as Perry's ships first came into the Detroit River were Tekamthi and many of his warriors, then camped on Bois Blanc Island, just off the Ontario shore. Angered by the inaction of the British, Tekamthi paddled across to Amherstburg and demanded an explanation. He was told in effect that this was a naval matter which Indians could not be expected to understand, that at the proper time Perry would be dealt with severely. Whether he believed it or not, Tekamthi had little choice but to tell his warriors that the English were making ready their great war canoes and would soon hunt down and destroy the Americans. The hopeful news temporarily halted defections among the warriors whose enthusiasm for the war was waning.

On September 9, judging that he had prepared as well as he could, Barclay left his sanctuary at Fort Malden. The next morning he found and engaged Perry off the Bass Islands, between Ontario and Ohio in the western end of Lake Erie. Perry had more ships (eight to Barclay's six) and more cannon but the British gunboats carried a few pieces which had a longer range than any he possessed. Barclay therefore attempted to pick off the American vessels while remaining sufficiently distant so they could not retaliate. However, Perry was able—principally because of some good luck with the wind—to close in on the British. The fight lasted for some four hours, during which Perry lost his flagship, the *Lawrence*. In a skiff, under heavy British fire, carrying his battle flag which was emblazoned with the slogan, "Don't Give Up the Ship," Perry transferred to his second brig, the *Niagara*. From that deck he was able to prevail. In midafternoon with most of his guns out of action, many of his men dead, and himself badly wounded, Robert Barclay surrendered. Having won what proved to be the decisive battle of the war in the west, Perry scrawled his famous message on the back of an envelope: "We have met the enemy and they are ours." Shortly after receiving it, Harrison started his army marching north, confident that the British and Indians at Amherstburg could not be supplied or reinforced over water routes.

*   *   *

Henry Procter, at Fort Malden, learned of Barclay's defeat two days after it occurred. His immediate reactions to the bad news led, among other things, to court-martial proceedings the next year and to his being remembered by Canadians as a craven and fool. Typically, at the trial, one of the men who served under him vowed that Procter was "the meanest-looking man I ever saw. He had an expression in which that of the murderer and cowardly assassin predominates; nor did he belie his appearance." Another junior officer testified to his "glaring imbecility."

Certainly in the month following Perry's victory on Lake Erie, Procter made a series of very bad judgments. However, the savage criticism of his character that followed (in part because a number of his colleagues were much in need of a scapegoat) seems, in retrospect, to have been excessive.

In the summer of 1812 Isaac Brock had found Procter to be a dependable, competent subordinate. Others had had the same opinion of him during his long, respectable career as a regular officer. Presumedly he was the same sort of man in 1813, a military bureaucrat whose modest ambition it was not to blot his copybook. During his first year as an independent commander in the west, he showed himself to be disinclined to risk much in pursuit of possible victories but much concerned with not losing—men, government property, and, most particularly, his reputation as a prudent, by-the-book career officer. "I feel the weight of my responsibility," Procter plaintively wrote to the governor-general of Canada after Barclay's defeat. "I shall act to the best of my judgement and hope I shall be fairly judged."

Unfortunately for Procter and many others, what was required in the fall of 1813 was someone to cope with a complex, rapidly evolving crisis in which conventional military regulations and wisdom did not apply. Procter's natural inability to improvise and take bold chances virtually guaranteed that he would, as he did, lose everything, including forever after the respect of his superiors, officers, troops, allies, and countrymen. A better man might well have put up a better show than Procter did and not been personally humiliated as he eventually was. But it does not inevitably follow— as many Canadians of the time suggested—that an Isaac Brock, for example, could have easily reversed the outcome of the final campaign in Ontario. The real problems which Henry Procter faced in the fall of 1813 were numerous and complex. The most critical ones were not of his own making.

. . . Harrison was rapidly approaching with more than 4,500 men. (Procter thought there might be as many as 6,000 Americans marching against him.) There were 1,000 British troops in the area. However, several hundred of them were either unfit for duty or garrisoning outlying posts. There were still 2,000–2,500 warriors with Tekamthi, but many of them were in the process of making up their minds about whether to stay and fight or go home.

. . . As he had repeatedly attempted to explain to his superiors, the supply situation at Amherstburg had been very difficult throughout the summer during which Procter, in addition to his own troops, had had to feed at various times some 10,000 Indians. "The quantity of beef and flour consumed here is tremendous," Procter glumly reported in late August. "There was such hordes of Indians with their *wives* and children." So long as local produce could be augmented with provisions shipped in across Lake Erie, Procter had managed, barely, to support his own men, the warriors, and refugees. After Perry cut the supply lines and isolated Amherstburg, Procter's quartermasters reckoned the food on hand would last no more than one month. Military stores were also very short.

. . . There was a corollary to the supply crisis, which understandably concerned Procter. The Indians were already complaining about how poorly they and their families were eating. If their rations were further reduced or stopped it seemed probable that they would begin helping themselves from white Ontario farmers or, worse, from Procter's standpoint, his depots.

. . . Even after Barclay's defeat, the British high command took no emergency measures to reinforce or provision Procter. Instead he received a good bit of rather vague, often contradictory advice. George Prevost, the governor-general, told him that at all costs he must keep his army intact. If the situation warranted, he could withdraw, taking Tekamthi's warriors with him, and join the main British forces north of Lake Ontario. Major General de Rottenburg, Procter's direct military superior, said that he appreciated the fact that the supply situation might be a bit sticky, but it certainly was no reason for immediate panic. Procter was directed to hang on as long as possible around Amherstburg so as to throw back the Americans if and when they appeared. De Rottenburg added:

> This interval [while Procter was waiting for Harrison to invade Ontario] you will employ by looking well at your situation in communication with Tecumseth, and the Indians, in ascertaining the impression which this [Barclay's defeat on Lake Erie] has produced on them, and in concerting with them the measures best calculated to lessen the consequences of that disaster. . . .

(Distant British officials had already begun to compare, unfavorably, their own general in the west with Tekamthi. This led to the belief often expressed in subsequent Canadian histories, that had Procter cooperated more closely with Tekamthi, or better yet deferred to this military genius, the outcome could have been much different. Again the premise that all that was lacking was a hero is a very debatable one.)

Procter's situation was more precarious than Prevost or De Rottenburg understood or at least were willing to admit, but it may not have been completely hopeless. Had Procter, after the defeat of his navy, immediately withdrawn from Amherstburg, it is quite likely he could have joined the British armies in the east with all of his troops and most of their movable equipment, escaping before the Americans coming up through Michigan could catch them. Or had he made preparations to engage Harrison somewhere in the open countryside around Amherstburg, there was a fair chance that the American invasion could have been halted. This was the strategy Tekamthi and Roundhead favored. The latter, as Harrison was starting north, encouraged his Wyandot and other warriors with a rousing speech. Now that the despicable Long Knives had finally come out of their holes, the fighting could begin in earnest, said Roundhead. He was confident that this batch of American groundhogs could be dispatched as so many others had been. Roundhead's opinion was based on more than bravado. Though Harrison had an advantage in numbers, his army was a hastily organized, mostly militia one and greatly inferior in artillery to the British. It was the sort of force which historically the warriors had often dealt with quite easily in ambushes and open battles.

None of which encouraged Procter, whose mind-set inclined him to think more about potential pitfalls than opportunities. With his limited supplies and dependence on Indians whom he did not trust, the risks of making a stand somewhere along the Detroit River were obvious to Proctor. He and his troops might be annihilated while the wretched savages disappeared into the woods. On the other hand, if he hastily retreated, he would surely be criticized for not having tried to defend western Ontario. Furthermore, even if he brought his own men out safely, the Indians—whose assistance Prevost and De Rottenburg seemed to value so highly—probably would not follow. In fact they would almost certainly defect, because they thought him a coward and had no interest in fighting for the British along the St. Lawrence.

Since the two bold choices plainly involved large risks, Procter, true to his nature, did not commit himself fully to either. Rather, he

attempted to pursue the two disparate courses of action simultaneously, thus making it inevitable that the worst possible scenarios
in both cases—fleeing or fighting—would come to pass.

Specifically, the day after he learned of the naval defeat on Lake
Erie, Procter decided to abandon Amherstburg/Fort Malden and
retreat eastward up the Thames River valley. However the withdrawal was to be made slowly, so as not to give the impression that
he was running away and to hold open the option, as he told his
officers, of fighting a defensive action against the Americans.
Procter also directed that information about this move should be
withheld from the Indians lest it make them "uneasy." Procter's
notion that he could somehow disappear from Amherstburg without the savages noticing or understanding what was happening
seems to have bordered—as his critics were to claim later—on the
imbecilic.

On the morning of September 14, Procter's engineers began
dismantling Fort Malden—ordered to do so in a manner which
would not "alarm" the Indians. An hour or so after they commenced, Tekamthi arrived. He was so clearly furious that, even
though they had no interpreter, the engineers halted work and sent
off a runner to get further instructions from headquarters. Procter
first responded in an odd, bureaucratic way, blustering that he had
"a perfect right to give any secret orders that he thought proper."
Then Matthew Elliott told him that unless Tekamthi and his
warriors were given some straight information they "might cut the
wampum belt [dissolve the alliance on the spot] and no man could
answer for the consequences." Much subdued, Procter agreed to
meet with the Indians in a general council, but said that because of
the press of other administrative business, he could not do so for
several days.

The next year at Procter's court-martial, a military prosecutor
commented at length on his behavior that day, charging among
other things that "the indignation of that brave and superior man
[Tekamthi] and the suspicions of the Indians in general arose
entirely from a want of frankness and candour in Major General
Procter."

Procter himself gave no real explanation of his thinking but there
is a strong sense that, having had several previous unpleasant
interviews with the intimidating Tekamthi, he was hoping, for very
human reasons, to put off another one for as long as possible. His
anxiety about what might happen was fully confirmed when the
meeting finally took place on September 18. Procter and his staff
and Tekamthi with many of his warriors, crowded into the Am-

herstburg municipal council hall, a large one in which during the previous twenty years the Indians and British had made much medicine.

Procter spoke first. He said that it was necessary to make an orderly, minor withdrawal to the Thames River. There under the proper circumstances he might well make a stand against the Americans if they came that far. He had no intention of abandoning his brave Indian allies and would coordinate his movements with theirs.

Tekamthi then answered. His remarks bear repeating at length not only for their substance but because, of all of his public orations, this was the one which was probably translated most accurately. A purportedly verbatim account of it was preserved. Said Tekamthi:

> Our fleet has gone out, we know they have fought; we have heard the great guns but know nothing of what has happened to our Father with the One Arm. [Procter had also thought it best not to tell the Indians that the one-armed Robert Barclay had been beaten and surrendered to Oliver Perry.]
>
> Our ships have gone one way, and we are much astonished to see our father [Procter] tying up everything and preparing to run away the other, without letting his red children know what his intentions are. You always told us to remain here and take care of our lands; it made our hearts glad to hear that was your wish. Our great father, the king, is the head, and you represent him. You always told us you would never draw your foot off British ground; but now, father, we see you are drawing back, and we are sorry to see our father doing so without seeing the enemy. We must compare our father's conduct to a fat animal, that carries its tail upon its back, but when affrighted, it drops it between its legs and runs off.

Procter made no response to the elaborate insult, but the warriors in the council hall and even some British officers began to snicker and laugh. When the crowd quieted, Tekamthi continued in a less provocative way:

> Listen, father! The Americans have not yet defeated us by land; neither are we sure that they have done so by water; we therefore wish to remain here, and fight our enemy, should they make their appearance. If they defeat us, we will then retreat with our father.
>
> At the battle of the Rapids, last war [at Fallen Timbers in 1794], the Americans certainly defeated us; and when we retreated to our father's fort at that place, the gates were shut against us. We were afraid that it would now be the case; but

instead of that we now see our British father preparing to march out of his garrison.

Father! You have got the arms and ammunition which our great father sent for his red children. If you have any idea of going away, give them to us, and you may go in welcome; for us, our lives are in the hands of the Great Spirit. We are determined to defend our lands, and if it is his will, we wish to leave our bones upon them.

XVI. The Shooting Star Falls

Following their public confrontation, Tekamthi and Procter met again, facing the fact that however much they might grate on one another, the need for cooperation was imperative. Tekamthi remained adamant that a stand should be made in western Ontario. If he and his people must leave their bones somewhere, it would be in their own country, not in the St. Lawrence Valley. However, after learning the true facts of the naval situation—that the Americans completely controlled Lake Erie—he made no objections to abandoning Amherstburg/Fort Malden. As a veteran campaigner, he understood the difficulties of trying to defend this blockaded outpost. Rather than have his warriors penned up within the fort, he wanted to keep them in the open, where they could employ their traditional tactics against the Americans.

Despite his humiliation at the public meeting, Procter was in a conciliatory mood. He not only vowed that he would fight but, on the spur of the moment, named the place—the village of Chatham at the forks of the Thames River some sixty miles east of the Detroit–Sandwich area. Procter had no particular information which recommended the place as a battle site but picked it, more or less at random, from the map, seemingly to demonstrate his decisiveness and belligerency. Tekamthi accepted the general outlines of the plan. His warriors would screen the retreat from Amherstburg and then rejoin the British when Procter had his men and artillery in place. The red noncombatants, including his son,

312

Pachetha, his sister, Tecumpease, and his brother, Tenskwatawa, would fall back with the British.

Meanwhile, back at the main Indian encampment, many of the men from the nations north and west of the big lakes had independently decided that Procter was indeed an untrustworthy cur, already dragging his tail between his fat legs. On the grounds that no good could come of going into battle alongside this white chief, large numbers of these warriors departed for their distant homes. The most serious defection was that of Main Poc, who took his Potawatomi braves first to Michigan and then on to the Mississippi Valley. By the end of September, Tekamthi and Roundhead were left with fewer than a thousand warriors. These were the true believers, many of whom had joined the red resistance in its first days, at Greenville, during 1806–1807. Unlike Main Poc's Potawatomi and others from the western lakes and prairies, they no longer had secure homelands to which they could return.

The last of Procter's troops left Amherstburg on September 26. Before they departed, they set fire to the shipyards and Fort Malden. The following day the first contingents of the American army were ferried across the Detroit River, under the protective guns of Perry's ships, and landed three miles south of Amherstburg. (Simultaneously, Harrison sent 700 men overland through Michigan to reclaim Detroit, which Procter had also evacuated.) Many of the men in the first wave of Long Knives to come ashore in Ontario were Kentuckians. Those who were with them later recalled that the troopers were jubilant and in many cases drunk as they marched toward Fort Malden, which for so long had been regarded as the nerve center of the evil British-Indian alliance. Some of them sang an awkwardly worded but passionate patriotic song then popular:

> Freemen, no longer bear such slaughters;
> Avenge your country's cruel woe;
> Arouse, and save your wives and daughters!
> Arouse, and smite the faithless foe!

The first prize, taken just south of Amherstburg, was Matthew Elliott's estate, which he had developed into an extensive and prosperous plantation as the result of forty years of trading with the Indians and raiding with them against American settlers in Ohio and Kentucky. The destruction of this property gave great satisfaction. Ever since he had left Pittsburgh to join the British at the outbreak of the Revolution, Elliott had been regarded along the American frontier as one of the worst of the traitors and racial turncoats.

The first of the Americans marched into Amherstburg late in the afternoon. Only two of their enemies, but the pair which most Americans judged to be the most dangerous of the lot, remained in the town. On a rise, on horseback, Matthew Elliott and Tekamthi watched the approach of Harrison's skirmishers and the smoke rise over Fort Malden. When the Americans came close, they turned and rode off into the twilight, Tekamthi to deploy his warriors, who were protecting the British retreat.

Tekamthi spent the last week of his life with his cadre of veteran warriors and a handful of Canadian agents such as Matthew Elliott with whom he had been acquainted for many years. Quite naturally many of these old companions who survived the campaign often told stories about their final encounters and conversations with the man whom they continued to regard as the greatest they had ever met. In contrast to most of the accounts of Tekamthi—which were made by observers who knew him only as a public figure, an orator, political negotiator, or military commander—those based on incidents which occurred in the early fall of 1813 describe him as he appeared to, spoke, and acted with intimates. Though some of them were embellished, as time passed and memories blurred, the last-days stories give a sense of why it was that he retained the loyalty and love of so many for so long.

A common theme in the recollections of those who made the retreat from Amherstburg is that, despite the confusion and precariousness of their circumstances, Tekamthi was unusually calm and reflective. Some later said that this was because he possessed the seerish qualities that seemed so pronounced in his family, that as had his brother Cheesekau twenty-five years before, Tekamthi came to have a clear, detailed vision of how he would end his days. Thus forewarned, freed of the uncertainties and fears which beset other men, he remained serene as he prepared to meet his fate in a manner befitting the last war chief of the free Shawnee.

Whether or not he benefited from supernatural insights, Tekamthi did, according to those who remained with him, make some realistic calculations and pessimistic projections about their immediate military situation. Things had gone so far that surrendering and trusting in the mercy of the Americans would probably be a fatal choice and certainly a cowardly one. Though their prospects for winning even one more battle, let alone the war, were poor, the sensible, honorable choice was to continue the campaign. They no longer had the means to shape events but might still have the strength to respond to them heroically and thus, according to their own philosophy and traditions, be successful. In this mood, as the retreat began, Tekamthi spoke with Jim Blue Jacket, the son of his old commander. He explained that Fort Malden was indefensible. Because of the supply problems, they must follow the British and hope that Procter would finally stand by them to fight the Americans in the open. However, Tekamthi warned young Blue Jacket that no matter what Procter did, he reckoned that few of the men in the red rear guard would ever see their homelands or even Amherstburg again.

Before burning Fort Malden, Procter had said that he would make temporary headquarters at Sandwich, twenty miles to the north just across the river from Detroit. When the Indians arrived there on the afternoon of September 28, they found the town empty of British troops. Seeking information, Tekamthi and Elliott went to the nearby farm of Francis Baby, a merchant and colonel in the Canadian militia. Baby was preparing to leave and join Procter, who was already fifty miles to the east on the Thames. However, Baby recalled that "Tecumseh requested me to stay till the next morning till we saw the enemy to which I consented. On the 29th early in the morning we sent a scout to see where the enemy was, and he returned in about an hour and a half and told us he had seen the enemy at Turkey bridge [about four miles south of Baby's farm] repairing that bridge which had been destroyed."

Tekamthi, with Baby, Elliott, and his warriors, left Sandwich that day. While continuing to skirmish with the vanguard of Harrison's army, they reached the Thames, just above the point where it empties into Lake St. Clair. There a message was received from Procter. The frantic British commander said that the Indians must hurry on for he dared not wait long for them. With growing doubts about Procter's intentions, Tekamthi remarked to Elliott, "There is no place for us."

On October 1, in a small action against an American patrol, Roundhead was killed. Beyond depriving him of his most able lieutenant, it must have been a bitter personal loss for Tekamthi. There are only a few brief, tangential accounts of their private relationship. (They laughed and joked during the formal dinner party at Adena. When Detroit fell, Tekamthi gave Isaac Brock's official sash to Roundhead.) But the two men had been together since at least 1806, and seemingly in complete accord about the organization and aims of the red resistance movement. Roundhead, a Stonewall Jackson to Tekamthi's Lee, had been the staunch field commander, content to leave large matters of strategy and politics to the more complex and charismatic man. It is unimaginable that they were not close friends.

During the first week of October, while Tekamthi and his men were continuously engaged, Henry Procter reached Chatham at the forks of the Thames. It was his first look at the place at which he had agreed, two weeks before, to fight a battle. On inspection Procter decided with good reason that the terrain was not suitable. Therefore he continued his retreat up the river, but without leaving word for the Indians. Closely pursued by the Americans, Tekamthi and his men arrived at the village of Chatham on October 3. They found some abandoned artillery pieces and baggage but not, as they had expected, British troops. Coldly Tekamthi asked Elliott: "What is taking this other man [Procter] away?" Elliott answered that he did not know. Rumors began to circulate that Procter had deserted his troops and was fleeing to save his own skin. Tenskwatawa, who had been traveling with the noncombatants, showed up near Chatham and said he would like to strip Procter of his uniform. No one paid much attention to the failed prophet, but some of the warriors began to talk about setting off after the British general and killing him. Surrounded by furious Indians, Matthew Elliott became fearful even for his own life. Finally he got word to officers in the British rear guard that unless some explanation for the continued withdrawal was made to the warriors, there would be no controlling their wrath, and, Elliott added, "I will not, by God, sacrifice myself."

Eventually word came from Procter that he would fight and was already preparing to do so at Moraviantown, a small settlement about fifteen miles upstream on the Thames. The Indians were asked to delay the Americans as long as they could, to give the British commander more time for deploying his troops and guns. Sending most of the wounded and straggling refugees on toward Moraviantown, Tekamthi remained behind with about 200 men. On the south bank of the Thames, along which Harrison's army was rapidly advancing, the warriors burned a bridge over a small tributary, McGregor's Creek. Then they took up a position in the brush on the far side of it. Shortly, about 1,000 Kentuckians came up but were unable to force their way across the creek because of the heavy fire from the Indians. Though he took a bullet in the arm, Tekamthi and his braves held back the mounted Kentuckians for nearly two hours. They were not dislodged until Harrison arrived with his artillery—two 6-pound field pieces.

On October 4, the Indian rear guard fell back in good order, from McGregor's Creek toward Moraviantown, occasionally halting to exchange fire with the leading units of Harrison's force. Eyewitnesses agreed that Tekamthi was literally the last man in the red army, waiting until all of his people had passed by safely. (There were still many civilians mixed in with the warriors, their own families and those of Canadian settlers who joined the Indians to escape the Americans.) Again observers were struck by Tekamthi's calmness and how he seemed to have been enjoying himself in an almost recreational way. Certainly he spent his last day in Ontario as he had so many of those of his youth in Ohio, Kentucky, and Tennessee—as a partisan patrol leader matching wits, man to man, with the Long Knives, concerned with small tactical and human problems rather than large strategic and geopolitical ones.

In the refugee column was a niece of his. As a young girl she married George Ironside, the cultured British trader-banker who had kept a post at the forks of the Maumee in the 1780s before the place was called Fort Wayne and was still Kekionga, the Indian metropolis of the northwest. After Fallen Timbers, Ironside moved his business to Amherstburg. The family fled from there as the Americans approached. When Tekamthi came upon his niece, she was distraught, having become separated from one of her younger children. Tekamthi scouted around and found the boy. He then warned his niece that she must keep the children close by her side and get them north of Moraviantown as quickly as possible, for there was almost certain to be a battle very shortly. He left, after saying that it was unlikely he would see her again.

Later he met a Canadian teenager, David Sherman, who was trying to find a strayed cow. Apparently Tekamthi knew him, or his father who was one of the militiamen still with Procter. Tekamthi told Sherman that he should get the animal, go home at once, and stay there. If the Long Knives came by, he should not tell them that his father was in Procter's army, for if they knew this, they would surely burn down the family farm.

Another Canadian youth, Abraham Holmes, recalled later that having heard that Tekamthi was passing by, he hurried off to catch a glimpse of the famous war chief. He found him talking to a neighbor, a Joe Johnston, who had done enough trading with the Indians to have become fluent in Shawnee. Johnston later told young Holmes that Tekamthi had said that it appeared as if Procter was finally going to turn and fight but had waited so long that the prospects for victory were no longer good. Holmes was struck by the "dignified demeanour" and "superior bearing" of Tekamthi and said he "wore buckskin leggings and a shirt of the same material which reached to the knees and was secured at the waist with a belt. He wore a large silver brooch at the neck but no other silver ornaments. . . ." Others recalled that on that day Tekamthi also carried two pistols and a hatchet in his belt.

When Holmes saw him, Tekamthi was at Arnold's mill, and he

spent the night there, so said its owner, Christopher Arnold. His reason for doing so was compassionate. The mill was a good one, and elsewhere warriors were destroying such properties to keep them from being used by the Americans. However, Arnold was another old acquaintance, and Tekamthi wanted to make an exception in this case. Therefore he with a small escort camped on the place to ensure that it would be spared.

Later a great many claimed to have been with Tekamthi during the last night, but those who most probably were included Matthew Elliott, Andrew Clark (the Shawnee reared interpreter), and the confusingly named Caldwell brothers, Billy and William. (Billy's mother was Potawatomi and William's was a white woman but both were sons of William Caldwell senior, the veteran Anglo-Irish soldier of fortune.) Among the warriors most likely present were Shabbona (a Tekamthi loyalist since the early Greenville days), Naiwash (another Ottawa), Caraymaunee (a Winnebago chief), several younger Shawnee, and Wasegoboah. Wasegoboah, the brother-in-law with whom, after the death of his own father, Tekamthi had lived as a boy, was by then his oldest and probably closest surviving friend.

The men who camped around Arnold's mill had been marching and fighting for a week with little rest or food. As was Tekamthi, others were nursing fresh wounds. Yet according to the testimony of survivors, their mood was more anticipatory, even elated in a fatalistic way, than despondent. Generally they had come to share the opinion that it was senseless and ignoble to retreat much farther. They were ready to throw the dice and see what the gods of war might make of them. Reasonably it seems that, if there was much campfire conversation, it must have been topical and tactical: about rations, powder, shot, and casualties, about what the Americans just behind and the British somewhere ahead were doing. But some later said—because they claimed to have heard him themselves or talked to veracious men who had—that Tekamthi spoke mostly of Pachetha, the son for whom he had previously shown little parental concern. One story had it that at the last Tekamthi said that if anything happened to him, he wanted Pachetha to have a saber which had been presented to him by Isaac Brock. He asked his comrades to help the boy become a brave chief who would use the weapon to benefit his people and honor the memory of his father. In a quite contrary version, it was recalled that Tekamthi advised that Pachetha would not make a good leader because he had, from his mother, Mamate, too much white blood. As for himself, Tekamthi was said to have said that he had only one remaining mortal ambition. He wanted to meet William Henry Harrison face to face on a battlefield and kill him. He thought the opportunity to do so might occur within the next day or so.

At dawn on October 5, Tekamthi sent the others ahead, upstream along the Thames. He himself remained at the mill to watch for the Americans. They shortly appeared and, according to Christopher Arnold, came close to catching him. Under fire, lashing a white pony, Tekamthi escaped the Kentucky dragoons by outrunning them to the river. There he was met, said Arnold, by a woman, who had been holding a canoe by the bank. Paddling furiously the couple, with the white pony swimming alongside and rifle balls splashing around them, safely reached the north bank of the Thames. Perhaps there was some such close call but the fine details provided by Arnold strongly suggest that the miller was well acquainted with the gaudier folk ballads of the Scots Highlanders.

(In the main it was whites who commenced—a few days later—and continued during the rest of the century to create Tecumseh legends. Christopher Arnold's escape story, those having to do with Tekamthi's dynastic concerns for Pachetha and his desire to meet Harrison in single combat are more European than Shawnee in style and substance. Grains of truth may be embedded in the tales but on the whole they sound much like what whites imagined a great king or hero, say an Arthur, should be thinking and doing at the end.)

A bit upstream from Arnold's mill, another, never identified, member of the rear guard was not so lucky as Tekamthi had been. Before he could cross the river, he was ridden down, shot, and scalped by William Whitley, a Kentucky scout. Whitley, an eagle-beaked, grim old man, had come to Kentucky in the 1770s, and helped Boone defend the first settlements. In 1813 he was sixty-four years old but, being unable to pass up the opportunity to have another go at the British and Indians, had enlisted as a private. He went to war dressed in the style which had been fashionable on the Kentucky frontier in Revolutionary days. Wearing a cocked hat, a greasy buckskin hunting shirt, and leggings, he carried a silver-mounted long rifle, powder horn, bullet bag, knife, pistol, and tomahawk.

Whitley was delighted to have taken the first scalp of the day and came galloping back to his unit waving the fresh trophy. "See here," the old woodsman told his juniors, "this is the thirteenth Indian scalp I have taken and I'll have another before night or lose my own."

*　　　*　　　*

Traveling up the Thames but through the woods at some distance from the river, Tekamthi and his warriors came to Moraviantown in midmorning. Again they did not find Procter waiting, but this time he was, astonishingly, in front of them, a mile south of the village and closer to the oncoming Americans. In his last significant act as a commanding officer, this customarily indecisive man had made a snap judgment and acted promptly on it. It was the last large blunder of his military career.

Procter had arrived in Moraviantown on October 3. Immediately he set his engineers to digging entrenchments and placing his artillery. On the fourth, learning that Harrison's cavalry had driven the Indians back from McGregor's Creek, Procter gave orders to halt the work on the defensive positions. With what remained of his army, he started back downsteam to meet the Americans, selecting, for no obvious reasons, a swampy section of woods as the best place to wait for them. At his court-martial, Procter never directly addressed the question of why, after having passed up much better places and opportunities to make a stand (when his strength was much greater), he decided to turn on the Americans below Moraviantown. The most plausible explanation is that he wanted, at the end, to project an image of himself—or perhaps confirm his self-image—as a bold, aggressive commander.

Tekamthi and his men retraced their path downriver and caught up with the British about noontime. Procter was deploying his troops on the north shore of the Thames to which the Americans had crossed earlier in the morning. On the right were two jungly swamps, separated by an isthmuslike height of drier land. To Matthew Elliott, Tekamthi was critical of this location, saying that the site Procter had first chosen near the village was a better one. However, there was no longer much point in trying to instruct or shame the English. Mostly he seemed relieved that, under whatever circumstances, they had finally decided to make a stand, and that there would be at least one more battle in the west.

When Tekamthi and Procter met for the first time since Amherstburg, they spoke civilly, without recriminations or much passion. An aide who was present later testified at Procter's court-martial: "I recollected the general asking Tecumseth which would be the best place for his young men to fight. His answer, I think thro' Colonel Elliott, was this place will be as good a place as any, pointing to the right [the brushy ridge between the two swamps]."

Later, to magnify their accomplishment, American spokesmen claimed that Tekamthi had some 3,000 Indians with him. This counted all the fleeing refugees as combatants. In fact, on the morning of October 5, there were no more than 600 warriors remaining. Procter had about an equal number of British regulars and Canadian militia and only one light artillery piece. (When he left Amherstburg, Procter had twenty field guns while the pursuing Americans had only two. During the ten-day retreat, the British, fearing they would be overtaken, had destroyed fifteen of the guns. Procter arrived in Moraviantown with five cannon, but when he decided to go downstream to fight, left four of them emplaced at the village.)

To oppose the Indians and British along the Thames, Harrison, in addition to his two field pieces, had about 3,000 troops. Other units of the original invasion army were guarding supply lines and keeping an eye on those Indians who, having earlier left Tekamthi, were still milling about in Michigan to the west of Detroit.

After talking briefly to Procter, Tekamthi went off into the soggy woods with the warriors. They needed no direction when it came to picking the best windfalls, hollows, and thickets in which to make their fight. These were his veterans, the first and last citizens, the parliament as well as the army, of the pan-Indian federation which he had envisoned. Among the warriors with Tekamthi that day were those who had been born into every nation of the Ohio Valley: Delaware, Wyandot, a few Miami, and his own Shawnee. Many were the sons and grandsons of men who had first taken up the hatchet against the Long Knives fifty years before. From farther to the west there were men who, before they were Tekamthi's, had been Fox, Kickapoo, Ojibway, Ottawa, Potawatomi, Sauk, and Winnebago. There were also thirty Creek, young Red Sticks, the only true believers from the south who saw reason to join the red resistance in the north.

Tekamthi took up his place among some large trees in the center of the Indian line. With him were members of what had come to be his personal staff. He gave them the bleak news about the position and temper of the English on the left, saying, according to Billy Caldwell, that they "are just like sheep, with their wool tangled and fastened in the bushes. . . . They can't fight—the Americans will brush them all away, like chaff before the wind."

Perhaps to lift his spirits, Capt. William Caldwell of the Indian service said that whatever the other English did, "I will stand by you till the last—I pledge myself not to run till you set me the example."

"Yes, you, I, and Billy Caldwell," answered Tekamthi, holding up three fingers and indicating William's half-brother, "I know we'll fight—but what can we do alone?"

(All of which was repeated later by Billy Caldwell and probably was a stretcher. The loyalty of the two brothers was unquestioned, but this was not a conversation which could have taken place when such men as Shabbona, the Ottawa, and Tekamthi's kinsman, Wasegoboah, were present.)

A few minutes later a runner came from Procter asking Tekamthi to join him, which he did along with Matthew Elliott. When they arrived at the British position, Procter asked Tekamthi to inspect his troops and make suggestions about how they could be better deployed. It was a gesture which, had it been made several weeks earlier, might have altered or at least prolonged the campaign. Tekamthi advised that the British were "too thickly posted—that they would be exposed to the enemy's rifle men, and thrown away to no advantage." He added that Procter should especially encourage the soldiers around his single cannon to be "stout hearted for the enemy would make a push at the gun." Finally, Tekamthi walked down the British line and, said one of those who was there, "pressed the hand of each officer as he passed, made some remark in Shawnee, appropriate to the occasion, which was sufficiently understood by the expressive signs accompanying them, and then passed away forever from our view."

When he and Elliott returned to the woods, Tekamthi did one final sentimental deed. Billy Caldwell, the charming boy who others said was a great favorite of Tekamthi, asked him: "My father, what are we to do? Shall we fight the Americans?"

"Yes, my son," said Tekamthi. "We shall go into their very smoke. But you are now wanted by the general." Billy Caldwell was then sent back to act as a liaison with Procter, and as he left, Tekamthi is said to have said, as he had to his niece the day before, "I never expect to see you again."

Tekamthi and the others lighted their pipes, stood talking and smoking in the woods while waiting on the Long Knives. There, something so odd occurred as to suggest that the story about it may not have been entirely an invention. Though none of the men later recalled having first heard a gunshot, there was a sound with which they were all familiar—of a bullet whining through the woods. Tekamthi started and grabbed his side as though in pain. William Caldwell asked if he has been hit. Tekamthi said, remembered Caldwell, that "he could not exactly tell but it is an evil spirit which betokens no good." When it was determined that Tekamthi was not in fact injured, Matthew Elliott told a story about his old companion-in-arms, Caldwell's father. The two had been together in a Revolutionary War skirmish. The senior Caldwell was certain that he had been shot but discovered, as Tekamthi had, that the bullet was imaginary. On the next day Caldwell was hit and badly wounded, the real bullet striking him exactly where he had felt the phantom one. Because of this spooky incident, some of the others urged Tekamthi to withdraw behind the battle lines. He refused, saying, "I can't think of such an act."

William Henry Harrison was never, rightly, judged to be a brilliant soldier on the order of an Anthony Wayne or Isaac Brock. On the other hand he was a commonsensical, calculating man who seldom did foolish things. Politically astute and attuned to the sentiments of his frontier constituents, he was able to build up and hold together his forces while refusing to take action until the odds were much in his favor. In 1811 he had waited until Tekamthi was out of the country to march against Tippecanoe. In 1812 he had hung on at Fort Meigs until the Indians grew weary of the siege. In September of 1813, after landing in Ontario, he dogged the British patiently, confident that in due time he could exploit their disarray and the incompetence of Henry Procter.

The Americans approached the swamps south of Moraviantown in midafternoon of the fifth. After receiving reports from his scouts, Harrison decided that, if he turned immediately on the British, he might quickly dispose of them and then deal with the more difficult problem of Tekamthi and his men in the woods between the two swamps. The best equipped and disciplined unit in Harrison's largely militia army was a regiment of Kentucky mounted infantry. The commanding officer was Richard Johnson, a popular politician—and therefore a Democrat and War Hawk—who had returned from the House of Representatives in Washington to take part in the invasion of Canada. Leaving the bulk of his men in reserve in case the British proved unexpectedly stubborn or Tekamthi's warriors came out of the woods, Harrison sent Johnson with about 1,000 dragoons on a charge against Procter. Later there were detailed investigations of what happened next. Some said the engagement lasted exactly one minute. The most anybody claimed for the British was that, after discharging a single volley and taking thirty some casualties, they surrendered.

Procter was to the rear. As Johnson was overwhelming his men, he turned and fled, rapidly, at a full gallop. In Moraviantown, without dismounting, he got a drink and told the men there (who were shortly taken prisoner) to do the best they could. Then he took to the road with such members of his staff as could keep up with him. Several days later, he reached the main British army above Lake Ontario. Practically, there was little more Procter could have done than to save himself. One aide said that he had, in fact, briefly considered joining the Indians, but could not, because Johnson's riders were between him and them. However, appearances were much against the unfortunate Procter, who lived the rest of his life reviled as a stupid coward.

There was some sporadic firing between snipers, but while the British were making their very brief stand, the Indians did not budge from the woods. After rounding up Procter's troops, Johnson and his Kentuckians turned on them. The first move was to send a party of some twenty scouts, later memorialized as the Forlorn Hope, into the thickets to draw sufficient fire so that the exact position of the warriors could be determined. In the party was the venerable William Whitley, who was killed before he could take his fourteenth scalp.

When the main body of Kentuckians came up, Tekamthi and his veterans made a counterattack, temporarily driving them back. American reinforcements were sent in and for the next hour, as they had so often in the past, the warriors and Long Knives fought man against man in the brush and bogs. At some point in the melee his brother-in-law, Wasegoboah, went down, but the Americans said that even above the din they could hear Tekamthi's war cry. He called to his young men, "Be brave, be brave!" much as had Cornstalk during the first true battle between the reds and whites in the west, at Point Pleasant in 1774. Then he was heard no more.

After October 5, 1813, no one ever again claimed to have seen Tekamthi alive. Men of both races were certain that he died that day on the rise of land between the two swamps. There came to be, however, many different and contradictory stories about exactly how he fell. One of them was offered to a white reporter many years later by Shabbona, who said he was at the side of his chief. Together they found a wounded white officer, entangled in the harnesses of his horse. Tekamthi raised his hatchet to kill the man, but before he could do so, the American fired his pistol and shot him. "On seeing Tecumseh fall," Shabbona told the interviewer, "I went off as fast as I could, and have been a good American ever since that day."

When the remaining warriors saw or were convinced by others that their chief was dead, they fled from the woods as Shabbona said he did. Thus ended the battle of the Thames and for practical purposes the civil war in the west.

XVII. The Resurrection of Tecumseh

When the War of 1812 began, Tekamthi was widely known among the red peoples of the northwest. Also some frontier settlers and most white officials involved with native affairs recognized him as the most able and dangerous red resistance leader. The fall of Detroit and other events during the first year of the war increased his reputation, but it remained essentially a regional one so far as whites were concerned. However, shortly after he was killed on the Thames the name "Tecumseh" was, as the saying goes, a household one among English-speaking North Americans. As Tecumseh, he became an instant celebrity, not because of things he had done while alive but because the circumstances of his death gave American opinion makers a great dead Indian, a very useful figure at that particular time.

During the first year of the war, American land forces had suffered a number of humiliations and enjoyed very few successes in the west or elsewhere. A glorious unqualified victory was badly needed to raise military and civilian morale. Harrison was clearly the winner at Moraviantown, but notable triumphs require notable opponents. Even the most creative dispatch writers could not find much to crow about in the defeat of the wretched Procter and his troops. In consequence attention turned to the Indians, who had given a reasonably good account of themselves. There was much patriotic jubilation in the United States when it was learned that Harrison's brave boys had routed thousands of savages and killed their chief, who, it was soon being said, had been the equal of a Napoleon or Hannibal. Naturally there was also intense interest in how the mighty Tecumseh had fallen and in the identity of the American Achilles who had brought down the red Hector. The demand for them being so brisk, a number of professional and amateur reporters commenced to supply Death of Tecumseh stories. They continued to do so for many years.

All of the men who claimed to have gone into the woods with Tecumseh on October 5, and later spoke about what happened there, agreed that he was killed during the battle. Otherwise, their stories varied. Shabbona and William Caldwell said that they left him where he fell and, as Tekamthi had prophesied to Procter, his body was consumed by the birds, beasts, and elements. Others said they carried Tekamthi away, either dead or mortally wounded, and buried him in a secret place. An Ottawa, Noon Day, said that after laying his body on a blanket in a grave, "We all wept, we loved him so much. I took his hat and tomahawk."

The difficulty with the Indian stories is that they were told, or at least recorded, long after the events had occurred. In some cases the same men had different recollections at different times. In addition to failing memory, another factor was involved. The death of Tecumseh remained a politically significant matter in the United States for more than a quarter of a century. Therefore the aging warriors had reasons of self-interest for pandering to the preconceived notions of white interviewers and telling them whatever it was they wanted to hear. (Gaynwah, the Shawnee historian—who said that his people had no compunction about lying to whites—hinted that none of the Americans had been or ever would be told the truth about the end of his great-grandfather, Tecumseh.)

The only man who could have been a first-hand witness and spoke about the death of Tekamthi immediately after it occurred was Andrew Clark, the naturalized Shawnee who served his leader as an interpreter. While policing the battlefield after the fighting ended, Harrison's men found Clark propped against a tree, terribly wounded. He said that Tecumseh had been killed and been moved someplace by his companions. Clark died before volunteering more information or being further interrogated. Then the Americans found a body which some thought was Tecumseh's. What happened next became a matter of dispute, but the most common and persistent story was that the troopers took souvenirs from this dead Indian, cutting off strips of skin from the thighs and chest. Throughout much of the nineteenth century, there were men who said they had razor strops made from the hide of Tecumseh. If there were as many pieces of this leather as there were stories about them, then he would indeed have been a giant of a man.

During the next several days, a half dozen people who had known Tecumseh when he was alive came by to look at the corpse, but none made, at that time, a positive identification. Simon Kenton said that these remains were not those of Tecumseh. Harrison said that the body had so deteriorated (he made no mention of the skinnings) that he could not be certain. Anthony Shane, John and William Conner, the three who were serving as scouts and interpreters, also initially had doubts. Later, questioned by government agents and journalists, they decided that the body had been Tecumseh's.

Despite what might be called the habeas corpus problem, speculation and arguments about who had killed Tecumseh began immediately. They have continued down to the present, at least among history buffs. Many candidates for the honor stepped forward or were proposed. The companions of William Whitley contended that this flamboyant old frontiersman should posthumously receive credit for the feat. They said that Whitley had engaged in a duel with a mighty warrior, such an impressive one that it could only have been Tekamthi. It ended with both men lying dead on the ground. Then there was David King, an eighteen-year-old Kentuckian who said—and was supported by others—that he had shot an Indian. After he did so, King turned to his mates and shouted, "Whoops! By God, I have killed one yellow bugger." The savage he bagged was so fine-looking that King and the men around him decided it was Tecumseh.

The man who came to have the most popular support was Richard Johnson, the Kentucky congressman/colonel who had led Harrison's dragoons into the battle on the Thames. Johnson's own story was that he had been badly wounded—as he was—and fallen to the ground, partially trapped under his dying horse. A warrior had rushed at him with the clear intention of finishing him. Johnson had been able to work loose his pistol and shot the savage at close range. Johnson himself never directly said that this man had been Tecumseh. On the other hand he never stopped his friends and admirers from making this claim, at length and in dramatic detail. Johnson was an active, ambitious politician, and supporters quickly realized what advantages would accrue if their man could be established as the Killer of Tecumseh. They did their best to do so, turning up eyewitness accounts (including, twenty-five years later, Shabbona's) and much circumstantial evidence. The question became a hot political one. Democrats, of which Johnson was one, were adamant that he had done the deed. Whigs suggested it was campaign puffery, and they supported the claims of people like Whitley and King.

After the war, Johnson was elected to the Senate to represent Kentucky as a Jacksonian Democrat. As a good many commentators noted, his service there was "inconspicuous." Nevertheless, in 1836 he was nominated to run with Martin Van Buren, and on that ticket was elected Vice President of the United States. During the campaign Democrats chanted the jingle, "Rumpsey Dumpsey, Rumpsey Dumpsey, Colonel Johnson killed Tecumseh." In some quarters he was admiringly referred to as "Razor Strop Johnson."

As the man who had finally outgeneraled Tecumseh, William Henry Harrison also benefited but not so immediately as did Johnson. After his triumph at Moraviantown, Harrison thought he deserved to be named the commander in chief of the United States army. However, he got into and lost a dispute with the War Department about the appointment. The job went to Andrew Jackson, whose success in the south soon overshadowed that of Harrison's in the north. During the next twenty-five years, as Jackson came to dominate the American political scene, Harrison's career declined. Money remained a problem for him and his family. For the sake of the salary involved, he was reduced to seeking, virtually begging for, small public offices—as for example, the clerkship of the Cincinnati court system. Finally his luck turned. In the 1830s the Whig party was made up of a collection of disparate politicians who were brought together largely by their dislike of Andrew Jackson and Martin Van Buren and the desire to share in the federal patronage system which these two Democrats had invented and monopolized. In 1840 the Whigs wanted a tractable candidate who had not taken any strong stands on the issues of the day but who could beat Van Buren and Richard Johnson in the general election. Though Harrison was then nearly seventy and enfeebled, the Whigs decided he was just the man to head the ticket. Their strategists ran a brilliant campaign. It is often cited as the first truly modern one, since the Whigs sold their candidate somewhat like a bar of soap or popular beverage. While Harrison's public appearances were kept to a minimum, he was advertised as Old Tippecanoe. The image created for him was that of a plain, simple backwoodsman, content to sit rocking on the porch of his log cabin, occasionally sipping on hard cider and thinking long, homely thoughts about old-fashioned frontier virtues.

Harrison was elected by a handsome majority. In January of 1841 he started east toward Washington, traveling through the icy Pennsylvania mountains across which, fifty years before as a young ensign, he had ridden west after the defeat of Arthur St. Clair.

During the hard stagecoach journey he caught a bad cold. By the time of his inaugural, it had worsened into pneumonia. He died after serving as President for less than six weeks.

The most direct and obvious influence of Tecumseh on American politics was the extent to which his career advanced those of Harrison, Johnson, Lewis Cass, and a number of other lesser-known public officials. Also it has been argued by historians that, had it not been for Tecumseh, the U.S.-Canadian boundary might well be further to the north than it now is. The reasoning runs that it was the prowess of Tecumseh and his men and the exaggerated fears of them which held the Americans at bay throughout 1812 and much of 1813. Except for the Indians, Hull, with his superior force, might have successfully invaded Ontario during the first weeks of the war and occupied parts of it permanently with little difficulty or expense. As it was, the cost of subduing Tecumseh and the fifteen months which it took to do so cooled the enthusiasm of the War Hawks for conquering Canada. This theory is supported by the fact that after the victory on the Thames, Harrison withdrew his army from Ontario. The militiamen were eager to go home and the western campaign had proved to be a major drain on the resources of the United States government.

While living, Tekamthi had no interest in benefiting any American politican and only a tactical one in defending Ontario. His responsibility in these matters was purely accidental. Otherwise, in terms of his overt hopes and plans for his own people, the material influence of Tecumseh disappeared quickly after his death.

During the fall of 1813 there was a brief flareup of fighting in the south as the Red Stick faction of the Creek captured Fort Mims in Alabama, killing 500 soldiers and settlers who had taken refuge there. The next winter at Horseshoe Bend on the Tallapoosa River, the Red Sticks were cornered and virtually annihilated by Andrew Jackson and an army of Tennessee volunteers. Bands of Seminole continued to conduct guerrilla actions in the swamps of central Florida, but Horseshoe Bend was the last major red-white military engagement east of the Mississippi.

In the Northwest the red resistance ceased when Tekamthi was killed on the Thames. After the battle, several hundred of his warriors and their dependents, including Tecumpease, Pachetha, and Tenskwatawa, escaped to the east. The men continued to fight for the British during the last year of the war but as mercenaries without a cause of their own. More of the people who survived Tekamthi returned in small groups to Michigan. There they joined several thousand other Indians who had drifted back from Ontario earlier in the fall. Lacking provisions, military supplies, and leadership they immediately agreed to a truce offered by the Americans. After giving hostages to ensure their good behavior, the displaced people were allowed to return to their former homes within the United States. Federal agents at Detroit and other posts provided them with rations to help them get through the winter. In the summer of 1814 there was a final general council in Ohio, held symbolically at Greenville. It was attended by remnants of all of the subdued nations of the Northwest. Harrison acted as the chief representative of the United States and offered a fairly innocuous treaty, which was accepted without objections. Essentially it required that the Indians agree to perpetual peace and accept their status as a defeated people who would henceforth be vassals of the United States. Nothing was said about the disposal of their lands in this last Greenville treaty, but Harrison certainly, and very probably the chiefs who met him, understood that this matter would be taken up later when the Americans had settled their differences with the British.

The first major postwar transfer of land was made in 1815, when 2 million acres in southern Michigan were ceded by reds to whites. During the next fifteen years similar transactions took place with increasing frequency throughout the Northwest. The negotiations were pro forma and involved little bargaining. When it became politically or commercially desirable to obtain a new tract, American agents set a price that they considered sufficient to be legal and ethical. There was occasional grumbling, but the Indians were no longer in a position to refuse any of these offers. The claims of Tekamthi, that the land was a racial possession which could only be disposed of with the consent of all red peoples, were not raised after his death. Also, as the rate of land transfers increased, less attention was paid to the former Indian nations and their leaders. American agents were able and pleased to deal separately with chiefs who represented only small villages or bands. John C. Calhoun, who became Secretary of War in the Monroe administration, summed up the situation, observing that in regard to the savages "helplessness has succeeded independence."

After giving up their lands, many of the reds were escorted by federal agents or soldiers to camps and reservations in Kansas and Oklahoma. Some were allowed to stay on for a time in their former homelands, living on marginal tracts in isolated communities, surrounded by white settlers. The quality of life in these red ghettos declined rapidly, as did the numbers of their residents.

The history of the Shawnee following Tekamthi's death is typical of that of the other red people of the Northwest. Immediately after the War of 1812, some of them left to join their kinsmen in Missouri without waiting to be told or ordered to do so by the Americans. About 1,000 of them remained at Wapekoneta on the Auglaize River even after the surrounding country was ceded to the Americans. They were permitted to stay mainly because the venerable Black Hoof had successfully kept them out of the clutches of Tekamthi and the British. In the process he formed close connections with federal agents, most notably John Johnston. During the 1820s the Wapekoneta community became a showpiece for progressive Americans who could point to its continued existence as evidence of their charity and liberality.

With Tecumpease, Pachetha, and a few other Shawnee, Tenskwatawa remained in Ontario for more than a decade after Tekamthi was killed. He was essentially a ward of the Canadian government but kept in touch with American officials, hoping that he might be readmitted to the United States and subsidized as a principal chief, or at least as the guardian of the only son of the great Tecumseh. In 1824, largely because Lewis Cass, the federal governor of the territory, took a scholarly interest in them, the family was allowed to settle in Michigan. Tecumpease died there, but with Pachetha still in tow Tenskwatawa went to Wapekoneta in 1826. Though tolerated by Black Hoof and his people, he was given no special privileges or respect. The next year he and his nephew moved on, finally locating along the Missouri River near what is now Kansas City. Tenskwatawa stayed there until he died, peacefully, in 1837. During the final ten years of his life, he became something of a tourist attraction as whites stopped by to look at, interview, and sketch the infamous Shawnee Prophet about whom there were so many old and terrible stories.

After Tenskwatawa left Ohio, Black Hoof was able to hold the Wapekoneta community together for a few more years but he grew increasingly pessimistic about the future. In 1830 when he was, according to some accounts, 105 years old, Black Hoof had a bleak conversation with John Johnston about the fate of his people. "He admitted," recalled Johnston, "that it would be best for them to go [west] if they could have assurances that they would remain undisturbed in the future; but he remarked, we know wherever we may go, your people, the American Farmers, will follow; and we will be forced to be removed again and again and finally arrive at the Pacific ocean and then be compelled to jump off and perish. There would no more be any room left for the poor Indian."

Black Hoof died early in 1832, and by midsummer of that year, preparations were being made to move all of the Wapekoneta people, the last 600 Shawnee in the east, west of the Mississippi. However, at the end, members of this community which had survived by being especially docile and obedient, demonstrated that they retained some of the traditional, obstreperous traits of the Shawnee. Selling off the possessions they could not carry, they converted the proceeds into whiskey. It was consumed regularly and in great quantities while they were packing. Alarmed at the prospect of trying to herd 600 drunken Indians through the white settlements, the federal agents in charge of the removal made arrangements to send them by steamboat, down the Wabash and Ohio to the Mississippi. The Shawnee refused to travel in this fashion. An ancient chief of the remaining women expressed the sentiment of the Wapekoneta people, saying:

> We will not go by steamboats, nor will we go in wagons; but we will go on horseback; it is the most agreeable manner for us; and if we are not allowed to go so, we can and will remain here and die and be buried with our relatives; it will be but a short time before we leave this world anyway, and let us avert from our heads as much unnecessary pain and sorrow as possible.

The federal agents did not press the matter, and the Shawnee were left with their horses. The last community act they performed in Wapekoneta was to plant prairie grasses in their cemetery so that no traces of "the graves of their fathers" might be seen under the green sod.

They finally departed in mid-September but camped for several days at Greenville so as to drink for the last time from a spring whose waters were thought to be particularly healthful. They continued down the Miami river valley, following what was still called Tecumseh's Trail, the path which had been so much used by the warriors and Long Knives a half century before. Refusing to be hurried, they stayed for sentimental reasons a few more days on the site of Old Piqua, the Shawnee community which George Rogers Clark had stormed and burned when Tecumseh was a boy. They reached Indianapolis during the first week of October and crossed the Mississippi toward the end of the month. There they divided, one party continuing directly to Kansas and the other striking off toward the scrublands of Oklahoma.

(Other reds who remained in the Northwest, the Chickasaw and Choctaw in the south were permanently exiled at about the same time and in the same manner as the Shawnee. Their removal reflected President Andrew Jackson's conviction that his predecessors had been too soft on Indians and that the time had come to clear all the savages out of the country east of the Mississippi.

This work was largely completed in 1837 when the Cherokee were driven westward along their Trail of Tears by federal troops.)

Even in the unfamiliar trans-Mississippi country, the Shawnee attempted to cling to their old wandering ways and did not adjust to reservation life as well as did the Chickasaw, Choctaw, and other more agriculturally inclined refugees. Pachetha, for example, remained a few years with Tenskwatawa in Kansas and then moved to the Sabine River in Texas. There he married, fathered six children, and died in 1840. The youngest of these grandchildren of Tecumseh was Wapameepto (Gives Light as He Walks), who was called Big Jim by whites. He was said to be the most conservative Shawnee of his generation and also seemed to have had some of his grandfather's radical traits of mind and character. When he became a man, Wapameepto said that, like his ancestors, he believed that the earth was his mother. Therefore, he told federal Indian agents, he refused to lacerate and scar Her by using the white man's plow. Seeking a place where they could hunt, forage, and farm in the traditional Shawnee style, Wapameepto left the United States with his family and a small group of like-minded followers. They settled in the mountains of northern Mexico, where he died of smallpox in 1901.

The immediate excitement about the defeat and death of Tekamthi was followed by a spate of journalistic features about the late Red Napoleon, Hannibal, or Alexander. The stories were as a rule extravagantly eulogistic. A typical one appeared in the *Indiana Centinel,* published in Vincennes. Though this community had been especially fearful of the living Tekamthi, a few years after his death an editorialist for the *Centinel* wrote: "Every schoolboy in the Union now knows Tecumseh was a great man. He was truly great—and his greatness was his own, unassisted by the science or the aids of education. As a statesman, a warrior and a patriot, take him in all, we shall not look upon his like again."

During the nineteenth century in the Midwest (as the Old Northwest came to be called) it was fashionable to give the name "Tecumseh" to topographical features, new villages, buildings, commercial products, and even children. The most famous of the latter was the Ohio-born William Tecumseh Sherman, who as a man and general marched the Union armies from Atlanta to the sea during the second American Civil War. There also grew to be an abundance of what can best be called folktales concerning Tecumseh which were circulated by word of mouth. By way of personal example:

According to undocumented family tradition, my great-great-grandfather, Cornelias Sparks, was an Ohio militiaman who served in the second Army of the Northwest under William Henry Harrison during the war of 1812. The story goes that after Tekamthi was defeated, Sparks settled around Fort Wayne. In 1817, as a matter of record, he, his wife Susanna, and several young children moved to southern Michigan. They took up a farm in Berrien County a few miles north of the Indiana state line in the St. Joseph River valley. Most of the descendants of the family stayed in this part of the country for at least the next century and a half. (My paternal ancestors came to the area a bit later but also arrived before Michigan was admitted into the Union as a state.)

I was born—110 years after Cornelias and Susanna Sparks pioneered into this territory—in Monroe, which had first been called Frenchtown and was the site of the River Raisin massacre, where many white prisoners were tortured and killed by the warriors in 1813. My father was born in Kalamazoo, and my parents moved back to that community from Monroe when I was an infant. I lived there for the next seventeen years. My grandfather owned rural properties in the southern part of the county, and I spent much of my time roaming about in the swamps and woodlands, which were still interspersed with farms and represented the remnants of the temperate jungle which had originally covered the region.

I was no more interested than the average schoolchild—which is to say very little—in the formal history of this country. As a guess I probably first learned that Tecumseh was a Shawnee, a bit about Tippecanoe, the fall of Detroit, and the battle of the Thames when I was in the late elementary grades. But well before that I had heard of Tecumseh. In fact, I cannot remember—and I have thought about this now and then while writing this book—when I did not know the name "Tecumseh" and understand that it had belonged to a great Indian. It would have been difficult to be ignorant about this in that place and time. When I was growing up, my parents still had close friends in Monroe, and when we visited them we passed through the town of Tecumseh. I also specifically remember a hill, lake, grocery store, restaurant, two roads, and a make of combustion engine which bore the name Tecumseh.

Now and then a man who did something especially impressive would be described as a "champion" or "captain." I had a great-uncle who used a different expression for the same purpose. He would speak of somebody he judged to be a great rifle shot, post-hole digger, or baseball hitter as a "regular Tecumseh."

I do not remember when and by whom I was first erroneously

told that it was a likeness of Tecumseh which was engraved on Indian-head pennies. The story was common in those parts and accepted as absolute fact. The corollary to the tale was that pennies were once in every citizen's pocket or purse and the face of Tecumseh appeared on them to serve as a constant reminder that his people had first owned the land and had gallantly defended it.

On schoolyards, at summer camps, wherever and whenever there were enough of us hanging out together, the crowd I ran with played, passionately, a game called Pioneers-and-Indians. It was a cross between kick-the-can and catch-as-catch-can wrestling. At least a dozen participants were required for a satisfying game. A great deal of time was spent in pregame arguments about who would get to be on which side. Everybody wanted to be an Indian. Therefore, while the pioneers had to be more numerous, according to the traditions of the game, the Indians were bigger, stronger, and the better debaters. After the sides were finally chosen, Indians tied red bandannas around their necks or arms, and the pioneers put on white handkerchiefs. Then the Indians ran off to lurk in bushes and other hiding places. The puny whites gathered at their camp, which was designated by a block of wood, bucket, or sometimes a flag. There were two objectives. The first was to scalp opponents by ripping off the red or white insignias. There were no restrictions on methods—gang tackling was popular. The Indians could also win by charging through the defending whites, scalping as they came, and capturing their goal.

Except during the initial arguments about who got to be who, Pioneers-and-Indians was less a competitive happening than a psychodrama. Especially aggressive gangs of pioneers would sometimes vow that it would be otherwise and put up a real struggle, but their role was to be victims while those who wore the red played the hero. So far as I remember, things invariably ended in the same way—with the victorious Indians sitting around the sacked camp, counting scalp cloths and boasting about how they had made the pioneer sissies cry and run away.

The captain and champion of the Indians was always called Tecumseh. Tecumsehs were selected somewhat as mayors of Chicago once were. Aspirants for the position hung around serving as brave, obedient warriors, hoping to be elevated to leadership when the reigning Tecumseh commenced growing pubic hair and went out for junior-high football.

In my set girls sometimes played this game but, with the exception of one truly formidable young female, they were required to be pioneers. Some forty years after my own playing days were over, I met a lady who was then in her eighties and had grown up along the Indiana line in an open section of Berrien County called Indian Prairie. In the course of conversation, she mentioned that in 1900 or thereabout she played Pioneers-and-Indians, but much differently than I had in the 1930s. She said: "My sister and I and our girlfriends bossed my brother and his friends around something awful. We girls were always the Indians. We'd hide in the woodlot or cornfield and the boys were supposed to find us before we ran in and tagged base on a big chestnut tree which grew behind the barn. If they did catch us, then it was their turn to be Indians. But lots of times we'd get mad and refuse to be Pioneers. I was crazy, demented may be the word, about Indians. Here I was this blond, curly headed, blue-eyed little thing, and I convinced myself that I was really an Indian girl who had been stolen when I was a papoose by the whites. I'd daydream that someday a big Indian chief would come to the farm and take me back to my tribe. You know the name I gave him."

"Tecumseh?"

"Of course."

I have the impression that my generation was the last to have Tecumseh games and fantasies, probably because it is the last generation which was directly influenced by people who were born in the 1800s. The formal interest in Tecumseh may also have peaked in the nineteenth century, but as this book testifies it has never abated. In the Library of Congress catalog, works indexed under the heading "Tecumseh" are approximately twice as numerous as those having to do with William Henry Harrison. Additions to this now sizable body of Tecumseh literature have been made in every decade since his death. Included are popular biographical and historical commentaries, scholarly monographs, novels, narrative poems, and occasional epic dramas.

The mortal Tekamthi was an able warrior, but during most of his military career served as a subordinate to more senior war chiefs or as the leader of very small partisan bands. Only in the last year of his life did he command what can legitimately be called an army. In 1813 he generally performed well in difficult circumstances but won no victories comparable to those of Little Turtle, Blue Jacket, and Cornstalk. It seems beyond dispute that Tekamthi was a man of exceptional intelligence, eloquence, and charisma, a clever political negotiator and propagandist. He had some loyal supporters among all the Indian peoples of the northwest but did not create a racial union nor even an extensive system of international military alliances. Given the weakness of his people, creating a following as

Tekamthi did was a remarkable feat but the red resistance movement delayed the westward advance of the Americans only somewhat and for less than a decade.

Nevertheless, it can be fairly argued that no man of his race has had such a strong and lasting impact on the American imagination as Tecumseh, the posthumous Tekamthi, has had. Any answers to the question of why this has been the case must be soft, speculative, and subjective, since they involve judgments about the nature and workings of the collective national psyche. My own conceits are as follows:

Everywhere, always, heroes—those who risk comfort, security, and even life for the sake of principles, ideals, and honor—have been considered intrinsically interesting and admirable. Very soon after Tekamthi was killed, he was recognized as a hero of the rarest and highest type—a populist leader of a lost cause who remained defiant to the end and died gallantly in battle. As more biographical information was accumulated, folk and formal historians concluded that Tekamthi had not only died but lived heroically, having since youth been a defender of the rights and territories of his people.

Rousseau, Voltaire, and the other eighteenth-century European philosophers of the romantic-humanist school argued forcefully that society would be much improved if greater emphasis was placed on natural laws and behavior. Some of the more devoted followers of these savants were North American colonists, members of the seaboard intelligentsia. This was a small but influential group which included Franklin, Jefferson, Paine, and others of the founding fathers of the United States. Largely because of them, the concept that the natural is superior to the contrived (as for example the inalienable rights of man were to the divine rights of kings) became a cornerstone of American political philosophy. A cardinal tenet of the romantic humanists was that civilization corrupted humans, while exposure to Nature ennobled them. To the intellectuals who advanced this proposition, the North American savages appeared to be the most natural of men and therefore probably the noblest.

Throughout the eighteenth century and during the first years of the nineteenth, the view that Indians were as good as white people and in some respects innately better was largely restricted to the elite classes. The great majority of Americans were engaged, directly or indirectly, in subduing the savages and regarded them as human varmints. Like wolves or bears, the Indians had to be greatly thinned out or eradicated if the continent was to be properly developed and civilized. After and to some extent because of the death of Tekamthi, views on this subject began to shift. The Noble

Savage theory grew more popular and respectable until finally it came to reflect—as it still does—the thinking of the majority.

Aldo Leopold, the influential natural historian and philosopher, once wrote that ethics begin after breakfast. The same might be said about nostalgia. Following the final defeat of Tekamthi, the Indians ceased to be a threat to most white Americans, that is for those who lived east of the Mississippi. (In the western regions the opinion that the only good Indian was a dead Indian was prevalent for another hundred years—that is, for as long as there were unsubdued savages.) Having had breakfast, so to speak, easterners, who made up 90 percent of the population, became more reflective and sentimental about Indians.

September 19, 1832, fell on a Sunday. On that day the last of the Shawnee in Ohio were traveling slowly down the Miami Valley heading toward exile in Kansas and Oklahoma. A white girl, Ann Bercau, who was a member of the nearby Piqua Presbyterian Church, played truant from morning services and rode to the river "to see the Indians who were on their way westward." Later the moderator of the church interrogated Bercau but concluded that while she had violated the Sabbath, her reasons for doing so were understandable, and that her apology gave "sufficient satisfaction for her offense."

Eleven years later a small straggling band of Wyandot who had previously escaped deportation, passed through Xenia, Ohio, on their way west. A reporter from the local paper, the *Xenia Torchlight,* came out to see them and wrote, on July 20, 1843: "Our citizens seemed to look upon the scene of their departure [the Wyandot] from among us with feelings of melancholy interest. To reflect that the last remnant of a powerful people, once the proud possessors of the soil we now occupy, were just leaving their beloved hunting grounds . . . was well calculated to awaken the liveliest sympathies of the human heart."

In this sentimental climate Tecumseh tales, factual, fictional, and mixed, flourished like sycamores in the Wabash bottomlands. From them grew the figure which has remained fixed in American folklore and histories. Tecumseh was the most formidable but also the most compassionate of warriors. He was a terror in battle but abhorred the abuse of prisoners, was protective of women and children and chivalrous with honorable white men. Though the most Indian—the wildest and freest—of Indians, he was a teetotaler, dressed plainly, lived simply, and comported himself with the dignity of a king or president. Tecumseh validated theories about the purifying and uplifting properties of Nature—which, like those having to do with the innate goodness of Indians, became and have remained popular after the wilderness was much reduced. Tecumseh, the untutored Child of Nature, was an incomparably eloquent orator, as knowledgeable about history and politics as civilized scholars, and as shrewd a debater as any parliamentarian or lawyer. In short, Tecumseh personified the Noble Savage.

There was a related phenomenon. As time passed, the virtues attributed to Tekamthi came to be associated with Indians in general. Memories of the drunks, sadists, cowards, and connivers among them faded and were replaced with the image of a race of natural paragons. Somewhat as would later be the case with Robert E. Lee, the perceived nobility of Tecumseh ennobled his followers and his cause. In regard to their historical reputations, there is another parallel between these principal leaders on the losing sides of the two American civil wars. Even among the descendants of the winners, Tecumseh and Lee are generally remembered better and more sympathetically than are any of the men who defeated them. I am the great-great-grandson of an Indian fighter, but I pretended to be Tecumseh. I am the great-grandson of a trooper in the 6th Michigan Cavalry. He lost a leg at Gettysburg in 1863, but as a boy the first full biography I read was that of Marse Robert.

Even during the pioneering period in North America, Europeans were afflicted by low-grade guilt feelings about their treatment of the natives. Basically the concerns were about property rather than human rights. The official and popular justification for taking lands away from the natives was based on natural law. It was the rule of the world, so the reasoning ran, that aggressive species, races, and nations should multiply, pioneer into new territories, and displace less numerous and efficient competitors. Allowing a few thousand savages to block the development of vast territories which could support millions of civilized people was contrary to common sense, science, and the intentions of the Creator.

Reasonable as this ecological defense was, an appreciable number of Americans, including many who had no philosophical affection for savages, were not entirely convinced that it answered the simple argument of the Indians: that, as Kekewepellethe said, "God gave us this Country. It is all ours." Using natural law to challenge the authority of an English King and Parliament was one thing. But many Americans were made uneasy by the proposition that natural law was also superior to the first principle—the rights of original ownership—of property law.

Doubts about the moral validity of land titles raised another disturbing matter. During the long, cruel racial wars, whites frequently rationalized their own atrocious conduct on the grounds that it was necessary to fight fire with fire, that they had to be vicious because the savages were so vicious. The possibility that they, as land thieves and swindlers, were the first culprits undercut this position. Shawnee warriors had eaten the warm heart of Richard Butler but there remained the nagging suspicion that the warriors were less wrong than Hugh McGary had been when he brained the harmless, trusting Shawnee chief, Moluntha. Defending their property was an underlying motive and perhaps excuse for whatever the savages did.

After the United States was organized, federal authorities were generally more concerned than their constituents about ethical issues involving the Indians. The first preference of all of the early Presidents was to pursue the "conciliatory" policy designed by George Washington and Henry Knox. Obtaining Indian lands piecemeal through treaties, which at least gave the appearance of willing seller—willing buyer, was inexpensive and also, as Knox pointed out, avoided the "blood and injustice which would stain the character of the nation."

Later Knox explained to Anthony Wayne why the Indians presented such a delicate moral or at least public relations problem. The Secretary of War cautioned his field commander:

> The favorable opinion and pity of the world is easily excited in favor of the oppressed. The Indians are considered in a great degree of this description—If our modes of population and War destroy the tribes, the disinterested part of mankind and posterity will be apt to class the effects of our Conduct and that of the Spaniards in Mexico and Peru together.

The preoccupation of the United States with projecting an image as the most righteous of nations has frequently been noted. In this regard the past treatment of Indians has been and remains a chronic sore spot in the national conscience. In the interests of spiritual therapy, Americans themselves have incessantly picked at this supposed blemish. So too, just as Henry Knox warned they might, have foreigners. For two hundred years the ambition of the United States to be recognized as an international role model and arbiter has been mocked by the question: "If you are so good, why did you do such bad things to the Indians?"

During his lifetime Tekamthi was remarkably adept at keeping whites on the defensive by probing at soft, tender places in their consciences. Repeatedly he made American and Canadian officials squirm as he cataloged the hypocrisies and deceits of the whites, the ways in which, by their own fine civilized standards, they had cheated and abused the Indians. Thereafter a central theme in the Tecumseh histories and legends was that the great Shawnee patriot had made a case for his people which was so true and logical as to be beyond rebuttal. The lesson taught to "every schoolboy in the Union"—or at least an appreciable number of them—was that with Tecumseh at their head, the Indians had captured the moral high ground and would hold it so long as there was any interest in the history of the United States. For catharsis, white Americans should look up, figuratively, to Tecumseh or, literally, down at the pennies in their pockets.

Tecumseh has been remembered, I think, because it is generally accepted that he was a hero, a noble man of nature, and one who was right. I also have the notion that the manner in which Tecumseh has worked on the imagination of white Americans may represent the great triumph and ultimate revenge of Tekamthi.

Notes

Complete information about sources cited in these notes appears in the bibliography which commences on page 351.

Page 5. SHAWNEE CUSTOMS. Clark and Howard are general references, published in the twentieth century. Accounts, by contemporaries, concerning Shawnee customs in the eighteenth and early nineteenth centuries appear in Heckewelder, David Jones, and Trowbridge.

Page 6. TEKAMTHI'S BIRTH. There have been numerous biographies and sketches of Tekamthi. As is this one, all of them are indebted for most of the information about his early life to Benjamin Drake, who published the first biography in 1841. Drake gathered Tekamthi material for many years and was able to interview contemporaries who had personally known the man. Drake's most notable informants were Stephen Ruddell and Anthony Shane. Statements by Ruddell and Shane, as well as additional information collected by Drake and others, are preserved in the Draper Manuscripts/Tecumseh Papers, Wisconsin State Historical Society in Madison, Wisconsin.

Page 8. PLACE OF BIRTH. After Tekamthi's death many conflicting claims were made about where he was born. Galloway (*Old Chillicothe*), pp. 107–18, summarizes and critiques these claims. Wheeler-Voegelin (Vol. II), pp. 380–81, in her detailed study of Shawnee communities in eighteenth century Ohio, makes the point that if Tekamthi was born near Xenia, it was at a hunting camp since no permanent village existed at this site until the mid-1770s.

Page 8. SHAWNEE NAMES. Alford, pp. 3–5; Trowbridge, pp. 26–28; C. F. and E. W. Voegelin, pp. 617–35.

Page 10. LALAWETHIKA. Edmunds (*The Shawnee Prophet*), pp. 28–30; Draper Manuscripts/Tecumseh Papers, File YY–12, p. 1.

Page 10. TEKAMTHI . . . Gatschet, pp. 91–92.

Page 11. WILLIAM HENRY HARRISON. Harrison biographies used here are Cleaves and Goebel.

Page 14. INDIAN NATIONS OF THE NORTHEASTERN WOODLANDS. A good general reference is Sturtevant (*Handbook of North American Indians,* Vol. 15). There are many other sources dealing with specific nations, cultural phenomena, and early red-white relations. Among those frequently used are Anson, Axtell, Clark, Berkhofer, Heckewelder, James H. Howard, Jennings (*The Invasion of America*), Loudon, Martin, Owen-Deetz-Fisher, Parker, Shetrone, Tantaquidgeon, Washburn, Wheeler-Voegelin.

Page 16. SMITH AND TECAUGHRETANEGO. Loudon, pp. 192–94.

Page 19. VISIT OF DAVID JONES TO THE SHAWNEE. Jones, pp. 54–78.

Page 24. POPULATION AND DISEASE. Kroeber, pp. 1–25; Martin, pp. 44–48.

Page 26. FUR EXPORTS. U.S. Department of Commerce (*Historical Statistics of the United States*), Vol. II, pp. 1183–84.

Page 28. RED-WHITE CASUALTIES. Moorehead, p. 108.

Page 30. JOHN QUINCY ADAMS. As quoted by Berkhofer, p. 138.

Page 34. SHAWNEE CREATION ACCORDING TO TENSKWATAWA. Trowbridge, pp. 1–11.

Page 38. CALLENDER. Sturtevant (*Handbook of North American Indians,* Vol. 15), p. 622.

Page 38. SHAWNEE MEETING WHITES. Spencer, p. 384; James H. Howard, p. 5.

Page 39. IROQUOIS WARS AND SHAWNEE. Anson, Hanna, Hunt, Jennings (*The Ambiguous Iroquois Empire*), Wallace.

Page 43. SOUTHERN SLAVE TRADE. Gibson, p. 41.

Page 44. OPETHTHA. Hanna, Vol. I, pp. 127–39.

Page 49. KISHKALWA. McKenney and Hall, Vol. I, pp. 34–43.

Page 49. SHAWNEE POLITICS ACCORDING TO TENSKWATAWA. Trowbridge, pp. 11–13.

Page 50. SHAWNEE CONSERVATISM. Clark, pp. 55–59; Spencer, p. 387.

Page 51. TENSKWATAWA'S GRANDFATHER. McKenney and Hall, Vol. I, pp. 75–78.

Page 53. GAYNWAH'S FAMILY HISTORY. Galloway (*Old Chillicothe*), p. 18 and pp. 37–40. There may have been several Shawnee leaders in the eighteenth century who were called Puckeshinwa or something similar and whose identities were confused by whites. See Hanna, Vol. I, pp. 155–57.

Page 54. TEKAMTHI AND MCARTHUR. Drake, p. 66.

Page 56. THE PROCLAMATION OF 1763 AND ITS CONSEQUENCES. Excellent, detailed accounts of red-white relations in the Ohio Valley during this period are given by both Downes and Sosin, and I have depended heavily on them. Other sources have been used as indicated below.

Page 61. JOHN FINDLEY. Beckner ("John Findley"), pp. 206–15.

Page 61. DANIEL BOONE. Galloway ("Daniel Boon"), pp. 263–77.

Page 62. CAPTAIN WILL TO BOONE. Downes, p. 12.

Page 65. LOGAN AND THE POINT PLEASANT CAMPAIGN. Randall ("The Dunmore War"), pp. 167–96.

Page 69. CORNSTALK TO SHAWNEE. Drake, p. 34.

Page 70. SHAWNEE VERSION OF CAMP CHARLOTTE TREATY. Norton, pp. 16–17.

Page 71. BLACK FISH AND TEKAMTHI. Edmunds (*Tecumseh*), p. 21. Galloway (*Old Chillicothe*), pp. 114–15.

Page 74. SHANE ON TEKAMTHI. Draper Manuscripts/Tecumseh Papers, File YY-12, pp. 12 and 31.

Page 74. INDIAN EDUCATION. Heckewelder, pp. vii–xiii and 115–17.

Page 77. JOHN M'CULLOUGH. Loudon, pp. 252–301.

Page 78. JAMES SMITH. Loudon, p. 125.

Page 81. WHITE CAPTIVES. Axtell, pp. 74–77, 171–80, 202; Crèvecoeur, pp. 208–10.

Page 82. ICE WATER AND HUNTING TESTS. Alford, pp. 23–25.

Page 84. UMSOMA HUMOR. Galloway (*Old Chillicothe*), pp. 194–95.

Page 84. RESPECT FOR THE AGED. Alford, pp. 20–21, 65–66; Heckewelder, p. 116; Trowbridge, pp. 46–47.

Page 85. KUMSKAUKAU. Draper Manuscripts/Tecumseh Papers, File YY-12, p. 12.

Page 86. SHAWNEE AND PROHIBITION. Alford, p. 48; Hanna, Vol. I, p. 152, Vol. II, p. 306; Anson, p. 52.

Page 89. MARTHA MOORE. Gilbert, p. 40.

Page 90. CANNIBAL SOCIETIES. Trowbridge, pp. 53–54, 64–65.

Page 95. CORNSTALK TO THE CHEROKEE. Brown, pp. 141–48.

Page 97. DEATH OF CORNSTALK. Thwaites and Kellogg (*Frontier Defense*), pp. 157–63, 205–209.

Page 98. BOONE WITH SHAWNEE. Galloway ("Daniel Boon"), pp. 271–72; Hinde, pp. 373–75.

Page 99. CLARK'S INVASION OF ILLINOIS. Downes, pp. 228–39; Sosin, pp. 116–20.

Page 101. SHAWNEE TO MISSOURI. Drake, p. 62; Edmunds (*Tecumseh*), p. 22; Galloway (*Old Chillicothe*), pp. 57, 61.

Page 101. BOWMAN'S RAID. *Ohio Archaeological and Historical Publications,* Vol. 19, pp. 446–59; Galloway (*Old Chillicothe*), pp. 55–65.

Page 104. RUDDELL'S STATION. Beckner ("Reverend John D. Shane's Notes"), pp. 166–73; Galloway (*Old Chillicothe*), pp. 50–54; Horsman (*Matthew Elliott*), pp. 28–29; Rothert, pp. 227–31.

Page 105. CLARK'S RAID, 1780. Galloway (*Old Chillicothe*), pp. 54–61; Sosin, p. 137.

Page 106. GNADENHUTTEN AND CRAWFORD. Downes, pp. 272–74; Heckewelder, pp. 284–89; Moorehead, pp. 64–72.

Page 108. CRAWFORD TORTURE. Loudon, pp. 1–15.

Page 109. BUILDERBACK. Sword, pp. 76–77.

Page 110. BLUE LICKS. Z. F. Smith, pp. 205–15.

Page 110. TEKAMTHI'S FIRST BATTLES. Drake, pp. 68–69; Galloway (*Old Chillicothe*), pp. 130–31.

Page 112. DE PEYSTER. Downes, p. 281.

Page 115. KEKEWEPELLETHE. Downes, p. 297.

Page 117. U.S. INDIAN POLICY. An excellent summary is given by Horsman (*Expansion and American Indian Policy*), pp. 3–32.

Page 119. FORT FINNEY TREATY. Downes, pp. 296–99; Sword, pp. 28–30.

Page 120. CLARK AND LOGAN, 1786. Galloway (*Old Chillicothe*), pp. 91–94; Sword, pp. 33–44.

Page 122. SHAWNEE MOVE TO MAUMEE. Horsman (*Matthew Eliott*), p. 56.

Page 122. MIAMI AND KEKIONGA. Anson, pp. 77–125; Griswold, pp. 85–97.

Page 125. TEKAMTHI DESCRIPTIONS. Galloway (*Old Chillicothe*), pp. 130–32; Hatch, p. 111; Siberell, pp. 12–13.

Page 127. CHEESEKAU'S DEATH. Brown, pp. 270–71; Galloway (*Old Chillicothe*), p. 131.

Page 127. TEKAMTHI IN THE SOUTH, 1787–90. Drake, p. 169; Galloway (*Old Chillicothe*), pp. 130–32; Draper Manuscripts/Tecumseh Papers, File YY-12, pp. 35–36.

Page 128. JAMES SMITH. Loudon, p. 177.

Page 129. SHAWNEE SEX EDUCATION. Voegelin, C. F., Yegerlehner and Robinett, p. 37.

Page 129. TEKAMTHI'S LIAISONS. Galloway (*Old Chillicothe*), p. 130; Draper Manuscripts/Tecumseh Papers, File YY-12, pp. 31–33, 58.

Page 132. WESTERN SETTLERS. Sword, pp. 47–58.

Page 135. U.S. MILITARY IN NORTHWEST. Prucha (*The Sword of the Republic*), pp. 19–28.

Page 135. HARMAR'S CAMPAIGN. Sword, pp. 92–116.

Page 139. RUFUS PUTNAM. Prucha (*The Sword of the Republic*), p. 22.

Page 140. DUNLAP'S STATION. Sword, pp. 126–28.

Page 141. RUFUS PUTNAM TO WASHINGTON. Hildreth, p. 280.

Page 141. GREATHOUSE. Sword, p. 138.

Page 143. BECKWITH AND HAMILTON. Burt, pp. 115–19.

Page 144. ST. CLAIR. Sears, pp. 41–57.

Page 145. SYMMES. Prucha (*The Sword of the Republic*), pp. 26–27.

Page 145. ST. CLAIR CAMPAIGN. A detailed account is given by Sword, pp. 145–200.

Page 152. POLLY MEADOWS AND HENRY BALL. Spencer, p. 96.

Page 153. TEKAMTHI IN WINTER OF 1791. Hildreth, pp. 221–23, 301–303; Draper Manuscripts/Tecumseh Papers, File YY-12, pp. 36–37; Withers, p. 400.

Page 153. HARRISON. Cleaves, pp. 8–15.

Page 156. WASHINGTON AND LEAR. Rush, pp. 65–69.

Page 158. PEACE NEGOTIATIONS, 1792. Burt, pp. 120–26; Sword, pp. 225–31.

Page 160. PUTNAM ON INDIANS. Downes, p. 320.

Page 160. TEKAMTHI SKIRMISH WITH KENTON. Drake, pp. 272–76; Galloway (*Old Chillicothe*), pp. 132–36.

Page 161. TEKAMTHI AT WAGGONER'S FARM. Withers, pp. 408–10.

Page 162. THE U.S. LEGION, WAYNE, AND THE FALLEN TIMBERS CAMPAIGN. The account offered here is based generally on Sword, pp. 201–312, and Wildes, pp. 349–430. Other sources are noted below.

Page 164. WAYNE'S DISCIPLINE. Prucha (*The Sword of the Republic*), pp. 32–34.

Page 167. PEACE TALKS, 1793. Downes, p. 327; Cruikshank, Vol. II, pp. 18–36.

Page 170. MARSHALL AND TURNER ON WILKINSON. Kohn, pp. 361–62.

Page 173. DORCHESTER'S SPEECH. Cruikshank, Vol. II, pp. 149–50.

Page 174. SUPPLYING WAR PARTIES. Horsman (*Matthew Elliott*), p. 97.

Page 174. ATTACK ON FORT RECOVERY. In addition to Sword and Wildes: Draper Manuscripts/Tecumseh Papers, File YY-12, p. 22; Cruikshank, Vol. II, pp. 310-17.

Page 176. LITTLE TURTLE AND COLONEL ENGLAND. Cruikshank, Vol. II, pp. 333–34.

Page 177. LITTLE TURTLE ADVISES PEACE. Anson, p. 192.

Page 178. FALLEN TIMBERS BATTLEFIELD. Cruikshank, Vol. II, p. 396.

Page 179. BATTLE OF FALLEN TIMBERS. In addition to Sword and Wildes: Dresden W. H. Howard, pp. 37–49, gives the account of Kinjoino, an Ottawa war chief; Draper Manuscripts/Tecumseh Papers, File YY-12, pp. 40–42.

Page 182. CAMPBELL AND WAYNE. Cruikshank, Vol. II, pp. 396, 405–406.

Page 183. MAMATE. Draper Manuscripts/Tecumseh Papers, File YY-12, p. 58.

Page 185. CANADIAN FUR TRADE. Cruikshank, Vol. I, pp. 310–13.

Page 185. GREENVILLE COUNCIL. Horsman (*Expansion and American Indian Policy*), pp. 99–103; Dwight L. Smith, pp. 239–55; Sword, pp. 323–33; Wildes, pp. 437–47.

Page 190. RED POLE AT GREENVILLE. American State Papers, Vol. IV, pp. 578, 581–82.

Page 190. BLUE JACKET AND TEKAMTHI. Draper Manuscripts/Tecumseh Papers, File YY-12, pp. 43–44. On pages 33–34 and 43–45 of same file, Shane describes Tekamthi's movements in southern Ohio between 1795 and 1802.

Page 193. JOB GUARD. Hill, p. 24.

Page 193. JOHN CONNER AND TEKAMTHI. Draper Manuscripts. Tecumseh Papers, File YY-8, p. 4.

Page 193. JOHN JOHNSTON AND TEKAMTHI. McKenney and Hall, Vol. I, p. 94.

Page 194. ABNER BARRETT. Drake, p. 85.

Page 194. REBECCA GALLOWAY AND TEKAMTHI. Galloway (*Old Chillicothe*), pp. 135–38; 276–83.

Page 197. TEKAMTHI AT MAD RIVER, 1799. Drake, p. 84.

Page 197. WOLF AND WAWWILAWAY. Brice, pp. 166–68; Norton, p. 172.

Page 198. JOHN M'DONALD. Drake, p. 85.

Page 199. JEFFERSON'S LETTER TO HARRISON. Esarey, Vol. I, pp. 69–73.

Page 200. U.S. LAND ACQUISITIONS, 1803–05. Cleaves, p. 42; Goebel, pp. 105–106; Horsman (*Expansion and American Indian Policy*), p. 146.

Page 201. JEFFERSON TO THE DELAWARE. Horsman (*Expansion and American Indian Policy*), p. 109.

Page 201. LITTLE TURTLE ON CIVILIZATION. Sword, p. 335.

Page 206. TEKAMTHI TO HARRISON. Tekamthi and Harrison met twice, in August of 1810 and again in the summer of 1811. On each occasion Harrison made detailed reports to the U.S. War Department. In some passages he directly quoted Tekamthi; in others, Tekamthi's remarks were summarized. These reports appear in Esarey, Vol. I, pp. 459–69 and 542–51.

Page 207. TEKAMTHI TO THE OSAGE, CREEK, AND CHOCTAW. No firsthand account of Tekamthi's trip to these nations in 1811 exists or, presumably, was ever made. Subsequently these orations were recalled by men who claimed to have heard or heard of them. These recollections came to be accepted and published as though they were verbatim reports. At best they are re-creations made well after the fact. However, the substance of the remarks Tekamthi purportedly made on these occasions is compatible with things he documentably said to American and British officials at other times. The "southern" speeches, or lengthy condensations of them, appear in Klinck, pp. 91–93 (Choctaw); pp. 94–97 (Creek); pp. 104–107 (Osage).

Page 212. TEKAMTHI'S EUROPEAN CHARACTERISTICS. Randall, p. 465.

Page 217. LALAWETHIKA'S FIRST VISIONS. Drake, pp. 86–89; Edmunds (*The Shawnee Prophet*), pp. 32–35.

Page 217. MESSIAHS. Mooney, pp. 657–61; Wallis, pp. 107–108.

Page 220. SHANE ON TEKAMTHI AND TENSKWATAWA. Draper Manuscripts/Tecumseh Papers, File YY-12, p. 40.

Page 222. DELAWARE WITCH TRIALS. Drake, pp. 88–89.

Page 224. HARRISON TO DELAWARE AND ECLIPSE. Drake, pp. 89–91; Edmunds (*The Shawnee Prophet*), pp. 47–49.

Page 226. THE PROPHET—RITUALS AND TABOOS. Edmunds (*The Shawnee Prophet*), pp. 35–41; Mooney, pp. 672–80.

Page 226. THE PROPHET AND SHAKERS. MacLean, pp. 215–29.

Page 227. TANNER AND THE PROPHET'S MISSIONARIES. Tanner, pp. 155–58.

Page 227. WILLIAM WELLS. Hutton, pp. 183–222; Volney, pp. 371–75.

Page 230. SHANE TO GREENVILLE. Drake, pp. 91–93.

Page 231. THE TROUT. Edmunds (*The Shawnee Prophet*), pp. 51–52.

Page 232. BLUE JACKET, 1807. Edmunds (*The Shawnee Prophet*), p. 60.

Page 233. MAIN POC. Edmunds (*The Shawnee Prophet*), pp. 63–66.

Page 234. HARRISON TO INDIANA LEGISLATURE. Esarey, Vol. I, pp. 229–36.

Page 236. ELLIOTT, CRAIG, AND GORE, 1807. Goltz, pp. 104–105; Horsman (*Matthew Elliott*), pp. 162–65.

Page 237. HARRISON AND SPIES. Esarey, Vol. I, p. 266.

Page 238. TEKAMTHI AT SPRINGFIELD, 1807. Drake, pp. 97–99; Edmunds (*Tecumseh*), pp. 93–94. Drake thought the incident occurred in the fall, but Edmunds argues convincingly that it was probably in the summer.

Page 239. NEGOTIATIONS AT GREENVILLE, 1807. Drake, pp. 94–96.

Page 240. DINNER AT ADENA. Galloway (*Old Chillicothe*), pp. 214–16.

Page 243. MOVE TO TIPPECANOE. Edmunds (*The Shawnee Prophet*), pp. 69–70; Esarey, Vol. I, pp. 290–91.

Page 246. TEKAMTHI AND GORE, 1808. Goltz, pp. 118–24; Horsman (*Matthew Elliott*), pp. 169–72.

Page 248. THE PROPHET AND HARRISON. Esarey, Vol I., pp. 299–300, 302.

Page 250. TREATY OF FORT WAYNE. Anson, pp. 153–55; Barce, pp. 352–67; Edmunds (*The Potawatomis*), pp. 169–70.

Page 252. TEKAMTHI AT WAPEKONETA, 1810. Esarey, Vol. I, pp. 430–36; Norton, p. 174–75.

Page 253. EXECUTION OF LEATHER LIPS. Curry, pp. 30–36; Drake, pp. 118–20.

Page 254. BROUILLETTE. Esarey, Vol. I, pp. 417–19.

Page 254. SALT BOAT INCIDENT, 1810. Esarey, Vol. I, pp. 426–27.

Page 255. BARRON AT TIPPECANOE. Esarey, Vol. I, pp. 456–59; Goltz, p. 189.

Page 256. COUNCIL AT VINCENNES, 1810. Draper Manuscripts/ Tecumseh Papers, File YY-3, p. 109; Drake, pp. 125–30; Esarey, Vol. I, pp. 459–69. In his report made to the War Department at the time, Harrison did not make mention of Tekamthi's saying that the two of them might one day meet in battle while President Madison sipped wine in Washington. Not until fourteen years later did Harrison refer to this exchange. By then many were romanticizing the life of the late Tekamthi. It has been suggested that this is what Harrison was doing. All that is certain is that in 1824 Harrison said that is what Tekamthi had said in 1810.

Page 259. TEKAMTHI WITH SHABBONA AND CALDWELL, 1810. Hickling, pp. 35–36.

Page 259. TEKAMTHI AND ELLIOTT, November 1810. Horsman (*Matthew Elliott*), pp. 180–81.

Page 261. WELLS AND TEKAMTHI, 1811. Esarey, Vol. I, pp. 512–13.

Page 261. SALT BOAT SEIZURE, 1811. Esarey, Vol. I, p. 518.

Page 261. VINCENNES COUNCIL, 1811. Esarey, Vol. I, pp. 522–24, 529, 532–35, 542–51.

Page 262. TEKAMTHI TRAVELS SOUTH, 1811. Cotterill, pp. 166–75.

Page 264. TEKAMTHI AND THE CHOCTAW. Draper Manuscripts/Tecumseh Papers, File YY-4, pp. 74–86; Whicker, pp. 315–31.

Page 266. TEKAMTHI AND THE CREEK. Debo (*A History of the Creek Indians*), pp. 76–78; Cotterill, pp. 171–75.

Page 267. TEKAMTHI AND THE OSAGE. Hunter, pp. 27–31.

Page 268. HARRISON ON NEED FOR PREEMPTIVE STRIKE. Esarey, Vol. I, pp. 548–51.

Page 269. BATTLE OF TIPPECANOE AND THE PROPHET. Edmunds (*The Shawnee Prophet*), pp. 108–15; Creason, pp. 309–18; Watts, pp. 225–47.

Page 272. TEKAMTHI RETURNS. Drake, pp. 156–57; Draper Manuscripts/Tecumseh Papers, File YY-12, pp. 57–58; Esarey, Vol. II, p. 18.

Page 273. TEKAMTHI AND ELLIOTT. Goltz, pp. 314–15.

Page 274. ASSASSINATION OF TEKAMTHI PROPOSED. Hill, p. 56.

Page 274. TEKAMTHI ON THE MISSISSINEWA. Esarey, Vol. II, pp. 49–53.

Page 274. TEKAMTHI AND CHAINE. Edmunds (*The Shawnee Prophet*), pp. 121–24; Esarey, Vol. II, pp. 50–55, 60–62. Among the Americans, Benjamin Stickney, the federal Indian agent at Fort Wayne, was certain that Chaine was a British spy. For whatever reason, Chaine was permitted to attend the conference and bring the message from Elliott to Tekamthi.

Page 275. TEKAMTHI AND STICKNEY AT FORT WAYNE. Thornbrough, pp. 141–43.

Page 279. HULL'S PROCLAMATION AND CANADIAN DESERTIONS. Klinck, p. 131; Mason, p. 33.

Page 279. CANARD RIVER ACTION. Chalou, pp. 98–99.

Page 279. BRITISH-INDIAN-U.S. MILITARY STRENGTH. Klinck, p. 128; Sugden, p. 21.

Page 280. BROCK'S REPLY TO HULL'S PROCLAMATION. Klinck, p. 132.

Page 281. BROWNSTOWN ACTIONS. Drake, pp. 163–65; Klinck, pp. 150–57.

Page 283. TEKAMTHI AND BROCK. Klinck, pp. 137–42.

Page 284. CAPTURE OF DETROIT. Gilpin, pp. 109–22; Klinck, pp. 158–62.

Page 286. CAPTURE OF FORT DEARBORN. Drake, pp. 166–67; Hutton, pp. 218–22.

Page 287. FRONTIER RAIDS, FALL OF 1812. Gilpin, pp. 136–42.

Page 287. AMERICAN RESPONSE/HARRISON AND WINCHESTER, Gilpin, pp. 126–45.

Page 288. EXPEDITION TO FORT WAYNE. Edmunds (*Tecumseh*), pp. 182–84; Horsman (*Matthew Elliott*), pp. 198–201.

Page 290. DESTRUCTION OF THE MIAMI. Chalou, pp. 157–62.

Page 291. TEKAMTHI AND TENSKWATAWA, WINTER 1813. Drake, p. 167; Edmunds (*The Shawnee Prophet*), pp. 131–33.

Page 293. RIVER RAISIN MASSACRE. Gilpin, pp. 163–71; Klinck, pp. 170–73.

Page 294. PROCTER AND TEKAMTHI. McAfee, p. 273.

Page 295. FIRST SIEGE OF FORT MEIGS. Gilpin, pp. 179–90; McAfee, pp. 256–82.

Page 297. TEKAMTHI SAVES AMERICAN PRISONERS. Drake, pp. 181–82.

Page 299. SECOND SIEGE OF FORT MEIGS, AND FORT STEPHENSON. Drake, pp. 183–85; McAfee, pp. 316–29.

Page 302. TEKAMTHI, PROCTER, AND LECROIX. Drake, p. 186.

Page 303. PERRY ON LAKE ERIE. Gilpin, pp. 208–12; McAfee, pp. 342–46, 354–60; Sugden, pp. 28–38.

Page 309. EVACUATION AND RETREAT FROM AMHERSTBURG. Sugden gives an excellent, scholarly account of the final campaign. Detailed references as to original sources are appended. Except where otherwise noted, the description here is based on Sugden.

Page 310. TEKAMTHI'S SPEECH AT AMHERSTBURG. Klinck, pp. 184–87.

Page 313. AMERICANS ENTER ONTARIO. Chalou, p. 282; Esarey, Vol. II, pp. 546–51.

Page 316. TEKAMTHI WOUNDED. Drake, p. 192.

Page 319. WILLIAM WHITLEY. Talbert, pp. 101–19.

Page 320. BATTLE OF THE THAMES. In addition to Sugden, see Drake, pp. 192–99; Gilpin, pp. 223–27.

Page 324. DEATH OF TEKAMTHI. Many politicians and historians have addressed the question, which has never been definitely answered, of who killed Tecumseh. The best summaries of the claims and counterclaims are by Drake, pp. 199–219, and Sugden, pp. 136–81.

Page 330. CALHOUN. Hill, p. 101.

Page 331. TENSKWATAWA AND PACHETHA. Edmunds (*The Shawnee Prophet*), pp. 165–90.

Page 331. BLACK HOOF AND JOHNSTON. Hill, p. 114.

Page 331. REMOVAL OF THE SHAWNEE. Hill, pp. 113–17.

Page 333. WAPAMEEPTO. Galbreath, pp. 149–50.

Page 338. LAST INDIANS. Hill, p. 116, pp. 135–36.

Bibliography

Alford, Thomas Wildcat. *Civilization*. As told to Florence Drake. Norman: University of Oklahoma Press, 1936.

American State Papers. *Documents, Legislative and Executive, of the Congress of the United States*, Vol. IV. Washington: Gales and Seaton, 1832.

Anson, Bert. *The Miami Indians*. Norman: University of Oklahoma Press, 1970.

Atwater, Caleb. *A History of the State of Ohio, Natural and Civil*. Cincinnati: Glezen and Shepard, 1838.

Axtell, James. *The European and the Indian*. New York: Oxford University Press, 1981.

Barce, Ellmore. "Governor Harrison and the Treaty of Fort Wayne, 1809," *Indiana Magazine of History* 11:352–67.

Beckner, Lucien. "John Findley: The First Pathfinder of Kentucky." *The Filson Club History Quarterly* 43:206–15.

———. "Reverend John D. Shane's Notes on Interviews, in 1844, with Mrs. Hinds and Patrick Scott of Bourbon County," *The Filson Club Quarterly* 10:164–73.

Beirne, Francis F. *The War of 1812*. New York: E. P. Dutton & Company, Inc., 1949.

Berkhofer, Robert F., Jr. *The White Man's Indian*. New York: Random House, 1978.

"Bowman's Expedition Against Chillicothe," *Ohio Archaeological and Historical Publications* 19:446–59.

Brice, Wallace A. *History of Fort Wayne, from the Earliest Known Accounts of This Point, to the Present Period*. Fort Wayne, Indiana: D. W. Jones & Son, 1868.

Brown, John P. *Old Frontiers*. New York: Arno Press, Inc., 1971.

Burt, A. L. *The United States, Great Britain and British North America*. New York: Russell & Russell, 1961.

Chalou, George Clifford. "The Red Pawns Go to War: British-American Relations, 1810–1815." Dissertation, History Department of Indiana University, Bloomington, Indiana, 1971. University Microfilms, Ann Arbor, Michigan, 1977.

Clark, Jerry E. *The Shawnee.* Lexington: The University Press of Kentucky, 1977.

Cleaves, Freeman. *Old Tippecanoe.* Port Washington, N.Y.: Kennikat Press, 1969.

Collins, Richard H. *History of Kentucky.* Covington, Ky.: Collins & Co., 1882.

Cotterill, R. S. *The Southern Indians.* Norman: University of Oklahoma Press, 1954.

Creason, Joe C. "The Battle of Tippecanoe," *The Filson Club History Quarterly* 36:309–18.

Crèvecoeur, J. Hector St. John de. *Letters from an American Farmer.* New York: E. P. Dutton & Co., Inc., 1957

Cruikshank, Brig. Gen. E. A., ed. *The Correspondence of Lieut. Governor John Graves Simcoe.* Toronto: Ontario Historical Society, 1924.

Curry, Wm. L. "The Wyandot Chief, Leather Lips." *Ohio Archaeological and Historical Society Publications* 12:30–36.

Debo, Angie. *A History of the Creek Indians.* Norman: University of Oklahoma Press, 1941.

————. *The Rise and Fall of the Choctaw Republic.* Norman: University of Oklahoma Press, 1934, 1961.

Downes, Randolph C. *Council Fires on the Upper Ohio.* Pittsburgh: University of Pittsburgh Press, 1940.

Drake, Benjamin. *Life of Tecumseh, and of His Brother the Prophet; with a Historical Sketch of the Shawanoe Indians.* Cincinnati: E. Morgan & Co., 1841.

Draper Manuscripts/Tecumseh Papers. The State Historical Society of Wisconsin. Madison, Wisconsin.

Edmunds, R. David. *Tecumseh and the Quest for Indian Leadership.* Boston: Little, Brown & Company, 1984.

————. *The Potawatomis.* Norman: University of Oklahoma Press, 1978.

————. *The Shawnee Prophet.* Lincoln: University of Nebraska Press, 1983.

Esarey, Logan, ed. *Governor's Messages and Letters: Messages and Letters of William Henry Harrison.* Indianapolis: Indiana Historical Commission, 1922.

Galbreath, C. B. "Tecumseh and his Descendants," *Ohio Archaeological and Historical Quarterly* 34:143–53.

Galloway, William Albert. "Daniel Boon," *Ohio Archaeological and Historical Society Publications* 13:263–77.

————. *Old Chillicothe.* Xenia, Ohio: The Buckeye Press, 1934.

Gatschet, Albert S. "Tecumseh's Name," *American Anthropologist* 8 (1895):91–92.

Gibson, Arrell M. *The Chickasaws.* Norman: University of Oklahoma Press, 1971.

Gilbert, Bil. *Westering Man*. New York: Atheneum, 1983.

Gilpin, Alec R. *The War of 1812 in the Old Northwest*. East Lansing, Mich.: Michigan State University Press, 1958.

Goebel, Dorothy Burne. *William Henry Harrison*. Philadelphia: Porcupine Press, 1974.

Goltz, Herbert Charles Walter, Jr. "Tecumseh, the Prophet and the Rise of the Northwest Indian Confederation." Dissertation, Faculty of Graduate Studies, University of Western Ontario, London, Ontario, 1973.

Griswold, B. J. *The Pictorial History of Fort Wayne Indiana*. Chicago: Robert O. Law Company, 1917.

Hanna, Charles A. *The Wilderness Trail*. New York: AMS Press, 1971.

Hatch, Colonel William Stanley. *A Chapter of the History of the War of 1812 in the Northwest*. Cincinnati: Miami Printing and Publishing Company, 1872.

Heckewelder, Rev. John. *History, Manners, and Customs of the Indian Nations*. Philadelphia: The Historical Society of Pennsylvania, 1876.

Hickling, William. "Caldwell and Shabonee," *Journal of Chicago Historical Society* 10:29–35.

Hildreth, S. P. *Pioneer History: Being an Account of the First Examinations of the Ohio Valley, and the Early Settlement of the Northwest Territory*. New York: Arno Press, Inc., 1971.

Hill, Leonard U. *John Johnston and the Indians*. Columbus, Ohio: Stoneman Press, 1957.

Hinde, T. S. "T. S. Hinde's Letter," *American Pioneer* 10:373–75.

Horsman, Reginald. *Expansion and American Indian Policy, 1783–1812*. East Lansing, Mich.: Michigan State University Press, 1967.

———. *Matthew Elliott, British Indian Agent*. Detroit: Wayne State University Press, 1964.

Howard, Dresden W. H. "The Battle of Fallen Timbers as Told by Chief Kin-Jo-I-No," *Northwest Ohio Quarterly* 20:37–49.

Howard, James H. *Shawnee!* Athens, Ohio: Ohio University Press, 1981.

Hunt, George T. *The Wars of the Iroquois*. Madison: University of Wisconsin Press, 1940.

Hunter, John Dunn. *Memoirs of a Captivity Among the Indians of North America*. Edited by Richard Drinnon. New York: Schocken Books, 1973.

Hutton, Paul A. "William Wells: Frontier Scout and Indian Agent." *Indiana Magazine of History* 74:183–222.

Jennings, Francis. *The Ambiguous Iroquois Empire*. New York: W. W. Norton & Company, 1984.

———. *The Invasion of America*. Chapel Hill: University of North Carolina Press, 1975.

Jones, Rev. David. *A Journal of Two Visits Made to Some Nations of Indians on the West Side of the River Ohio in the Years 1772 and 1773*. New York: Arno Press, Inc., 1971.

Josephy, Alvin M., Jr. *The Patriot Chiefs*. New York: Penguin Books, 1976.

Kellogg, Louise Phelps, ed. *Frontier Advance on the Upper Ohio, 1778–1779*. Madison: State Historical Society of Wisconsin, 1916.

Kinietz, W. Vernon. *The Indians of the Western Great Lakes, 1615–1760.* Ann Arbor: University of Michigan Press, 1965.

Klinck, Carl F., ed. *Tecumseh, Fact and Fiction in Early Records.* Englewood Cliffs, N.J.: Prentice-Hall, Inc., 1961.

Kohn, Richard H. "General Wilkinson's Vendetta with General Wayne: Politics and Command in the American Army, 1791–1796," *The Filson Club History Quarterly* 45:361–72.

Kroeber, A. L. "Native American Population," *American Anthropologist* 36:1–25.

Loudon, Archibald, *A Selection of Some of the Most Interesting Narratives of Outrages Committed by the Indians in Their Wars with the White People.* New York: Arno Press, 1971.

MacLean, J. P. "Shaker Mission to the Shawnee Indians," *Ohio Archaeological and Historical Society Publications* 11:215–29.

Martin, Calvin. *Keepers of the Game.* Berkeley and Los Angeles: University of California Press, 1978.

Mason, Philip P., ed. *After Tippecanoe: Some Aspects of the War of 1812.* Westport, Conn.: Greenwood Press.

McAfee, Robert Breckinridge. *History of the Late War in the Western Country.* Ann Arbor: University Microfilms, Inc., 1966.

McKenney, Thomas L., and James Hall. *The Indian Tribes of North America.* Totowa, New Jersey: Rowman and Littlefield, 1972.

Mooney, James. *The Ghost-Dance Religion and the Sioux Outbreak of 1890.* Washington: *Fourteenth Annual Report of the Bureau of Ethnology to the Secretary of the Smithsonian Institution, 1892–93.* Washington, D.C.: Government Printing Office, 1896.

Moorehead, Warren King. "The Indian Tribes of Ohio—Historically Considered," *Ohio Archaeological and Historical Publications* 7:1–109.

Norton, Major John. *The Journal of Major John Norton, 1816.* Edited by Carl F. Klinck and James J. Talman. Toronto: The Champlain Society, 1970.

Owen, Roger C., James J. F. Deetz, and Anthony D. Fisher, eds. *The North American Indians.* New York: Macmillan Publishing Co., Inc., 1967.

Parker, Arthur C. *Parker on the Iroquois.* Edited by William N. Fenton. Syracuse, N.Y.: Syracuse University Press, 1968.

Prucha, Francis Paul. *American Indian Policy in the Formative Years.* Cambridge, Mass.: Harvard University Press, 1962.

———. *The Sword of the Republic.* Bloomington & London: Indiana University Press, 1969.

Quaife, Milo Milton, ed. *The Indian Captivity of O. M. Spencer.* New York: The Citadel Press, Inc., 1968.

Randall, E. O. "Tecumseh, The Shawnee Chief," *Ohio Archaeological and Historical Society Publications* 15:418–97.

———. "The Dunmore War," *Ohio Archaeological and Historical Publications* 11:167–97.

Rothert, Otto A. "John D. Shane's Interview, in 1841, with Mrs. Wilson of Woodford County," *The Filson Club History Quarterly* 16:227–33.

Rush, Richard. *Washington in Domestic Life*. Philadelphia: J. B. Lippincott and Company, 1857.

Sahlins, Marshall. *Stone Age Economics*. Chicago and New York: Aldine-Atherton, Inc., 1972.

Sears, Alfred B. "The Political Philosophy of Arthur St. Clair," *Ohio Archaeological and Historical Quarterly* 49:41–57.

Shetrone, H. C. "The Indian in Ohio," *Ohio Archaeological and Historical Publications* 27:274–507.

Siberell, Lloyd Emerson. *Tecumseh*. Chillicothe, Ohio: The Ross County Historical Society, 1944.

Smith, Dwight L. "Wayne's Peace with the Indians of the Old Northwest, 1795," *Ohio State Archaeological and Historical Quarterly* 49:239–55.

Smith, Z. F. *The History of Kentucky*. Louisville: The Prentice Press, 1886.

Sosin, Jack M. *The Revolutionary Frontier, 1763–1783*. New York: Holt, Rinehart & Winston, 1967.

Spencer, Joab. "The Shawnee Indians," *Transactions of the Kansas State Historical Society* 10:382–402.

Sturtevant, William C. ed. *Handbook of North American Indians*, Vol. 15. Washington: Smithsonian Institution, 1978.

Sugden, John. *Tecumseh's Last Stand*. Norman: University of Oklahoma Press, 1985.

Swanton, John R. *The Indian Tribes of North America*. Washington, D.C.: Smithsonian Institution Press, 1969.

Sword, Wiley. *President Washington's Indian War*. Norman: University of Oklahoma Press, 1985.

Talbert, Charles G. "William Whitley 1749–1813," *The Filson Club Quarterly* 25:101–19.

Tanner, John. *A Narrative of the Captivity and Adventures of John Tanner*. New York and London: Garland Publishing, Inc., 1975.

Tantaquidgeon, Gladys. *Folk Medicine of the Delaware and Related Algonkian Indians*, Anthropological Series, no. 3. Harrisburg: Pennsylvania Historical and Museum Commission, 1972.

Thompson, Charles N. *Sons of the Wilderness*. Indianapolis: Indiana Historical Society, 1937.

Thornbrough, Gayle, ed. *Letter Book of the Indian Agency at Fort Wayne, 1809–1815*. Indianapolis: Indiana Historical Society, 1961.

Thwaites, Reuben Gold and Louise Phelps Kellogg. *Frontier Defense on the Upper Ohio, 1777–1778*. Millwood, N.Y.: Kraus Reprint Company, 1973.

Trowbridge, Charles C. *Shawnese Traditions*. Edited by Vernon Kinietz and Erminie W. Voegelin. Museum of Anthropology Occasional Contributions no. 9. Ann Arbor: University of Michigan Press, 1939.

U.S. Department of Commerce. *Historical Statistics of the United States*. Bicentennial Edition, Vols. I and II.

Vanderwerth, W. C., comp. *Indian Oratory*. New York: Ballantine Books and University of Oklahoma Press, 1972.

Voegelin, C. F. and E. W. "Shawnee Name Groups," *American Anthropologist* 37:617–35.

Voegelin, C. F., John F. Yegerlehner, and Florence M. Robinett, "Shawnee Laws: Perceptual Statements for the Language and for the Content." *The American Anthropologist* 56:32–46.

Volney, C. F. *A View of the Soil and Climate of the United States of America.* New York and London: Hafner Publishing Company, Inc., 1968.

Wallace, Paul A. W. *Indians in Pennsylvania.* Harrisburg: Pennsylvania Historical and Museum Commission, 1964.

Wallis, Wilson D. *Messiahs.* Washington, D.C.: American Council on Public Affairs, 1943.

Washburn, Wilcomb E., ed. *The Indian and the White Man.* Garden City, N.Y.: Anchor Books/Doubleday & Company, Inc., 1964.

Watts, Florence G., ed. "Lieutenant Charles Larrabee's Account of the Battle of Tippecanoe, 1811," *Indiana Magazine of History* 57:225–47.

Wheeler-Voegelin, Erminie. *Indians of Ohio and Indiana Prior to 1795: Ethnohistory of Indian Use and Occupancy in Ohio and Indiana Prior to 1795.* Vols. I and II. New York & London: Garland Publishing, Inc., 1974.

Whicker, J. Wesley. "Tecumseh and Pushmataha," *Indiana Magazine of History* 18:315–31.

Wildes, Harry Emerson. *Anthony Wayne.* New York: Harcourt, Brace & Company, 1941.

Witherell, Hon. B. F. H. "Reminiscences of the North-West," *Third Annual Report and Collections of the State Historical Society of Wisconsin, for the Year 1856* 3:299–337.

Withers, Alexander Scott. *Chronicles of Border Warfare; or, A History of the Settlement by the Whites of North-Western Virginia, and of the Indian Wars and Massacres in That Section of the State, with Reflections, Anecdotes, &c., by Alexander Scott Withers.* Edited by Reuben Gold Thwaites. Cincinnati: The Robert Clarke Company, 1895.

Woodward, Grace Steele. *The Cherokees.* Norman: University of Oklahoma Press, 1963.

Index

BIL GILBERT has published eight previous books (the most recent being *Our Nature*) and some three hundred articles in major magazines, including *Audubon, Discover, Esquire, Smithsonian, Sports Illustrated,* and *Time*. Most often he writes about American natural and social history. His books and essays on these subjects have won numerous national awards and he has been called "our best full-time environmental journalist" by the *Washington Post*.